KU-286-300

A Divided Life

MOHAMMED KHAN

Grosvenor House
Publishing Limited

All rights reserved
Copyright © Mohammed Khan, 2014

The right of Mohammed Khan to be identified as the author of this
work has been asserted by him in accordance with Section 78
of the Copyright, Designs and Patents Act 1988

The book cover picture is copyright to Mohammed Khan

This book is published by
Grosvenor House Publishing Ltd
28-30 High Street, Guildford, Surrey, GU1 3EL.
www.grosvenorhousepublishing.co.uk

This book is sold subject to the conditions that it shall not, by way of
trade or otherwise, be lent, resold, hired out or otherwise circulated
without the author's or publisher's prior consent in any form of binding or
cover other than that in which it is published and
without a similar condition including this condition being imposed
on the subsequent purchaser.

A CIP record for this book
is available from the British Library

ISBN 978-1-78148-620-7

Contents

Front cover

'A spectacular TRICHMIR (soars to 25,264 feet), about eighty miles away from the view point in Chitral. Located in the magical and breath taking Hindukush Mountains; in the mystical and glorious North West Frontier of Pakistan.

On its left is where the famous 'Tora Bora Caves' are located (in which Al-Qaida Chief Osama Bin Laden and his Mujahedeen once took shelter, during the American punitive aggressive Campaign in Afghanistan, where B52s' Carpet Bombings took place and later smoked out Bin Laden.)'

Acknowledgements

First and foremost I must thank my neighbours and close friends Matilda and Ramakrishnan for inspiring and rousing me to embark on this lonely trail... Without their gracious lead and insight, I would not have thought of narrating any of my memoirs or historical moments.

Additionally I have been more than fortunate over the last thirteen years to be associated with my most brilliant and caring tutor Stephen Smith as well as contemporaries in the creative writing class at Scola, who have been the watershed for this book. I sincerely tender my gratitude to Stephen for his reviews, and editing and for his ongoing guidance to sharpen and polish my narrative of events.

Last, but not the least, I must thank my beloved wife Shuda for her unwavering support and diligence over the long chain of strenuous years; without her dogged effort I wouldn't be as I stand. I am also grateful to my children and grandchildren for displaying their terrific exhilaration and interest and also lending me their computer skills to create this book over the last few years, especially Hazik and Ameer for helping with the final production of the book and its design.

Mohammed Khan

Preface

I was born in British India on the penultimate day of December 1939, just four months after the advent of the Great World War Two. Although I was an infant during that period, I observed and realised the horrendous impact of the war. I noticed some of my aunts shrieking and wailing in the Grandma's village on the sad news how their sons drowned on the high seas or shattered to pieces in the unknown trenches in foreign lands. I also observed the happiest mothers celebrating when their sons returned home safely after being released from the Japanese concentration camps and stared at the distribution of sumptuous freshly cooked spicy and aromatic food and sweets. Later I met my own first cousin in his early twenties, having just been released from his active British Indian army service from Singapore, almost empty handed. All those young men fought for the protection of the British Empire without getting any significant compensation, like any other young men from India as well as other countries under the British Empire; the same situation applied to the other colonial empires. The reason could be that Great Britain abdicated control of India at the end of the Great War after having suffered colossal financial losses. However I have the conviction that there would be no more World Wars because there would be no more empires run by any powers or super powers or no more low paid coolies or mercenaries would be on hands to fight for their masters. The main reason for granting independence to various countries all over Asia and Africa was not their contemporary leaders, but the gravity of weakness of the European colonial powers. It was just like a domino effect that the empires crumbled one after the other.

I was not born in a village, but in a most modern town called Montgomery, in West Punjab. When I reached the age of two, unfortunately my mother died in Montgomery during maternity and my father being in his early thirties married again. Subsequently due to some pragmatic reasons or due to some love and hate,

I was despatched to the far distant and remote village where my maternal grandma lived. My three elder brothers and sister still stayed with my father and the step mother and the paternal grandmother (a widow herself). As a result my way of living changed dramatically and tilted towards the worse and primitive standard. My maternal grandma's village was located in the East Punjab, and at the time of Independence and subsequent partition of the Punjab, was unfairly given to India by the British imperialist and colonial masters. But luckily during the summer holidays at school in 1947, my eldest brother was on a visit to my grandmother and just few days before the partition, fetched me back to my father's place safe and sound, but what happened soon after my departure from the village is impossible to describe and who could escape if there was collaboration between the politicians, religious leaders and the army, especially in the East Punjab. Most of my descriptions and narrations of the grotesque scenes at the time of the partition are of my personal observation as a young child or of my closest relatives and friends. They are free from any politics or malicious propaganda or being biased in any sense. To me Hindus Sikhs Muslims Christians atheists or pagans living in that area, have the same blood and the same culture and I cannot see any reason to hate any one on the basis of some one's belief or ethnic origin. This is the age of freedom and enlightenment. If the European can live as one nation, after fighting with each other for hundreds of years and fighting World Wars with each other, why do the Indians having the same blood and flesh, not live in peace and harmony?. This is one of my main themes.

The other biting issue for me is the terrific size of the armies, sustained both in India and Pakistan; over two million soldiers, plus more fighting personnel in the most advanced Air forces and navies. They hardly fight with each other, but billions of the Dollars are consumed every month drawn from the tax payers to maintain and update them, perhaps on loans under compound interests. I can recollect vividly only one full scale major war fought between them in 1965, which lasted for only seventeen days and then both collapsed on the knees. There is no doubt in my mind that the soldiers stand eye to eye against each other like the 'Idol Warriors', but how much money is being burnt for some aimless target. I think they need to reduce their armies at least by half and resolve any disputes amicably and then become prosperous at the grass root level. Any atom bombs, missiles, going to the moon or mars are not fruitful to the common man, these might be good for some chosen people, but not for the indigenous residents of the subcontinent. It can still become a golden sparrow by reducing the defence budgets. The only legitimate daily targets for these armies are their own poor civilians, not the enemy. These two countries hate each other so much that they even have the highest battle field in the world on a glacier located at an average height of 20,000 feet or higher, the soldiers simply lose limbs by frost bite or perish in the crevasses. These invaluable funds must be used to build up the infra-structure like controlling the explosion of population, building up dams to store precious water and to control the floods and to generate environment friendly and pollution free hydroelectricity, provide the best and cheapest education to all desiring people, provide them with welfare systems and means of earning their livelihood. These measures can provide peace and security in the subcontinent on a far firmer and harmonious footing than the armed forces are providing to their nations at the moment.

However the main objective for me is to highlight vividly the environment and unique way of life and cultural traditions which prevailed from the cradle of the lap of my mother to the end of my full time education, it will take me to the age of twenty four. At the beginning I have given a brief introduction on the movements of various races into India and subsequent development of various civilisations and what sort of impact was made by the invaders like the Aryans, Arabs, Turks, Persians, Afghans and last but not the least the British as well as after the independence. So I begin with my place of birth called Montgomery. I describe in full detail this magnificent and well-built settlement on a European scale and under British planning. It is an example of the glittering ingenuity and excellent gift left behind by the British. I think that the British used their omnipotent and colonial royal power to build up these new settlements, irrigation systems, build barrages on the rivers, build railways and roads on a massive and industrial scale and nobody could challenge them anyway. But now the local selfish politicians and petty feudal lords refuse to build any dams, railways or canals on the pretext that it will have adverse effects on their areas of political power. Rather since independence quite a few rail tracks have been uprooted and railway stations dismantled in Pakistan. Since then only two significant dams have been built over forty years ago, but there is a great non-cooperation and squabbling to build new dams and hydroelectric projects between the provinces and millions of cusecs of water is wasted by letting it flow to the sea. I think if the British were still there they would have developed the country without being challenged by anybody and made the country self-sufficient in hydroelectricity, railways and irrigation canals which would have been sufficient for the need of the ever exploding population. The indigenous people always moan and groan about the shortage of water and electricity, but no action is taken by the lame duck rulers to build up new dams and hydro-electric projects; these leaders pay more attention building up their own palaces in the country and abroad by siphoning off the funds from the national exchequer.

While I stand over the bridgehead of the mighty canal, enjoying the roars and sizzle of the waterfalls and whirlpools, my thoughts glide towards my grandparents and parents, who would have stood on the same sacred site and spot for the first ever wonderful glimpse of the canal or would have crossed the bridge on a tonga (horse coach) to catch the train from the station opposite. As the mist and breeze of plunging water flies in the air, it refracts and glistens into a beautiful and sparkling rainbow, which actually illustrates and depicts the glory and glitter of this magnetic and colourful country and its people. The great archaeological site of Harappa is not far away from Montgomery, the artefacts of which lie in all over the major museums of the world, being the cradle of the Indus Valley Civilisation about which so many books have been written by the Western scholars and documentaries prepared, along with its twin city of Mohenjudaru. As I hold my grandmother's jewellery next to my heart, I can see lot of dust rising to the sky. I can hear the sound and noise of the hooves of the donkeys and horses trotting and soldiers scurrying towards Iran, as well as load-full of gold and diamonds carried on the thousands of camels and bull-carts. In the midst of the storm, I can see the Indian virgins solemnly carrying The Peacock Throne over their shoulders, loaded safely in the Dolees, plundered by the Muslim marauding nomadic Iranian general Nadir Shah, from the Mughal Red Fort of the Muslim capital of Delhi. Montgomery is located on the old camel or silk routes leading from Delhi to Iran. My heart flutters like a buzzard and I splatter and flap like a shot down golden gosling.

My own life as a whole for this particular epic and historical period was exceptionally unparalleled in itself as a kid or a growing youth and luckily I recollect various tones and tempos of the unique momentous incidents, traditions, landscapes, seasons and wild life which the reader will, I hope, find captivating and enlightening. I had travelled myself through the passage of freedom as a kid of seven and also witnessed the caravans of refugees departing and arriving and had listened to their unfortunate stories and watched their sad faces trickling with tears and with rising sighs. These are all drawn from my personal observations, but there is no doubt that every individual in the same boat would react in a different way according to one's personal circumstances. It's worth noting that this variety of cultures is not only because of the caste systems, but also because over one thousands different languages are spoken all over the subcontinent, they wear different dresses, eat different food and of course they have different beliefs and even in the same belief, there are countless subdivisions and factions; and apparently they are all right. The subcontinent and its people are very colourful and possess countless cultures and life styles and the good news is that every single person thinks that he or she is superior to the others and as well he or she is right and everyone else is wrong. I have highlighted the ancient customs and tradition of the caste system, being someone automatically superior or inferior, the abuse of women and children, particularly if some children run away as a result of mistreatment of their parents or poverty. They can be easily trapped with the mafia or criminal gangs and there are hundreds and thousands of such victims. They can be deformed, maimed or sexually abused or turn into slaves for rest of their lives. They can easily be used as begging tools till they die, can be drugged for committing crimes or for lust. Such abused children roam in the shape of 'Mafia Gangs' and well-coordinated by their own hierarchy and with the cooperation of the police. It is shocking that no religious leader or mullah object to such grim abuses and no government department question any one committing these grim crimes with the innocent and wretched young kids and none of the criminals are ever charged or imprisoned. Abduction of the young children is quite rampant for such grotesque crimes. The parents of the victims cannot do anything as the government institutions or courts appear insensitive or unconcerned. However it is even more shocking that some parents donate their own children at the time of their infancy to various shrines and gangs, in return for some blessings, forgiveness or the meanest amount of remuneration. More shocking are some of the feudal lords in Pakistan who marry their daughters with the Quraan to save their inheritance or wealth for their future male off springs, although it is not a part of any religious belief. There are no significant welfare and rehabilitation institutions which can help such abused kids and women. It is more startling that in case of adultery, only female are killed or punished, but not the male involved in the incident. This is called honour killings and is definitely not a part of the religion because in such cases, both persons must be dealt with equal justice and severity, male or female.

The other issue I have highlighted is the arranged marriage system and treatment of woman as subordinate can be very compelling and a burning issue; and is questioned quite openly in this fast developing, modern and free world. I think this is based on the old pagan culture and is quite disturbing and full of problems.

Although with the enlightenment and influence of the developed countries, the situation is improving, but still persisting. I have quoted some examples from my own experience as a kid or growing up to an adult. My misery as an orphan could have been reduced to a greater extent if I had received inheritance of agricultural land and the house entitled to my late mother or if we had property in lieu of my father's urban assets left behind in the East Punjab. This is even more vital in the absence of the welfare system in the developing world because the religious leaders, imams and relatives pay only superficial lip service, but rather exploit them as subservient or unpaid slaves if someone is in that dire situation. In most cases the property and wealth of the parentless infants or kids is simply swallowed in a very mysterious way.

It is a well-known fact or perhaps an open secret that during the grim communal violence in the East Punjab, hundreds and thousands of young girls and women were abducted by the hordes of Sikhs and Hindus militants and although most of them stayed back with their oppressors out of embarrassment, but hundreds had returned to Pakistan, but even they were treated as underdogs and employed as maids or concubines by the wealthy people and the young orphans did not know who their parents were and what happened to their properties. Those unfortunate victims simply melted away in the furnace. I recollect one beautiful young pregnant woman retrieved from India after partition and visiting my sister's house in Lahore with her mother and aunt, but tears continuously trickled down her silky and apricot cheeks while her eyes gazed mournfully at her toes out of shame. Almost at the same time, I saw the long queues of the orphans being escorted by some young men in their twenties, while I lodged in the Gurdawara in Depalpur. The kids were forced to walk in straight line completely dumb like cattle. It is quite possible that they belonged to some very honourable families, but now wiped out and deprived from their parents in the communal atrocities and they had no one to turn to or express their feelings. But now they were forced to sing and beg wandering aimlessly from place to place. How awful and painful sight it was at that pitiless moment and still is! Why did the British genius fail miserably in their obligations to protect their own loyal subjects or were they somehow forced not to?

First of all I thank my stars for my safe escape from the grandmother's village, especially my eldest teen age brother Yaqub who brought me to the safe place, he definitely saved me from becoming a fossil. After having arrived back to my father's house and staying with my brothers and sister and paternal grandmother, I felt much better placed and looked after. There is no doubt that being a youngest person in the family, I was almost being treated as a lesser. But still that built up my confidence and I developed myself as a better person. I missed one year from school as a result of the upheavals of the partition, but started in my class one again with a greater vigour and stature and topped the class up to the end of my school studies. However I was hardly nine years old, when my father died at the age of forty four and soon my paternal grandmother followed him. Although my father was a senior civil servant, his bereaved family did not get any pension, perhaps soon after partition there was no money in the exchequer, most of the funds were still held by India and release of them was still being negotiated. It was also possible that we were not entitled to any state pension because my father died prematurely before the pensionable age. Within two years from the death of my father, all our funds ran out and we were evicted from our house because we were unable to pay the rent and started living in the abandoned Gurdawara, the Sikhs holy temple. This was the place where I met with the King Cobra and I have devoted one chapter in his memory. However before this I parted with the ever breathtaking daughter of the potter in our neighbourhood and I dedicate one chapter in her sweet memory. By this time whole of our joint family disintegrated as well, my teenaged brothers discard their studies and commenced doing some sort of low grade jobs to earn money and even each one got married, including my lonely elder sister. For the next seven years I stayed with my middle elder brother Sarwer and his wife Mumtaz, until I passed my two years pre graduation course in the college. After that at the age of nineteen I left the college and performed a clerical job in a government department to earn some money for my higher studies and rejoined the college at Montgomery to do my graduation, but this time I dwelled with my eldest brother Yaqub and last but not the least, I continued on my post-graduation studies in Lahore and lodged there with my sister and some noble family. After all those upheavals and turmoil, by the age of twenty four I was lucky to achieve a comfortable and a respectable job as a lecturer in the government college and this was the moment for the end of my restless and uncertain times. So many incessant calamities fell on me and for such a long time and with such ferocity that everything else looked nice and easy then. After teaching for four years in the college, I resigned my job and then migrated to the United Kingdom on 2 May 1968. Since then my life has flourished for the better each day, but the story does not fall in the scope of this book and hopefully will continue.

During those early years of my life, I had gone through some most noteworthy and epic historical moments on this uncertain planet, like the World War Two, the independence of India and its partition and consequent communal violence; and personally the premature death of my parents, my upbringing by different people and in different environments and circumstances, the death of my maternal grandmother in the refugee camps; they all bite hard and are painful to remember. However in the midst of those turbulent moments are many more sweet memories as well, that is captivating and ever fascinating and hurt even more than the former. It was a growing up age, there were excitements and delights at each new and pleasant moment, like gazing at the flash floods or movement of the monsoon clouds and later thunder and lightning with the heavy downpour of rain over the Himalayas, like meeting the fawn in the green fields of sweet corns, like gazing at the leveret nibbling in the fields or observing the peacock prowling in the meadows, like myself wandering alone in the dry river bed or the fields or in the dust storm, those are a few moments I have quoted, which also bite for their bliss, freedom and happiness. In that growing up age every moment was full of thrill and excitement like travelling in the steam engine train or wandering in the Anakali Bazar and staring at the beauties carefree or in tuition, when I was full of blood and at freewill. Jumping in the canals and rivers in the company of the friends for swimming was a unique thrill and exhilaration by itself. Only few people experience the hurricane Monsoon clouds and their savage melodrama over the highest mountains of the world. Those extraordinary and exceptional moments are there with me all the time and I yearn for them fruitlessly. I perceive that life is definitely full of charm and excitement and worth yearning. Most of those moments were so sensuous and ever refreshing like green lemons that they surpass the evil moments of that era and I keep on dreaming, but unfortunately everything is changed now including myself and there is nothing remaining apart from the nostalgia and captivating feelings and emotions. If per chance I am born again, that time and space will never be the same, so I have to live with the yearnings, echoes and the inspiration of those magical moments.

Chapter I

Grandma's Jewellery

It was a pleasant November morning, 1885 in Victorian India. The remote village was located on the edge of the great soaring wall of The Himalayas mountain range. The hazy, brownish dark barrier pierced through the sky only a few miles away covered with an ever white turban over its head. Even the skies stooped down to kiss its forehead. The village was split by a dry-river bed. The sand was soft. The banks of the river were overgrown with reeds and wild bush; shelter for deer, rabbits and lizards. The cool and fresh air blew in the mornings from the icy mountains. The soil was fertile and alluvial. Over here the pea-cocks prowled in the green fields and fawns jumped and rabbits hopped around in the meadows. At that moment, the lush green fields were exploding with yellow a carpet of Linseed flowers. The pomegranate buds were blossoming into light pink and violet blooms. The dew drops washed the face of the sprouting crops and glistened like glittering diamonds. The atmosphere was full of colours, fragrance and glitter. Although it was a Muslim dominated village, some Sikhs and Hindus families also mingled happily together. The terrain was decorated with meadows of tall grass, and many orchards and groves of mangoes and oranges. There was abundance of thorny acacia trees as well as green stumps of wild pulpy cactus plants and clumps of tall cane bush.

That day it was a special occasion and everyone in the village was in a vibrant mood; preparing to receive the bridegroom and the party. The wedding party had stayed overnight in a neighbouring village, as they had come from afar. Great effort was put in by the hosts for that historical moment. The relatives and friends had arrived from far and wide to attend the wedding. Grandma's parents and family had made special arrangements for the lodging of the guests as well as for their meals and welfare. Everyone in the family especially the children and women flashed special and colourful new clothes. There were regular late night gatherings for singing and dancing by the girls and their mums. The atmosphere was full of romantic emotions and excitement. The cool and silvery light of the glowing full moon enhanced the charm and tranquillity of the special event. The white floating clouds tried to shroud the face of the moon, but still it was lured into peeping down on the earth.

The men were not far behind they were enjoying the festivities too, rather in a better manner. They had not only invited the local singers but also the town singers as well as the female dancers for the entertainment of the guests. There was an open invitation for the whole village at family level and they shared the same sentiments as well as responsibility to look after the guests. The artists seemed highly professional and charged hefty rewards, especially the female singers and dancers. Any interested people were welcomed from the neighbouring villages as well without any prejudice against their creed or background. They all celebrated the festivities together and with same excitement and spirits, Fresh exotic food was cooked by professional chefs at each meal time in huge cauldrons, under glowing fire of the logs in the open fields and served by the local people in a simple and co-ordinated manner, as if their own daughter was getting married. The air was mellow from the food being cooked and filled with the aroma of spices and herbs. It made the mouth water and one felt desperately hungry.

It was the fact of life that most of the co-inhabitants in those villages belonged to the same tribes, whether they were Hindus, Sikhs or Muslims. Changing the belief did not change one's genealogy; rather it is part of evolution and human development. It is based on human freedom, individual choice and democracy. They eat the same food, speak the same language and wear similar clothes. They had the same caste system and the same culture. Changing the ritual of belief should not create any enmity, one must be allowed to practice as one pleases so that people could live in harmony and peace. It is the politicians and high priests, who create hatred and exploit the masses for their own personal glory, power and wealth, common people do not perceive this and when they do, it is too late! There is a very popular Punjabi song: 'Innaan muzbi thakadaran ne aye lut lai dunya sari aye'; highlighting the same theme, 'These religious contractors have plundered the whole world'. Having a particular belief does not automatically guarantee any one to be a superior or inferior, but it is the individual actions what matter. The same principle applies to the pagans, atheists or non-believers.

That was an historical moment for the glorious British Empire as well. It was the era when Bob Bahadur (English Warrior) would come galloping on his horse along with the dusty road, under the shade of lofty trees, while the subjects waited by the route for a glimpse. At the other end, in the villa miles away, the Mem-Sahib supervised daily chores performed in earnest by a pack of workers; To name only a few, Behras (Food servants), Dhobiwala (Clothes Washer), Pankhawala (Man who pulls the fan), Chokidar (Watchman or Gatekeeper), Chahwala (Man who serves tea), Aya (Lady who looks after children), last not the least Mali(Gardener), plus drivers, cleaners, barbers and horse -stable coolies.

I quote from the memoir of Margret 'Recalling the Raj'; who is one of our senior most colleagues in the Creative writing class, "My mother's role as a white Memsahib married to the army officer, was clearly defined. She was expected to run a household of Indian servants, the size of which increased with each of my father's promotions, attend regimental balls and dinners, and idly speculates about the comings and goings of the other Memsahibs (White-Women). She was not encouraged to fraternise with the local population. In fact there was total segregation of the races, in the dying days of the British Raj, with separate trains, buses, and restaurants. Despised by both parties were the unfortunate of mixed parentage, who often made desperate attempts to conceal their origin." She was two years old when set sail for India, Edward VIII had yet to abdicate and Second World War was three years away. Her father was an officer in the British Army. She herself later retired as a teacher in England. Margaret has shown me a memorable picture of her, sitting in the lap of her Aya, while her elder brother stood next to her holding hand. There is a clear picture of their lodge in the background.

At the time of Partition the younger daughter of Lord Mountbatten, Pamela, had accompanied her parents to India and stayed there for eighteen months. She would normally join the viceroy's entourage to attend all important functions and meetings; and thus luckily had managed to maintain a meticulous daily diary herself. At that time she was only seventeen years old and was so thrilled that she immediately packed up her studies and became a part of the great epic historical moment. In her unique and unusually enlightened book 'India Remembered' which is derived from the entries of her 'Daily Diary' and she describes without any false pretence or prejudice:

'The Viceroy's House compound had 555 servants, so with their families, there will be several thousand and a separate school. There are swarms of servants and endless cocktail parties and people to meals and there seems to be five thousand attached to the Viceroy' house, it was completed only 20 years before the partition in the heart of a magnificent Mughal garden'. She further reminisces, 'I do not know what to say to these servants and how to say and why?' Back home in England, she was not used to any!

This was the era when the army captain's entourage would accompany more than two hundred coolies and backed by a caravan of camels, bull-carts, horse-wagons, carrying provisions, boxes of whisky and wines and in addition some concubines waiting at the next campsite. That was the time, when the Sahib would shoot out dozens of tigers and send their skins back home to Great Britain as souvenir.

However at the time of her wedding, Grandmother was only a fourteen years old, but well trained and mature for her age and looking forward to settle down in her new home hundreds of miles away. She was expected to stay in a joint family and pay less frequent visits to her parents. She sprang up like a delicate blossom of pomegranate and clad in a traditional - bridal dress of red silk, with lot of fancy gold embroidery on it. It was also a local tradition for the Indian bride to wear Hina on her hands and feet, filled with exotic perfumes. Her parents had made special sets of jewellery for her on order. The ear-rings which I am lucky to hold at the moment are part of them. They are made of pure gold and created by a very skilful family goldsmith. Its stem is clustered with small rectangular petals of gold swaying down the edge. It shows up a combination of three inverted canopies, fixed on top of each other, each one bigger than the other as it goes down. Additionally their value and beauty is enhanced by jutting and encrusting colourful rubies and sapphires around the stem and the petals. It is indeed a very skilful and beautiful design.

Although she was very beautiful herself and did not need any ornaments to enhance her charm, but those were the traditional gifts from her parents, as well as family members to remember their love for her, as well a sign of warm welcome from the bridegroom's side. In fact the ornaments dangling in her ears or fixed on her forehead or in her nose blot like a scar on the full glowing moon. However it was a local Indian tradition and had to be fulfilled. Everyone in the family looked forward to seeing those glittering gifts and in turn appreciated them .They also expected to see that bride was laden with different sets of good quality designs and taste. No doubt that her friends and relatives, especially the bride-groom and her in-laws admire them and of course her as well, laden with the wonderful jewellery. Unfortunately the groom's side would normally reap all the wealth, but the bride's side had to sacrifice as per Indian culture. If someone from either side cannot afford because of financial crunch, then heads would roll. Her skin was piercing and silvery like the first rays of sun falling on the horizon and the glitter of jewellery on her body made her more stunning. Someone hovering over my shoulders at the moment has just gestured and whispered in my ears and I must quote, "When the maker will peep down the sky, He will wonder as to who has had made her!" But there is no doubt that I feel proud to be her offspring.

In the Indian culture it is a common practice and tradition all across the board that there is a special time assigned at the bride's house as well as at the groom's house for exhibition of dowry, clothes, gifts and especially jewellery to all the female guests and a great appreciation and adverse remarks are showered in the gathering depending upon the quality of the displayed items. Visitors and family members ask lots of questions who has given the gold or who has not and why and why not and shower comments in favour or against. According to the typical local, traditional and pagan Indian belief, the possession of gold is considered to be a sign of good luck. Just imagine the tons of gold being consumed annually in this unfairly impoverished region and later lying dormant in the vaults waiting for rainy days. This paradox pairs very well with the caste system. It does not matter whether someone is the Muslim, Hindu, Sikh or Budhist or a Christian. There are lot of instances where brides are burnt alive or divorced on the spot or disfigured, if they do not come with dowry or valuables and it can cause serious family feuds. There are numbers of incidents when the wedding party is returned without the bride, as a result of such disputes, especially if the groom arrives without any jewellery for the bride. Over here two 'Ws' are involved, woman and wealth; wine just simmers and shimmers inside. It is one more deep rooted irony of Indian culture after the Caste System.

As soon as the wedding party headed by the bridegroom and his parents was in sight, the hosts at this end go forward to welcome them. They had trailed by bull-carts, horses, on foot and as well as by Dolees (Children and women only) raising lot of dust clouds in the air as well as arousing storms of sentiments, especially for teenagers.. The grandmother, sisters, mother, children and females, all peeped and gazed through the gap of their entrance or from top of the stairs or their flat roof. Instantly all members of the wedding party are garlanded with strings of fragrant roses as is typical of Indian custom and then followed by embraces, cuddles and kisses, exchange of laughs, smiles and introductions. The female guests are taken inside straight away, followed by the bridegroom to meet the family and the bride. The bride and groom can hardly restraint themselves and their hearts beat like hawks. An excellent seating arrangement had been made by erecting tents and laying down the furniture on the red carpet. As is traditional the guests were helped to wash their hands or to refresh themselves and entertained with live music. To start with a variety of refreshments including hot and cold drinks were served to all guests. Quite a few of the visitors liked to have few puffs of the newly prepared hubbly-bubbly while at the same time they had a casual gossip with each other. The atmosphere was very relaxing and there was a magical blend of the laughs, jokes and personal exchange of emotions. There were lots of giggles, titters and glees; glimpses, stares and pleas. This is the only time when everyone was free.

The wedding party was welcomed by the thump of the Dholki (typical Indian wedding drum) and songs by the girls, followed by dances inside the house. The outside gathering was equally amused by the professional musicians and dancers. The Mullah was also waiting solemnly amongst the wedding party to perform the wedding ceremony and for endowment of his blessings. However grandmother was well pleased to gaze at her spouse, and he was more than thrilled to have a quick glimpse of her. At that moment the tradition went that the people used to marry in the same village and within the same tribe, but the horizon had been widening steadily after the introduction of the railways and motor transport. Now the indigenous people could migrate to other parts of India with ease or indeed to abroad for business or jobs and even for further education... This is also becoming an era of competition and money makes the mare go, people are becoming more and more aware about the status, education and looks. The tribal and caste noose is steadily loosening at this moment, but not quite yet. It is still being resisted and sticking like an adhesive or a gum.

I must narrate one particular eye opener's incident relating to one of my uncles, who was very handsome and noble; and got married to one of my aunties, who was not good looking or attractive. Obviously this was an arranged marriage. They never saw or met each other before getting married. So on the first night, in the bridal room, he was shocked to find her waiting for him in the bed under the bridal decorated and perfumed canopy. He immediately retreated out of his room without touching her or having a word and disappeared into the oblivion for good. She has been still waiting for him from her first wedding night over the last fifty years and has died since. It was speculated that he ran away with the gypsies or nomads from central Asia or Afghanistan, who were camping in the tents just out in the nearby jungle or a barren strip of common land. Their girls are stunningly beautiful, with fair skin and with blue, green, brown and hazel eyes. For thousands of years Afghanistan was a part of India or India was ruled from Afghanistan. The first Mughal emperor Babar who is buried in Kabul, also adventured to Delhi from there. So were the many rulers of India for many centuries before. Even in my youth I used to observe camel caravans of gypsies and nomads coming to Pakistan and perhaps going further to India for doing business or construction work in the winter season. The border between Pakistan and Afghanistan was never controlled by the border police of either country. The simple reason is that the people on either side of the border line are the same and relatives to each other. Later when I visited central Asia, I found those people resembling us, wearing the same kind of dress and eating similar kind of food. The imaginary border line between Afghanistan and India (over 1200 miles long) is highly porous and rugged. It was drawn by Sir Henry Durand in 1893 to divide the warlike Pathan tribes into two zones on the paper, but still the British and indeed the Pakistani could not control them. This tribal belt is over 100,000 square kilometres in area and has been declared as a free zone and untameable even at the time of British empire.. However my uncle's parents have been in a terrible turmoil and there are many rumours and speculations that he might have drowned himself in the river or plunged into a well or might be sheltering into the remote areas, but the best known popular speculation was that he had fled with the nomads, vanished with the gypsy girls and perhaps had sunk, soaked and choked in there......

At grandma's wedding party some colourful and sensuous rituals had taken place as well. The young sisters and nieces of the bride had gathered around the groom in full force and had snatched his shoes while he was sitting snugly next to his bride in front of the female audience and concealed them somewhere in their laps, but had promised to return them in exchange for a substantial sum of money. The bridegroom was naturally tempted by so many beauties clad in colourful dresses and full of fragrance and with captivating smiles. However he had already been briefed what he had to do in case of such bloodthirsty callous assault and he pretended as if he was not bothered and gave the girls some funny cool smiles with teasing gestures. He had already some reasonable figure in his mind, but kept the girls in suspense and let them speculate. There was lot of exchange of bargains and haggling before the final figure was revealed. But he had come to the final figure after lot of booing, slogans and sensuous remarks by the ever demanding and boisterous girls. On top of that he kept on staring and smiling at the bride as well as the girls. Those were the last few moments of his freedom and that was a kind of bridal training how to deal with the bride and also to make him familiar and her as well with each other. After all it was an arranged marriage. Grandmother was enjoying the magical scenario and she played both ways, but was mainly interested in the welfare of the groom already. At that moment her feelings were a blend of missing her parents, family, friends and the village itself, but looked forward to a happy married life, to have her children and a comfortable home. Sometimes she smiled, sometimes tears filled her eyes. The whole family and friends were there to bid her farewell. The touch of her ear-rings, bridal clothes, the sight of her spouse, the aroma of food being cooked and served in the open fields and the hustle and bustle everywhere, everyone in a celebration mood, aroused her feelings and she forgot she was leaving her parental home for-good, far away and forever.

With tears trickling down her cheeks and with her heart fluttering, she bade goodbye to her village amidst tears and hugs of her parents, family and friends. She travelled over two hundred miles, over the fields, dusty paths, sandy tracks, by train and finally by horse-coach. To begin with she was carried from her parental home by four men on their shoulders in the 'Dolee'. This is the only comfortable transport available in this remote village, as all the paths, tracks and roads are bumpy and dusty; and scarred with pot-holes. She was accompanied with her aunt to look after her during the course of her virgin journey. Some other female members and children had also used Dolees as well. Most of the males travelled on foot or trot on the horses or by the jerky and bumpy bull-carts, but they all raised lot of clouds of dust. The newly constructed railway station was few hours away. The bridegroom travelled on a decorated horse and escorted his bride's nest. The whole of the wedding party had travelled together in the shape of a caravan. They trailed as if on a picnic. They had lot of excitement, warm emotions and pleasant feelings.

The Dolee resembles a wooden cabin built on a ship and can carry two to three persons, squatting comfortably with cushions, and could even sleep, just like in a bed. It is normally embedded on two thick wooden rods, beams or shafts. It looks like a doll-house or a tent or a nest of birds perched on the twigs. Traditionally it was an ancient practice to carry brides, even in the centre of the village or a town. It used to be also a common routine to carry women and children of the noble families from one place to the other or from one village to the other or carry them in the town or a city. The same conveyance was used to carry sick, lame and lazy or old. However I was privileged to have travelled once or twice by a Dolee with my grandmother when I trailed from my maternal village to the paternal village which were about ten miles apart from each other. It was fascinating to be carried by men, one feels high and lofty. (In the USA, the expatriates from the Indian subcontinent, sometimes use these exquisite lifts on their daughter's wedding; In this scenario they only cruise from six to seven stars, as the newly wedded couple normally spend their wedding night in the hotel. It is difficult to say what happens to the groom, perhaps he trots on a horse back, walks on foot or use an exotic car or perhaps snug with the bride!)

Dolees were also used in the siege of Delhi, at the time of mutiny in 1857, carrying the Honourable East India Company's injured soldiers. Amongst the war heroes thus carried was Brigadier–General John Nicholson from Ulster who was fatally wounded during the assault and breach of the great walls of the Red Fort. Nicholson was escorted to the field hospital by his most trusted body guard named Hayat Muhammad Khan, a tower like figure with big moustaches and a fearsome man. The general died on 23 September 1857 at age of 34, just 9 days after his injury and still buried there. Later Khan was promoted to a post of commissioner, in his native Punjab and awarded a huge estate. He also carried a huge booty of fair ladies and piles of wealth with him returning home. Also among the injured and carried in the Dolee was Neville Chamberlain, then military secretary of the Punjab Board of Administration Lahore, later called Field Marshall Sir Neville Chamberlain, died in 1902, a year after the Great Queen Victoria.

Delhi's brand new red fort and the thick walled city with mighty gates was built by the Mughal emperor Shah Jahan (King of the World), the man who had built Taj Mahal and Shalimar Gardens in Lahore and Kashmir. Before the Mughals, there were other Muslim Sultans or rulers, who had shifted their capital to Delhi, almost over seven hundred years before them. They did that because of its central position thus making it easier to look after the empire. They too had built magnificent palaces, forts, tombs, mosques and they ruled happily with the indigenous Hindu population. There was never racial or religious tension between the rulers and their subjects, rather there were lot of inter marriages.

The grandpa was riding the decorated horse, galloping alongside the entourage of grandmother sitting erect. His turban pierced to the sky. His bridal attire flashed like a feudal chief and he appeared to be submerged in emotions, while grandma peeped through the slit of the curtain. The Dolees kept the bride and other passengers travelling in them away from the dust, away from miscreants or harsh weather. At that moment the sun shone bright and crisp, over the wild bush and semi alluvial plain. The temperature was mild and mellow. The whole wedding party was trailing in great harmony. The old people sank in their nostalgic reminiscences, while the young ones were surged in excitement and submerged in fantasy. Some youngsters, ladies and old men were travelling by the ox- wagons; their ride was rather bumpy and jumpy because of pot-holes and uneven terrain and they had raised lot of dust clouds with the rattle of the wooden wheels. The oxen were trudging hard along the route with huffs and puffs and trickles of liquid foam were oozing and dripping from their mouths, their eyes were rolling and tongues were dangling with the fierce toil of their drive. But the tinkles and peals of the bells dangling from the necks of the bulls blended very well with the dust of the wedding caravan. Although the journey was full of fatigue, it was enchanting like a picnic of a life time and glimpsed like a romantic dream. They meandered and swayed like a stream cascading down the slopes of the romantic green valley.

Not long ago, one of our great uncles while leading his wedding – procession on the back of his horse, disappeared somewhere soon after the wedding party paused for a short convenience break in the wild bush area. The men proceeded on one side and the women and children on the other direction. When everyone who wanted to be relieved had finished and refreshed; they got ready to march again. But before the departure of the caravan there was lot of panic and disturbance in the wedding camp because they could not find the bride-groom anywhere and the wedding pony was still tethered with the stump of the tree waiting for the bridegroom. They searched the groom in every bush, clump of trees, every field, potholes or troughs, but no luck. In the confusion a young boy had heard some giggles and grunts filtering through the Dolee. Eventually they had found him squatting in the Dolee, sharing milk with his bride. It is alleged that he was so keen to get married that he used to caress and play with the oval shape reclining jumbo –pillow. However their thrill and zeal continued and the couple had managed to produce some twelve sons and a lonely daughter just like the Biblical prophet. The eldest sons and the mother produced children concurrently. Unfortunately the great uncle died earlier than his beloved wife, perhaps he was too exhausted, but she was still resilient. However an old man in the wedding party smiled and gestured, "I wish that I become a young man again, I like this." Perhaps this is the heart beat of every bridegroom in the wild, why wait for the intensity of the dark night or flickering of the moonlight or even the twinkle of the stars!

At last the railway station was in sight, the wedding party had been trailing for more than six hours, the sun was dipping down the horizon, changed its colour from silver to red, to orange and violet, from pink to green and finally to grey dark. Soon it was twilight. The whole journey floated across in fantasy and the hours sounded like a flash or a fraction of it! It resembled the shadow of the cruising cloud in the blue sky. Now it was complete dark, getting quite chilly and a bit windy, green signal was already down. The train luckily was in time. The signal man had struck the strokes to the metallic disc to alert the passengers that the train was arriving within a matter of minutes, every -one including the coolies carrying the luggage, took positions on the platform to enter the coaches. Grandmother had viewed a train for the first -time, in fact she had come out of her village for the first time. To her it appeared like a glittering shooting star falling from the sky with great sizzles, hisses and thrusts, heading towards the horizon. The glaring beams of steam engine's lights were too dazzling and choking for her eyes. Her eyes squint and she puts her hands on her forehead to view how the engine or train looked. She kept on staring at the approaching train. It cruised into the station with the usual hiss, sizzle and thrust of the mighty steam engine. She was sure that an Englishman was driving it. Later I ask her, "Ma, how did you feel when you first saw the train and travel in it?" "Oh it was an amazing experience. The train was so far more comfortable and faster compared to the bull-carts, horses or Dolees. There were bright lights inside the train as well. All long distant passengers came with their blankets and quilts as well as plenty of food. It was just like having a picnic in some rest house. The trees and fields were whirling and twirling around the train. I even did not realise whether I was travelling. It was really wonderful, although there was still lot of dust coming in the train, because so many passengers were leaving the windows open for sightseeing the terrain and villages around us, even in the night time." She recollected. "How did you feel about the grand dad?" I asked reluctantly. "I found him very impressive and full of goodness. He kept on coming to our compartment with excuse to bring fruit and drinks. First I felt a bit embarrassed, but soon I got used to him, in fact looked forward to seeing him. I was sitting comfortably in the train and I felt as if I was sitting in the lounge of my house." She narrated. "There was lot of smoke coming up the funnel of the steam engine and the engine looked like a bowler hat, I thought that the Englishmen were smoking lot of cigarettes while having a chattering in the engine room." She gestured in a kind of her own joking and laughing mood.

The train had separate compartments for male and female passengers, so grandma proceeded to her coach along with other females. She was being supported by her aunt and got her settled in her seat. They had carried food and blankets with them for the night sleep and also had secured their valuables, which were comparatively safer in the woman' compartment. The culture of night time train robbers had already begun. This brand new station was built only ten years ago, but the robbers who used to intercept the trade caravans had now moved to the trains. Over here they enjoyed the free ride to their destinations as well as the soft target for their plunder.

However the train journey was not direct, so the wedding party had to change at two more train junctions, but eventually arrived safely to their final destination at Montgomery. As usual the coolies dressed in baggy uniforms unloaded their luggage from the train and escorted them to the waiting tongas outside the station. The wedding trail from the station back home to her new home was most pleasant of all. They crossed over the main bridge of the mighty canal, went across the parks and through the gardens; they found no dust and it was very clean all the way to her new and permanent home.

Montgomery was named after and founded by Sir Robert Montgomery in 1865 just eight years after the Indian Mutiny. He was a very fine colonial administrator of the East India Company. Robert was born at New Park, Moville, County Donegal, Ireland in 1809 and died in India in 1887 (aged 78), just one month after the birth of his grandson Bernard. He was the Lieutenant Governor of Lahore, Punjab at that time. At the age of seventeen he set off for India, initially to work and earn fortune for his family who were a family of Anglo Irish priests and preachers. At that time India was a golden sparrow and far more prosperous as compared to Europe, Britain or Ireland. Robert became a celebrated fine soldier, an excellent planner, a commissioner and later enthroned as Lieutenant Governor of the most prosperous province of Punjab based at Lahore, who later developed this semi-arid alluvial plain and transformed it into a bread basket of India. His grandson was Field Marshall Viscount Bernard Montgomery (Monty of Alamein). Even 'Monty' who was born in Kennington, London on 17 November 1887 to the second son of Sir Robert called Reverend Henry Hutchinson Montgomery, at the time the Vicar of St Mark's, Kennington, started his military carrier in India as a second lieutenant by joining The Warwickshire Regiment in September 1908, seeing service in India until 1913. He used millions of Indian soldiers fighting in the World wars One and Two all over the globe including Europe, Africa and the Middle East and thus made far reaching changes over the planet. After about fifteen years another similar town was created on the right bank of River Ravi some sixty miles away from Montgomery, which is located on the left bank of river Ravi. This is called Lyallpur which is named after its creator and another British genius called Charles James Lyall.

Lyall was born in London on 9 March 1845 and progressed on the lines of Sir Robert Montgomery and rose to the greatest prestigious and sought after job of the Lieutenant Governor of the Punjab. At the time of its foundation Lyallpur was merely a canal colony sprawling with few thousand houses, but now it boasts of being the third largest city of Pakistan after Karachi and Lahore. Lyallpur is also named to be the twin city of Manchester for being the greatest industrial town of Pakistan famous for its textile mills and other manufacturing industries and now its population soars to over three millions. The design of Lyallpur is even more amazing, which is based on the Union Jack, with eight roads radiating from a large clock tower in the centre. The eight roads developed into eight separate bazaars. The town and its vast district or rural area is provided with railways as well as a vast canal passing through the town, barraged from River Chenab as well as its hundreds of miles of net worked distributaries for irrigation.

However the brand new settlement of Montgomery was developed on a modern British scale and its grid and layout was beautiful, with a magnificent railway station, coal-power house for generating electricity, as well as civil courts of justice, Christian Mission Hospital and a church of gothic design with a lofty spire. The roads were of broad grid, planted with good quality trees. They built separate hospitals for ladies and gents, veterinary hospital for the animals, canal colony, a high security central jail, where most dangerous prisoners from all over India were brought in and, police offices and Post offices. They also built local municipal offices, library, water supply towers, an excellent sewerage system, modern drains and rubbish collection system. At that moment the settlement had about 15,000 residents, my grandfather, a practising lawyer, was one of them. This brand new colony consisted of government and civic centre buildings, stables for the horses, playgrounds, schools, bungalows and lodges for the officials, rest houses, clubs, and a sports stadium to mention only a few. The settlement was dotted with gardens, parks, orchards and private metalled roads, planted with lofty and imposing rows of trees. Cleanliness was immaculate, just the opposite to other Indian towns and cities. I was favoured to be born in Montgomery on a foggy and glistening morning of December 1939; delivered by a midwife called Bharri, in the local maternity hospital near to our house.

The main character in this settlement is the major canal dug out, bigger than River Thames and its vast network of distributaries, passing through the heart of the new town. Punjab means land of five major perennial rivers, but many more other rivers fall into them. They fetch down colossal quantity of water from over a thousand of miles, some as far as Tibet, West China, and Afghanistan, from the highest mountains of the planet, such as Himalayas, Hindukush, Karakarum and many more ranges of mountains. Although most of the water is from the melted - glaciers, some is also from the Monsoon rains and as well as Westerlies. This canal was part of vast network of irrigation system, which fans all over India, particularly in the Punjab, especially in West Punjab, which irrigate millions of acres of land. There are excellent barrages built over the rivers to harness water and as well as bridges over the canals. They also supply hydro-electric power. The canals, roads and railways are spread parallel to each other and most of the villages, towns and cities flourish around them. The arteries of the canal and its distributaries supply water to each single bush and tree in the settlement.

The town had some segregated or 'No Go Areas', assigned exclusively for the white residents who had huge bungalows and offices of the top officials with private roads and gardens; and that arrogance still continues for ever as far as the Pakistani Englishmen are concerned. The only difference is that Pakistani Englishmen do not dig any new irrigation canals or build any new hydroelectric projects, but they rather prefer to build their own palaces with the public funds and keep the public in the dark of load-shading. However the British ingenuity glittered and glowed just like grandma's ear-rings. At the time of the empire and even long after that a visitor to the Deputy Commissioner's office would read his title, highlighted in bold capital letters on a gigantic erected wooden white painted board, and flashed as below:

"Office of the Sir, the Honourable, the Deputy Commissioner Sahib Bahadur (English Warrior) of Montgomery District." In addition to this his huge secluded lodge was fully guarded and loaded with a variety of anxiously waiting servants, drivers and caretakers. They were all clad in smart and immaculately pressed uniforms and enhanced with erected turbans and stood in a shipshape readiness and waited for the order from the Memsahib or the Sahib. Those titles, facilities and protocols increased or decreased along the line of hierarchy in a spectacular and splendid manner and still continue doggedly in Pakistan.

Montgomery is located about 15 kilometres from Harappa, the cradle of Indus Valley Civilisation and the grand -canal cruises directly to it from Montgomery. In Harappa, there is not much left now, because the site has been plundered or ransacked over the centuries. Most of its valuables and artefacts are now displayed now in all major museums of the developed world including the Great Britain, USA, Russia, China, France, Germany, Spain and Italy. Its twin city Mohan- Judaru is located some five hundred miles down to the south on the banks of the gifted 'Indus River'. India got its name from this river and from this civilisation. Great British archaeologists Alexander Cunningham (1864) and john Marshall (1913) discover and excavated these sites buried under 6,000 years under soil. It is difficult to say as to why they perished, it could have been due to the flash floods in the great rivers or perhaps destruction by invaders, as this destination was always popular for foreign marauders or possibly by the earthquakes. These great archaeologists also discover Taxila, near Islamabad, where Alexander the Great fought the Indian ruler Porus and from where he turned back to Greece. Taxila was the capital of ancient India from where The Great Ashoka and Kanishka ruled, not only in India, but also over Central Asian territories as well. Budhism and Hinduism spread from here to other part of Asia during this golden era. There is a magnificent museum at Taxila which was established by the British and worth visiting; it is indeed a very popular itinerary for the international and local explorers. It is easily comparable with the concurrent Egyptian, Chinese, Persian and Iraqi Civilisations.

However it was not only me who was born in Montgomery, but also the Chief Air Marshall Arjan Singh (A Sikh himself) of The Indian Air Force, was born over here as well. His bombers had attacked some military positions in Montgomery during the war of 1965 and as a result one of his shot down bombers is hanged in a newly developed square, between the railway station and the great canal and displays like a dead bee, reminding the onlooker what Montgomery can do when attacked. Montgomery is very famous for its fine pedigree of cows and bulls, oranges, mangoes, cotton, wheat, and Basmati rice and exported all over the world, especially to Great Britain, Middle East Canada, Europe, South East Asia and Japan.

There is another landmark, called Mitchells Farms, an ever glorious British genius, worth mentioning in our district of Montgomery; situated fifty miles upstream along the great canal. It is the great orchard or plantation for 'Red Blood' oranges as well as different other high quality varieties of oranges, mangoes, grapefruit and apples. It stretches about twelve miles long, miles wide and has three railway stations dotted along its length located at an interval of about four miles each. This is laid mainly on the left bank of the great canal. It is very pleasant for the eyes, while zooming by the train, to gaze at the deep orange colour shining and blazing on the skin of the fruit and the umbrellas of the shining green leaves in the crisp, cool and bright winter weather. The trees are planted in straight rows and at fixed intervals and again for miles. The soil is well tilled and clear of any weeds or under growth. The workers patrol the plantation just like soldiers; they pick up the fruit and load them in the wagons for processing, sale and marketing. There is a huge factory inside the vast plantation called Mitchell factory for bottling and canning the fresh juices and pulps. They also prepare different products from the oranges as well as from other exotic fruit; thus employ lot of local working force on a permanent basis. They also produce their own honey, jams and squashes of great purity and flavours and in great demand. Now quite a few other competitive private landlords with huge agricultural estates have developed their lands on a similar pattern, although not as compatible and mass producers of oranges of different varieties as well as other exotic fruit just like mangoes, apples, pears, apricots and cherries and export them all over the world earning foreign exchange for the national exchequer, as well as consumed locally in abundance at a grass root level because they are sold at a cheaper rate, although very sumptuous and delicious and of high quality, and affordable by almost all indigenous people.

In addition to the above there is one more feat of the British excellence in civil engineering and land development in Montgomery area. They diverted a flow of water from the main canal and looped it one mile before it enters the main canal again. Over this loop they build a hydro-electric power house at Renala Khurd, where Mitchell Factory is located as well as a canal colony, which generates 1.1 Megawatts of electricity by fixing five turbines. This is almost at nil cost and is environmentally friendly. Thus it is a glamorous piece of jewellery for the people of our area. This project supplies electricity not only to the large settlements nearby, but also to the vast Mitchell fruit farms and factories. There is a potential to generate five times more hydro-electricity, but Pakistan has not done an iota to harness this potential, perhaps they are waiting for the British again! Even the single rail track from Peshawar to Karachi (over 1200 miles) and passing through Montgomery still remains single, although the population has exploded almost to six folds since independence. There is a colossal potential to improve the irrigation system in Pakistan and also to generate cheaper and more environment friendly hydro-electricity by building up new dams over the mighty perennial rivers by following the British skills and initiative, but it would appear that Pakistan is an almost a virgin country from this perspective. They need to divert attention from children productions to the generation of hydro-electricity and building up new dams and barrages and then no one would be able to match with them. At the moment the country and its people drown in load-shedding of electricity, flash-floods and corruption, which need to be rectified sooner rather than later in order to survive with dignity and self-reliance.

After arriving in Montgomery Grandma was happy to be there and settled very well within no time. She found the new place very pleasant and comfortable. She liked the modern town with wide open roads, lofty trees and the gardens. Now she had electricity in the house which was being generated from the coal power plant situated on the embankment of the canal. She was also pleased with the modern civil and maternity hospitals for the ladies not far away from her house. She was rather amazed that a mighty canal and its distribution network were passing through the heart of the town. Soon she had forgotten her magical maternal village and even her parents. She appreciated the modern sewerage system as well the refuse collection arrangements. She was also thankful for getting fresh and clean water supplied by the local municipal corporation on a nominal charges basis. Even the modern shopping bazaars were conveniently located nearby. They often used to go for a walk along the wide avenues as well as on the embankment of the canal lined up with lofty Cypress, Eucalyptus, Poplar trees as well as decorated with flower beds and bushes. The smiling blossoms of roses, jasmine, crocus and chambaili flowers tossed in the bright and crispy sunshine filled the atmosphere with pleasant colours and fragrance. While the gardeners toiled tirelessly to keep the park tidy and trim. The flowers bush laden with blossoms stooped down the embankment to have a glimpse in the icy clean water coming from the melted glaciers. The fish rose and jumped in the air, wiggled and waggled against the flow of the current. Not far away in the horizon the ducks fluttered and slapped in the canal and rose to the sky. The canal and the lines of lofty trees disappeared straight in the horizon like a blissful, everlasting, Jewel in the Crown. It gives life and support to the millions, makes the soil able to grow a great variety of grain, vegetable and fruit from the most fertile land on the earth.

The bridgehead over which I stand at the moment is opposite to the railway station and is fascinating. It has been constructed with red bricks and joined with special waterproof cement. There are strong embankments and speed breakers contiguous to the main structure of the bridge. I often pause and reflect at its unique design and admire its structure. Unfortunately some of the brick work is piteously crumbling away now and the irrigation department has paid very little attention to rectify it, which is terribly distressing and perturbing for the pilgrims to this celestial canal which perhaps exists nowhere on this planet, especially in the middle of the town.. From the rear of the bridge the water level is raised by building barriers like that of the Thames Barrier which is located in the suburb of London and in the front it turns into waterfalls. It is a miniature of the great Niagara Falls, the water swoops and plunges through the seven gates with a celestial force. The roars, the thrusts and the gusts are full of deafening thunder. The water jumps in white steam and silvery sun rays refract water breeze and glitter like diamonds and splash showers of clouds in the air forming rainbows. Over here the water-falls twirl and swirl; foam and spume like serpents. If anybody falls down, then there is very little chance of survival. It is colourful and enchanting like an Indian Bride. The British being highly organised, had employed full time professional divers, who would squat over the bridge, day and night in shifts, just in case any admirer or a dejected lover falls down the bridge. Few such incidents of suicide, in the sizzling and whirling waters had been brought occasionally to the notice of the Sahibs during the empire days. Now it does not matter, the fertile land is exploding with the population.

While I reminisce and relax over this magnificent bridge and admire the British ingenuity and perseverance, enjoy the roars, thrusts and sizzles of whirling eddies and hold my grandma's ear-rings next to my heart, my thought goes to the legendary Koh-I-Noor (Mountain of light) Diamond and Takht-i-Taus (Peacock-Throne). In 1739 Iranian nomadic general and ruler, Nadir Shah, had invaded India and ventured up to Delhi. He ransacked the Red Fort, the Mughal court and the city of Delhi, had massacred hundreds and thousands of its inhabitants. The Mughal Emperor surrendered his glorious and magnificent throne to the Persian marauder to save his life and his Indian subjects. This has happens exactly two hundred years before my birth and the start of great World War Two. The route he followed was the same route on which I am standing at this moment. It is difficult to surmise whether he had taken this priceless throne, as well as the Koh- I -Noor Diamond which was encrusted to the throne, on the horse- coaches, bull-carts, camels or elephants, but perhaps most probably on the shoulders of Indian slaves just like a Dolee. I am sure he was over thrilled and rushed to the secured border of his country. Still it would have taken him a few months or so, as more atrocities and ransacking was supposed to be done on his caravan routes, while returning home with the priceless gift and an extraordinary plundered booty and spoil of war.

The name of the one only Peacock Throne came from the shape of the throne, having the figures of two peacocks standing behind it, their tails being expanded and the whole so inlaid with sapphires, rubies, emeralds, pearls, diamonds and other precious stones of appropriate colours as to represent life, created for the Great Mughal Emperor Shah Jahan (King of the World), in the 17th century. In fact the Peacock Throne was twice as costly as the Taj Mahal, built by the same emperor of India. This was the most glorious, dazzling and refined single piece of craft ever created by man on this planet. It also shows unparalleled aesthetic sense and love of art by the Emperor Shah Jahan. This will never be afforded in the future and no one had ever made such a stunning and an amazing item in the past. This also shows great skill of craftsmanship and taste of the designers, as well as the richness of Indian culture and wealth. One can hardly visualise the beauty and glow of it. Koh-I-Noor was part that exotic settings, along with similar priceless diamonds, rubies and valuable stones, jutted on pure gold.

I must quote from an article printed in the Sunday Tribune. 'It was, accordingly ordered that, in addition to the jewels in the imperial jewel house, rubies, garnets, diamonds, rich pearls and emeralds in all weighing 230 KG should be brought for the inspection of the Emperor and they should be handed over to Babadal Khan, the superintendent of the goldsmith's department. There was also to be given to him 1150 kg of pure gold. The throne was to be three yards in length, two and a half in breadth and five in height and supported by 12 emerald columns. Of the 11 Jewelled - recesses formed around it for cushions, the middle one was intended for the seat it for the Emperor. Among the historical diamonds, decorating it, were the famous Kohinoor (186 carats), the Akbar Shah (95 carats), the Shah (89 carats), the Jahangir (83 carats), and second largest spine ruby in the world-The Timur ruby (283 carats).

A -20 couplet poem by the Mughal poet- Laureate, Qudsi, praises the Emperor in emerald letters, was embedded in the throne. On March 12, 1635, Emperor Shah Jahan ascended for the first time to the newly completed Peacock Throne. It was usually at the Hall of Private Audience known as Diwan-i-Khas, although it was also kept at the Hall of Public Audience, known as the Diwan-i-Am, when larger audience was expected. Shah Jahan's throne was guarded by smartly dressed guards; Mughals, Indians, Africans and Turks. Any Rajas, rulers and feudal lords would come stooping in front of the Emperor. All movements were rigidly controlled. Foreign dignitaries had to wait for months before they could get audience with the emperor, they too had to stoop and bend in front of the Emperor. While Shah Jahan would relax and recline cross-legged against the peacocks, beautiful young maidens with low necks and marble chests, would stoop with swaying bunch of flowers and seek his majesty's attention.

I was so fascinated by the Peacock Throne that I paid a visit to Iran for a pilgrimage to the Peacock Throne in Tehran, but I could only have a glimpse of the deposed Shah's throne plumped in his discarded palace, now a museum. Unfortunately it exhibited just like a chair embedded with gold and jewels. It was quite disappointing and depressing for me. However it had turned up that after few years of the fateful expedition in India, a terrible feud broke out between Nadir Shah and his lawless generals; as a result of which he was assassinated in 1747, just 8 years after the possession of the Peacock Throne. Subsequently the Peacock Throne was shattered and torn into pieces and distributed amongst the war lords. This must be a tragic moment for our glorious and glittering planet, as the dazzling and magnificent unique throne had disappeared forever. Subsequently The Mughal Empire also started crumbling, disintegrating and became highly fragile and frail. There were rebellions after rebellions, locally as well as from abroad. The Punjab became a part of Afghanistan's empire. On top of that the trading companies like East India Company, started encroaching from the East and the South. There were also other Europeans like the Portuguese, Dutch, Italians, French and Spanish, missionaries as well as trading companies, even fighting between themselves, to have access to the treasures of India. The humble mercenaries and traders of the Mughals' glorious Empire started killing their masters and occupied their domains and treasures. Thus there was a great chaos and lawlessness which followed after the invasion of Nadir Shah.

However after the assassination of Nadir Shah, Afghanistan had invaded Iran and occupied it. It is quite possible that they had invaded Iran for The Peacock Throne, but Afghans arrived a bit late and could not plunder the glorious throne. They just managed to get hold of the Kohinoor Diamond. Later the Afghans had appointed a very humble twenty years old Sikh Chieftain called Ranjit Singh; a man with one eye, the other eye had allegedly been damaged with the small pox, as their Governor of Lahore. They provided him with the guns and arms to protect their domain of the Punjab. After some period, the Afghan war lords had feud among themselves and their rule crumbled even in Afghanistan and had been divided between different factions of war lords who kept on fighting among themselves. As a result one of their princes called Shujah Shah later had taken shelter in the citadel of Lahore, with his governor Ranjit Singh for protection of his life. He carried Kohinoor under his turban, until one day Ranjit's courtier saw it. From that time onward, Kohinoor became the possession of the Sikhs, now firmly independent rulers of Lahore. Afterwards The British fought wars with the Sikhs and became rulers of the Punjab and Kohinoor was sent to London in 1851, as spoil of war. I wish it could have been Peacock Throne as well! At least the legendary throne would have been in the safe custody of The Beef-Eaters, in Tower of London!

I have linked grandmother's ear-rings with the Peacock Throne, the Grand Canal, the Koh-I-Noor and the Great Indus Valley Civilisation and Budhist and Hindu Civilisations, to me they are all part of my heritage, may be related directly or indirectly. All these have profound effects on our forefathers, to the people currently living and generations to come. I have the same reminiscence and emotions about them. These have had a deep impact on our culture and our way of thinking, and reacting and have become a part of our blood circulation and a source of inspiration in the depth of our minds.

The Grand Canal embankment is just like a sacred shrine to me. I like the great deep and quiet flow of water, birds diving to catch fish, fish jumping in the air at the bridge head and pushing upstream like a submarine. Whenever I visit Montgomery, I daily perform my pilgrimage in the early mornings and in the twilight, to the bridge-head and listen to the sizzle and roar of waterfalls, walk miles as usual on the embankment. I feel emotional, but keep to my heart, just like I keep the grandmother's ear-rings. I mesmerise myself with the rainbows, gaze at the lofty trees, admire the beautiful flowers, inspire from their fragrance which lifts my emotions. It also reminds me about my forefathers, when

I stare at the decaying trees, some half stooped, some fallen and rotten, some decaying trunks immersed in the canal. I stare at the ripples and waves which rise and fall in the deep water and then fade and merge with the main flow forever. I see life just like ripples which begins and melt without any controls and goes with the flow of the meanders. Although the canal appears to flow with great harmony and smoothness giving goodness to its people animals and crops, it soon disappears in the horizon, just like the humans wither after their trail of life!

Chapter II

Village School

It is difficult to surmise how and why I was there, but it was a unique magical place located in a wild bush area. The village was scarred by a vast sandy- dry and a flash- flood river bed. It was the village where my mother was born, brought up and got married. It was the place where my widowed maternal grandmother lived at that moment with her lonely son and younger daughter. Although both of her offspring were married, grandma lived with her son. They lodged on the left side of the river in a minor portion of the village, the major part of the village was located on the higher ground, on the right bank, my school was located there and that was where the bulk of the residents lodged. The soaring dark brown and hazy wall of The Himalayas appeared only a few miles away. To me the village appeared like an island, located within the sprawling and melting sheet of the flash floods. At the time of the Monsoons or rainy season, water poured and tumbled from all directions, as if into a bowl. Naturally the terrain was sandy, a mix of clay and loamy soil, which comprised of a fine and a fertile soft soil.

The neighbouring villages were separated from each other by that network of sandy dry river- beds. They stretched out down the slopes of The Himalayas, where the rivers meandered, joined and departed, like arteries and veins of the heart, fanned out and sprawled across the gradient of the plain. Flash flood waters crumpled and slithered like an agitated serpent. Waves upon waves rushed and gushed with great thrust and sway of hurricane winds and finally embraced the main river bed flowing gracefully scores of miles down the plain. However some deep perennial rivers intercepted the young and agile flash flood rivers and cruised between them. There was abundance of wild reeds around the banks of the rivers, as well as a carpet of green pastures with tall, soft grass and forests, spread along the cultivated fields. There were also clumps of mangoes, lemons and orange groves, as well as thorny Kikkar trees, speckled with thorny bushes. There were also soaring rows of wild Aloe Vera plants and cactus along with the dusty tracks, although green and thorny, but with plenty of pulp. Overshadowing all of them were the Bur trees. They spread like umbrella, grew very tall and had immense girth. They were evergreen, with wide leaves, and had dense and cool shadows underneath. On top of that the village was dotted with natural lakes made by the flash floods and lot of fish were caught by the village folks from them, by using jute nets. In addition the water buffaloes cooled down in them in summer, and cattle: cows, bulls, sheep, goats and horses drank water throughout the year. Sometimes children jumped in for splash and splatter and caught some fish.

The above wilderness of flora attracted and gave shelter to a great variety of wild life, which was captivating and fascinating .The wild life included many beautiful birds and animals, especially rabbits, deer, peacocks, wolves, foxes, chirping birds, snakes, neolas, lizards, colourful parrots, singing Koels, woodpeckers, to name only few. We often climbed the trees and picked up young chicks of parrots from the deep holes dug on the trunk of the trees, played and cuddled with them while they screeched and then later released them. We liked their red curved beaks, green feathers and bluish tails. We fancied to observe them how they nibbled the fruit, rotated their eyes and necks. We also tried to chatter and talk to them, caress them in our lap, sometimes they seemed to response to our chat and questions... We liked the melodious singing voice of the Koel, while she perched and fluttered over the fragrant Mango trees, especially in the romantic monsoons. While playing in the jungle and wild bush, we picked up some peacock eggs, prepared a bonfire from twigs and grilled them in the fields. We sat around the smouldering flame of fire, sniffed the billowing smoke, giggled and gossiped amongst ourselves while turning the grass and twigs for making the fire stronger, till the eggs were fully cooked. Once they were fully grilled, they automatically exploded from their shells and indeed a very refreshing exotic fresh and an aromatic meal to enjoy. Their taste and flavour was everlasting, nice and hot. Occasionally some of our elders observed us as they passed by and their mouth watered by the whiff of the wild cooked eggs. However they got amused by our amazing picnic. They paused for a moment and gestured at our ingenuity and skill; then trailed about on their daily chores. However they departed us with a warning, "Do not eat snake's eggs, or anything which resemble them!" The only difference between the two species was that peacock's eggs were pure white and large, while those of snakes were slightly smaller, a bit rusty and dabbled. We were made aware and warned. However the kids in our village were rather adventurous and tended to wander around and enjoyed ourselves without the company of the adults. We simply did not pay any heed to such warnings. My grandmother sometimes used to go on foot to meet her relatives in the nearby villages and took me with her, she often advised me, "Do not go to the jungle or wild bush, on your own, there were ghosts in them!" For a moment I was a bit scared in my mind, but later the magic and charm of the bush, orchards, fields, peacocks, rabbits, deer, parrots, green fields and flowers, overtook me. Sometime I used to stroll on my own, sometimes with other friends and sometimes with my uncle. The peace and tranquillity thus achieved was everlasting. Each moment, each wandering step appeared spellbound and magical.

Only a few days ago, I was startled by a boisterous chase of a mighty lizard by the men on the embankment of the flash flood river, but she was too strong and fast. The lizard managed to hide in the sugarcane field nearby. They did not give up either and called for the hunting hounds. The hounds searched into the sugarcane field along with the hunters, while some men laid a siege and kept vigilant over the perimeter of the field. I observed them as usual at a distance and waited for the outcome. At the end with diligence and perseverance they managed to chase the lizard out. While that drama of hot pursuit was raging, the lizard found a deep furrow or a hole and tried to squeeze herself into it.

The lizard seemed about three feet long and well fed. However she could not hide herself completely and rear part of her body, especially the tail remained dangling out of the hole, wiggled and waggled and thus became an easy target for the assailants as they had no fear of being attacked by the lizard.. At that moment the lizard was easily overtaken by the hounds and the men were using sticks and finally overpowered the lizard and battered her to death.

In Grandma's village, I recollect one enchanting sunny breezy morning when I criss-crossed alone in the cool and green fields of corn, admiring the natural goodness and peace. I got entranced with the cobs protruding upwards from the upper part of the stems with their dangling dark brown bushy tails and wrapped cushion of green fibrous leaves over them. I was so immersed in the green refreshing fields and the cool blue sky that I did not remember where I was standing. However momentarily there appeared a young fawn waggling its tail and dappled yellowish brown. He jumped and hopped just next to me and then vanished like a flash. His ears were tiny and he was huffing and puffing. It was roughly of my size, but rather lean and skinny; and perhaps a bit younger. I felt myself fiercely thrilled and extremely lucky to have such a close and wild view of him and wanted to grab and cuddle him. I quietly and carefully sneaked after him. I searched him everywhere in the fields, but alas I could not find him, perhaps he had gone miles away. I was still looking for him, he was still there, but where I did not know! I just gave up. Still there is a supreme innocence about this, a fascinating moment in my mind. It just jumped and ran across the river meadows and the lush green fields. I find it an amazingly beautiful and magical animal. This reminded me of my own loneliness and my plight. But this hypnotic moment is with me forever, Irresistible, charming and unforgettable. That cute and lightening fawn is still with me. I still yearn to find him, caress and cuddle him.

In the village I always liked the magnificent view of the graceful and colourful peacocks prowling in the fields, flying from one tree to the other, even dancing on the flat roof of the houses. Their croaking in the spring and the romantic monsoons aroused lot of feelings and emotions. Their presence over the trees or meadows reminisces like bluish green blotches on the horizon and their spread out plumes appealed to the eyes like a colourful shower. While on my way to and from the school, I also used to witness the innocent looking leverets with their doe hopping and jumping around in the bush and the fields; nibbling and eating the vegetables and plants. Again as I tried to catch them, they simply frisked away, but the pleasant nostalgia of their presence and hopping about still remains in my mind forever. I still see them with their beady- eyes and fur- coats crunching and sniffing; and with their ears and whiskers in the air. Unfortunately they were easy target for the village hunting hounds. The villagers liked their soft meat and their furs as well.

The snake charmer shared the wild life too with equal zeal and enthusiasm. He used his musical Bein to seduce and lure the snakes out of their lairs and shelters and later harnessed them with his pet Neola. Neola looked like a larger version of a cross -breed of a mouse and a squirrel, but with a thicker and a longer hairy tail. When the snake slithered out of the den, the snake charmer let loose his Neola and sets up a fight. It resembled a bloody fight between two cockerels or bull-dogs. However Neola was a genius, when the snake dilated and tried to bite, Neola used its tale as a defence and poked it into the snake's mouth .This device made the snake ineffective and he lost his biting capability. That was the moment when the snake charmer could snare the beast without the fear of being bitten. I think that the trading officials and administrators of East India Company had used the similar device and had learnt their empire building skills from the snake charmer. Initially they would make the two feuding indigenous factions to have a bloody fight between themselves to exhaust themselves to death. Then they would themselves land a few more punches on each of their bleeding noses. Then with a bit of bribery and threats, they would make them subservient and coolies. Then further they would use their resources and mercenaries to subdue the next indigenous factions. So this domino effect of subduing other nations continued with ease and speed. They very cleverly used the other people manpower and money to rule not only over them, but also over the far bigger, richer and stronger states.

A Bein is a kind of flute made from the outer shell of the pumpkin with wooden pipes fixed at its either end. It is a wonderful musical instrument, very cheap and effective to charm snakes and it has an intoxicating impact on them. There have been countless Indian Film songs in which this wonderful musical instrument has been played. The snake charmer normally wore yellow or green or an orange long cloak and same colour muslin turban to camouflage from the snakes. Lot of youngsters, including myself, as well as grown -ups followed him in the fields to witness the fight between the snake and the Neola. It was very thrilling, exhilarating and sensuous. One's eyes got fixed and hearts started beating fast; and waited in awe for the moment when the snake would come out and the battle would rage between him and the Neola. At the end the snake charmer was the winner and that was a great thriller for the crowd. Normally the farmers and gardeners informed the snake charmers about the location and the site of the snakes' shelters.

Although the village was located in the Muslim dominated area, there was a happy blend of some Sikh and Hindu families as well, who lived in their own separate communal areas; Though Sikhs and Hindus remained segregated from each other. Each indigenous religious group had their own worshipping place: a Temple, Gurdawara or a mosque. Apparently there was a unique religious tolerance and harmony in the village at that moment. Each community shared each other grief together, as well as enjoyed and celebrated each other religious and social events, just like a family. They had lot of common names, especially the first names, for example a Muslim name might be Kartar Bux, Menhdi Khan, while a Sikh or Hindu could be Kirtar Singh or Menhdi Ram. There appeared to me, as I recollect, some Hindu relatives living in the village, perhaps close blood relations. I remember going with my grandmother and aunt to pay condolences to the bereaved Hindu family .I noticed that the women in that family were wailing and beating their heads and breasts while standing over the coffin of the deceased, while we stood in silence staring at them. After some time an elderly man died in our family and subsequently the Hindu-relatives came to our house to pay the condolences. However there is no doubt in my mind that there were different mourning and burial rituals for each creed. For example in case of Muslims, they would take the deceased person to the graveyard for burial, in this case final prayers are performed by the Imam, but in case of Hindus, the rituals would be performed by the pujari(Priest), then the deceased person would be taken to the crematorium and burnt, and the ashes would be collected and thrown in the river. I am sure that the Sikhs also followed the rituals of the Hindus, but they would have their own religious leader to perform the final ceremony.

I recollect vividly that on two or three occasions, I accompanied my grandmother and aunt with some Hindu relatives, to a deep perennial- river, a mile away from our village. They floated some candles in the paper boats, which to me seemed fascinating seeing the flames floating and burning in the river and I can still visualise the peaceful sight of their flow and flickers. After the floating ceremony, they gave sweets to all, especially to the children and then returned home together on foot. Roughly in the same period a unique and queer ritual took place in our family as well. On the eve of the death of my great uncle, women from the Muslim community in our village (I believe they were all relatives), gathered each afternoon, for forty days at a stretch, in the vast dusty- courtyard of his house. They squatted cross-legged on the carpet or reed –mats, covered their heads and faces with white-Dopattas and began wailing collectively and continued the session for half an hour. Sometimes I joined them too with my grandmother and aunts, perhaps a wolf amongst the sheep. I spied into their hidden faces and tried to sense or evaluate the intensity of their grief. In nostalgia I feel sorry for the women who had to wail or at least pretend to cry or shed tears to keep the deceased person happy. However the good news is that they were not plunging down to a mass Sati pyre. I never noticed any mass weeping performed by the men when a woman passed away. At the termination of the self-imposed wailing session, I used to note who had the genuine tears. Not many, only one or two; perhaps none. The whole of the congregation seemed fake to me, but they all endeavoured to blow their noses and wipe their eyes. However it is quite possible that in this disguised routine most of them were laughing hilariously. Often I look back and think that such ideas and practices had been derived from the old pagan and ancient beliefs. After that episode, I had never encountered that kind of practice again. The reason could be the change of the venue due to the partition or perhaps the effect of the modern enlightenment in the society.

Our great uncle who had died was free at leisure and unconstrained. I have a feeling that he never married and had no children. He was a very rich man and had lots of estate at his disposal.. The story goes that he used to go to Simla to stay with his concubines, which was just over thirty miles away from our village. He used to come to the village for a short time stay to pick up the harvest money and off he went again to Simla. However I do not think he was in any way connected with the entourage of the viceroy. So when he died, there were plenty of prospective living beneficiaries to celebrate his death; thus they could not be shedding tears in grief, but could be in extreme exhilaration. At the end of forty days' mourning, a great feast was thrown for all the village folks celebrating his long and a happy life.

Simla was the glorious summer capital of British India and Viceroys had a very pompous and ever glittering stay over there. For the last Viceroy Lord Mountbatten it was even more enjoyable and powerful. The lives of the presidents and prime ministers and millions of Indians were under his golden feet. There were plenty of polo games, romantic dances, sumptuous and dazzling banquets. He had Pandit Nehru and his daughter Indira as his frequent guests in his palace. So there was more exchange of sensuous and fluttering moments. There Nehru used to stand on his head next to the swimming pool of the Viceroy's palace wearing his shortest possible underwear, but his white muslin hat was still covering his head and legs revolved nicely around his neck. Over there he used to teach skills about Yoga exercises to the inmates, especially to the females. His right hand man was called Sardar Patel. The Viceroy's wife Lady Edwina fell in deeply in love with Mr Nehru and those fragrant relationships lasted for a long time even after Independence. Plenty of cream rolls rolled immersed in the exotic Simla tea. It is difficult to say how Mrs Kamala Nehru might have reacted in those charged emotional circumstances as normally she had been left alone back home in Allah Abad (pure Muslim name), perhaps she would have her own free and exotic time, quite a few stories were rumoured about her as well. Fatefully Kamala died on February 28, 1936 in Lausanne at tender age of 37 while on tour of Europe. There were frequent chattering and discussions behind the scenes about the hidden and high romance between the amicable parties on give and take basis. It was also alleged that one of the mysterious aides to Mr Nehru called V.P. Mennon had drawn the boundary line of Partition of India as directed by his charismatic leader and then passed on the map to the Viceroy for his perusal and then in return His Excellency took it by hand to the parliament in Westminster for the final British authority and Royal final consent; then followed grotesque communal violence in the history of mankind.

In grandma's village the Untouchables performed most of the dirty and menial chores for all the other communities and dwelled in a poor and neglected area of the village. Their living standard was far below than the other groups, but they lived together as a close and a united people. As far as I can remember, they were called Chumars, who performed sanitary, street cleansing and toilet clearance work. They even disposed of dead animals and also scrounged for food and thrived on left overs. They also collected timber and logs for the cremation of the deceased persons for the Hindu and Sikh communities, which took place in their own open crematorium, although executed under the blessings and prayers of each individual religious leader. As a child, I thought Hindus and Sikhs were of the same belief and culture. The only anomaly and difference I noticed from my school mates was that a Sikh boy would lock and knot his long hair on the top of his head, while a Hindu boy normally would have a pony- tail or a pig-tail at the back of his head, with rest of his head shaven. In case of a Muslim, there was no visible physical distinction, apart from circumcision, which is normally hidden from the view of the public.

In grandma's village most of the houses were built from the mud and bricks, but some were built purely of bricks and some of mud, depending upon the status of the owner. Most of the families lived in a joint system; although they would have a common flat roof, but had separate entrance to their lodging. I also remember the local Imam with a long dark beard, slightly lame, short and wore a turban, but his wife a tall and a beautiful woman from Turkey. They were happily married and had a beautiful daughter and a handsome son. They lived comfortably in a large high walled house. Everyone in the village, especially the Muslim folks, gave them a great respect and they were also happy to teach their off-springs free of cost. The tradition went that her parents in Turkey had a vision to go to this Indian village and settle there to enlighten the local Muslim population. After getting their daughter married to this local Imam, the parents headed back home to Turkey. I also recollect that almost every household in the village had a fruit-tree, especially of oranges, lemons, mangoes and pomegranates. There were pomegranate and lemon trees in the backyard of my grandmother's house as well, I always looked forward to seeing their pink and white silky buds and blossoms in the winter and then observed how did they ripened in the beautiful crispy sunshine of the spring. I enjoyed their fragrance. Those trees were always fascinating and appealing to my mind and also their fruit was refreshing and delicious.

I recollect that those residents belonged either to one caste or a sub-caste and as far as our community was concerned, the main caste seemed to be Rajput and sub-caste Naaru. In the neighbouring village the pedigree might be same or of a different tribe or sub-caste. It is amazing to observe that each caste or sub-caste perceived themselves as superior to the others. Its hierarchy also depended on the size of the village, or the estate of the family or an individual's wealth or success. Normally the higher the status, the better was the caste. Later on I found out that this was even worse in case of Hindus and Sikhs. There was a lot of pride and prejudice linked to that, on the basis of religion, the family background, the tribe and also what language they spoke and what was their profession. Those people believed seriously in the quality of blood and tried fanatically to maintain its purity! In our tribes there was a widespread practice that a family story teller, of great enlightenment, would narrate the family tree and genealogy, quoting full ancestors' names and complete breakdown of their status in a special ceremony attended by a huge gathering, a very important part of wedding ceremony. In the case of Rajputs, it either started or ended with god or king Rama, this included the Muslim Rajputs. These narrators were highly paid and appreciated and well known to the tribes as a charismatic magical person, just like the ancient sacred men.

There are countless fascinating sagas about the origin of the Rajputs (The self-alleged ruling elite and warrior race of India) and how they had evolved. One tradition goes that the Rajputs were created from three different origins. Their tribal elders and scholars narrate that one of the three tribes came from the moon, another one from the sun and the third one from the volcano. Some Muslim Rajput zealots and fanatics believe they are the descendants of Hindu god Rama! The Rajput Associations from Pakistan have regular meetings with the associations living on the Indian side. Apparently they are emotionally closer to each other than any other bindings. However some of the Raput scholars in Rajasthan, India, do not accept conversion of Rajputs to Islam or having inter- marriages. One of the guides in India told me,' Rajputs never accepted the dominance of the Muslims. They hid in the mountains and prefer to perish in the desert, rather than accept their lordship and obedience. They never gave their daughters in the marriage to a Muslim, rather the women preferred to commit suicide (perform Sati), whenever Rajput-men were in defeat.' he continued arrogantly. However I get baffled how the Rajputs flourished for over twelve hundred years of the Muslim rule in India? While these tribal nobles squabble among themselves about their superiority or inferiority, the fact of the matter is that they were both enslaved and subservient to the British! But I always felt empathy and tenderness for the Untouchables. It is difficult to say for how long and why they have been in these iron cages and shackles. It must be for hundreds of years. Those people who call themselves Pundits or Brahmans or top of the hierarchy as well in the caste system, it is difficult to surmise why they are superior and who raised them to their throne; and for how long and why? These questions equally apply to the different castes of Hindus, Sikhs and Muslims alike. It would appear that I just got carried away by the genealogy of the tribes and their origin, also pride and prejudice of indigenous castes, their ancient beliefs, as well as the complexity of the human nature. And perhaps these devices will drag on forever till some miracle happens. There is no doubt in my mind that brain-washing and exploitation of the masses would continue for the glory of few handful people amongst the religious and political elites.

However before dwelling in the Grandma village, I was happily living with my parents in Montgomery and then after the death of my mother had migrated over here. My grandfather who was a professional lawyer and the original settler in Montgomery, died at a comparatively young age and had little chance to build a house for his family or attain some agricultural land which was going very cheap in that newly developed irrigated fertile land. He left behind four young sons and a young widow. This was his second marriage as his first wife had died at the time of her maternity. His eldest son was from his first wife and became the family's bread-earner .My father was the youngest and he had abandoned his studies earlier than planned. The other two elder brothers also started to work in the local newly established courts -of -justice. At that time it was the prevailing custom that the boys got married before the end of their teenage years, I wish I was one! The girls were married even earlier. I think that was not fair for the parents of young married couples and could have caused extra strenuous parental responsibility and financial resources could be stretched to the poverty line. The reason could be that the average life expectancy was no higher than the mid-forties at that time in India. Premature death of either parent could cause calamity and disaster for the young surviving family. I think I fall into this particular category.

For my parents time passed on like a flash and my father's two real elder brothers died at a relatively young age, one left behind three sons and a young widow and the other one left behind a teenage widow, as he died in his early twenties, but luckily, he had no off spring. The burden of responsibility fell on my father's shoulders as well as on my mother. Her domestic and private life was in a terrible mess and dilapidated. Even though at that moment my father was doing a good job in the civil service and working as a Tax-Inspector. My parents had three elder sons apart from me, a sister as well as my paternal grandmother. One or two other widows also lodged with them with their children. My parents resided in a high walled rented dwelling, where my grandmother dominated the management of the house. Grandmother was tough and towering, although not too tall.. My parents had shown lavish and excessive generosity in an open handed manner to the needy persons. That was all at the cost of their' own freedom and a terrific sacrifice.

After the untimely and tragic loss of her husband and her two elder sons, my paternal grandmother was in deep turmoil and often yearned in nostalgia, wailed and shrieked in the sweet memory of her great beloved and noble husband, as well as two youthful and handsome deceased sons. She cried on an almost daily basis after shrouding herself in her dopatta, when she was not occupied. People in the house would often hear her cries and moans, "If he was alive, as well as my lovely sons, I would never be so miserable and in so much trouble, but I would be far more prosperous and relaxed. This was the time for us to enjoy." She would continue the cries in a rhetoric manner, "I want to come to you sooner. I do not like this world anymore. Where have you vanished?" She continued with the rupture. She was also more concerned about her young widowed daughters-in-law and orphaned grandsons. She showered her full attention and love to them; and gave them the best possible food and clothes. My own mother and her children were normally bypassed.

My father slaved away earnestly to earn, clogged up within his family and the clan, the conglomeration of scroungers, widows and orphans, I found my mother the first to wake up and last to sleep in the family. From dawn to dusk, she was busy like a bee. She performed daily chores with great dignity and patience. Although daily she was burdened and exhausted, but she was sublime and sweet. She sometimes did complain in whispers and gestures, to her visiting friends and relatives, "I have hardly any time to relax or to look after my own children or husband, even she (mother-in-law) keeps on pestering and nagging." Sometimes she was in tears and continued, "He does not stop producing children, eight so far, three have already died as infants." She reiterated with a sombre gesture. She was an excellent cook and prepared delicious meals especially favoured by my father. "I think he is overfed and getting a bit plump and heavy", she remarked casually with her sisters-in-law. Her two widowed elder sisters-in-law were real sisters and were married to my father's two real elder brothers. My two great aunts seemed to be quarrelsome and hot-headed and that could be out of their frustration. They normally stuck together and huddled themselves with their children in their spacious rooms. Both of them fed themselves and their children in a secluded manner and hardly gave any helping hand to my mother. Rather sometimes they would go to the neighbours or visit nearby relatives and directed backbiting comments against my mother, those ill remarks flashed back to her in no time.

My great aunts had the right feelings that my mum's home was not their house and they had no sense of belongings with our family. I do not know why my great uncles died at such a young age, perhaps those two sisters were too harsh and demanding, but unfortunately they were highly depressed and frustrated at that moment. They did not have their own home or independent income and were desperately dependent on our family's support. One of our widowed aunts, who had three sons, drank or puffed Hubly-Bubly, that kept her stomach going, but the elder sister who was issueless sometimes kindly lent her hands to my mother. Infrequently my aunts had terrible feuds and squabbles with my mother as well and shouted abuses at her. They even had pronounced and declared my father as the poodle and a slave to his wife; but my grandmother shut them off and suggested to them to leave our house and stay with their parents.

Our house resembled to a stadium or at least a play centre, seven boys wrestling with each other's, running upstairs and downstairs, beating other boys in the streets, playing hide and seek, laughing and joking and last but not the least, playing football or cricket. Grandmother seemed very tolerant to them, made special food for them and adored every single one of them. When the cockerels in the house used to crow, she infrequently remarked with a burst of smiles, "When it crows 'Kukrun Krun', it is calling for Akbar Khaaannn", all her grandsons names ended with a suffix 'Khan'. 'Kukrun Krun' is the sound of a cockerel's crowing (in the Punjabi language) and Akbar Khan was the name of one of my tallest cousins. The boys were all demanding, spoilt and aggressive. On top of that they consumed lot of chapattis, curries, butter, milk, meat, fruit and eggs and rather used to bet who was going to eat more therefore it involved lot of cooking as well as plenty of shopping, washing, cleaning and expenditure..

However my parents had managed a separate bed room, but some of the young children also shared the same room. They hardly had a private moment, except in the heat of the blazing summer or the freezing dark of the winter. In summer everyone slept outside either in the vast dusty courtyard or on top of the flat roof for a cool breeze. In winter it was extremely cold and dry, they used coal fire to warm up inside the rooms, as well as wrapping up, in heavy duty cotton wool quilts. So they cooled down in burning heat and warmed up in freezing cold and the family survived on the basics.

Daily activities denuded my parents of their comforts and welfare. Wearing by the platoon, worn out by the cares, exhausted by the responsibility and tormented by the plague, sometimes they manage to slip away quietly for a walk in the evenings. For both of them life was hectic, bustling and boisterous. There was lot of hassle, interruption and disturbance. They sometimes escaped to the park and to the embankment of the mighty canal for few moments of relief and solitude; shrouded by the twilight and shelter of the lofty trees. They trailed alone in the dim light, hand in hand to soothe the pain. Cool breeze waited for them giving soft hugs and healings. Flowers welcomed them with fragrant smiles. Eucalyptus trees stood on guard and greeted them with open arms. In the canal eddies, waves and ripples; slurped and slithered in excitement. Fish and ducks dived in glee; petals spread tenderly under their feet. The moon gazed and gestured under the clouds, and stars swung with glitters. At the same time gigantic glaciers hundreds of miles away and miles up in the sky melted to show the warmth of their love. I forget so many when I ponder upon this single moment. It is indeed a happy tranquil moment, a lucky blissful event.

The time passed away quickly in this hassle and tussle. I was less than two years old, when my mother was expectant again for the next baby. That time it turned out to be fatal. Her maternity pains were more complicated and she was taken to the nearby newly built maternity hospital. The British had constructed two separate civil hospitals for men and women. Mother was taken to the hospital in a tonga (horse driven coach) suffering with terrible pains. The maternity hospital was located at a walking distance of only ten minutes away from our house. She thought that those were normal delivery pains and she would return home soon. Mother was escorted to the hospital by my aunt, while my father stayed at home with the children and waited for the good news regarding the new baby.. My grandmother and other aunt had prepared the meal together and served to the whole family. It was a daily routine for our gigantic joint-family to eat meals together. They used to squat comfortably on the mats, made from the fibres of the canes and spread them on the dusty floor. Normally my mother and aunt would serve the meal to them first and eat themselves later. This is provided anything was left. It was a very humble, caring and compassionate gesture indeed shown by my mother and the aunt. But this time my grandmother and aunt served the meal together. My father had just broken off a morsel of chapati and dipped it into the curry prepared from goat's meat and potatoes; and was about to put it into his mouth when someone arrived from the hospital and whispered something in his ears. His wife was no longer in this world. He left that bit of chapati in his plate uneaten and departed without saying a word!. It was further reiterated that the new baby was gone with her mother too. My mother was only thirty two and had produced at least eight to nine children by now, amongst them three or four were already dead and this included the latest baby. My father was a widower now at roughly the same age as my mother.

Consequently my father married again without wasting any time. He and my frail grandmother could not cope with the young family. He himself was still young and red hot like an active volcano. Within a year or perhaps may be nine months, his new wife had produced a new son. With our new mother and new brother, lot of competition and family rivalry began. A great many hidden agendas and conspiracies sparked off the feelings and hatred. However it was lucky for one of my widowed aunts that her two sons got respectable jobs in the police and the bank respectively; so they became independent and thus abdicated the new responsibility of looking after our young family. As a result, being the weakest and an infant, the axe fell on me. Three of my elder brothers and my elder sister could sustain the turbulence and pressure of our new family set up. When my maternal - grandmother came for the condolence of her daughter, she felt pity about my negligence and took me to her beloved village. As I mentioned before that was the same village where my mother was born and bred and got married. There is no doubt that this village was a magical, captivating and hypnotizing place. However I cannot recollect the exact day, month or year of my departure being too young. How can I remember that historical moment, and yet I even cannot recall the presence of my own mother?

In my maternal grandmother village life was just basic and primitive. There was no proper sewer system, no metal roads, no civil courts, no railway station or police. The roads were dusty, sandy and infested with pot –holes. The means of communications were bull-carts, horses or Dolees and sometimes horse wagons. There was no canal irrigation system. The growth of crops was dependent on the rainfall, although the soil was fertile and soft. The area was sparsely populated. Only few houses had water pumps. Water was supplied to most of the houses by a professional water carrier. He filled his leather water carrier, an oblong bag, by drawing water from the well attached to the mosque and then slung the carrier on his back by dangling it from his either shoulder and then delivered water to his customers by trotting from door to door just like a delivery milkman or a postman. However I am not sure who used to supply water to the Hindus, Sikhs and Untouchables, although they were not many; this was meant for the Muslims only. I presume that they had their own water suppliers and supply systems. I have a feeling that there was a conviction amongst the Hindus and Sikhs lodging in that village that supply of water by other believers might pollute the water!

One day my grandmother's favourite buffalo died, after eating some poisonous bush or perhaps bitten by a serpent. The news of her sudden death spread like a wild bush fire in the neighbourhood, people rushed to the scene and paid condolence to the grandma. I stood amongst the crowd next to my grandma, holding the left hand of my uncle; they both looked baffled and sunk in grief.

Every mourner speculated, minced around and squabbled about the cause of the calamity, but no one genuinely investigated the real cause of death. The buffalo lay plump on her side with her tongue dangling out and her eyes were staring and fixed to the sky. There were continuous trickle of tears pouring down my grandma's cheeks and she kept on the rhetoric of grieved emotions, "This is my best buffalo, I do not know what has happened, she is very healthy and produced a great quantity of milk, she is the best and of fine pedigree." Someone amongst the relatives interrupted, "It has happened and this is a fact of life, it is better to dispose of the dead beast". However Grandma was a bit reluctant and still did not believe that the beast was dead. Chumars were called out and they tied the ropes round the gigantic beast, weighing hundreds of tons and soon started dragging her. The grandmother started wailing again instantly, while patiently she bade farewell to her favourite buffalo. She caressed the buffalo for the last time and kept on stirring her tongue with a thin twig of a bush. Soon the buffalo disappeared towards the jungle, having been dragged across the dry river bed and in the midst of tears of my grandma, where the Chumars removed her hide and abandoned the carcass in a remote place for sumptuous dinner for the anxiously waiting vultures, who were already hovering above the sky, as well as to the delight of dogs, foxes, tigers and wolves.

While staying in the purity of village life, something unusual and weird happened to me. One late spring afternoon my grandma handed over a long reeds stick to me and ordered me to escort one of the buffaloes to the pasture located on the other side of the river. That was my first experience of handling a buffalo on my own and leading her to the pasture. I thumped her on her backbone to make her stagger towards the pasture, but that proved to be fatal. The long hollow spoke bounced back on my head and instantly I started bleeding like a fountain. The blood trickled down my head and face faster than expected. Whole of my white cotton shirt became red in no time while grandma was still standing there gazing at me. Momentarily grandma was startled on the sight of the blood. She immediately tore a part of her muslin Dopatta, burned it quickly into ashes, put the ashes over the wound and wrapped my head like a dressing with the rest. I felt the sting of the injury and cried at the first sight of my own blood. The women and children from the adjoining houses came out on hearing my shrieks and stared at me and sympathised with me and that made the grandma more and more embarrassed and repentant. Luckily for the grandma and for myself, it was not a deep wound, the blood stopped trickling after few minutes, but the dressing remained in place for the next few days and the ache of the wound also persisted for the next few days as well.

On some other fateful day I was asked to take a goat, three times of my size, for grazing. At the start, I held her harness in my hands and led her to the grazing fields. I felt myself confident at the beginning and was enjoying my new experience, I was rather thrilled. But after sometime, the goat was frustrated by my continuous control over her and tried to stretch out for more grass and bush. In that tug of war, I tried to pull her back and keep her next to myself. The simple reason was that I did not want her to enter anybody else's fields and damage their crops. Soon a more strenuous tug of war developed between me and the goat. She pulled and pulled further and further, dragged and dragged away from me towards her target for grazing. In the strife I thought of a better device to reduce pressure on my arms, which were intensely tired and stretched to the maximum by now and fully strained.. I put the loop of the harness on my neck, so that I could use hands as well as the support and strength of my neck to control her. The beast got frustrated even more and hurtled me with a fierce force over the thorny bush and wild grass. However I was extremely lucky and one of the acquaintances was passing by and rescued me from the beastly disaster of being strangled and wounded or perhaps saved me from the gallows.

On another occasion and a memorable day and at the time of the wheat harvest, my uncle's cousin put a load of wheat grain over my head and it was a substantial load and ordered me to march towards the village. At the beginning of my trauma I managed to struggle and stagger for few hundred yards and then collapsed with tears in my eyes and my body was frozen in shudders of gravity. I was crying and refused to carry the load any longer; but he was abusive and he was ultimately forced to pick up the load himself. However my neck is still hurting and legs are still shaking under strenuous and painful memory of that burden as a slave child.

In the village, there was no hospital and cures were through natural ingredients, Hakeems (Herbal specialist) and family traditions. When I used to have terrible cough and chest spasm, my grandmother used to roast few spoonful of white sugar in Ghee (concentrated butter) and then rolled that up into an almost burnt state and it resembled like a dark brown chocolate, a kind of black ball of concentrated sugar, it tasted slightly bitter and gave it to me for slow nibble or sucking and that was perfect treatment for my terrible cough and I used to recover within a day or so. In the blazing heat of the summer, I often had sore eyes, as I did not wear any hat or protective clothing or sunglasses and strolled carefree in the burning sandy bed of the flash flood river and in the midst of the fields. My grandmother used to put a thick coating of pulp of the opium on the lids of my closed eyes and I had to sleep or rest at least for few hours, as my eyes were completely sealed and shut. After I woke up the eyes were thoroughly washed and I felt fully normal. For stomach upset and malaria, grandmother used to pick me up, dangles me around her shoulders and breasts; and went to the Hindu Hakeem, he used to give me some Sherbat and I was perfect within days. If I had just the temperature, my grandmother, again picked me up around her shoulders, went to the Hindu Pandit who used to own a soda water factory. He made the fizzy Soda Water bottle for me instantly in his factory, while she was still chattering to him and kept me caressing as well. As soon as I used to drink this fizzy soda- water, the temperature was almost gone and I felt normal before reaching home. So it was all magical and fascinating in the village life in India at that historical time and to me it was completely harmonious.

Our school was situated on the other part of the village. It was constructed by one of my grandmother's cousins, named Babu Fazal Mohammad. People called him Babu (a nobleman or a man of distinction) because of his great service to the community by building and donating this middle school for the service of the community at large. Babu had earned a great fortune in Burma by doing some building projects like railways through British companies. He had been very generous and charitable to share his wealth with his village people, later that school was upgraded to a high school and subsequently upgraded to a college and his name is still displayed in bold letters on the walls of the great learning institution. When I visited his house with my grandmother and with my aunt's daughter adjacent to the school, we discovered that his wife was physically cleaning the wheat and rice for their meals. She would normally grind the wheat for making flour herself. It is an arduous and rigorous task. I could not believe that she was so rich, but prepared the flour and rice herself, although she could have easily employed a few servants and cooks. They also ran a school for girls from their own home and were desperately campaigning for the new admission. However she was disappointed that not many girls have come forward.

In the school class, we used to squat on the jute mats, but in straight rows and used to remove our shoes outside the room. Teachers were very strict and disciplined. The lessons were tough and demanding. In my first year, we had learnt tables up to sixteen while the whole class stood solemnly as if saying a prayer; as well as tables of quarters and halves between one and three. During the course of practice, if a mistake was made, one got hit on the head with a light cane and the rhetoric of learning tables had to be at top of the voice and at one go; and sometimes students could get choked. We used wood planking or tablet (twelve by eight by half inches) for writing, which used to be coated with some sort of refined clay, as well as on slates.

We used to carry inkpots with us, as well as pens made from the sharpened cane offshoots. Normally there was no use of note books in my class, perhaps there was no supply of them available in the remote village or perhaps they were considered to be too uneconomical.

On one odd scorching summer day, at the end of my class, I was unable to find my shoes. It was month of June and blazing hot. I had to go bare- footed to my house. It was most painful and burning walk of my life. I first sprinted few steps and then stood on my wooden writing plank called Takhti. Takhti is just a thin sheet of wood resembling like an Egyptian scroll. Unfortunately those stolen shoes were my brand new leather shoes, made by the local shoemaker and grandmother had done a special effort to get them made only two days ago. On the way, I had to cross the sandy Cho {river} as well, so that was a furlong of hell to cross. The wooden Takhti kept on sinking in the loose fluffy sand under my weight, but for me, "It is excelsior and river of death has brimmed its banks". I staggered to reach home, just like a wounded soldier under siege. Once I reached near our home, grandma was already waiting for me, in the middle of the burning street, aiming just like a tigress would do, ready to pounce on a young buck. "You idiot! You scoundrel! Where are your shoes?" She startled. "I got them made only two days ago. I have no money left now to buy new ones. You have to go back and find them." She continued bursting. Then a terrific and ferocious smack and thump on my right face, one more on the left and two further at the back of my head. My cheeks become further rosy, ears are on fire and my head reels and I fall curling on the dusty burning street. The neighbourhood women heard my cries and pleas and came out running from the other sides of the houses. "Do not be silly Rahmatay (as they call to my grandma), do not smack him. It is not his fault, some kid has stolen them. Go and talk to the teacher tomorrow." They pleaded.

On the following morning she escorted me to the school with my old pair of shoes which I used to wear after the school time and had a sharp word with the teacher. "Where are my grandson's shoes? Were you sleeping?" She said as she jumps in the air swinging her arms in front of the class. "It is your responsibility to look after the kids and their possessions!" She argued in a boisterous tone. "Yes Mam. I tried hard to find his shoes everywhere and ask all the kids, but in vain. I am extremely sorry for the loss of his shoes and I will keep on endeavouring to find them." He reassured my grandma in earnest, holding his Muslin white turban. "I will keep extra vigilance on the pair of his shoes in future, so Mam do not become too much anguished" he reiterated.

I normally used to trail to the school with my class-mate named Mohan Singh, a Sikh boy from our side of the village, through the Cho (flash flood river} and across the mango groves and orange orchards. We used to trot along the dusty and diagonal path passing through the fields, a kind of short cut to the school. He was very brilliant and top of the class. Whenever the teacher used to ask any questions, he was the first one to raise his hand, his cheeks and eyes flashed like a beacon glittering on the shore and he used to answer correctly straight away, before any other student could have responded. I always envied his performance and capability. He was simply a rising star, but I did not know how to match him.

One day we were trotting on our way to school and chattering in light conversation as normal. He fired a surprise question on me, "How many Gods, do you think there are?" "There are two, one for the Muslims and one for the Hindus" I responded instantly. At that time I had an impression that Hindus and Sikhs were of same kind of race and creed. But he reacted sharply, "No! There is only one God. If there were two, then there will be a terrible feud and turmoil. Gods will be fighting with each other and there will be no peace on this earth." No doubt he was an enlightened and a genius compared to me, I thought in my mind and responded without prejudice, "You are certainly right, I agree with you that in that scenario there will be lots of trouble and turbulence."

At that time both of us were not aware about the high priests, war lords or politicians; as well as super-powers, oil, bombers or missiles. Well I certainly wasn't anyway!

However some days later, during the course of our usual hour lunch break and while we chose the shade of a tree to relax because it was a hot sunny day and were about to unwrap the chapattis and ready to eat. I inadvertently touched his chapatti, which was still intact and nicely wrapped by his mum in a rag. He momentarily got disdainful and disgruntled by my casual touch of his rag and had slung his chapatti immediately to the dog which happened to be just crouching opposite to us and his mouth was dribbling. I was baffled as well as embarrassed for my stupid folly. I underestimated his negative reaction against the other creeds and also that was not what he was preaching to me earlier. It would appear that because a Muslim child had touched the chapatti, although it was still wrapped in a rag, it had become impure. Then I got more enlightened and still remember that vividly just like a flash and crackle of the lightening which had earlier swooped on the nearby green tree.

In the monsoon season, I enjoyed the flash floods in the Cho (dry river bed). I appreciated the power, glory, abundance and goodness of nature. In the summer it used to be very hot and stuffy in the village and the subtle touch and feel of cool breeze gave lot of hope and relief. As soon as the dark clouds rushed and rumbled towards the Himalayas with growls and roars, sooner there would be lightning and thunder. Soon there would be flashes, flares and heavy downpour of rain over the mountains which happened to be only few miles away from our village... The water rushed and gushed from all directions and used to arrive in the village within an hour or so. The flood would first flow with a sizzling noise, just like an earthquake, accompanying any load on its route. It tossed trees and bushes just like straws. Gushing water rippled and waved and meandered with a colossal roar and thrust. The sandy dry bed of the Cho used to become like a tidal ocean and nothing could stand its thrust and sway. I just used to stand and stare on the edge of the bank of the swollen river along with the grownups and enjoy the great freshness and excitement and power of nature. All fields, meadows, groves were submerged within a matter of minutes. The flash floods also brought in lot of fish and snakes to the village. The wild rise of ripples and waves, the spume and foam swaying with the waves, the water slurps and slaps against the embankments and the hissing sound of the fresh water like the slithering serpent, tumbling from the Himalayas created a unique fantasy and magical sounds of music.

Although life in grandma's village was serene, magical and peaceful, It passed away like a flash flood. Soon I had to abandon not only my grandma, but also the peaceful village forever. There were man-made painful waves, tides and storms on the way descending from the horizons. The peace and harmony which prevailed over here for centuries would soon be shattered.

Chapter III

Great Escape

In summer, blazing heat from the overhead flaring sun turned Grandma's semi-arid village into a furnace. Most of the men, youths and children escaped from their houses to take shelter under the mighty clump of Bur trees, adjacent to the mosque and public baths attached to it. They left behind females at the mercy of the heat. The ladies and girls shut themselves off in the dark of their rooms, stirred Pankhas (Manual straw -fans} to cool themselves down and then had a bit of nap. The females had their own way of chattering, backbiting and holding serious discussion about family politics or politics at large. The villagers laid their 'charpies', under the shade of wide and dense leaves of Bur trees. They tethered their buffaloes, cows and horses under the shades of thorny Kikkar trees, on the embankment of the Cho. However there was an occasional gust of fresh breeze coming down from the mountains, groves, meadows and fields to the shadowy shelters. Some of the water buffaloes preferred to cool in the lakes, while the sun glittered bright over the zenith. The Bur- trees were of such a colossal girth and height that they also covered a good part of the dome of the adjoining mosque. Normally the men drank Huqqa (Hubly- Bubly), the youngsters played cards and children fought duals, played with marbles or just hopped about. So everyone could relax one way or the other and had different leisure activities under the mighty Bur tree.

As this communal relaxing place was on the edge of the flash flood river, there was plenty of sand to splash and stir about for the activities of the kids under the mighty tree. One day, one of my friends showered a fistful of sand into my eyes and made me blind, as I was unable to open my eyes and made me cry. It was very painful and it felt like a sand paper grinding in the eyes. I plumped tormented and distressed on the sand with my hands on my eyes, calling for help in agony. Soon one of the elders heard my shrieks and came to my rescue and helped me to clear my eyes by splashing water into them. That sandy turmoil still hurts me, although my friend was just having fun or playing a game for a laugh. He felt so ashamed at seeing me suffering from the turmoil and was rather embarrassed.

While relaxing under the shade, the men also discussed political turbulence in the country, breeding of their animals, domestic situations or any social activities. There were open and frank daily discussions and hot debates about the British Rule, the number of fatalities during the World War Two, debate on the difference in opinion of the various politicians and political parties. They also debated on the pros and cons of going to Pakistan or staying in India, once the partition was done. Some Muslims favoured the Congress Party, some liked the Muslim League. Some wanted to stay where they were, but some preferred migration to the new country, after thinking about their long term perspectives. But most of the residents intended to stay in their mother land, where their great -great ancestors lived and are buried. Most of the Mullahs favoured staying in India and they were deadly against the Partition.

One of our great uncles in the village, who was over six feet tall, was a soldier in the First World War. He had a white long-beard and walked with a bamboo stick, perhaps he damaged his limbs in the battle. He was very compassionate and friendly with the kids. As soon as I used to see him on the embankment of the Cho, I used to rush to him for a ride on his walking stick. He simply smiled and giggle and I immediately climbed on his walking stick, just like a monkey would do and he made us laugh by rotating the bamboo stick with a great thrust and making some funny grunting noise like an engine. It was a great thrill and mesmerising for all kids to admire his strength and we enjoyed the bamboo-ride given by the ex- world war veteran. His eldest son nick-named 'Rala', joined the army too in the Second World War, but unfortunately was killed, when his ship was torpedoed by the enemy. He left behind one younger brother, named 'Jean'. I often used to gaze standing next to my great aunt, while she kept on narrating the dramatic tragedy of her son, to the visitors, who kept on visiting to pay their condolences to her, on her son's tragic death. Rala's mother shrieked and wailed in an erratic and rhetorical manner. I do not know who had told her about his last moment's floating in the sea, but she kept on reiterating about his last moment and what was his alleged last wish or a dialogue! And I must quote. "One of his mates, who was rescued, told me that when he was floating on a plank of the ship-wreck, he wanted to see his younger brother Jean and while calling him, he simply perished in the high sea, swallowed by the mighty waves or perhaps pounced on by a shark!" She kept on reiterating while tears trickled down her cheeks and her eyes covered over by her Dopatta... In our neighbourhood another soldier had returned home safely last week, his house was located on the other side of the lake, to this part of the village, after having been released from the prison of the Japanese in South East Asia. He had brought some Aluminium pots for his family as well as some clothes and perhaps some money. He brought these gifts in tin-suite cases and in some jute sacks. His mother was so excited and thanked her stars. Relatives and friends rushed to his house to greet him back safely and to say congratulations to his parents. Soon there was a special celebration by his family and a special feast was thrown for the relatives and friends. Soon his mother searched for his future wife and preparations were on hand to marry him at the earliest moment.

Some two million British Indian soldiers died in the Great Wars and not much compensation was paid to their families or to the survivors. One of my first cousins from Montgomery joined the army and fought all over, especially in Singapore, Hong Kong and Malaysia. When he had returned home after having been discharged from the army, he became unemployed and survived on subsistence given by my father. He earlier had discarded his studies to join the British Indian Army and hardly received any pension or a compensation for fighting in the war as a conscript. The reason could be the political uncertainty in India or its raging turbulent Independence - movement. While strolling in the fields or playing in the sand or sitting under the shade of the mighty Bur tree, I often used to listen to the patriotic war songs in Punjabi, sung with great rhythm and enthusiasm, equally by the ploughing farmers and the village youth. Those songs were sung in order to protect the Motherland and the Empire. Below are some of the verses which used to be aired in every agricultural field of the Punjab; and echoed in Punjabi language as thus:

Surely I want to join our army, I want to be a conscript

Over here we wear tattered shoes, over there we wear boots

Over here we eat pickle- Chapati, over there sumptuous meals

Over here we walk bare feet, over there wear socks

Over here we lay wretched, over there we trail abroad

Over here we die of poverty, over there play with wealth

Surely I want to join our army, I want to be a conscript

In the afternoons and mornings, I used to roam and prowl in the Cho {river bed}, play and run about, frequently with friends, but occasionally on my own as well. In the Cho one does not need any companion, the company of the Cho on its own was more than sufficient. It was pleasant, comfortable and mesmerising. The sand cooled down faster than the clay. The layers of loose and soft sand over there were quite thick, brought from the Himalayas each year and it was enjoyable to walk bare-footed, rather than with shoes on. The loose cushion of silver-grey sand gave a soothing massage to the soles of the feet. People could easily relax and enjoy sitting in the Cho and walking without shoes was even better. One could relax and be tranquil for hours by sitting, walking and gossiping on the sand and forget tension and pressure of life. The grown - ups, men and women alike enjoyed the soft and relaxing walk with the same comfort and tranquillity. In the rainy season, as well as the dry season, we trailed for miles along the river bed, staring at the wild bushes, canes and reeds, cultivated agricultural fields, as well as meadows, pastures and groves. On our trail we could see prowling peacocks in the fields, sometimes dancing, with spread out plumes, appearing like colourful showers. Occasionally we used to observe deer flashing like lightning, leveret hopping and foxes running.

In the summer our house appeared like an oven and the village sizzled like a furnace. I always yearned for a sand or dust storm. It felt romantic and peaceful to see the mighty storm approaching and rubbing against the scorched and burnt river bed. The wind gushed with a great speed and thrust. It carried with it all the dry bush, sand, and dust. It was a symbol of freedom, vastness and natural glory. It also took away the heat from the atmosphere and brought in a cool air to the area. It was thrilling to see the sand storm stretching from the earth to the skies. It was overpowering and captivating and came with a great speed, sway and magnitude. As a young kid I used to welcome it with open arms and with lot of smiles on my face. It cooled my body down and gave me a soothing, relaxing massage. At the sight of the dust storm, I simply stood still and waited for its impact on me and the landscape. Within seconds the horizon was shrouded by a dust cloud, trees swayed and everything was simply swept away. The sand, straws and dry thorny bushes were mercilessly dragged across the river bed and across the fields. I used to stretch my arms in exhilaration and appreciated the cool freedom and goodness of the mother earth. I realised I was not alone, but those wonderful natural forces were with me.

While the sand and dust storms raged with gusts of wind, I frequently observed quite a few thorny bushes roll, rumple, tumble and fly across the undulating sandy bed. I instantly used to move out of their way to escape being scratched or avoid having painful multiple wound stabs from their thorns, but those lonely and tactful agile manoeuvres now seem everlasting and fascinating moments in the mind. On one pleasant day while we were playing around and fighting duals amongst ourselves, a big Kikkar - tree's thorn, pierced into the sole of one of my feet. It was about two inches long, sharper than a sword and harder than a needle. It was hidden somewhere in the deep layer of loose sand. I immediately dropped on my other foot, as it appeared to have penetrated up to the top side of my foot. The pain was unbearable and intolerable. I toiled and trudged to my home, on one leg and one foot. I explained to my grandmother about my latest misery. She rushed to my aunt who used to live in the next street, as she could not pull the thorn herself because I was constantly shrieking. Her heart was sinking with compassion hearing my dreadful groans. I did not let her to pull the thorn because I was suffering from a terrible pain and drenched in fear. They all caressed and tried to handle me together, but I never came within their grasp. I shuddered and shivered like a fish out of water and stopped everyone coming near to me.

At last my aunt went to the Imam's house and fetched in his daughter. She was stunningly beautiful and charming and must have been about sixteen years old. She asked my aunt to hold my head in her lap, grandmother to hold my arms and cover my eyes, others to hold my legs. She herself held my feet in her lap and made me unable to move and pulled the thorn in the midst of my cries, their yelling and chatter. Momentarily I was relieved and tears stopped falling from my eyes. However, I was so lucky that the most beautiful girl in the whole world had cured my grief by holding my troubled foot against her breasts and what a lucky thorn to be removed by such a fine lady. She was so pleased that she cuddled and kissed me followed by some more kisses and cuddles from my grandmother, aunt and others with loads of smiles and relief, but that painful, romantic, epic moment flashes forever and enrage my emotions. Normally thorns or prickles did not bother me much and I removed them with ease, but this one was a monster, extra-long, greyish dark colour. It was just like a cone, its head like a pincer, but gradually its diameter increases in the other direction. It seemed drilled in with great stubbornness. When we tried to pull it out, it carried the sole's skin, nerves and muscles with it. That was the reason for the great pain and agony in that instance. I was highly obliged to the Imam's daughter for relieving my pain, as well as my grandmother, aunt and others. When I stare and sniff at the fragrant roses, protected by the thorns, I infer from my observation that the protection of the flowers was not possible if the thorns were made of velvet or silk. This particular incident reminds me of many beautiful roses, so many sincere and loving relations. It also a moment in my life, which accompanies me all the time and unique sensuous chilly feelings go down my spine, when I think about my escape from the thorn.

On another sunny afternoon, we were just wandering as usual in the fields which were not far away from our village and the adjacent wild bush area, along the right edge of the Cho. Momentarily, we heard a man sprinting and running at top his speed after a dog suffering from rabies. The dog was running at the top of his speed as well towards us, his tongue hanging out and dripping with spume and foam. The man had a long Bamboo stick and appeared exhausted. It came to light later that they had poisoned the dog to kill him, but the dog was trying to escape, although while running, the dog seemed out of normal rhythm of movement and was dangling. The sprinting man with the long stick yelled loudly, "Get out of the way. The dog will bite you. Run. Run, Run out of the way!" Being young, we could not appreciate the seriousness of the danger, ignored the warning and kept on gazing at him and the mad dog dumbfounded. Even if we had run, we were no match with the mad dog. Luckily the dog ran at a far distance from us and the man still kept on sprinting and yelling the warnings.. While he passed near us, he shouted, "The dog is mad or suffering from rabies and I am trying to kill him. He is very dangerous, he has been poisoned, but to no effect." The man had no time to relax, he kept on sprinting. Soon they disappeared in the horizon and in the haze. The dog appeared losing control, but still running. Again as far I am concerned, it was a lucky escape for us. It is difficult to recollect from the distance whether the hunting man was a Muslim, Hindu or a Sikh. However, death from rabies is said to be very painful and wretched. However that startling moment is still with me and the thought of that hazy scene still scares me.

While trotting and playing in the open countryside, I infrequently used to observe dog and a bitch mating, just like foxes. They got stuck back to back, wiggled and waggled to and fro and that lasted for hours. Between the pair there seemed an emotional tug of war, pulling each other in opposite directions and they continued over a greater stretch of the hot ground. They also continued squeaking, with their tongues out dribbling, till it was all over. I also noticed the farmers bringing a special bull for mating the buffaloes as well as the cows, sometimes they would help the bull to fix in. The reason could be that those special bulls had to be hired and paid for their pedigree and no attempt was to be fruitless. One other thing I recollect is that those mating bulls would only be called for when the cows or buffaloes started crying for them and it happened only when they were in a special phase or mood and in a particular season of the year.. In case of horses, even extra care was taken. The hind legs of the mare were tied up and a horse of special pedigree was brought in and he got a helping hand from the farmers for the ride over the mare. In case of donkeys, it was carefree and relaxing, the rides were unlimited, they did not need any helping hands. It would appear that the females were very resilient and stayed doggedly cool at the same place. However she would occasionally wrinkle and crinkle her ears during the mating process. To me those were all wonders of nature and those thrilling creative moments are well preserved forever.

I remember one domestic crackling and fuming squabble as well at the normally peaceful Cho, this time pertaining to the complexity of human nature. My maternal grandmother had only one son named Ali. He was a very handsome man with red white cheeks and of a fine delicate skin. To me he was completely spoilt and irresponsible at that time. He was married to a woman of average beauty and she was not compatible with him. As usual and as per tradition, this was an arranged marriage, which normally gives more importance to the marriage between the families rather than between the young couples. From this marriage my uncle had two lovely kids, at that moment. Her father was a Subadar- major (the most senior and powerful non-commissioned officer) in the British Indian Army, a giant towering figure. I used to notice that my uncle normally came late in the night and did not use the main entrance to the house, but sneaked through a side window at the back of the house. This could be because my grandmother refused to let him in so late in the night. In the day time, he used to spend time playing cards, gossiping with friends or enjoying cockerel – fights. He did not appear to be caring for his wife or children or even his mother. Perhaps he had a relationship, somewhere, I do not know. But I did notice him relaxing under the Bur- tree, playing cards, busy in cockerel fights, drinking Huqqa or just wandering carefree with his friends.

However on one crispy, glittering winter morning, I witnessed an amazing encounter in the peaceful Cho. It would appear and I am merely speculating that my uncle had sent a message to his father-in-law to take his daughter away, as he had no intention to keep her and wanted to get rid of her... The father arrived in panic, clad in the khaki uniform and with an erect turban over his head, pleading for clemency. They lived few miles away from our village, in a far bigger and a more dominant village. My grandmother and my uncle stood with their backs against the village and my aunt and her father overlooked the village, as well as faced my uncle and grandmother. I just stood as a minor observer. My uncle was in a boisterous mood and yelled, "Take this wretched woman away from my sight, I cannot tolerate her any more, she has been backbiting against me." The women are just like a pair of shoes, just change them for new ones. People replace them as required. He kept on bragging and neighing about his manhood and status.

"Ali, could you please care to peep into my eyes for a second. I will admonish her. She will never do it again." Her father kept on pleading for clemency. My grandmother stood in silence and kept on reminding her son to be rational, especially for the sake of his children. "Stay in your senses and do not be mad!" She kept on admonishing him. "No she has to go, I will never keep her, she is completely useless, she is just like a bitch!" He reiterated without any heed and kept up his boisterous tone. His arms staggered in the air and his body shuddered and shook. My aunt's father clasped his hands in front of his son-in-law in a typical Indian way, but my uncle did not bend. He continued the shower of abuse and shouts without any compromise. We all stood in the comfort of the soft sandy Cho on the edge of the mosque and public baths. My uncle's father–in-law looked frustrated, his heart fluttered in awe and drummed loudly. Eventually he removed his erected army khaki turban and put it on the feet of my uncle and began pleading with more humility. Even my aunt (his wife) prostrated in front of him and begged for his clemency by clenching his feet. Soon the squabble cooled down and they started living as normal at least for the time being. Their married life lingered and undulated on for another thirty years and between them they produced four sons and two daughters. Their eldest son died in the refugee camps due to multiple infectious diseases and malnutrition.

After arriving in Pakistan uncle had become the headman of the new village and also became more mature with the age. Being the headman he was privileged to have direct contact with the government officials, on top of that he was one of the biggest landlords in the village. He hired the local farmers to till his lands and did the harvesting on a fifty –fifty basis and he himself enjoyed socialising and wandering about. But still he often used to flirt with the good looking and attractive wives of the simple farmers. The culture and social set up in the village was quite secular and hardly any woman wore any Hijab or stayed in Purdah. The indigenous people were a harmonious blend of all pedigree of people like farmers, landlords, ironsmiths, carpenters, mullahs and shepherds to name only few. Uncle liked to smoke his huqqa and always carried it with him when he visited the farmers or other people's homes. Normally he would have a casual chat with them and especially with the beautiful wives of the farmers while the farmers were away working in the fields. He only came to his house to have his breakfast, lunch, dinner or in the evenings to relax with other visitors who used to come to have an audience with him in his back courtyard. Although our aunt always cooked fresh meals for him and the best possible which he had demanded, but from time to time, she was still got beaten with his shoes and sometimes she got lashing with the sticks. It happened few times in front of me when I was visiting them at the weekends or during the holidays and I really felt pity for her, but could not help and just watched in silence. I think that all this turbulence happened because he was having a relationship with other women outside his marriage.

The most memorable moment in the whole village was the spectacle between the monsoon clouds and the Himalayas. While I used to stroll about or stayed in the house, I used to observe the soft and dense clouds floating faster than the birds, and then mingling together into folds, and later those sometimes appeared stationary and sometimes hurrying towards the Himalayas. Then those miles of steamy and icy fine cotton wool would lie and mingle on top of each other layer, wave after wave and pile after pile. Soon the turbulence in the atmosphere made mountains and heaps of cotton wool dark, then darker and darker. Those mountains of ice, vapours and miles of thickness steamy violent -blankets, uplifted and surged to a colossal height, breadth and girth with a latent force of gradients in pressure and temperature. There was a visible rumble and grumble of the black clouds while driving towards the Himalayas.. Hidden in the fast cruising clouds was the lightening, waiting to be unleashed at an appropriate moment. It is fascinating how negative and positive charges cluster together, in the sky, at their poles and create a spark mightier than atom bomb. It is also incredible to perceive how the unity of a humble and lightest spec of steam can cause such a powerful spark and explosion and make the human run for cover or hide their eyes from its glare. However I was always fascinated and gazed at the gripping and captivating spectrum and smoothness of the rainbow and yearned to have a ride in it.

Sometimes I used to hear distressing news that lightning had burnt a farmer or its buffaloes who had taken a shelter under a greenwood tree, or some one's family had been struck by the lightning and every -thing has been turned into ashes. I also got carried away by the hail storm and admired how the earth was being bombarded by the frozen white balls. It used to be an unusual and a rare opportunity to observe a white carpet in the streets and in the yard of the house, a change to cool down the temperature and an unusual blessing from mother -nature. I thrived on this wonder of nature too and its colourfulness. I did not mind being hit hard on my head by these celestial white balls; this is provided that they would not damage my skull.

I sometimes start scratching my head about the wonders of the clouds how millions upon millions of tons and litres of water turn into this an amazing gift from nature and their goodness is delivered free, door to door. The clouds are oceans of distilled water, floating and rambling in the sky and they reflect nicely in their source below and eventually rejoin and recycle. This is a free vital ingredient of life, donated from mother –nature, a selfless benefactor for the planet. It is incredible to note that every moving creature is created by the flit and flutter of water, some may crawl or slither on their bellies, some of the creatures may walk on two feet, some others on four feet. Some of the creatures can fly, some can dive and some of them can swim. All humans are made from half a cell, mingle with the other half and there are trillions and trillions of these cells in one human body. It is food for thought for those who neigh or brag about themselves being super or mighty!

The dark or greyish white clouds flashed and growled cruising towards the great wall of the Himalayas, They took only less than an hour to fly from our village and then soon the battle raged between the mighty mountain-walls and the gigantic storm of clouds, as soon as the free movement of the clouds was blocked. The clouds became agitated, turbulent, rose up and down, bounced and blazed. There was lot of turbulence in the air, movements in the fronts and rears of the clouds, squeezes, folds and uplifts. As I stared from the edge of the Cho, gazing at the dark clouds, soon there were lot of flashes, flickers, lightning, thunder, grumble and growls over the vales and the slopes. The clouds were so dark and dense that it was not possible to see one's own hands. It seemed the greatest battle of all times. Forests and bushes swayed and crumbled. The water poured from the sky with great ferocity. The roads were blocked with landslides and by falling debris from the slopes. The boulders and waterfalls tumbled and stumbled, tugged and jumbled together .The clouds might be lighter or delicate, but they showed unity of power. Everything was upside down. There were spasmodic and unpredictable crackles, explosions and fires from the clouds. While the water rushed and gushed, boulders rocked and rolled, birds, reptiles and animals took shelter. But who can fight the highest mountains on the planet, especially if someone is soft and light, it does not matter, how agitated and boisterous it had been. The clouds had no alternative, but to cool down and shed their tears.

At a glance from our village, the mountain wall sprang up hazy and dusty. This could be because of dust or sandstorms, but after the cloudbursts and soaking rains, their face was thoroughly and completely washed and now they appeared dark brown. The Himalayas arose like a great barrier and the skies kissed their forehead. It still turned up ever young this is in spite of wear and tear by the weather, passage of turbulent times and evolution in the civilisations. The rivers, streams and waterfalls came down thumping from the great heights with sonorous singing, sometime hitting the rocks and sometimes escaped to the sides. Within less than an hour, the flash flood reached our village with a great surge, sizzle and roar. It was a magical sight for all, every wave and ripple rose and fell with a fresh sway and swing. The Cho which was normally barren used to become full of life and glamour. All pastures and fields around it used to get submerged under sea of forceful water,. The trees and bushes tumbled and tossed like straws. The water rushed and gushed with eddies, whirls and waves; spume and foam floated up and down with great rhythm and sway. All onlookers smiled and got excited. Some daring young men persevered to wade through the rising tides, but most of the times fell off balance and got driven away by the forceful waves. However when the pressure is reduced in the river, some of the bravest men tested their strength, but still they had to struggle to reach the fields to pluck some delicious sweet corn cobs or get some exotic, juicy and fragrant mangoes from the groves, to please their mothers, wives and children. The panorama was full of romance, excitement and far more than a picnic. There used to be peace and tranquillity on the horizon, mingled with the roars of the mighty flash flood river. If there was a heaven on the earth, then it was over here, it was over there, it was here.

A famous Panjabi poet called Waris Shah has said once and I must quote, "The moment just gone, the joy just surged and the ripple just rose, will never return again." However, once the main flow of flash flood was over after few days, there used to be still some remnant of crystal clear water flowing over the top of fully cleaned and soaked sand, In fact some water also used to ooze out from the over saturated quilt of sand and its delicate ripples used to glisten in the bright sunny day... At that moment I used to jump in and flap through the river with friends. Normally we used to swim naked, lie flat on our backs or fronts, splash water in the air with both hands while staring at the blue sky. We trudged and trampled, slopped and sloshed, waddled and waded, slugged and slurped in the river slump. We felt great comfort and tranquillity from the soft cushion of sand and also enjoyed the crystal clear ripples of smooth cruising water and we used to be highly excited. On top of that we used to make sand castles, huts, as well as dams. We massaged our feet, legs and indeed the whole body and enjoyed its soothing effect on our feelings. There used to be some pot -holes near the embankments and they were watersheds for some fish. We dived and delved into those tiny ponds and we thrilled at the slippery catch, but sometime we used to get startled when they thrashed about. However there was a lot of exhilaration, happiness at each success at catching.

Before moving on further I must narrate an incredible true tale about my far distant uncle, who only dwelled three doors away from my grandmother's house. They had hounds and guns for hunting ducks, deer and rabbits. One of their sons was only a year older than me and he sometimes used to give me the cotton white fur-skin of the leveret or hare. Sometimes they also used to bring meat of the deer to my grandmother, which tasted very delicious and tender, especially if it was of a young buck or a fawn. One day I was sitting in their house with my grandmother and uncle; and I happened to listen to their social chat. My uncle began by asking his distant cousin, "How did hunting go last week?" "We heard some funny story that one of your mates died in the hunting expedition, we cannot believe the way he died!" My uncle's cousin became anguished and replied with a smile, "Yes brother, it was very strange and unbelievable the way he died. The animal was snared and shot at close range, with three –not –three rifle. That deer was a godly animal when he was shot. It would appear that the bullets rebounded and hit at the throat of the hunter. The result was that the deer escaped miraculously and sneaked into the wild bush, but unfortunately, the man got killed instead." The cousin sighed with grief. It is alleged that Hindus have thirty three million gods, it is difficult to speculate which one of the gods had transformed into the form of a young deer!

Luckily the ancient beliefs do not apply to the British judiciary justice laws and logic of crime investigation and procedures; therefore an inquiry was launched by the police for this mysterious murder... Before any arrests could have been made, the cold blooded communal turbulence had already begun. There was forced mass expulsion of the people from their beloved ancestral villages. As a result many families were wiped out completely and many more were killed and a kind of new life pattern was in sight. In the light of those mass atrocities some odd single mischievous killing was completely forgotten. It faded away like the flame of a lantern in the dazzling glare of the June sun over the zenith.

My aunt used to live in a cul-de-sac, where houses were made of bricks and mud. Those houses had protection of high brick walls and had been fixed with strong wooden entrance doors. The Imam and his family also lived in the same narrow alleyway. Opposite to her house lodged another relative's family and with them also resided a scary and a cranky woman. She must have been in her mid-thirties and was quite beautiful, tall and wore nice deep colours clothes. She appeared to be a deranged and a ghostly creature. She was said to be suffering from some sort of dementia. Normally she was bound in shackles and chained in a dark cell, within the enclosure of the high walled jail of their house. However outside one could easily hear her loud wails and shrieks and also shouts of her captives. To me she was spooky, eerie and frightening. Sometimes she used to break out from her shackles. Sometimes suddenly she would have a fit of madness and rush out like a Spanish Bull in the arena. Her eyes flashed like Monsoon lightning and her face used to glow like a glass furnace. She used to break the sound barrier in the narrow strait. The earth shuddered and shook, as it does with the beat and trample of the wild beast. It was the moment when the cockerel would stop crowing or hen would drop her eggs, or the pigeons would buzz in panic. This was the moment when children would run for shelter and mothers rushed to the street to be vigilant. That was also the moment when the cattle stopped grazing, the air did not breathe and trees did not swing. This was the moment when I shivered and quivered and splintered from afar. I used be terribly frightened of her as she could have easily strangled any child to death.

That stark woman's family sounded quite well off and were arrogant people. They were comparatively more sophisticated and educated than other residents of the village. Naturally because of her traumatic disease they were fiercely depressed and under severe strain. It is difficult to surmise about the cause of that pitiable situation, but it would appear that this just happened momentarily and she started having fits of madness. It is possible that someone had abused her while she was a kid in her house or she might had some other hidden deep scar in her mind, perhaps a dejection of pure deep love with someone which she never disclosed to anybody being a female and in male dominated society or perhaps due to some erratic adverse secretion of biochemical fluids or neurones in her brain. She was a tall, fair and an attractive woman and it is really sad that she was in this eerie and ghostly plight. However I am not sure why she was kept shackled in her house and by her own family; and whether she was getting any medical treatment for her tragic ailment. At the time of the partition as the most cruel and savage communal rioting began with great ferocity and all Muslims in East Punjab, whether belonging to the Congress or Muslim League, had to flee in a great chaos to join any camps and gathering within matter of minutes and seconds. Panic stricken people left behind not only their own off springs; but also sick, lame and old relatives as well. There was no time to think or plan ahead. Again I am not sure whether that lady was abandoned behind in her shackles or let loose. But one thing is certain that the wild and drunken hoards of Sikhs and Hindus would have pounced on her being an attractive and beautiful young woman.

In our village and again next to my aunt's house on the right, there was another elderly weird and creepy person who resided with his family. At that time he gave an impression of being in his sixties, well-built chubby, almost seven feet tall, but blind. People mentioned about him as being a great soldier who had fought in the Great World War and returned home safely. Over the passage of time, something happened to him and he lost his normal conscience and awareness. He was not strong when I had seen him and occasionally used to creep slowly in the street, mumbling something on his own. He was a towering figure and always entirely unclothed, but he was totally harmless and not much mobile. When he rarely tramped in the street, he cautiously tried to feel about or groped on top of the brick walls, as if in the dark. At that moment he was not much confident about himself. I used to observe him once in a blue moon dotted just few feet away from him, while he prowled steadily in the street. After surveillance of the high wall and a bit of exercise, he used to return to his fort. Any passerby in the street would sometime have a casual look at him and some even tried to share conversation with him, especially the ladies peeping out of their main entrance. However sometimes he would respond to their chattering in a short code, mumble or a whisper, but frequently he did not react. In his house, there was a vast rectangular dusty yard, where he felt safe, relaxed and sunbathed. I used to watch him over there in his house. However in his house the ladies used to grind their own wheat and corn flour for making chapaties. They used to grind the clean grain in a kind of primitive and ancient stone grinder, which was made of two thick stone discs, lying on top of each other, with some gap in between them and a wooden handle fixed to top edge of the upper disc. There was a hole carved in the middle of both discs about two inches in radius for pouring the grain in the grinder. The rotation of the discs was done manually by the women and needed lot of muscular power. I was told by my aunt that Baba (Old man), did help some times in grinding the grains and he did so with the perseverance, speed and tireless energy of a soldier. However it all depended upon his state of mind.

So the life in the village was quite colourful as far as its inhabitants were concerned. Unfortunately all good things come to an end, but luckily bad ones as well. However during my stay in the village I got enlightenment and became more mature with a greater variety of experience. It was a blend and mix of mostly beneficial impacts, but as well as occasional injurious episodes too. Although living in grandma's village, where my mother was also born, was full of charisma, fascination and charm, there is no doubt in my mind that this was a wild bush area. In the earliest few years of my life and stay over there, I observed and learnt an amazing colossal amount of knowledge about human complexity, the forces of nature and a greater variety of wild life. The Himalayas, The Cho, The flash floods The Monsoons and the dust storms are only a few to mention here again. In this place of wilderness, turbulence and natural beauty, I had hardly remembered my mother. To me my maternal- grandmother was my mother. The simple matter of the fact is that I had never seen my mother or her photograph. Therefore I had no recollection of her and I was not emotionally attached to her. I never remembered the comfort and warmth of her lap or softness of her breasts or charm of her cuddles.

At the end of the month of June 1947, schools and colleges closed as usual for the normal summer holidays for duration of over two months. At that time the landscape simmered and sizzled with the sun which glittered over the zenith. My eldest brother named Yaqoob, an 'O' level student and only of sixteen years old arrived in the village at the end of June to visit the grandma, uncle, the aunt or most probably to have a glimpse of his gazelle like fiancée. She also felt excited and was over the moon. She kept on asking me, "Where is Yaqoob? What is he doing in grandma' house. When is he coming to see us?" However, I just smiled back with a little nod, because I had no clue, but I surmised that she was desperate to see him. Even my aunt and her whole family kept on asking me about his whereabouts and everyone smiled and looked excited. Nobody told me the reason, but I understood their psychology by gazing at their faces and noting the tone of their gestures.

That June and the coming few months were very historical, crucial and epic moments not only for me, but also for my grandma, her family and for the whole village. That was the turning- point for the glorious and Great British Indian Empire and indeed for the whole of the British Empire as well, which encompassed one quarter of the planet directly and the other quarter indirectly and no doubt that was the turning point for the other global empires as well.. Soon there would be an end to the hoards of the servants, cheap mercenaries and World Wars. Soon the sun would be start setting over the Great Empires. Soon there would be an advent of dark politics, gruesome massacres and grisly occupations. Soon a submissive, tame and humble people would turn stone-hearted, treacherous and warriors.

It is difficult for me to speculate, just like the political turbulence in India at that moment, why my brother had come to East Punjab from the West Punjab at that dangerous, violent and uncertain moment; on his own and at such a young age. I was seven years old at that time and I later discovered that I was the only beneficiary and had a great escape from the gravest moment of all times, which soon had developed in the history of the grandma's village. That was the period in which the most humble and simple people on the planet had become cruel and blood thirsty to their own friends and neighbours within a twist of the moment.. They had planned themselves meticulously well in advance and were given full support by their democratic leaders to ensnare the helpless and unarmed people. These hoards and drunken hooligans committed maximum cruelties and atrocities to their own blood relations. They had developed their hatred on the difference of religious beliefs. This episode becomes even more grim and terrible because no one in the UNO has ever burped or bothered to make any investigation and hang the culprits thousand times each. It does not matter who was guilty and from which background.

At that particular moment there were already some tales circulating about a Muslim being killed on a farm overnight or his cattle having been robbed or their horses taken away. While I prowled as usual in the fields or orchards, I observed and gazed on some lonely Sikhs walking with their eyes down and with swords slung on their backs. Stories of some odd skirmishes, atrocities and communal rioting from far distant places also were filtering in and discussed in each house, gatherings or fields. However In that remote village, there was no means of communications, no trains or buses, no radio set or a newspaper. The only means of information was on personal basis circulating from village to village or from the travellers, sometimes speculated or rumoured. While the village folk sheltered under the mighty clump of Bur- trees, there were hot debates about what was happening and why? Everyone was worried, anguished and in a frenzy. However, nobody could predict or foresee any barbaric and horrifying treacherous communal -violence, which was going to be unleashed at any moment, especially under the genius of the British expertise. However most of the residents wanted to stay in their beloved villages and lands. In the past time it used to be a routine and normal practice by the farmers to narrate an incident whenever their sheep, goat or a lamb was plundered or eaten by the wolf or a tiger; but now those bloodthirsty incidents related to the humans. As usual whether I was sitting alone or with the family or while playing with my friends, I always listened and observed unnoticed and would digest the turbulent remarks.

Soon after the dusk when the red and orange and grey colours faded away from the horizon and then the gloomy discussions in the dark about the hush-hush of political disturbance and jiggery-poker of the politicians, engulfed and shrouded the emotions. I used to get disturbed and startled by the harrowing sagas. Under those depressed sentiments I would ask my grandmother if she could accompany me to the charpies, which lay on the flat roof upstairs. However once I lay in my charpie, still I could hear low whispers going on downstairs between my uncle, his wife, my brother and the neighbours. The village condition did not look promising. After making my bed and making me almost asleep my grandma used to go downstairs again to join the gathering. It was late in the night when she returned to the roof with my brother. At that moment the stars twinkled deep in the sky, but no glowing moon. I felt scared, muddled and dizzy and was unable to sleep. I constantly stared beyond the stars and the milky-way, fanciful that my mum was there, staring and smiling at me, from a spooky and a foggy place, but unable to reach me. However that provided me with thoughtful consolation and a momentous mirage of hope. Thus for few moments I got immersed in a deep reflection and fantasy. While I was lying in my bed alone under the dark blanket of sea, in this muffled and fuzzy state, I had a kind of vision and hallucination. While engulfed in those repressed and baffled emotions, I could hear jingle-jangle and clink of swords, a mix of shrieks and wails, barks of dogs and howls of wolves. I heard people chasing each other, fighting and killing. I visualised dust storms and the thorny bushes rolling with the gusts and I became glum and gloomy. From those tense and excruciating emotional dark dreams, I visualised that my grandma's village did not like me anymore and perhaps I would be saying good-bye to it.

However the circumstances in the East Punjab were getting more and more tense; day by day. There was no time to be wasted now and my brother decided to take me back home as soon as possible. The journey across the East Punjab was becoming more and more unsafe and dangerous, at each passing hour. Soon, on one day in the last week of July, 1947, we departed early in the morning. It was burning hot, even at such an early time in the morning. Most of our epic initial route was dusty and sandy, infested with pot-holes. The railway station was some ten miles away, but luckily the train station was located on the outskirts of my father's ancestral home, located in a tower within a strong fortified citadel. It took us two days to reach there with one overnight stop.

We parted facing each other in our beloved Cho, the grandmother and my aunt with their backs to the mosque and the village; my uncle, my brother and I faced the village and the mosque and its public baths. It was an extremely sad and sombre moment. We stood few yards away from each other. My grandmother had earlier cuddled and kissed me for the last time in her lifetime and my lifetime. Her face ruffled and flustered. Tears trickled and showered her silky and wrinkled cheeks. She steadily persevered to wipe her face with her muslin dupatta while her hands trembled and sometimes covered her eyes with it. She stared and glared at me with her eyes of a gazelle. Her body shivered and shuddered and her heart drummed fast. "I will plunge into the well, if you take Anwer from me. I cannot live without him." She exclaimed with tears and wiping her nose. Her last dialogue and gestures now resonate and bite me again and again. I think she had the prior feelings at that moment that she would never be meeting with me again

I myself stood dumb like a statue or an idol, completely denuded and sinking in the sand. My eyes soaked in tears and stared mercilessly at her withered and frail face. I did not want to apart from her. I stand still in chill, stunned and with a broken heart. My legs were frozen, eyes did not flicker and I stood like a mute. Only the soft cushion of sand gave me a bit of comfort. My brother had tears in his eyes as well and he comforted grandma. He reassured her by caressing her and wiping the tears, "Ma don't worry, you will see him soon."

With those pitiable sentiments we started drifting away slowly across the dry river soft sands and say good-bye for the last time to my grandmother and the magical village and the Cho. I started walking along with my brother and my uncle. She was still standing there while we were trailing away from her and kept on waving .Soon we disappeared in the horizon and never met again. At this moment I do not know for how long she would have been standing there as she was adamantly refusing to go home and rather wanted to plunge into the well and I even do not know how she was feeling afterwards! While reminiscing and recording that historical moment, my heart sinks again and again and I choke, but to no avail and I wonder why the human species do this to each other! We continued crossing my beloved Cho, trail through the diagonal dusty- path, pass through the mangoes - grove, we troop along to the school and other part of the village. The mangoes were fully ripe now and swayed in the cool breeze with their exotic juice, ready to be plucked and sucked, along with their goodness and fragrance. The black bird called Koel, fluttered and flitted perching on the clump of the mangoes and kept on singing with its usual melodious rhythm and expressed her best wishes for our safe journey. It is said that the Indian ever most celebrated female melody singer Lata, who has sung well over hundred thousand film songs and whose songs still make me sleep every night, had copied her voice from this melodious bird.

We trotted for few hours along the sandy and dusty road sprawling through the middle of the fields and pastures, full of pitfalls and

submerged in painful emotions and arrived at a small municipal
town, where my uncle' in-laws lodged. It was just before noon and
was scorching hot, the silver disc of the sun glittered just over our
heads at an angle of ninety. I recollect travelling along this route
before when my father came to pick me up with my grandmother,
but that was a peaceful -time, about two years ago. However that
time I had travelled in the Dolee with my grandmother, snug
and comfortable in her cushy lap all the way to the railway
station, some Ten miles away, while my father trotted on the back
of a horse. along with my uncle. I also recollect how my sister
at the other end had taught me how to wash my face and the
hands properly; and I felt rather embarrassed when my paternal
grandmother and my brothers made fun of me and ridiculed me
over my uncouth and primitive village manners.

However in that small municipal town, my uncle's father-in-law
welcomed us, he was in his full military uniform, along with his
two wives and a son. They resided in a large house, with a high
brick wall. They gifted me two Paisas, as pocket money and asked
me to buy some sweets from a corner Hindu shop. That was the
first ever time that I remember having a hard cash and felt very
rich. I rushed to the shop with one of his wives and purchased
some sweets, but still had a lot of change left over. It surprised me
how much difference money could make; it was full of power.

Back in grandmother's village, all shops, medical clinics and
utility stores belonged to the Krars (Hindu Banias), as well as the
lucrative money lending business. They are alleged to be the
equivalent to the Jews in India and rather surpass them. I recollect
one dark night, on the eve of Hindu Diwali festival in a freezing
winter I forced my grandma to buy some fireworks for me. She
enfolded me on her shoulders and went alone all the way in the
dark to the other part of the village and knocked at the door of
the Krar, whose shop sold those fireworks. He came out specially
and opened his adjoining shop and was kind enough to sell the
fireworks to us. We returned home in excitement with the supplies
and I enjoyed the fire displays in the Cho with my friends. In the

remote village all inhabitants lodged like friends and relatives. However there might have been some exceptions which I did not know at that time.

I must quote a parable about an intensely soaked and a highly charged female lover, who was unable to reach her beloved because her neighbours and local community women used to keep a strict vigil on her movement. The local Punjabi poet expresses her frustration and depressed feelings like this:

Let Krar's shop blaze, where lantern glows all night

Let the beggar's bitch die, who howls all the times

Let five or seven women die, who lodge nearby

Let the rest perish, by the terrible deadly fever

The next few miles of my journey were more perilous and painful. While my brother and uncle kept on walking, they decided that my uncle's brother-in-law should carry me on his bike to my father's town. In between those small towns was located the railway station and the main metalled road. In the villages located on our route, there was a proportional blend of Hindu, Sikh and Muslim communities. In this area some more punitive and aggressive attacks on the Muslims had already begun, although not in an open manner, but rather in guerrilla skirmishes. It could have been a rehearsal for what was going to follow in the next few weeks. However the idea was to cover the trail in the shortest possible time and make me less tired. Later my uncle informed me that on his way back, he had to be escorted on a horse by other armed horsemen, as that route became more dangerous to walk on his own or even in a group, if unarmed.

Although I would have preferred the walk rather than going on a bike, but I had no choice. We drove on an un-metalled footpath infested with lairs. He peddled rather faster because of fear of a surprise attacks, the attackers normally used to hide behind the bush or lie low in the fields, then ambushed when the target was close by. First I perched on the back seat of the pedal-bike which was made from a network of thin iron rods, but with the thumps and bumps, it was terribly painful. During the course of drive, my uncle asked me, "Are you alright? Tell me if you are not comfortable." I burst in agony and responded, "It is hurting me and not comfortable."

He immediately applied breaks on his bike and then shifted me to the iron rod fixed in the front of the main frame. This time he even drove faster, as if in panic. I jumped and thumped and held the handle tight so that to avoid tumbling down, but it got worse; more painful and miserable. That made my thighs and bum bruised brutally and later I noticed some blood on my shorts. However thankfully we arrived safely in my father ancestor's home. My uncle's brother-in-law, returned to his home immediately.

My ancestor's home was not a simple flat-roofed home, made of bricks or mud. It was a strong medieval citadel made of small bricks and secured with a series of massive strong thick-wood and iron doors and series of thick concentric walls. We entered the main gigantic door and passed through narrow streets with towering strong buildings on both sides. When we reached near our main enclosure or cluster of buildings, it had a queer entrance. It was a tall and thick wooden door, tightly locked and its entrance was via a steep, slanting hump-slope, which I had to struggle to ascend. A special message was sent in to gain access. We had to wait for few minutes before the access was granted. That entrance was the main door to a set of independent high walled - houses inside the common bricked compound. Then there were further separate strong doors and high strong walls to each independent house. Our house was in the main pavilion, again enclosed with thick and high walls and three stories tall, decorated with upper balconies and steep covered stairs leading up the balconies. Still there was a high wall on the top roof and toilets were located on the top floor. The structure of toilets is worth mentioning. They were fitted with a shaft leading down from the third floor to the base of the foundation, where containers were provided and fully covered. The untouchables would come in the street below for sweeping the streets and cleaning the toilets. One of the untouchable ladies came inside the main pavilion for cleaning as well as pouring water down the shaft to flush the toilets downstairs. In the inner clump of the houses, there are so many concentric walls and doors that even a sparrow could not flutter. However in the heat of the summer, it felt like an oven or a furnace.

In our house, which was a kind of magnificent ancient palace, I found that only my great aunt was living there. She became a widow when she was only fifteen or so because my great -uncle who had married to her, died at the young age of about twenty. She herself never married again, although later she got many offers, she just followed the ancient tradition of our Hindu ancestors and lived as a spinster for another seventy years. This great fort belonged to a Hindu Raja called Sham, who had an estate of eighty four villages. Therefore this small municipality is known as ShamChorasi (Sham of eighty four villages}. However Raja Sham converted to Islam under the influence of a mystic, along with his subjects. The magnificent shrine of the same mystic, who converted him, is still there and well looked after by a dedicated Hindu family, who lodge within the complex of the shrine in a comfortable accommodation. At the time of my visit later to my ancestor's home, I was informed that some dedicated devotees of the saint now living in Pakistan are providing for the funds not only for the caretakers, but also to maintain the shrine.

After having few days rest in my ancestor's fort, we departed on our final leg of the journey, this time by train. We said good-bye to all our relatives, uncles and aunts and unfortunately some of them I never met again. We reached the local station by a horse wagon or a Tonga, as it is called. The railway station was about two miles away from our fortified town. The train entered the station with the usual thrust and sizzle of the steam engine. This station was not on the main line, thus did not sound busy or it could had been a potential trouble in the pipeline. One of our aunties called Shahzada had wrapped a good stock of kebabs and chapaties for us to eat during our long journey in the train. Also one of our uncles called Abdul was escorting us up to Amritsar, the holy city of the Sikhs, where we got our final connection of the train to Lahore. In total we had to cover over one hundred and twenty miles or so to reach our destination. As we trailed to the west, we went far and far away from Simla, the summer capital of British India, where the Viceroy and political elites were lusting at the glorious sumptuous heights and also far away from my grandma's village.

However the train journey was far more comfortable than travelling on the bike. After about two hours in the slow train as it had to pass through various crossings and junctions, there rose a mighty dark dust storm, which metamorphosed the day into a night. The train stopped straight away, as the driver was unable to see any signals or even the track. In fact there were series of dust storms, one after the other. Although I used to enjoy the dust storms in Grandma's village, but this particular dark dust storm was more eerie and frightening, especially when the train halted in the middle of the wilderness in the night. Each time the train came to a halt, again and again after steady cruising for an hour or so, we just wondered what was about to happen. In that natural calamity the whole network of train services had been disrupted in that region. As I mentioned earlier normally I used to yearn for the dust-storm as it took away the peril of heat and sweat, but this time they were frightening because of their ferocity and dark colour. To see the smooth train journey coming to a sudden halt in the middle of the wild bush-terrain; creates some more fear and suspense, especially in the blanket of dark night. But thankfully the train reached to its destination without any sad mishap.

After the dust storm was over, a Sikh entered the train at the next station and seated next to me, while my brother was seated just the opposite. Soon my brother started a gossip with him, in a usual relaxed Punjabi way. He turned up a bit drowsy and covered his eyes and nose. It was quite possible that he was exhausted of waiting for the excessive delayed train or he wanted to protect his face or head against the dust gusting outside the train. I hazard to guess he had gone with the wind. It came to light that his stomach was fermenting with whisky and garlic or onion pickle. There was a continuous emission of Carbon Mono-oxide gas, at an interval of every few seconds. The pungent puffs and whiffs choked my breath and nose, as well as of my brother. My brother held his breath, as well as myself without blocking our noses, during the time of the bombardment and its pungent impact in the coach. We just stared at each other as well as at the Sardarji (Chief) without any visible reaction. It was a mental as well as a physical torture. The train was manufactured by the Englishmen, so it must have been provided with toilet facilities and he could have easily relieved himself or perhaps he was too lazy. Normally people of the village and mostly in the towns at that time preferred relieving themselves in the open wild bush or fields. He was pretending to be fast asleep, but held the back tail of his turban to cover his nose and eyes. My brother kept on looking at me and him and made sarcastic gestures. My reaction was rather more subdued and at least it was not killing me, just choking. However we were unable to escape this gas attack although we are only inches away from the gas chambers. I wish I was wearing a turban as well so that I could have covered my nose. Obviously we did not talk about that pitiless trauma or perhaps it was a necessary evil. In that crisis we kept our lips sealed and we managed to keep cool. My brother just wanted to continue chattering with him, but he soon pretended as if he was fast asleep or was that a bad omen for new commuters who would be fleeing in the next few weeks, it is anybody's speculation. There were some other Sardarjies (Sikhs, as we call them in Punjabi) sitting as well, on the other seats and with other indigenous passengers, they must be feeling the sting and stink as well, but not with as much intensity because luckily they were far away from the polluted air, and its ferocity must be diluted. However those pungent fumes still choke me to death and attack like a nerve gas.

However thanks to the steam engine driver, the train arrived safely in Amritsar, the Holy city of the Sikhs. Here we shifted to another train and caught her from some other platform at the main station for our onward journey to Lahore. The platforms were full of collies, wearing red shirts and turbans and white trousers. To me they were a happy blend of Sikhs, Hindus as well as Muslims and apparently there was no tension.

Amritsar was the twin city of Lahore and not far away from it; now the holy city of the Sikhs, was equally fascinating, although comparatively far younger and bustled with equal proportion of Hindus, Sikhs and Muslim inhabitants and they had fought for the freedom as one united people. The Sikhs holiest shrine called The Golden Temple was designed on a pattern of a mosque with lofty minarets and its architect was a Muslim; even the land for this site was originally donated by the then Muslim rulers. That was very historical moment for the glorious province of the Punjab and its Punjabi people, then living happily together, but unfortunately this would soon be shattered. However I must thank my eldest brother Yaqoob for bringing me to safely and who had endeavoured to help me to a miraculous escape from the terrible communal violence which was about to be unleashed and had been planned over the great heights as well as in the lairs. He had done so even at the risk of his own teenage life because odd skirmishes were already cindering right across the board in the remote areas of East Punjab. From Lahore we got another train for further half a day journey to Okara some eighty miles away towards Montgomery and our nearest railway station and from there we got a bus to Depalpur which was located some fifteen miles away from the railway station where my parents were living. When I had reached home I felt I had come completely to a foreign land. However everyone in the house welcomed us for having a safe journey and I looked forward to start a new life in a more civilised manner. Soon I had forgotten grandma's village in the East Punjab.

Chapter IV

Road to Freedom

I commence with an extract from a report by a special correspondent of a western daily newspaper who happened to be travelling from Lahore to Delhi at the time of the Partition of India. Whatever he had observed, he would have had given an eye-witness account....

"Only those people would hear my story who would have had the guts and strong hearts. I had the information already that a lot of atrocities were being committed to the extremes in East Punjab. After reaching Lahore, it became more evident to me because on the same day, a train number 15-Up, arrived in Lahore full of corpses and with dripping pools of blood. In that train, hundreds of passengers were mercilessly daggered to death in Bathinda, in the Sikh State of Patiala. From that train, only eight passengers were picked up alive, but even they were badly injured. That train comprised of nine wagons, in which one thousand passengers could have been easily accommodated. In that train, Muslim migrants from India were being transported towards Lahore, but it was stopped in the middle of its journey. As soon as the train is stopped, heavily armed Sikhs and Hindu extremists let themselves loose with a great ferocity. The soldiers escorting the train just stood aside as spectators. The passengers were cut into pieces and thrown into the canal flowing nearby. Hundreds of the passengers flee to the fields in panic, but they too are chased and massacred. That carnage continued for an hour. The guard and the driver are spared, because they professed themselves to be Hindus. The oozing and sloppy train in dripping blood arrived with a slump and slosh.

When our train left for Delhi from Lahore, I witnessed quite a few horrible scenes. Flocks of vultures were hovering and feeding on the carcasses in every village adjoining to the railway line. In the old British India's garrison town of Ferozepur, the flames were rising to the sky. The dogs were lurching on the dead bodies and trying to pull the meat away with shudders and shakes. I was not yet fully aware of the intense ferocity of the atrocities, when we reached Bathinda at 4 PM. In this most remote and ghost railway junction, the locusts and hoards of Sikhs were everywhere. The trains loaded with massacred migrants; stacks and piles of slithering and fluttering humans were approaching from all directions. When we arrived at the station, two trains, loaded with two thousand people were parked over there. Although there was a small police guard present at the station, they were warned by the Sikhs that if they interfered, their families would be killed. Hardly ten minutes had passed, when I noticed a Muslim beggar being stabbed to death by a Sikh with his Kirpan (small double edged dagger). Soon I realised what the meaning of freedom was.

The clump of human's carcasses could be seen plumped, just next to our train. While I was staring at them, two policemen arrived on a bull-cart, already loaded with the dead bodies. On top of the heap of corpses, one injured man was also wailing with colossal deep wounds. The policemen saw him, but they kept on piling up the bull-cart with the new load of dead humans. That slithering and fluttering human, just simply got choked under the cargo of the fresh load. Another Muslim farmer was breaking his breath lying nearby. His throat was bleeding and his hands were cut off. His legs were shaking and shuddering. There was a dog and a vulture gazing at him under a tree and waiting for him to die.

As soon as our train started moving towards Delhi, then what we had witnessed became even more frightful and painful. We observed that four Sikhs were beating six Muslim girls in a very vicious and violent manner and they had already killed one or two of them. On the next station, we saw another irate and boisterous swarm of Sikhs. Those people were armed with Kirpans, daggers, axes, spears, hammers and knives. Some of the Sikhs had leather whips, on which heavy lead- bullets were sealed in. There were more hoards of Sikhs converging on their horses, camels and mules. On the other stations, were the similar frightful and grim scenes. The corpses were littered all across the track, which had been dragged from the train. While we continuously witnessed those horrific scenes, we arrived at Delhi."

But before I describe more harrowing stories from the narrations of the victims of the partition, I want to give an introduction to the origin of the actual people who were involved in the conflict; they were mainly Hindus, Sikhs and Muslims. However it would appear that the most of the Christians, Parsies, Anglo-Indians and Budhists remained neutral.

Let us commence with the Hindus who at that moment made up about 60% of greater India's population, most of them call themselves descendants of the Aryans, who arrived in India over four thousand years ago. They allege to have come from central Asia, but the Untouchables (original Indian inhabitants) were already there and easily conquered by the war like Aryans. That was at almost the same time, when the Prophet Abraham would have migrated from Ur (Iraq) to the Palestine and simultaneously Aryans would have migrated to Germany, Iran and Afghanistan. The Aryans came from the harshness and extremities of the desert and wilderness of Central Asia to the most fertile Indus and Ganges plains, to the vast and green alluvial landscape. They also found the highest mountains in the world, beautiful and romantic valleys and largest perennial rivers in the world. They also found a great variety of crops, exotic fruits, a great variety of trees, beautiful flowers; in addition to this a fascinating and teeming wild life. They must have been dazzled by its gold, diamonds and a great wealth of precious colourful stones.

They overran the Indus Valley Civilisation on the banks and plains of the Indus, which had been flourishing in Harappa and Moheinjudaru (both currently in Pakistan) over two thousand years before them and pushed the original inhabitants to the far extremities of the south and the east. In order to control and manage this gifted country, they devised the caste system.

They split the population into four tiers or segments. The top of the hierarchy came the Brahmen(a kind of god like and blessed people), second came the soldiers, the third working or administration class and at the bottom, the Untouchable(a kind of subservient and inferior to all above three).Vertical movement on the ladder was forbidden and anybody breaking the regulation was stringently admonished. Each segment of population lived in a separate section of the settlement far away from each other. For example the untouchable could not draw water from the well of the upper castes, if someone was caught or observed, the village of the untouchable could be burnt or the offender could be killed as a punishment.

It is surprising that Hinduism is a name of a religion like Islam, Christianity or Judaism; it is a mixture of set of traditions, stories, gods, rituals, beliefs, actions or prayers. Some Hindus believe in one God, some in gods (Human kings), some worship idols, some do not. However most of the Hindus worship idols in various shapes, deities and attributes. Few among their gods are moon, sun, stones, fire, trees, plants, snakes, cows, elephants, monkeys. They believe in reincarnation, being reborn in a new body. The soul is sometimes born in a human body, sometimes in an animal and sometimes in a plant. The new birth depends upon the Karma (Action) in the first life, so the status changes according to the previous actions in life. Hence cycle of life continues eternally. The name Hindu or Hindustan was given by the Persian, Afghan, Turks or Mongol rulers of India. The language of the Muslim invaders and rulers to India, from Central Asia, Afghanistan and Iran was Persian... The Hindus holy scripture are written in Sanskrit, like Veda (The spiritual knowledge directly revealed by God) and Bhagvat Gita (Song of God taught by Krishna), but only Brahmin are supposed to know the holy language of Sanskrit, it is forbidden to the other castes. Most of the Hindus are vegetarians, but some of them eat meat. However there was ritual of Sati (Woman burning herself to death, along with the cremation of her deceased husband).However if the wife dies, the husband can marry more than one wife. Normally inheritance only goes to the males and also the practice of human sacrifice was not uncommon.

After the Indian Mutiny or the War of Independence in 1857, rift and division existed between Hindus and Muslims. At the time of war against the British East India Company, they fought with great valour and unity. Both communities gave colossal sacrifices under the command of Bakht Khan, held the Red Fort and Delhi for almost six months. As the British had taken power from the Muslim- rulers all across India, starting from Madras, Deccan, Gujrat, Bengal and Delhi; they tried to give preferential and favourable treatment to the Hindus against the Muslims, perhaps to win the support of the majority of the population and also to have less fear of Muslims' revival.. The Hindus also found this a unique opportunity to rise with great effort and downgrade the ex-Muslim ruling race to an unprivileged society. The Hindu Brahmins and Banias took most areas of business, education and lands as fast as they could, under an organised and biased umbrella. Now Hindu Pandits and Banias were the elite of the society, money lenders and bankers, as well as the top intellectuals and civil servants. They also had achieved that success through bribery, corruption and flattery. The majority of Muslims became underdogs and subservient, apart from the feudal lords and few business families. Those Muslim elites also abused the Muslim masses. As a whole the Muslims had become superficially arrogant and over confident on the basis of their past glorious ruling record and a prolonged history over India. They were soaked in their idle dreams and glories. They simply lay dormant and decadent, littered in their dead past. They had perceived Hindus as meek, cowardly and a subservient mass, over a long period of their domination in India, lasting over twelve hundred years.

Indian Congress Party was founded in 1885 by a Scotsman called Allan Octavian Hume in Porbandar (Gujrat); its membership was open to all Indians and without prejudice against any religion. Its presidents and secretaries were Muslims, Parsies as well as Hindus and they worked together and in co-ordination, under one leader, whosoever it might happen to be. All those officials of the Congress Party negotiated and dealt with the British Imperialists for one united and gifted country, called India. They fought together for its previous glory and prosperity without any prejudice or suspicion against each other. However at the advent of the 20th century and during the First World War, the British became weaker and weaker and the Indian congress party became stronger and stronger, especially its majority of Hindus, who now thought themselves as the sole future rulers of mother India. The Hindus also established further political or militant groups like RSS, JanSingh, ShevSina, Hindu Mahasabha or Bhartia Janta Party. Their members received proper military training in using fire arms, explosive, swords and spears, to name only a few. Those groups definitely played important roles in one of the greatest calamities in the history of mankind which took place in India, at time of the partition in 1947.

The history of Muslims in India began in earnest in the year 712 AD, when a young Arab general of seventeen, named Mohammed Bin Qasim invaded Sindh (now Pakistan), commencing from Daibul (currently Karachi).The story of Mohammed Bin Qasim's adventures is one of the romances of history. The young general had at least six thousand picked horsemen to his back, chosen from the caliph's veterans from Damascus and was supplied with a baggage –train of three thousand Bactarian camels as well. Marching through Mekran coast line (Baluchistan, now Pakistan), he was joined by the provincial governor with more troops and five stone-slings for siege work were sent by sea to meet him at Daibul, the great medieval port of the Indus valley. The ruler of Sindh called Raja Dahir, met the invaders along with his chiefs and soldiers, mounted on the war elephants, in the comfort and safety of the Howdahs. The Arabs stormed the enemy positions with lightning speed and with great courage and skill. Soon the ruler of Sindh, his chiefs lay slithering between blood and dust. Most of the defenders were butchered, if they were still fighting, but luckily most of them were on the run and later became mercenaries for their invaders, for they got better human treatment from them and shared the booty equally.

Soon the grieved widows, princesses, queens and concubines in the Harem and the citadel got together wailing and shrieking and plunged to death in the inferno, blazing down the edge of the great security wall. They had performed Sati in a joint ceremony and jumped down the great wall into the colossal wood fire fuming like a volcano. Soon they perished and smothered like red roses and fragrant petals, joined their husbands, even before they could arrive there. So many enchanting beauties glow and melt like rubies and glass in the furnace. They were very brave, beautiful and charming ladies, even braver than their husbands and men, who had plunged to death in the honour of their late men. However, it is noticed that the male folks have never committed Sati, when their beloved wives had died. In fact they yearn for more wives, concubines and far younger, if possible. The Indian women used to show the desperate courage for which they were famous. They used to refuse to owe their lives to the 'vile cow-eaters', at the price of dishonour, instead they used to set their house ablaze and perish themselves in the flames. Later the great Punjabi romantic poet Waris Shah had become emotionally depressed, agitated and critical of the tradition of Purda (Hijab) observed by the Muslim women. He had felt denuded, deprived and thus had consequently gestured and even protested, "we should never imprison the eyes in the cage (Burkha) and we should never deface and ruin the jewels, rubies, emeralds and roses by trampling them in the dust!" He admired the invaluable charm and gift of nature; it must not perish into the dark oblivion; it must be allowed to glitter and glisten." However going back to the Hindu episodes the chiefs in the delta and lower Indus Valley had surrendered at their discretion, but not without a tough resistance and a prolonged siege. The fighting men were either massacred or on the run, but later had become subservient, that was if their lives were spared.

Raja Dahir and his chiefs were cruel and oppressors; they treated their subjects as slaves and were fiercely clenched in the terrible squeeze of the caste system. The people of his empire had welcomed the young general and his soldiers for their generous behaviour, for their justice, equality and fairness. They did not persecute anybody because of their religion or culture. They allowed them to practice their religion or beliefs as they wished. Quran clearly dictates, "Your religion is your religion, our religion is our religion" to be a Muslim does not give a certificate to be a good person and the same thing applies to the other beliefs or creeds. Its teaching emphasises personal performance and deeds, not mediated through any priest or prophet or caste. It completely rejects and refutes any such self-important claimants or self-preserved groups or self-appointed agents. There was no forced conversion, the proof of the pudding is in the eating. At this moment there are about 15-20% Hindus, still living in the Sindh, although Sindh is called the 'Gateway to Islam' in India. There was no slaughter or inquisition. There was no burning or water boarding or tearing away their bodies, for purpose of purification... The people were allowed to practice, whatever was their choice and they had progressed as they wished. There is no doubt that everyone had to obey the law of the land, sometimes there could be a Hindu governor or sometimes an Arab, depending upon the ability and loyalty of the individuals. If the Muslim or an Arab had committed treason or rebellion, they were sorted out according to the seriousness of their action. To the rulers every law abiding citizen was equal, there was no division of caste or hierarchy in the religion. Islam got assimilated quickly, because it was simple to practice. They just believed in one 'Supreme Being', they could simply pray in the fields, pavement, forest, or a desert; without a high priest, without a deity or a god, even without an Imam. They did not need gold idols or diamond statues, there was no discrimination between colours and background. Any knowledgeable person was entitled to be a Mullah or an Imam, but there was no top Mullah, who controls other Mullahs. Their religion did not involve any gods, deities, icons or a monopoly or strata of holy-men or gurus. It was left to the democratic system or to the ability and choice of the individual. To those people, the Arab was not superior to the Persian or a Persian not superior to the Arab, but could have been superior or inferior according to their actions, not by their colour or creed or background.

In Sindh all traditions, cultures and beliefs flourished concurrently without any restraints. They meandered and flowed together just like the waves, ripples and currents of the river, only constrained by its banks.

The story of Mohammad Bin Qasim's military expedition into Sindh becomes even more interesting when we ask ourselves as why particularly he had invaded India? The tradition goes that at the time of the Umayyad Caliphs in Damascus, there was a very able and tough governor based in Basra (Iraq) named Hujjaj Bin Yusuf. It would appear that during the time of his tenure, some pilgrims' ships from Mecca were intercepted and plundered by the sea pirates in the realm of Raja Dahir, near Daibul(Currently Karachi) and it happened a few times. Those Muslim pilgrims were returning home to Sri Lanka, Malaysia, Indonesia and the Philipines. The pilgrims were imprisoned and their property was confiscated by the sea pirates. Those pilgrims included men, women and children. The reports of such incidents reached the governor and he sent series of messages to Raja Dahir, demanding the return of the prisoners and their confiscated property immediately, but no response was forthcoming from the Indian ruler of Sindh. He simply shrugged his shoulders and responded, "These pirates are not under my control, I have tried hard to find and locate them, but I am extremely sorry to say that I have failed to harness them, thus I am unable to help in this case." Hujjaj was furious and he sought permission and help from the Caliph, which was granted without any delay. Mohammed Bin Qasim reached up to Multan (two hundred miles south of Lahore) in the Punjab, just like a dust storm and was welcomed with open arms by the indigenous inhabitants. Sadly due to some political dispute in the family back home, he was recalled back and the expedition came to a halt.

In 1875 almost a decade before the Indian National Congress was founded, Sir Sayyid started his potent Muhammadan Anglo-Oriental College at Aligarh, some sixty miles southeast of Delhi. Modelled on the Cambridge residential and tutorial collegiate system. Sir Sayyid himself was knighted in 1870, devoted his mature life to service in the British Empire and was appointed by the viceroy to his Imperial Legislative council; Sir Sayyid argued from that powerful platform in 1883 against the introduction of the principle of election, pure and simple into the body politics of a country like India, where caste distinctions still flourished, where there was no fusion of the various races, where religious distinctions were still violent. That was the earliest modern articulation of the two nation theory, which was to become the ideological basis for Pakistan. Jinnah joined Indian Congress Party in 1896.The first annual session of Congress attended by Jinnah was its 20th held in Bombay in December 1904. Jinnah's involvement in Congress politics was a by-product of his flourishing legal career and social life in Bombay as his earlier commitment to Dadabhai had been in London.

During Lord Curzon's half decade of rule, the Muslim dominant province of Bengal and Assam was partitioned into Hindu and Muslim sectors, dividing a population of 85 million (largest populated province of India) in 1903.This first partition ignited Muslim political consciousness throughout the subcontinent, providing a provincial cradle in Dacca for the birth of the Muslim League in 1906.At this moment the money lending, politics and the land ownership mostly belonged to the Hindus and Muslims were treated as underdogs. This was the moment when hatred started between the Hindus and the Muslims, even the hatred by the Hindu's elites against the British. However the partition of Bengal was annulled in 1911.

Jinnah did agree to join Muslim league in 1913, but he insisted as a prior condition that his loyalty to the Muslim League and the Muslim interest would in no way and at no time imply even the shadow of disloyalty to the larger national cause to which his life was dedicated. In 1914 Jinnah was chosen by the Congress to chair a Congress deputation to London to lobby members of Parliament and Whitehall. Later the elder Nehru (Motilal) called Jinnah as a keen nationalist and champion of Hindu-Muslim unity. However the difficulty arose for Jinnah, when Gandhi arrived in India from South Africa in 1915 and also the change in the attitude of the senior Nehru, who wanted himself or his son to become the sole leader and wanted Jinnah as an assistant. However Jinnah, the Lincoln's Inn barrister, would never rest content simply to assist a provincial pleader, no matter how great his fortune or caste happened to be. For decades he helped Congress and Gandhi; but kept on observing the shift in the Hindu ideology. He kept a balance between the Congress and Muslim League and pleaded to the British masters for a unified free India, without monopoly of any sect, caste or religion. He believed in equal rights and opportunity for all, including any minorities; but by late 1920's Motilal and Jinnah became bitter rivals, slowly and gradually Jinnah's loyalty shifted as required. The historic Pakistan Resolution was passed on 22 March 1940 in Lahore; and In 1942 the Congress party, under the leadership of Mahatma Gandhi, passed a resolution against the British to Quit India. Later in 1944, Quaid-i-Azam and Mahatma had talks together in Bombay and reached a settlement so that India remained undivided.

However because of Second World War, the British had become very weak in India, the political squabbling multiplied; and racial violence flourished and became out of control. In August of 1946, there was deadly rioting in the street of Calcutta and thousands of Hindus and Muslims were butchered in three days of racial violence. Later there was rioting in Behar and Orissa. In April 1947, there was similar violence in the West Punjab, near Rawalpindi or Taxilla (Ancient capital of India) and thousands more were killed, this time Sikhs, Hindus and Muslims; a greater mass murder was to follow in East Punjab after the partition, where one million Muslims were killed and ten millions had to run for their lives, this is provided they could!

In the circumstances the imperial rulers of Great Britain had made up their mind in 1946 for partition and were committed to a policy of complete independence for India. At that time Field

Marshall Lord Archibald Wavell was the viceroy of India since September 1943. The new labour government of Clement Attlee terminated Wavell's job before his term and appointed Lord Mountbatten, who was said to be more a charmer, pragmatic and charismatic. Pamela Mountbatten wrote in her diary,' On Tuesday 20th February1947: Daddy was to become Viceroy read by the P.M. House of Commons was fully crowded, and before everyone had become very uproarious during Question Time so that it dissolved into complete chaos. Winston demanding, "Why Wavell was to be recalled?"; and Attlee refusing to give further explanation. She continues, "Nehru himself had put my father's name forward as a potential candidate in his meeting with Sir Stafford Cripps during the Cripps mission of 1946." He had royal family ties, born in the Windsor Castle in 1900 to the granddaughter of Queen Victoria. According to Pamela, "My mother Edwina, was the daughter of Lord Mount Temple. She and my father were married in 1922. In 1947 he was 46 and she forty-four. He was enthusiastic, pragmatic, extrovert, a raconteur and fascinated by his family connections. She was introvert, but fearless and excited by action. And of course, her special relationship with Pundit Nehru was very useful for him. He had a very unusual wife."

In her much enlightening book 'India Remembered'; Pamela narrates some more impartial and honest details about her parents, "My parents had met Pandit Nehru in 1946 when he had travelled to Malaya to meet the Indians living there. My father was Supreme Allied Commander and some of his staff warned him that there might be trouble and against his meeting Nehru. One of his staff had already refused to provide transport for the visit. When he heard this, my father was furious. He drove with Pandit Nehru in his official car to the YMCA in Singapore, where the meeting was being held. My mother was already there with a group of Indian welfare workers. As she came forward to be introduced, a crowd of Panditji's admirers swarmed in behind him and she was knocked off her feet. She crawled under a table from where Panditji rescued her. Towards the end of the fifteen months we spent in India, the immediate attraction between my mother and Pandiji blossomed into love. Nehru was a widower and was alone. She became his confidante. Nehru would never write to her until about two in the morning."

Pamela continues, "My mother had already had lovers. My father was inured to it. It broke his heart the first time, but it was somehow different with Nehru. My father wrote my sister in June 1948: 'She and Jawaharlal are sweet together, they really dote on each other in the nicest way; Pammy and I are doing everything we can to be tactful and help. Mummy has been incredibly sweet lately and we've been such a happy family.' The relationship had deepened in May, when we had gone to retreat in Mashobra (Shimla)." She also quotes from the letter written by Nehru to Edwina, "Suddenly I realised (and you did also), that there was a deeper attraction between us, of which I was dumbly aware, drew us to one another, I was overwhelmed and at the same time exhilarated by this new discovery. We talked more intimately as if veil has been removed and we could look into each other's eyes without fear and embarrassment."

The famous Indian writer Narendra Sarila remembers them in these words, "Mountbatten was cousin of the King Emperor George VI and married in July 1922 with one of the richest heiresses in England, Edwina Ashley, who was considered one of the most sought after girls in London for her fierce brilliance and elegance. Her grandfather Sir Ernest Cassel; a Jewish banker, had migrated from Germany to London at the end of 19th century and had left behind a great fortune. It was in New Delhi in 1921 that Mountbatten got engaged to Edwina Ashley. He was pleased with the elite life style of the rich Indians, like playing Polo, pig-sticking, hunting, shooting, the pageants, the ball room dancing, as well as merry making in the courts of the Indian princes. In 1946 Jawaharlal Nehru was guest of the Mountbattens in Singapore and discovered Lady Edwina and indeed rescued her after she had got knocked down to the ground in a melee of enthusiastic Singaporeans at a reception!"

Lord Mountbatten became Viceroy of India on 24 March 1947, with the date for transfer given as June 1948 (fifteen months). He was accompanied by his wife Edwina and seventeen years old younger daughter Pamela. 'India Remembered' is a pure evocation of this key period of India and Pakistan's history. Using diary entries and extracts from the meticulously kept family photo albums as documentary evidence, Pamela has written this book brilliantly; it is informative read and a chance to witness first hand a generation of characters whose actions were to change the fate of the Indian Subcontinent.

After arriving in India with his family, the new Viceroy Lord Mountbatten enjoyed tiger hunting and pageantry of Sikhs's Maharajas of East Punjab and enjoyed the breathtaking scenery of Kashmir Vale escorted by Maharaja Hari Singh himself. There were cocktails parties and ball-room dances and festivities. Charismatic Nehru performed private Yoga sessions in the Viceroy's Palace and while Gandhi purified his devotees through his unique and mysterious meditational rituals with full sport of virgins under the comfort of his armpits.. While next to my grandma's village, the king Cobras were planning in their lairs to wither and bleed the red-rose petals. It would appear that within two months, Nehru himself had drawn road-map for partition of India, by dividing most powerful Muslim Provinces of Punjab and Bengal and Assam, as he desired; and handed over the plan to his Excellence Lord Mountbatten for implementation..Partition was done rather in a hurried and mysterious manner, under the smoke screen; and had baffled everyone in the Subcontinent. Jinnah originally had demanded undivided provinces under Muslim rule and to remain within the Federation of United India coupled with power sharing in central government directly proportional to the Muslim population in the Subcontinent.

Pamela wrote about Vallabhbhai Patel: 'He was Nehru's Congress colleague; he was a hard trade union man. He too was disciple of Gandhiji since 1922. I remember a funny incident with this severe man at lunch one day. My mother was forever taking her shoes off under the table because she had quite high heels. And Vallabhbhbai had taken his sandals off and we could see that she and he were chuckling. Lots of chuckling was going on and of course he was trying to get her shoes on and she was trying to get his sandals on.'

'One of the other players who contributed in the partition was Krishna Menon, who later became the first Indian ambassador to the U.K. He was settled in London. Menon then headed the India League in the U.K, was a member of the British Labour party and the sole interlocutor on behalf of Nehru with the British Socialist leaders. He was the first Indian, whom Lord Louis Mountbatten sought out on being appointed as the viceroy of India in March 1947. Narendra narrates.

Pamela describes, "In 1946 Krishna Menon had put his name forward as Viceroy; acceptable to Congress and Attlee perceived him as an extremely lively, exciting personality. He had an extraordinary faculty for getting on with all kinds of people and was also blessed with a very unusual wife."

She describes Mohammed Ali Jinnah, "He was a fastidious man. He was extremely sophisticated and unlike the other Indian leaders always dressed in an immaculate English style, rather than national dress. He was a Muslim, but only spoke in English, perfectly. He had been intent in creating Pakistan ever since 1933 in London. He did not fall for my father's charm offensive. My father could not crack Jinnah and this has never happened to him before."

"On 7th May 1947 Panditji arrived to stay with us as a friend. After couple of days my father began soul–searching and decided to show Nehru the Mountbatten Plan to get his feedback. Nehru was incandescent and kept Krishna Menon up until dawn the night he arrived, dictating the 'bombshell' letter dated the 11th May to my father, which rejected many points of the plan. My father rethought and with the incredible and brilliant V.P. Menon (one of Mountbatten's counsellors), redrafted the whole plan and resubmitted it to London; much to the India Office and Attlee's confusion and perturbation." Pamela informs.

"Thursday 8th May 1947: We had lunch in the garden alone with Mr Nehru........Evening alone with Pandit Nehru! On Friday 9th May: We walked and talked in the garden with Panditji. Saturday 10th May: Krishna Menon came to stay."

On Sunday 11th May 1947: She wrote in her diary; in Simla:

'Yesterday evening Panditji gave us a demonstration of standing on his head, Actually he really is marvellously fit and had three of us down on the floor during the most extraordinary Yogi exercises. I had chat with Krishna Menon. He had been up all night with Panditji previously.'

Pamela has shown many memorable pictures of charismatic Jawaharlal Nehru, two of them in his black tight swimming trunk; one standing on his head and the other strolling along the swimming pool, while he still wears his cotton white –cap over his head.

It is difficult to speculate what role Indra had played, political, physical or moral, in the success of her romantic and handsome father She frequently accompanied him on most of tours.. She definitely proved herself as a formidable and a shrewd politician after his death and carried the banner of his family brilliantly.

Narendra Sarila, who was one of Mountbatten's ADCs; describes, "In Simla 10th & 11th May were the days of high drama. The plan sent to London on 2 May reached back with HMG's approval on 10th May 1947. That night Mounbatten gave it to Nehru to get his reaction. The step was against the advice of the staff, who felt it should be shown to all the parties or none at all. V.P Mennon and Nehru draw a new plan together and re-submit to London.' I had only two or three hours in which to prepare an alternative draft plan and I sat to work on it at once.' Wrote V.P. Mennon."

On 18th of May Mountbatten flies to London for discussion with the Government and opposition, following Nehru's rejection of the original plan; and return to New Delhi on first of June with the final plan and approval.

Narendra narrates, "When Mountbatten went to London, he visited Churchill (opposition leader of Conservative Party) on 22 May 1947, he did not consult Jinnah about the new plan, but assumed he will accept whatever will be given, and rather be thankful. Churchill lambasted the Labour Party for its India policy... Later in the year, when Mountbatten came from Delhi to attend Princess Elizabeth's wedding in November, Churchill refused to talk to Mountbatten, nor did he do so for many years thereafter. Churchill hurled angry words at Mountbatten suggesting his former protégé had led him up the garden path; Then Churchill turned and walked away in full view of the assembled guests..." Earlier Churchill had appointed Mountbatten as Supreme Commander of the Allied forces in SE Asia over the head of many senior and able officers; and he had based his headquarters in New Delhi's Faridkot House (property belonging to a Sikh chief).

On 3rd of June agreement was reached by all parties and the administrative consequences discussed. The date of Independence was set as 14th for Pakistan and India (Bharat, its new name) on the 15th of August 1947. This date came ten month earlier than the scheduled time. An announcement was broadcasted on All India Radio by the Viceroy himself, addressing all his subjects for their benefit and the audience at large over the globe. On 18th July the Parliament passed the Indian Independence Act. At this time India consisted of 565 separate states and provinces ruled over by feudal princes. In the plan, the Muslim dominant provinces of the Punjab and Bengal were agreed to be divided on the basis of the indigenous population. Boundaries Commissions were set up to fix the partition. The Muslim League insisted that the partition of these provinces should be done through the UNO, but Nehru rejected it. On the 8th of July Sir Cyril Radcliffe, a barrister by profession, arrived in New Delhi to arrange the boundary lines, but his decision was not announced till the 16th of August. It would appear that he had given some vital Muslim areas in the Punjab to Bharat. These were the areas adjoining to Kashmir, the districts of Gurdaspur and Pathankot, District Ferozpur and perhaps the district of Hoshiarpur as well. Within minutes of his announcement, the Holocaust of Muslims in East Punjab began.

One of our relatives and a renowned writer Sardar Ali Ahmad Khan recounts in his chronicle, "Akali Sikh leader Master Tara Singh, Giani (Sikh religious leader) Kartar Singh and many other Sikh leaders stood on the stairs of the Punjab -Assembly Building in Lahore and yelled threats against the Muslims and forewarned them about the grave consequences by brandishing swords in their hands. The Hindus and Sikhs swarms became warriors, sponsored by their leaders. After this, the holocaust sparks off on the Muslims of Delhi, East Punjab and Sikhs–chiefdoms in the East- Punjab In this terrible and inhumane campaign at least one million Muslims were killed, fifty thousand women were abducted and thousands more were converted under swords; millions of the Muslims were robbed of their possessions. In the biggest Sikh-State of Patiala alone, 60% of Muslims were killed out of total population of 500,000. The total population of the state was about 1.5 million, equally inhabited by the Hindus, Sikhs and Muslims. Only few people survived from the rural areas. The Sikhs had blockaded all exits. People were picked out from the buses and trains and massacred. They had left the Crusaders and the Mongols far behind. Countless men, women, children and elderly were burnt alive sheltering in their homes. The young children heads were cut off and swayed in the air on top of their spears. The women were paraded naked in the public to degrade them to the extremes; their breasts were slashed and sown into the garlands. He reiterates that he cannot believe how a human being falls below the level of the carnivorous. However he does not deny that even the Muslims in the West Punjab and Frontier had committed atrocities on the Sikhs and Hindus to some extent, but these were not done under the umbrella of government establishments; they were in reaction to the atrocities committed on the other side of the border. The Muslims in the west were just looting the valuables of their victims, not killing them. While in the East, Hindus and Sikhs first slaughter the Muslims and then plunder... The Muslim blood was drained away just like from the cattle in a slaughter house and their life was less than a dog or a cat."

Narendra Sarila reiterates, "The Akali (Immortals) originally constituted a famous regiment in Ranjit Singh's army. Later in the twentieth century, a militant Sikh political party gave itself a name 'Akali Dal' and started to struggle against the government sponsored priests of Sikhs-shrines, including the holiest of all, the Golden Temple of Amritsar." In 1947; even before the Radcliffe Award, the armed Sikh horse riders used to invade the surrounding villages at night time from their training and base camps in Amritsar and other main towns in East Punjab. They used to throw first fire bombs, when Muslims run in panic for shelter, the invaders used swords, spears and guns to kill them; then they plundered. They did under religious fervour as well as a desire for booty. However Narendra narrates, "Hindus and Sikhs were well prepared and planned far ahead, but the Muslims simply did not bother. The Muslim League somehow did not expect any such grave communal rioting and killings in such an organised and coordinated manner." The Hindu and Sikh politicians religious leaders, as well as military and police, made necessary preparations, a few months ahead for the war against the unarmed and wretched people. The Maharaja of Patiala gave lots of support by providing his police and army to begin the training and arming of the rioters. It was not few individuals' effort, but the action of a well-trained army and the police.

According to one of my uncles, Major Abdur-Rashid Chaudhary, a resident of Jallunder, the cultural town of the East Punjab, "At the end of World War Two (1939-45); I returned to my home in 1946 after falling sick and becoming disabled. I was shocked to learn that the environment had completely changed. The Hindu and Urdu Newspapers were slinging insults on each other and stirring emotional hatred. They spread false, malicious and poisonous propaganda to create enmity among the people; who have been living happily together for hundreds of years, they had the same blood and genes. Now they did not trust each other. All the top civil administrators were British, Hindus, Jews or Sikhs. In such circumstances who would hear the voice of a Muslim? It would appear that as a consequence of political violence and turbulence, the Hindus and Sikhs instigated preparations on a large scale. The proposals and plans were drawn in May & June for communal violence. The Hindu Maha Subha was the centre and they had set up a special secret branch as well. They gathered all cadres of Hindus and Sikhs, collected huge sums of money and arms; arranged special camps for training in the use of proper military equipment under capable army generals and police chiefs. The Muslims falsely perceived the Hindus and Sikhs the most subservient, timid and humble people, so as normal they under estimated them and showed a 'couldn't careless attitude'. Most of the Muslim League leaders were over confident and highly selfish, they did not plan an iota to protect the masses of the Muslims. I am sure they knew what was happening behind the scenes. Most of the Muslim League's leaders were feudal lords, they had means to protect themselves, but not their subjects."

The World War Two veteran continues, "the night of the 18th & 19th was the end of the world (August 1947). From the sunset, gun fire crackles and exactly at 10 PM, a convoy of four vehicles start rambling in our area. First vehicle had petrol sprayer fixed in it. Four men sat in it with guns in their hands and their faces camouflaged. This vehicle sprinkles a thick shower of petrol on the walls and doors of the houses. Behind this vehicle was another vehicle cruising behind at the same pace, it would throw fire bomb to ignite the fire; it also had four men with guns ready in their hands. Behind the second vehicle was the bigger van with twelve people inside, holding machine or bren guns. When the baffled and panic-stricken residents rushed out, they were simply gunned down. In addition to these three vehicles; another official truck, manned by police, Sikh and Dogra soldiers followed behind.. If any fire returns from inside, the house was besieged and inhabitants put to death mercilessly and house plundered. Apart from these convoys, there were also other bands of thugs, clumps of three or four, on intent on carnage and rampage. They were given police or army uniforms, as well as guns. Such organised gangs and convoys were also sent to the nearby villages and campsites in the wilderness. However I give a great credit to the leaders who had planned these attacks." He proclaims. The World War Two Veteran observed these horrendous scenes from the grill of his gallery; but unable to help the victims and worried about his own life.

My mother-in-law, who lived in the USA at that moment, remembered quite vividly, "At the time of partition I was only in my mid-twenties and lodged jointly with my in-laws; in a huge, newly built magnificent house, comprising of numerous rooms, a swimming pool, stable for the ponies and the horses. There were lot of servants, including chefs and behras who used to prepare and serve food, dressed in smart uniforms. The house was spread over four acres of land in the suburb of Jallundhar. (The poet laureate Hafiz Jallundhary, who later composed The National Anthem of Pakistan, was also born and lived in Jallundhar)." She reminisces in nostalgia, "In one acre was the actual building, the other three acres were orchards of exotic fruit trees and colourful fragrant flowers for all seasons... When I got married, I was only thirteen and the bridegroom was eighteen; I did not know what to say, how to say, what to eat, what not to eat and how! I used to forget where my bedroom was. I had just come from a simple and modest family." She recollected. "I used to become a bit blushing, nervous and panicky at the beginning." She describes with a pause. "There were gardeners to tend the garden. Each servant and their family was provided with their living quarters, if they did not live locally... On top of that there was a nice black Rolls Royce car for our family, as well as a private driver."

Although she was over ninety at the moment, her memory and speech was still like a young maiden; perhaps this could be because of her happy and comfortable living. My wife was less than two years old at that time and I myself was hardly seven years old, but we lived far apart. Mother-in-law recalls, "In Shamchorasi (her parents' home town), I had a nice friend called Chandra Devi and I liked her very much. Her family was in our neighbourhood and we had grown up together since we were toddlers. She often came to our house and I used to go to her house, almost on daily basis. We used to skip ropes, sing and dance; laugh and joke. Chandra was a nice and a charming girl, we also learnt cooking and knitting in the local school. We resemble each other in habits and features and could hardly live without each other. I am certain that not long ago our ancestors must have been the same. Our food, clothes and language are same, apart from some variations in the religious rituals, although we share celebrations and look forward to each other's festivities. I must have been about twelve or thirteen, this is just before I got married; I remember one day, when I entered their kitchen, I just followed my friend. Her mum observes me and startles, 'RAM, RAM'. I was startled too and slipped back quickly. I felt embarrassed and blushed; my cheeks were red and I was almost shivering. My friend was embarrassed too and enlightened me that non-Hindus cannot enter the kitchen, it is not allowed. 'It is nothing to worry about', she gestured, 'they believe that some evil spirits can spoil the environment', but at the same time she just caressed and cuddled me to uplift my spirits. My friend's mum disinfects all contents in the kitchen and also gives a thin quoting on the floor with the mixture of cow's urine, dung and clay to purify the kitchen." She just gasps with a smile; raising her right arm in the air with her palm open to the sky and wipes her leaking nose, with a white handkerchief which normally crumples in her left hand.

Mother–in-law reminisces in nostalgia, "We had a Persian wheel water-well in our house in Jallundar; driven by a camel. It was fascinating to observe the glitter and hear the shrill silvery water pouring down from the tin-containers and tumbling into the big flat wooden trough. It was magical and peaceful." She continues with her thoughtful eyes and occasionally wiping her nose, "My father-in-law was a genius and had reached to the top grade of Chief Engineer Sahib Bahadur, Irrigation Department and had bought thousands acres of fertile land." Mother-in-law narrates some more interesting episodes of her life, "Before I got married to his eldest son, our Abba Jan (beloved and honourable father, as she calls her father-in-law), he got married again with a new and young bride; almost of my age. People used to call Abba Jan a 'Black Englishman'. He used to wear expensive suits, bowler hats and go hunting on his horses. He had already six children from his first wife; three sons and three daughters; and she was still alive. Luckily for the family, the new wife did not produce any children; but still turbulence and family feuds began. It would appear that while the old man was enjoying the 'merry-go-round', just like the Persian-wheel, the old happy family bond started to crumble and wither away." She gestured with a wet and subdued smile on her lips.

After the Radcliffe Award, Jallundhar came under India, although the Muslims were expecting the opposite; but even then the Muslims wanted to stay in India, just as Muslims in other parts of India; as most of them had voted for Congress. In the Punjab Muslims were Muslims, but might belong to the Congress party or Muslim League; they had no say. It is worth remembering that the Muslim League was originally started by the Nawab of Deccan (now in India) and the Nawab of Bengal and Sir Agha Khan; not by the Punjabis. In the Punjab, up to April 1947 was the Coalition government of Hindus, Sikhs and Muslims in its capital Lahore, headed by a Muslim, who was anti-Muslim League, rather an enemy of Jinnah, named Khizr Hayat Khan Tawana. From inside he was supporting the Congress and no preparations or contingency arrangements were made by the government of the Punjab for the protection or safe passage of the Muslims. In NW Frontier, Congress and Unionists were the ruling party. The leader of the Congress party in Peshawar Khan Abdul Ghaffar Khan, used to be called Gandhi of the North Western Frontier felt degraded if he ever talked to Jinnah.

He hated Pakistan so much that he preferred to live in India after partition and later died in Afghanistan and buried there as per his will. There were definitely no plans ahead by the Muslims for the mass carnage of the Hindus or Sikhs. Any odd killings or slaughter was done on an individual or local basis. Also the Mullahs all over India were against Quaid-i-Azam. On top of that the Muslim militant parties like Ahrar and Khaksars were against Quaid-i-Azam (Jinnah). All these pathetic parties or groups considered him not even a proper Muslim, but rather an Englishman or a Parsi. So Quaid-i-Azam had to face a dilemma even on the Muslim front. Twice some members of Khaksars (Muslim militants) tried to murder Jinnah and each time he had a narrow escape. His daughter still lives in Bombay..All these Mullahs and militant groups wanted a greater strength in a United India; but after the announcement of the Partition of India by the British, their loyalty tilted overnight towards the Muslim League. However it was too late to get organised on a war footings.. The Hindus and Sikhs proved themselves as formidable warriors and the Muslims as wretched cowards; although the way massacre and carnage has been done in a treacherous way is most detestable and cowardly an act,; not even a meagre sensible person will call, massacre and carnage of unarmed and beleaguered people, bravery. Unfortunately it was all swallowed up without a burp and it is quite obvious that justice never prevails on this planet! International War-Crime Tribunals, memorials and museums are set up to strengthen and enhance the image of the super powers; not for justice or remembering the victims. I am sure still it is not too late for the UNO to investigate and highlight the culprits involved in the slaughter and butchery of the helpless innocent people. I am certain if those victims had been armed, then those self-alleged warriors would have been cowards and run for their lives, as their past records show.

In Jallundhar my mother-in-law and her joint family were startled by sudden dramatic and frightening announcements which were broadcast on the loudspeakers, on all local Indian Radio Stations and drums were beating in the localities, bazaars and streets; "All Muslims are warned that they must leave their homes, businesses and jobs within twenty four hours; after that a carnage will begin and no guarantee would be given on their safety. Special camps have been set up near the cantonment, they must assemble over there; they have to make their own arrangements to reach there. They will concentrate in the camps at their own risk; there will be no escort or guards provided. This order is given by the government of India and the East Punjab. —— ORDER! ORDERR!! ORDERRRRRR, BEWARE. BEWARE. BEWARE. BE ALERT, BE ALERT, BE ALERT!!!" Mother-in-law reiterated with her pale face. "The following day, genuinely communal rioting and atrocities began, odd killings started on the roads, shops and houses. Everyone ran to a safe place, some rushed to the camps, but was found dead soon; some were intercepted and killed mercilessly, got cut organ by organ. The young girls were dragged out and raped in front of their parents and some were abducted. Houses were torched and people fleeing for their safety were daggered, shot dead or burnt alive. That bloodshed continued for days, nights and for weeks. The oppressors felt proud and boisterous. If anybody retaliated; the army and police were there as a backup team for the gangsters." She wonders. "Earlier, my younger brother-in-law; Qari Muhammad Anwar Samadani, an advocate from Aligarh and a senior Muslim League member had escaped to Lahore; he had been blamed by the Congress for having distributed 200 guns to the Muslim League supporters." She mumbled with a little sniff of her nose.

She further added, "We had contacts and means to reach the relative safety of the nearby town of Kapurthala and stayed there for three weeks in one of our friends' house, although he himself had already fled to Pakistan with his family. The State of Kapurthala was the second largest Sikh State in East Punjab, adjoining to Pakistan and the Maharajah had proved himself to be a protector of the Muslims at the beginning; but during the turbulence; the law and order situation deteriorated over there as well. My eldest son Imtiaz, ten years old at that time, had broken his elbow and was admitted to the hospital in Kapurthala; but even in the hospital, the rioters had started picking up the injured and sick Muslims; and started slaughtering them mercilessly. So at nightfall, we managed to get him out of the hospital, otherwise on that night, he would have been killed because most of raids took place in the dark. The situation was becoming even tenser with the continuous influx of refugees from Pakistan. These refugees needed land, houses and businesses in the East Punjab. One of my brother-in-laws was a young captain in the army and luckily based in Jallundhar; also my father-in-law was an influential person. Special arrangements were made to transport us to Pakistan by a special army convoy of tanks and six armoured carriers. When we passed through Amritsar, there were thousands of armed Sikhs shouting wildly, brandishing their swords and spears. We were so scared that we stopped breathing. I have a feeling that even the Sikh women were involved with the rioters and killers. We were ordered to stoop low for fear of being attacked, but we just sneaked around out of curiosity. The women might be performing some ancillary duties like spying on the Muslims' targets or looking after the booty; which is said to have been divided into four portions; one for the fighters, one for the priests, one for the politicians and one for the services. We heard the horrendous noises of shrieks and wailings, people were being stabbed in their stomachs, and chests; their noses and ears were chopped as well as their fingers and arms and hands; one by one, while the victims pleaded for mercy and prostrated themselves in front of them. More were the pleas for mercy, more were the atrocities; more was the severity; added by dances and songs; under the beat of the drums. It happened in big courtyards, with massive gates and a colossal inferno of logs and petrol were raging to the sky. Some of the victims were pushed alive, some hurled half alive, along with the rotten corpses. The air was pungent and choking." She describes sadly wiping her eyes.

The ten years old boy who was admitted in the hospital with his broken arm in Kapurthala, is in his seventies now and he happens to be my brother-in-law. I felt so lucky to see him in person in London while he was recently on his holidays to Great Britain and the USA; this is exactly at the same time when I am writing this particular episode of my autobiography. He recollects quite vividly what had happened in Kapurthala hospital and narrates, "On the Eid's night (celebration day at the end of Ramadhan's fastings) our grandfather who was retired as Chief Engineer Sahib Bahadur from the irrigation department, hired a private bus on an emergency basis and loaded the whole of our family in it and we departed towards Kapurthala from Jallundur. This was the day when the then Viceroy of India Lord Mountbatten had announced the details of partition of India and the boundary lines of the new born sovereign states of Pakistan and Bharat (now normally called India). We locked all our doors and stored all the valuable goods in a safe in a secured manner. There was lot of Jahez (dowry) for my Phophie's (father's sisters) weddings; we locked them in the more safe rooms. There was lot communal violence already started and there was a rumour of a bigger attack that night, especially this time hooligans were said to be backed by the police and the army. The intention of this sudden evacuation was to escape from the communal rioting for the time being and when peace was restored, we were supposed to return to our beloved home." He continued...

"We were staying in a friend's house which was still being built and it was situated near to the palace of the Sikh Maharaja of Kapurthala, so apparently it sounded quite safe. One day when youngsters were playing hide and seek and building castles in the sand; and I was just standing on the ledge of the iron-bars window and dangling. My two years old younger sister Shams (nicknamed Shuda) tried to pull my feet and I just hurtled on my right arm on the concrete floor. I have a feeling that at that fateful moment I was not concentrating within myself and was baffled with the communal violence. And as result of this sudden fall I had a multi fracture on my arm at three points. I was immediately taken to the hospital and admitted after fixture of bones and dressing for recovery and further medical care. Earlier when we were travelling on the main road from Jallundur to Kaprthala, we witnessed lots of dead bodies, some still fluttering on the branches of the trees.

I am sure the Sikh and Hindu hooligans were disguising themselves in the nearby bushes enjoying themselves with a peg of alcohol or a dose of opium. Those scenes had a depressing and frightening impact on my nerves and really I was not in myself, but with the unfortunate dead or dying people. That lack of concentration caused misery for me as well. I just got startled when my sister touched me." He reiterated.

"I had been in the hospital for two days when I overheard someone asking the nurse, 'how many Muslays (Muslims) are in this hospital and where are they? We want to .... tonight.' The nurse replied, 'There are only two persons. One is a young boy in this ward and the other one is a doctor over there in the ward.' I was immediately alarmed and sent an urgent message to my mother through my visiting cousin to the hospital. First they thought I was having a nightmare, but my mother did not want to take risk. She came rushing to the hospital wearing the usual straight white baggy Burkha with a charpie carried by some young men from the family. It was almost getting pitch dark and they smuggled me out pretending to be carrying a dead person over the walls of the hospital as the main gate of the hospital was kept locked in the night time because of security reasons. That same midnight the attack took place and they killed the doctor. I had a very lucky escape because my mother took personal daring action to save my life; although my grandfather did not agree with her, arguing they would never attack in the hospital. I am simply lucky to be talking to you..." He narrated thanking his mother.

That ten years old boy later came to the UK to complete his BSc in maritime studies in 1971 from the University of South Wales, Institute of Science and Technology Cardiff. Then he became Captain of the merchant ships for international companies. After that he became Director General of ports and shipping for the Government of Pakistan from 1974-98. After his retirement he has established a college of Nautical Studies in Karachi since 1998 to impart his expertise to the young generation. His institute is recognised not only by the government of Pakistan, but also approved by the Lloyds Classified Society UK. His younger brother Ayaaz who was travelling with him at the time of partition became a medical doctor and a child specialist from Edinburgh University. He worked in the UK for five years and has now practices in the USA as he has done for the last forty years running his own surgeries. He also became the President of the Medical Association State of Wisconsin. He is still very popular with the young mothers because of his excellent delivery records and he has hundreds and thousands of them spread not only across USA, but all over the planet. Some of his patients come from overseas when they hear about his reputation. I am sure he has become immune by now and I feel envious. His daughter Uzma is a top neurosurgeon in the USA. That two years old naughty girl who pulled her brother's legs and tumbled him down is my wife now since 1966 and still with me and I think I have been trapped; even though I am almost worn out, but she keeps me going.

Mother-in-law harks back and recounts, "While we were being escorted from Jallundhar to Kapurthala, we passed by some of my uncles' and aunts' settlements and villages, most of them belonging to the Muslim's population, although some had a mix of Hindus and Sikhs as well. Only three days before, two of my uncles living in Hadia-Abad were mercilessly killed; in the main square of the town, no one was safe anywhere whether a city, town, village or a farm. What we see on this trail of freedom will never be seen again by anyone; we notice human bodies hanging from the trees, some tied with the stumps, some fluttering on the ground near the roots of the trees. The culprits must be hiding nearby for some more prey. We had no time to investigate, help or pause; we could have been easily dead ourselves or hanged on the trees. To me it looked like a slaughterhouse and really frightening; the trees and fields appeared like oranges or red roses. Those grotesque images had stunned us and we started looking around our vehicles, if someone was following us or might be hidden up the trees or in the adjoining fields with the guns and swords ready to attack us. I will never be able to forget that gruesome, grotesque and monstrous scene. It was clearly a sign of great cowardice, poverty of mind and extreme hatred. Why would those people commit atrocities against the unarmed, wretched and miserable people? I was so startled that no more feeling or fear was left." She paused with tears in her eyes and with deep sighs. Unfortunately mother-in-law herself passed away in Chicago on 28 February 2010.

One of our relatives named Rafiq, who retired as an H.M. Inspector of Taxes; and lodges in Watford; was twelve years old at that time, recollects vividly, "We used to live in Ludhiana (named after a Muslim, Sultan Lodhi of Delhi) in a rented property owned by a Hindu and used to pay five Rupees per month to the landlady. My father was a senior officer in the police. In the first week of October, 6-7 Hindu hooligans came to our house brandishing swords and started yelling slogans against us and told us to quit the house and go to Pakistan; they had even earlier approached the landlady to kick us out, but the landlady said, 'These people are nice and pay their rent in time and I need rent for my living.'" Mr Rafiq continues, "Before that the chief of the police had made my dad redundant and had taken his arms and uniform away. That day, one of my dad's subordinates named Harnam Singh (a Sikh), who had a fully loaded gun and luckily was passing through the street; he noticed and pointed the gun at the hooligans and warned them that if they do not push off immediately, he will shoot them down. They had to leave, the Sardar was ready on the trigger." He narrated with a relief. However, he admires the loyalty of his dad's colleague and still thankful to him for saving their lives. "Everyone was not bad, there were some nice human beings as well." He pointed out.

Rafiq reminisced, "Even in the normal times, there used to be separate drinking water positions for the Hindus and the Muslims; and it used to be highlighted quite clearly. If by any chance a Muslim had touched the water container of Hindus, then it had to be purified by yelping 'RAM, RAM'". He further reflected, "We had a cow and we were requested specially by the Hindu neighbours to save urine of the cow, as that was normally used for purification and for blessings. Similar routine was used for the chapatti oven and so on." He remembered, "Most of those racial and religious conflagrations and communal violence in the East Punjab were unleashed by the Akali Dal (headed by Master Tara Singh), Maharaja Yadovinder Singh of Patiala and by so many Hindu fundamentalist parties and armies, but the scale of killings like this was never heard of before and were exceptionally unprecedented. After the partition, the Sikh extremist chief Baldeo Singh became the defence minister and Sardar Patel (Hindu extremist) became the interior minister of India and they had provided full police and army support to those hooligans; that had caused the colossal damage and slaughter of the Muslims... I am sure that they had full blessings of Nehru, as well as of Gandhi; but it is necessary for the UNO to investigate, which has been overlooked since a long time!" He emphasized, "But the problem is we are not the Jews!" He declared with a chuckle on his witty cheeks and with his glittering eyes.

One of our friends named Latif, has very vivid memories about the communal violence in the East Punjab. He has been living in London for almost fifty years and he is one of the business tycoons of London and one of his grandchildren is a doctor. We ourselves have lived next to them for almost over forty years. He describes gruesome events with his eyes sunk in sadness, "I must have been about thirteen and we used to live in a good sized village in the district of Jallundhar; in full harmony with Sikhs and Hindus. Most of villages around us were of Muslim population, but they were intermingled with the Sikhs as well as Hindus. The communal violence had already started before the announcement of division, but the bad news was that the Muslim inhabitants and their houses were searched thoroughly and their arms or weapons taken. This was initiated by the local Hindu or Sikh administrators. For the Sikhs and Hindus, it was just the opposite. The Muslim Chief Minister of the Punjab Khizr (he headed a coalition government) was against Pakistan, so he purposely left the Muslims unprotected; the Muslim League not being in power in the Punjab, could not help either. It was simply bad news for the Muslims! Anyway, all these troubles were planned somewhere higher and far ahead in time; it was not a task to be done by a group or individual organisations, but by organised forces like army and police; as well as politicians at large. The Muslims proved themselves to be too dumb to foresee the oncoming dangers or too much overconfident or perhaps most probably too much insensitive." He described with sadness.

Mr Latif said, "We used to play Kabaddi, (fight wrestling) and do Bhangra together with the Sikhs and Hindus, just like brothers. Once the partition was announced, we could not find worse enemies than them. We were ordered to evacuate our homes and march to the camps, where the others were also arriving. While we were in the camps, some of our elder cousins and friends went to the orchard to pick up some fruit and that included some girls as well. Unfortunately it would appear that the Sikhs were waiting in the lairs and some on top of the trees. They jumped on us, one of our cousin's friends (a Sikh) even came trotting on a horse; and stabbing and beating began. While this carnage was taking place, some of us tried to hide in the fields, some just sprinted as fast as they could and reached the camp. The girls were abducted and raped. Most of the youths lay in the dust and blood; and fluttered to death. It was a lightning and a treacherous attack, we lost quite a few friends and relatives. Most of the girls were recovered from the neighbouring villages, but some just vanished. I was simply lucky to escape as I was standing a little bit farther away. Later the security men went to recover the dead and bury them nearby. However one of the injured persons, who was very strong and athletic, managed to survive. His body was in a harrowing condition. They had cut his toes one by one, arms one by one, ears one by one, nose at one go. He must have had over eighty wounds, but he survived. The Sikh horse-rider was his close friend and a wrestler. He pleaded with him that they were close friends, but unfortunately, more pleas for clemency were answered with more stabs. The youth survived on his crutches and with artificial limbs and with an artificial nose, minus ears for another forty years, but the tragic memory still hurts." Latif expressed with great pain. "Whilst on our trail to freedom, we found countless dead human and animal corpses soaring all along the river beds and banks; and the canals were choked, as well as the fields. Vultures and dogs were overfed with the Muslim flesh." He described in a sombre and subdued mood.

I must kindle the conscience of the world by narrating another terrifying and disturbingly gripping tale of Partition, this time described by one of my colleagues who had been manager in the Royal Mail called Nazeer Ahmad and who is two years senior to me and lodges prosperously not far away from us in South London. He remembered in his soaked slithering emotions, "We used to live in a village called Kangana in District Jallundar. It was purely a Muslim village and owned huge agricultural fertile lands. There were no Hindu or Sikhs lived there, apart from one Hindu Sunyara (goldsmith). Majority of surrounding villages also belonged to the Muslims, although some of the other villages belonged to Hindus and Sikhs communities as well and co-existed amicably. I was nine years old, was in class three of my school taught by a Muslim teacher called Khair Din and had three uncles one of them was so dark that people used to call him Kala Kaan (black crow)." He pondered. "Fourteen days had elapsed since Eid-ul-Fitr (end of fasting) and the full moon was glowing on the horizon and stars twinkled and the Milky Way littered the sky. There was already hullabaloo in the air about the impending assault of Sikhs and Hindus, but not of army and police. The villages in the north belonged to the Sikhs and they commenced a surprise attack on our village one afternoon... On the first attack we killed two Sikhs with spears and sticks and the attack was repulsed. But it became a regular occurrence every afternoon and the ferocity and magnitude became more co-ordinated and organised. They used to come in hoards, drunk and ferocious; kill, loot and run in a lightening manner. On the third day they were joined by the regular army, paramilitary and police, then a large scale massacre of burning and looting began before retreating to their base. At this moment my father climbed to the flat roof of our house and shouted to all our neighbours, 'The army is there now and there is no chance of survival and run for your life and hide wherever you can!' People ran in panic towards the south and hid in the sweet corn fields, perhaps dispersed in any direction and were snared by the merciless killers in the fields nearby. There were echoes of 'tha, tha' ('bang, bang') and mingled with wails of victims being slashed and stabbed; as well as hails of bullets and glares of swords. The bodies were cut into pieces and most of them left fluttering between life and death. After sunset the village fell into a blanket of grim darkness, the blazing flames and billowing smoke speckled all around the parameter of the village and killing continued late in the evening and then the hooligans retreated to their camps. By now they bound to be exhausted and needed fresh reinforcement for the next day."

He recollected. "We hurriedly huddled up into a stable adjoining to our house along with some other families and someone put up a lock from outside giving impression that no one had lived there. He did it in a clever way by pulling out the wooden door frame's knob from its base and then fixed it again to its hole at its wooden plank after re-entering the massive room. We could hear eerie activity of the hooligans outside, they all appeared drunk and charged with boisterous emotions. Some of them even yelled, 'Allah Hu Akbar (God is Great in Arabic)' to lure the hidden people out for slaughter and plunder. Someone even tried to break the lock of the door, but the other one yelled, 'Salia (you buffoon) the door is locked, there is no one inside, don't waste your effort'. The inmates in the stable, where we used to tether our buffaloes and bulls, were expecting massacre, rape and plunder any fraction of a second and by sheer luck had a narrow escape, the calculated gamble just paid off. Someone inside also had suggested to kill all the children because they shriek in panic and could easily attract the hooligans; but the mothers refused to accept his grim plea and he had desperately abandoned the room without saying anything to secure his own life. Just visualise the heart and feeling of a mother; my mother instantly had thumped us into one of the mangers and lay cushioned on top of us just a hen would do to her chicks if she observes any vultures hovering up the sky. She declared solemnly in a blatant manner, 'Before they slaughter my children, they have to kill me first as I wouldn't be able to handle this callous and cowardly atrocity in front of my own eyes in any circumstances'. By midnight it was all calm and peace, the invaders had left the slaughter house and we decided to sneak out in utter chill and awe heading to the security of the south. We herded ourselves dejectedly towards Nikodar (main civil town) located few miles away. We had to tread through the sweet corn fields in disguise and with caution. Even the peaceful green fields glowing with golden moonlight appeared shockingly grim and utterly ghostly. The fields were littered with dead corpses as well as heavily injured. Some victims had lost their arms, legs, eyes, noses; and had injuries all around their bodies, but still managed to survive and pleaded to us to inform their relatives or loved ones to come and pick them up; but who would have dared to retrieve those pitiably injured destitute people. After reaching Nikopdar, we joined the other fleeing masses and camped in the open fields. Soon Monsoon rain commenced and swamped our camp and cholera, diarrhoea, dysentery and malaria was rampant. Within few weeks my beloved mother passed away, along with thousands others and nowhere to bury the decaying corpses. She was merely forty years old. While we rushed out in panic, we lost our grandfather in the village, but somehow he managed to survive hidden in the ditches, bushes and crops; he joined us after four days. It was an amazing and emotional moment to see him alive and everyone had tears in their eyes. He was holding his shoes on the tip of a lathi (bamboo stick), hoisted on top his shoulder blade; he might have done so because of mud and water in the fields or slippery dirt pathways". He speculated.

Nazeer narrated these tragic and tortuous events while we were having a lavish lunch in Lahore Spice Restaurant, located in the serene and posh suburb of South London called Sutton. It meant to be a relaxing and casual dining table conversation while munching meal. In curiosity I asked, "How did you feed yourselves for over two months in the concentration camp in your own beloved motherland? Did you have any provisions or money or water? Was there any help forthcoming by any government's authorities?" "None, We arrived penniless, there was nothing planned or any advance warning. However my parents had buried some cash and jewellery under the trough of manger; while fleeing they had un-tethered the cattle so that they can feed themselves, For the first few days we survived with borrowing from others or nicking from the nearby fields or voluntary help from some Sikh or Hindu families who resided in the nearby villages; some of them were very humane and merciful and gave us flour, milk and other provisions. However after few days my father and uncles made a daring attempt to go to Kangana and retrieve the jewellery and money as well as some provisions. When they arrived in the suburb of the village, the air was extremely fouled and contaminated with pungent and breath-choking whiff emitted from the decaying corpses and they had to cover their noses to enter the village. Upon their arrival in their house, they found all the floors of their bedrooms utterly dug up by the hooligans, but luckily the valuables were hidden below the manger and survived. They all returned to the camp safely during the night. From that time onward, we were reasonably comfortable to spend money or to buy food from the surrounding friendly farmers of Sikh or Hindu community. Honestly speaking these people gave us so much grief and torture and in such a treacherous and cunning manner; that I didn't want to shake hands with them; but who can mend my grief?" He reiterated. While narrating his scourge his eyes were fixed to the wall, eyelashes were soaked in tears and hands were shuddering and he stopped munching and was almost choked with torturous emotions, even after sixty six years. Pakistan was not far away and only a few days trail on foot, but they were besieged in the concentration camps for months.

I was so carried away by the treacherous politicians, as well as religious extremists and the mass massacres of innocent unarmed people; that I simply forgot about my beloved maternal Grandma and the magical village where I had such a wonderful time; the village named Rehana or Ahrana was located in the district of Hoshiarpur; just over a 120 miles away from Lahore, to the east. This was the village where my mother was born and got married.

It is worth mentioning that this village was only thirty six miles away from Shimla (bird's eye view); summer capital of the British India. This is the place where the fate of the East Punjab's Muslims was decided while intensive romances were taking place. Shimla was so romantic that even 'the great uncle of my uncle' used to go to meet his mistress and forgot the family. As I have mentioned earlier; even the glorious flash floods came from that area. Anyone with good eyesight or with a telescope can easily see from Shimla (height around 7,500 feet) what is happening in the village. For further details on partition, I quote from my real uncle, who normally sits on his charpie, but sometimes in his wooden chair; having a round of his Hubly-bubly with his village folks chattering around him; underneath a tree or in his reception room located in the great back-yard of his house He has a pinkish pure white face with a fine skin and lot of glitter in his eyes. When he is really serious, he always has a few puffs from his freshly prepared sheesha (Hubly-Bubly) to relax and keeps on rubbing his head intermittently with one hand as if massaging and clasps the pipe of his Hubly-bubly with the other. He wears a pure white, fine cotton shirt and dhoti; and additionally wears a fine muslin erected turban, when he goes out to attend social events.

My uncle began by massaging his head and taking a few puffs, "The communal violence began soon after you left, you were very lucky indeed. There was lots of panic and some family members were left behind; luckily we managed to retrieve them later; stranded in other camps. We picked up only a few items like flour, rice, sugar, some money. The Sikhs and Chumars started to burn our houses and began the slaughter especially at the night time. They came in great hoards yelling slogans, brandishing kirpans, axes, hammers, Lathis and spears. The local police had earlier searched our homes and took away all kinds of arms including any Lathis, axes, spears and of course guns. So we had been left with no protecting weapons. There was no time to fight back, we simply ran to the safety of the more secured buildings and then later were concentrated in the camps. There were different camps for different clump of villages. We shifted from camp to camp just like prisoners, but with no security. Luckily our local Hindu-Rajputs were on the guard for us, after all they were our relatives and proved themselves sincere to us. One of local Hindu Chief named Rana Ram-Chander escorted us for few days up to the next few camps, he provided us with food and other supplies. He said to us, 'I will perish any Sikh or Brahmin to dust, if anybody tries to harm you.' He was a brave person; and a man of pure blood. He warned and scared off any miscreants long before they tried to approach near us." Uncle describes with a glow on his cheeks; and with a continuous rub to his head and with an intermittent puffs of his Hubly-bubly. "Maa always talk about you and wanted to see you; but she was so pleased that you escaped in good time." He recollected. "The Sikhs were simply coming in hoards, on horses or on foot, ransacking the houses, burning the people alive who clustered inside and coming back again the next night. However the sick, lame and lazy were left behind at the mercy of the killers. We could not even get our bull-carts ready or drag any cows or buffaloes with us." He gasped.

"What happened to the Old Baba and that Psychopath Woman?" I enquired. "They were left behind, perhaps the woman had been picked up by a Sikh, yes she was a beautiful beast; and the old Baba, I am told was looked after by the Hindus as a sacred god, he was innocent and harmless. The Hindus worship such kinds of odd people; they believe such people are next to gods." He explained. I further asked my uncle, "What happened to your cousin who had killed a man with his bullet while hunting the deer in the jungle?" "Oh. Do you still remember him; he hurried to Pakistan even before the partition, his case was being heard in Shimla. However it would appear, he had a lucky escape as well." He gestured by sliding his hand over his skull. I further asked my uncle in curiosity, "How did you travel to Pakistan and how did Maa (my grandmother) cope with the miserable journey; after all she was quite frail and old?" He responded, "I had to pick her up on my back infrequently, but luckily, occasionally someone gave her lift in the bull-cart, along with young children, pregnant women and old men. It was just a question of survival. Some women had even dropped their children in the river to avoid them being slaughtered in front of their eyes by the Hindu extremists as well as by the Akali-Dal thugs." He reminisced, "Those drunken hooligans enjoyed slashing the head of a child in front of the mother and then raise it in the air on the head of their spears; they were really cowards and cruel in the meanest way; the Sikh and Hindu armies were helping these bands too; they were in civilian clothes." He declared.

"We were huddled for months in one camp, then for weeks in the next and the next. It took us over six months to cover a distance of 120 miles. We were taken by the northern route; right on the edge of the Himalayas, via Kangra, Pathankot, Jammu, Gurdaspur, Salkot, Lahore and then Montgomery. At the beginning we travelled on foot, then by buses, if you could cram in, and at the end zigzagging by different trains from Pathankot onwards; but there was danger all the time. In the north The Hindu Dogras from Jammu and Gorkhas were helping the Sikhs. We do not know how we survived! We were deliberately treated worse than animals. At the beginning there were monsoon rains, flash floods, and lot of refugees drowned and flowed away in the gushing and roaring sways of the rivers. There was water everywhere, especially at the beginning when we were camping in the Choes (dry river beds) and numerous animals, children and women were just swept away like straws and bushes, but most sheltered on the safety of the high grounds. It is also possible that the perennial river banks were breached purposely to cause maximum collateral carnage. Whatever the case was, it would appear that the gods of flash floods and the Monsoon were in a rage and floods soared all along the refugee-camps; in all areas of East Punjab."

He describes with chilled emotions, "In the camps there was no sanitary system, the dead bodies littered the roads and fields, the air was full of the pungent smell; the dogs squelched and lurked, the vultures could not fly because of being overfed and choked with human flesh. The atmosphere became dark with the plunge and swoop of locust like flies; and whistling swarms of the buzzing mosquitoes. Soon malaria, cholera and dysentery spread. There was no proper medicine available, therefore many more died, especially children and old people. Each camp-site became a graveyard, a burial place for the dead, either from the casualties committed by the humans or by natural calamities. The sad story is that even the wells were poisoned by the thugs so that some more deaths might happen. There were lots of snake bites as this was the season for the snakes to come out from their lairs where they relax in the winter, but they come out in the rainy and hot season." He added, "Some migrants jumped in the soaring rivers to escape the assailants, but they were sometimes eaten by the crocodiles. No human beings, in their troubled history, have suffered like this before. Trains coming from as far as Delhi, overflowing with thousands of refugees were stopped somewhere in the middle of the fields and every single child, woman, old and young were daggered or speared to death. They were so cruel that they first slashed the belly and breasts of the pregnant women and then killed her; the baby just fluttered out from the womb. The more victims cried; the more they were overjoyed. Soon this kind of carnage spread to the main stations and at junctions. There are countless incidents of these slaughters, especially around Amritsar, Ambala, Shimla, Jallundhar, Ludiana, Kapurthala, Bathinda, Sirhind, Bangla Fazalka, Ferozpur and on top of all Patiala. Over hundred thousand refugees were mercilessly killed in the trains alone, however some people survived hidden under the heaps of the squelching bodies. All their valuables were plundered and shared by the thugs, politicians and religious leaders. If they could not remove any piece of jewellery, the finger, arm, ear or nose was simply slashed from the victim's body." My uncle simmered.

"But uncle please tell me about my Maa, how did she travel and how did she cope in that wretched calamity; did she get sick as well?" I asked him in curiosity. Uncle gasped a bit, and then he pulls the pipe of Hubly-bubly towards him, had a few puffs; rubbed his head sometimes with his right hand and sometimes with the left hand. He appeared agitated, but tried to relax as much as he could, sometimes tears simmered through his eyelashes. That clearly showed he was under intense emotion. His pink cheeks rustled like autumn leaves and his face had drained; eyes fixed to the horizon and he responded, "Yeah! She was ok at the beginning, but with the lack of comfort and constant fear of being killed in the open camps, she had become very weak, then weaker and at the end the weakest. It was worse than being prisoners; we had no shelter, no security, no meals, no roll–call; it was one's own responsibility. After the announcement of partition, Sardar Patel became the Home minister and he was very cruel, he had controlled the police and Sardar Baldeo Singh became the defence minister; so they both took charge of the rioters and gave them maximum support. Those two leaders were the cruelest. I do not know what Lord Mountbatten was up to; after all he was the Viceroy first and later Governor General of India? Did he become vindictive and revengeful because Quaid-i-Azam did not accept him as Governor-general of Pakistan as well; or perhaps it could be that his wife was a deep friend of Nehru. Who knows?" He continued, "There was no proper food, clean water or any reasonable place to sleep. We were open to the scorching sun, monsoon's rains, flash-floods; as well as, susceptible to attacks of swarms of flies and the mosquitoes. Many people were killed by the snake bites and even by drinking poisoned water." I interrupted him and said, "Uncle please, tell me about the grandmother!" He just smiled and continued, "Sorry I got carried away." He then orders one of his mates to put new supply of tobacco in the Hubly-bubly and also asked him to bring a jug of Lassi; (a kind of cultured milk) for all of us and after a thoughtful pause he narrated, "Everyone suffered in the camps, but Maa especially. First she suffered from Malaria and then because of extremely poor sanitary system, there was a severe widespread of cholera; many refugees died and were buried in the wilderness; luckily Maa survived the epidemic, but became very weak. On the last leg of the forced exile, she had developed some sort of chronic dysentery and then she never recovered. We tried very hard, but there was not appropriate medicine or doctors available; she became almost lifeless and hardly mobile. I do not know how she survived, perhaps she was very tough and resilient; and more than that, she was yearning to see you after reaching Pakistan. Sadly she died in Montgomery within two days; after leaving the camps. To the last breath she was asking about you and wanted to see you; but you were almost fifty miles away in Dipalpur." After that a silence prevailed and I escaped to the canal bank for a lonely walk and on my own, sunk in helpless and biting emotions, reflections and yearnings.

In my paternal town called Sham Chorasi, (District Hoshiarpur), the situation was slightly different. It was an ancient citadel town secured by formidable high walls made of small red and grey bricks; and provided with mighty gates, made of iron and thick wood. It had concentric barriers, humps and hurdles. It had narrow streets and flanked by towering strong buildings. However outside the old fort, there were lot of new settlements and houses. Considering it a relatively safe place, the refugees from the surrounding villages rushed to its security and inhabitants inside just soared. All Sikhs and Hindus fled for their own safety; they were not many anyway. However Radcliffe had given it to India, even then the residents wanted to stay in India, some of them were strong supporters of the Congress, but in case of the East Punjab, it did not make any difference, the Muslims had to evacuate or be killed. Like any other city, town, village or farms, this place was under siege by the hordes of drunken hooligans, armed with guns, Kirpans and spears. They tried hard, but were unable to breach the walls; and retreated after suffering heavy casualties; but later returned with more reinforcement. My uncles (one of them British Bravery-Award Winner in the First World War) were killed in the mosque outside the main centre. We were told that someone was spying round the corner of the mosque and called in the thugs. They (Muslims) locked themselves inside, but soon the doors of the mosque were broken and the terror raged. The faithful inside were cut into pieces, while they were still alive; copies of Quraan were torn into pieces (although Quraan did not shriek or bleed). The veteran of the Great War had saved his British commander's life, fluttered between his shattered body and the prayer mat.

He must have been over-confident about his fighting skills. However, some men of the congregation sneaked to the security of their homes and were lucky to be alive. Inside the citadel, they prepared their own explosives, missiles, swords and guns; and fought till the last minute and later they were evacuated by the Pakistan army or Gurkhas and escorted in military convoys to Lahore. In some other far stronger Muslim places like Phugwara and khnur, more heavy casualties were suffered by the Sikhs and Hindus, including the Indian soldiers My uncle told me that even The Indian Air Force was used to dislodge them. Again they were evacuated in military convoys and escorted to the other side of the border by Pakistan Army. However these besieged warriors were very lucky as they were directly taken to Pakistan in military convoys, without having suffered the filth, diseases and uncertainty of the camps. They were far more less-susceptible and resistant to mass slaughters in the trains, caravans or the camps; this is on top of the achievement that they had killed quite a few of the drunken, shameless and blood-thirsty hooligans.

One of our relatives named Aleem Khan, who has been settled happily in Great Britain for over forty years informed me that his village called Saroa (District Hoshiarpur) was situated on a bit higher ground in the flash flood area and near to the edge of the mighty Himalayas and not far from Shimla and as well as some twenty miles away from my grandma's village. He recollected, "I must be about thirteen years old at the time of partition and our village was swarmed by the refugees from the surrounding small villages as the Sikhs and Hindus had already started killing the Muslims in the small settlements; so they came to us for some sort of protection. Quite a few small villages scattered around us were completely destroyed and the Muslims were either burnt alive huddling in their houses or massacred mercilessly to the last man; the young women, girls and children were abducted; some of the women even plunged in the wells to protect the integrity of their families and preferred to perish, rather than be degraded. Frankly speaking this act of dying was worse than Sati, but there was no alternative; it was a necessary evil. In our village, the houses which used to have only four or five residents had now about forty or fifty residents in each house. After the announcement of the independence, about twenty seven thousands Sikhs and Hindus had besieged our village from all directions. We had fourteen exits from the village and they were all blocked by the invaders; ready for the killing and booty. Luckily for us we had a few uncles or relatives who were retired army and police officers; and we also had a hoard of guns and machineguns hidden somewhere in the basements. We already had the advance information about the pending attack and we were ready. One of my real uncles who was a Zaildar for twenty five villages (headman or powerful person); appointed by the government, and although not on government payroll, he got some benefits from a free holding of fifty acres of public land as remuneration, to collect revenue for the government's treasury from the farmers; and used to be a top most liaison person between the government and the villagers. This particular title or grant used to be carried in the same family for generations after generation. He had prior information about the assault even before us. What was more shocking was that he simply had pushed off with his own family to Pakistan without informing us, the reason was just in case we would insist to him to take us with him; it was a grim treachery with his relatives and utterly shameful to his subjects. It is very strange that such people pretend to be saviours for the masses in the peace time; to win respect and glory, but when the time comes for the real; they simply vanish and abdicate. So in case of calamities and tragedies, even the closet relatives become strangers and selfish; how can we blame the Hindus and the Sikhs." He continued. "I am still annoyed by his selfish behaviour. As occurred in the other villages, the invaders mistook us as soft target and initiated an invasion after a siege of only two days; we were completely surrounded. However we were fully vigilant and took our own defensive positions, so the opposite happened; we gave a great surprise to the doped and drunken thugs. There was retaliatory counter attack towards the invaders and we must have killed at least five hundreds of them in four hours battle. Most of the invaders were drunk or under the influence of opium. They must have consumed many barrels of alcohol as well as many bushels of opium. For us it was a question of 'Do or die'. We knew that if we had surrendered, we would definitely be killed and our women would have been raped and all our wealth plundered. So why not put up a fight and die as martyrs rather than be killed mercilessly at the hands of the infidels. On surrender, death and degradation was certain, just like the other villagers who earlier had surrendered and pleaded for mercy, but grim atrocities took place with those innocent and beleaguered people." He reiterated.

"I had noticed those invaders fleeing away wildly from our village towards the mountains like wild beasts. You will be amazed and would not believe that I have seen those cowards excreting dung or sprinkling diarrhoea from their backs. They had to crawl on their knees and elbows to escape death. While stooping they left behind their turbans and dhoties.. They were really in terrible panic and completely startled." He proclaimed with a proud smile on his cheeks and glitters in his eyes.

Just to change the subject, I asked him "Do you remember the Choes (dry river beds) and the flash floods?" "Oh, do you know about them as well?" He was taken by a surprise. "Yeah. I do. How can I forget the exhilaration and freshness of the waves and ripples tumbling from the Himalayas? They are part of my mind and blood circulation. I used to live with my grandma in the first few years of my childhood and her village was not far from yours. I think those natural scenes were magical and full of thrill; they do not exist anywhere in the world. I used to swim in them when the main thrust was passed; even catch fish." I added with a smile. "That's amazing. They were the happy days. We will never be able to forget them and those days will never come back again." He reacted. "I was a top sportsman in my school and I liked to wade and waddle in the flash floods; it was very powerful and thrilling. If someone enters the river, it was not possible to go straight, but ended somewhere half a mile down the stream. It was not only water dragging you down, but also the sand was sliding and drifting under your feet; so it was not possible to shoot straight at a right angle. One had to dangle and often raise your arms to keep up a balance; sometimes even frightening because of the great sway and flow of the currents. I remember the gazelles coming down the valleys of the Himalayas, the peacocks, rabbits, parrots, as well as the juicy and flavoured mangoes, the exotic and colourful pomegranates, apricots to mention only few things, but now it is thing of the past." He recollected.

"How did the people manage to escape from your village?" I interrupted. "Oh Gosh. I just got carried away by the Choe." He exclaimed. "Yeah. We survived for few days, the thugs were deadly scared of us after that heavy loss, at least for the time being; luckily the news reached our relatives in Pakistan and a military convoy was sent to transport us to the other side of the border. So our family quickly jumped in the army trucks and it was only four or five hours journey (nonstop)."He remembered. "How about the other thousands of the villagers who were taking shelter in your village?"I asked anxiously. "Yeah. They were not abandoned and they were all escorted in the shape of caravans, some trailed on bull-carts, some by walking, but fully guarded by the army or by our own armed guards. It was not possible to take them all in the military trucks. Thankfully none of them were killed or looted, but we had to evacuate at the earliest possible moment." "How about Mountbatten or other British officials, were they not of any help to the refugees?" I questioned him again." "Brother I was too young to notice any action, but whatever happened, it was all under the British nose. I am certain they could have easily avoided the pains and agonies. The problem was that the Nehru's were close friends of the Mountbatten's, in love with each other (including Indira); they were alleged to be in a deep romance." He simply sighed. "Everything is fair in love and war." He continued. "Why would a Hindu kill his Hindu god?" I refer to the killing of Mahatama Gandhiji by a Hindu; "In my opinion it was a political murder, instigated to clear the line of power rather than taking command from the lame boss. He suffered for over forty years, including going to the British jails to achieve freedom for his people." He expressed his thoughts with shrugs of his shoulders and raising his eyebrows. "Were there any Hindus or Sikhs living in your village and if any what happened to them?" I questioned Aleem "Yeah. It was mainly a Muslim Rajput village, but there were some non-Muslims as well. I am sure they were fully aware about the planned attacks and they had sneaked out well in advance; perhaps they were busy doing the carnage in other Muslim villages!" He responded. "I'm sure that most of the influential Hindus and Sikhs had already evacuated Pakistan's side well in advance of partition; after all they were drawing the maps and also planning ahead for the massacres." I commented. "Yeah. You are certainly right and I fully support your view." He nodded.

One of my elder cousins called Ashraf, who used to dwell with his family next door to my grandma's house in Ahrana attended the same school where I had commenced studying at the age of six. At that time he was a student in his 6th class, but I was in the first year; I think he is about six or seven years older than me. Although at the moment he lives in Lahore and enjoys a retired life, he had spent most of his working life in Saudi Arabia. He gave me more details about the turbulence and communal rioting in the East Punjab. I began with by asking him, "Why did you leave Ahrana and when?" He responded, "We were happily living in our beloved village and did not want to leave at any cost. The land was so fertile, plenty of greenery, Himalayas just there, abundance of fruit and wild life; it was an enchanting area. Flash floods spread new soil every year and the area was developing at great speed. After the announcement of partition, Master Tara Singh instigated the ferocious attacks on the villages, he had ignited the Sikhs. They were angry that some of their Gurus were killed or executed by the Mughals or by the Pathans. They wanted to take revenge and also some of the Sikhs were killed recently in communal rioting in the West Punjab; so some more revenge; not in West Punjab, but in the East." He surmised. "The Sikhs started their assaults on our neighbouring villages of Khnora and Phuglana, and killed almost all the Muslims, except for some women and children, which they abducted. They looted and plundered the villages with a tremendous speed. They normally invaded in the night time when people were fast asleep. Those were surprise ambushes and had shocked and baffled everyone. The remnants of the surviving people started rushing towards the major villages and our village was one of them". He narrated.

"The boundary of Sikh state of Kapurthala was only ten kilometre away from our village. The other powerful Sikh State of Patiala from where most of the hordes of warriors were swarming was not far away from our village either. They sent in small aeroplanes which had sprinkled petrol on our houses and set them ablaze. This followed the ground assaults; the invaders came on the horses, camels, donkeys and even walked. They were armed with swords, rifles, machine guns as well as axes and lathis. They were in hoards of thousands and under coordination from the regular army; who were disguised in the civilian clothes. It was not done by one group or village, but by a vast network of armies. They were attacking millions of strong communities, attacking their own relatives and their own mates. It was simply unbelievable. It was done at such a great speed and at such a colossal scale that it can easily surpass the Jewish holocaust; and what is more shocking is that no one in the UNO has raised any question so far! That was the greatest human crime of all times and still hidden under the blanket of diplomacy." He moaned. "It was the Monsoon season. We concentrated in the high grounds and fields; there was water everywhere, mosquitoes and flies. On daily basis people were dying and being buried in some shallow pits. Each campsite became a graveyard as well as a killing ground. It took us over three months to cover a trail of a hundred miles. We moved from one camp site to the other and at each location would stay for weeks."

"Why couldn't you continue trailing after overnight?" I enquired. "We were controlled by someone and we had to get prior clearance for the next move. However luckily we had about twelve foot soldiers of the Baluch regiment; they had two jeeps and a truck in our camp... They kept on patrolling round and round of the camp. There were hundreds and thousands of different camps dotted all over the East Punjab." He described. "What did you eat and drink over this tragic period?" I asked. "We only got a meagre supply of some roasted grams, corn or wheat grains; which were distributed only in the mornings and evenings, nothing else, no clean water; most of it was rain water and flood water. We were living just like primitive man; in the open and at the mercy of the nature. Even the major rivers were brimming out of their banks and flash floods were raging like serpents. Thousands upon thousands people drowned, especially women and children and the old. My own grandmother died in the camps as well and is buried there somewhere." He informed me. "Did you accompany my grandmother and her family?" I wondered. "No. I cannot remember. I think in the great confusion and panic, we became out of touch; in the chaos even the family members got separated, some were killed, some were abducted, some were left behind, some joined in the other camps. It is difficult to speculate what happened to our neighbours or friends. We were so happy living in our beautiful village and wanted to stay forever. Our ladies never went out of the village without Purdah; they even travelled to the neighbouring villages in the Dolies; but now they were walking on foot for months and without any privacy or dignity. We did not have any charpies or any shelter to have baths, sleep or relax. There were no cooked meals or drinking clean water; it was extremely degrading and humiliating. It was a Muslim village for centuries and we had great status and respect in the whole area. My grandfather was retired inspector of police and well admired by his British bosses, but now we were all prisoners of war; rather this should have happened to the perpetrators of those serious crimes and they should have been the prisoners of war who were committing those grim crimes and forcing us out of our homes and ancestral lands... We suffered because of grotesque and sickening politics or coldblooded politicians and callous religious leaders. They are all dead and down in the sewage drain now." He grumbled in immersed emotions. "However some of our local Sikhs and Hindus friends felt sympathy for our wretched condition which lasted over three months." He recollected.

"We passed through Hoshiarpur, Jallundhar and Amritsar before reaching Wagah (Lahore)." He added. "It was the most frustrating and terrible journey of our life and the most barbaric."

Last but not least, one of our closest friends as well as a relative called Lal Hussain has some more harrowing and painful stories to tell about the tragic chaos of the partition. He recollected that he was over eleven years old at that moment and was living comfortably with his parents and grandparents in Jallundar, in a joint family, spacious home. One day we heard a big bang on the far corner of the town and everyone rushed out of their house or climbed up their flat roofs to find out what had happened. Within a second, there was a great flurry of people in the streets and bazaars. Some community leaders yelled frightfully that attack had been launched by Sikh' hooligans and Jathas; in a co-ordinated manner, which were armed with Kirpans, axes, Lathis and guns. They were allegedly burning the Muslims' houses and shops, dragging out and slaughtering the Muslims and looting their valuables. Everyone seemed to rush about in panic, informing each other by banging at the doors and raising an alarm. Within a matter of minutes we all gathered and headed breathlessly towards the British built Jallundar Cantonment for protection, located some ten miles away from our town. My father had immediately grabbed his bicycle (a Hercules model manufactured in 1928), seated up my step mother, who was suffering from cancer, on the front part of the frame and plumped some valuables including some grain on the back saddle. My elderly grandparents and I sprinted as fast as we could along with my father's racing bicycle. There was a huge mass of tormented refugees steaming and staggering like sheep towards their self-created safe haven. In the chaos and confusion some of the frail, old and sick people were abandoned and discarded to the mercy of the invaders. There was no time left to worry about their missing loved ones and they came out empty handed; some even left behind their valuables and cash. While hopping like a startled gazelle, I got lost from my family and endeavoured on my own like a straw would toss in a flash flood.' He continued that Sikhs, Hindus and

Muslims used to live in their own segregated localities, but in fairly equal proportions. "Before that incident we used to gather round the radio sets in the bazaars and listen to the developing news about independence, but nothing so serious was forthcoming. At that time not many people had a radio set in their houses. However, it was expected that there would be a peaceful and orderly transfer of power to all India's citizens and as decreed by Great Britain. However no one had expected the partition of the Muslim provinces of Punjab, Bengal and Assam; especially no one had foreseen a fateful dispute in State of Jammu and Kashmir (85% Muslims).However it had taken place far ahead of its scheduled time and all momentously in a dramatic fashion. So no preparations were on hand for mass migration from their town to other parts situated in the West, some fifty miles away." He exclaimed in a thoughtful manner.

He recounted that his own real mother had died earlier at the time of the birth of her baby, when he was only a few years old. He continued to describe that when they eventually arrived at the cantonment, there had been no preparations or arrangements for receiving any refugees, no tents, no food or public toilets or even water. As a consequence all refugees had to survive with their own resources, sleep on the soil under the open sky, cook their own food or eat a bare minimum; some of the refugees even started going back to their homes to get some supplies of provisions under the protection of some local Hindus and Sikhs or to buy some food from the nearby shops and villages; or some volunteers and sympathisers amongst the Hindus and Sikhs also provided food for a time being. However, it took some time before a minimum, once a day meal started, having been provided by the army. "How did you re-join with your family?" I interrupted.

"I was wandering around the camp which was teeming and overflowing with the refugees, when suddenly one of our acquaintances saw me and said, 'Lal what are you doing here? Your parents are looking for you everywhere and wailing. Come with me. I will take you there'. As soon as my parents saw me, they cried wildly in great jubilation and kissed and cuddled me overwhelmingly; their bodies shuddered and hearts fluttered like doves." He was overcome with emotions and almost choked.

While describing those highly grotesque and painful moments, tears trickled down his pale and faded cheeks, as well as from his nicely trimmed silver white beard, like pearls and flooded his shirt. He is over seventy four and a well-known public figure in Great Britain, especially in London. He was so choked with those intense tragic sentiments that he had to stop for a few seconds. This is in spite of the fact that he himself is a brilliant public speaker. The beleaguered refugees had to provide their own security against surprise attacks and were not aware how to exit to safety from those joyless camps and whom to approach for advice. The refugees only got relieved from those concentration camps when Baluch- Regiment's soldiers from Pakistan arrived two months later and transported them in military trucks to the safety and security of Pakistan; they had reached their new country in less than two hours. "On reaching Pakistan's borders near Lahore, they were herded to the refugees' camps again. Those camps were highly unorganised, filthy and full of disease. No proper sanitation, toilets and tents were provided; food was supplied by the volunteers as the new government had no institutions or money to cope with such a colossal calamity and wretchedness. There was no proper housing or sheltering arrangements for millions of destitute refugees who were pouring in from across the new border." He remembered.

"My father decided to shift on to Karachi as the flow of refugees was still ongoing next to the border areas in the Punjab. We clambered over the roof of the train as the insides of the coaches were choked with the refugees, some were even hanging with the handles of the doors; my father decided so to take shelter with one of his cousins who was already living there, but unfortunately, we did not know his address. It took us three days to reach Karachi by squatting on top of the roof of the train. On our trail, we did not get any proper food, but only a supply of roasted grains of wheat, chanas (grams) and pulses. On arriving Karachi, we were put in the camps again, but this time in the army barrack or sheds. However the concentration and flow of refugees was less and management by volunteers was more effective and organised. One day while we were lazing in our camp, our cousin turned up as a volunteer; we were so excited and shifted to his house instantly. He offered a part of his house to us and then we relaxed for the first time on the charpies after three month 'turmoil; and we were lodging again in the comfort and tranquillity of our house. My father gave me some money to spend; and the first thing I did was to buy the crispy bread which I used to eat in Jallundar and I was so overjoyed to eat my favourite crispy bread again and that delight lasts forever, even today. In Karachi we had had to struggle for some more months before we shifted to our own rented accommodation". Lal recalled.

That young boy later arrived in Great Britain in the early sixties and performed as a science teacher for over thirty years. He became a property tycoon, a councillor for over ten years in the London Borough of Sutton and had been honoured to be elected as Mayor of Sutton. He was also endowed with the title of MBE for his social work to the community, by Her Majesty, the Queen.

Jallundar was a garrison town of the British Indian army in the East Punjab and this is the same cantonment from where Brigadier General Reginald Dyer had departed with his soldiers; comprising of 100 Gurkha, Sikh, Pathan and Baluchi riflemen on 13 April, 1919 for Jallianwala Bagh Amritsar. There were about 5,000 people including Muslims, Sikhs and Hindus protesting against the British Raj and in favour of independence. The soldiers fired at the relatively peaceful, although slightly volatile, crowd without warning and had killed over 379 people and injuring 1200 in a matter of few minutes.

"For centuries, Bengal and the Punjab had been melting-pots of cultures, a jumbled variety of Muslims and Hindus living side by side, with Sikhs, Budhists, Animists, and Christians fitted in too. As Jinnah himself had admitted, most people within the regions tended to consider their local identity before their religious affiliation. But the British policy of 'divide and rule' had created religious divides. In an extraordinary speech delivered to the constituent assembly on 11 August 1947, Jinnah made it very clear that he intended all along that Pakistan be a secular state. You may belong to any religion or caste or creed- that has nothing to do with the business of the state." He declared, guarding equality for all faiths and communities. Among Hindus you have Brahmins, Vashnavas, Khatris and also Bangalee, Madrasi and so on. In Muslim communities, you have Pathan, Punjabi, Shia, Sunni and so on. He said further still, "In course of time all angularities of the majority and minority communities will vanish." "Religiously speaking, the population in India was far too integrated and too complex for a straight partition of their land; and was an amorphous mass of different cultures, lifestyles, traditions and beliefs." Alex Von Tunzelmann commented. "Indians were commonly called as natives in the eighteenth century, coolies by the end of nineteenth century and niggers by the beginning of twentieth century. British attitude hardened, rather than liberalised as the empire went on." She reflected in her most captivating book 'Indian Summer-The Secret History of the end of an Empire'.

Alex continued. "Jinnah was no fundamentalist. His Islam was liberal, moderate and tolerant. It is said that he could recite none of the Koran, rarely went to the mosque and spoke little Urdu. He never pretended to be anything other than progressive Muslim, influenced by the intellectual and economic aspect of European culture as well as the teaching of Mohammed. Margret Bourke-White described Jinnah with his razor- sharp mind and hypnotic, smouldering eyes. He was described by the New York Times as undoubtedly one of the best dressed man in the British Empire; his public speech rich with quotations from Shakespeare; was part of British elite. Jinnah was without question one of the most brilliant politicians of his day. He made himself a figurehead for

Hindu-Muslim unity .He joined the Muslim League in 1913 confident that he could act as a bridge between the political parties. But it was emergence of Gandhi as a spiritual leader of Congress in 1920 that began to elbow Jinnah out. 'I will have nothing to do with the pseudo- religious approach to politics. I do not believe in working up mob hysteria. Politics is a gentleman's game. He clashed with Nehru like his compatriot and friend; the great poet and philosopher 'Sir Allama Muhammed Iqbal'. He disdained the atheistic socialism of Jawaharlal. Islam is our guide and complete code of our life." He asserted.

According to Jeremy Paxman, in his most brilliantly revealing book 'What Ruling the World did to the British', In December 1946 Churchill, while talking about the Hindu Raj said, "The political class were 'men of straw', of whom in a few years, no trace will remain." He hated the presence of Hindu priesthood in the Congress.

The Hindu Congress described Nehru as godlike figure, perhaps the reincarnation of the God Krishna. Nehru did not believe in God at all and declared that religion, "filled me with horror and was the enemy of clear thought." But he certainly believed in the 'Caste System', especially as he belonged to a superior Brahman caste. His ancestors had migrated from the ancient Brahman city of Lahore and his grandfather was a constable in the Muslim capital of Dehli at the time of Mutiny in 1857 and his father Motilal, a successful lawyer and a moderate Congress leader flourished in the Muslim city of Allah Abad with his son Jawahar and two daughters Vijaya Lakshmi and Betty. It is alleged that because of being a free thinker and political activist, Jawahar could not manage close relationship with his wife Kamala and his two cosmopolitan sisters had viewed the uneducated Kamala as something of a bumpkin. He had been away from his family because he had been frequently imprisoned by the British or sometimes had travelled around the country leading the freedom movements. In his absence a Muslim called Mahmud, a friend of Jawahar since his time at Cambridge, had supported and shared her feelings, just like a family member. However Kamala's beauty and spirit had ensured that, outside her marriage, she had had no shortage of admirers. Most significantly among them was a Parsi called Feroz Gandhy. In 1930, Feroz had been an eighteen –year old student, watching the beautiful, fragile Kamala, twelve years his senior, lead a demonstration at Allahabad. He left his college (dropped out) to volunteer for Congress work. Too much raising of eyebrows from those who had observed his devotions to Kamala, Feroz first proposed to Indira three years later and finally she agreed in Paris in 1937, after completion of her education in Oxford. Indira married him in spite of Nehru's disapproval in a Hindu ceremony in Allahabad. Even the new couple had their romantic affairs outside their marriage; sometimes questions were raised in the Indian Parliament who was the son-in law of Nehru. A captivating private secretary of Nehru called M.O. Mathai had later claimed long relationship with Indira in his memoirs; "she could not care, anyway." He boasted. Feroz himself had fallen into oblivion just like his mother–in- law, but his name still dominates the Nehru dynasty.

'Mahatama Gandhi's lean and dark figure had flashed like a beacon across the globe after his dogged hunger strikes, rotting in British Jails and boycott of British goods; and ''Quit India Campaign on 8 August, 1942'. He used to meditate in his Ashram (a semi-monastic community retreat), sometime located in Cleaners' huts, sometime in the richest man's mansion like Birla House. His son Devadas was the editor of the Hindustan Times and owned by his patron, G. D. Birla (one of the richest man in the world); and got maximum publicity for his propaganda and campaign against the British Raj and Muslim League. This had allured the attention and sympathy of the USA, British Labour Party and USSR. He also became very popular by his 'Brahmacharya experiments' during 1946 -47.The aged Mahatama (a great soul) had been testing his view of celibacy by sleeping at night in bed with a naked or partially clothed woman. The object of the experiment was to transcend physical arousal. One night, when the police turned up to arrest him; they found him in bed with a girl of eighteen. Amongst the other devotees to Gandhiji were Jawahar's two sisters Nan pundit and Betty as well as delicate daughter of Sardar Patel called Maniben and Amrit Kaur(a Sikh woman). Mahatama Gandhi, a tiny, fly weight figure also rested his hand on the Vicereine's shoulder- a gesture of fellowship, acceptance and trust; when Edwina and Mountbatten posed for a photograph in their palace. Earlier Gandhiji's eldest son Harilal had converted himself to Islam against Mahatama's teachings and had caused his Bapu a series of nervous breakdowns'.

'Nirmal Kumar Bose, a distinguished anthropologist who had volunteered his services to Gandhi as a secretary, wrote a detailed memoir of the experiments. According to him, several women were involved, and many among them became personally passionate of Gandhi; some at the point of personal crisis. Gandhi's grandniece Abha, who started sleeping next to the Mahatama when she was just sixteen and he seventy-four, spoke of experiences in her later life. 'I don't remember whether he had any clothes or not.' She told an interviewer. I don't like to think about it. Sushila Nayyar said that Gandhi had told another of his young relatives, Manu, that they both needed to be naked to offer the purest of sacrifices, because 'we both may be killed by the Muslims at any time'. There was a disquieting incident with Nayyar herself, when cries and loud two slaps on flesh were heard from Gandhi's hut. If anybody questioned Gandhiji's purity in respect of sex, he could fly into an anger'. Along with several others, Bose felt he had no option but to resign from Gandhi's services'. Alex Von Tunzelmann continued.

'In 1930, a group of Indian Muslim students at Cambridge University, led by Chaudhari Rahmat Ali, had brought out a pamphlet called 'Now or never'. Ali and his colleagues set forth a demand for what they called Pakistan – comprising of the provinces and initial letters of Punjab, Afghania (N.W. Frontier), Kashmir and Sindh and a 'tan' from Baluchistan. 'Land of purity' and was presented to Jinnah by a student group in the late 1930's.

Before 1901 the Province of Punjab stretched from Delhi to Kabul, but in that year the British had split it into two for administration purpose; this segregation was on paper only, but the people of the area still remained united because of their common culture or beliefs.

'Jinnah's wife Rutie died in 1929 at age 30 and he was devastated and moved to London from Bombay with his daughter Dina. He took a large house in Hampstead, was chauffeured around in a Bentley, played billiards, lunched at Simpsons, and went to theatre. He earned millions from his enormously successful legal practice and just the opposite to Gandhi's career. His sister Fatima was a qualified dentist from Calcatta. It is interesting to know that Rutie belonged to a successful Parsi family, but converted to Islam after her marriage His daughter Dina was married later to a Parsi in India and had preferred to remain in Bombay even after the partition. Jinnah had a magnificent lodge in his beloved cultured city of Bombay and throughout his political career had preached for the unity of India and against partition. Jinnah went on very well with Motilal Nehru, but soon after his death in 1931, he was steadily going on a collision course with Congress which was now led by the chauvinistic Caste- Hindus; and he fought in a single handed manner, reviving Islam as a modern political force'.

'On 15 February 1942 the Allies-and Britain in particular had received a devastating shock when the supposedly 'unconquerable' Singapore was taken by the Japanese. The parallel with 'Lawrence of Arabia ' s capture of Aqaba in 1917.Without firing a single shot, Colonel Hunt surrendered with 60,000 troops of the Indian Army. This brought Japan right up to India's doorstep and Britain was in real danger of losing Indian Empire; with incalculable consequences to the future conduct of war (the joint planners had warned Churchil)'. The situation was only brought under control when the USA had exploded an atom bomb on Hiroshima on 6 August 1945 killing 140,000 people and one more at Nagasaki which killed, thankfully, only 64,000 people.

Churchil had sent the Labour M.P. Sir Stafford Cripps to Delhi on 22 March 1942 on a fact finding mission about independence. Then the right of Muslim provinces to stay out of a Congress – dominated India had been acknowledged. In the general election of 1945-46, the Muslim League would win 75% of all Muslim votes, but Congress under the presidency of Nehru had won a great victory overall. Jinnah had not expected to win overall, but had pinned his hopes on achieving a strong enough share of vote that Congress would have to offer the Muslim League seats in its cabinet and wanted to stay within the federation of Indian States; this is in spite of separate Muslim administered Provinces. Viceroy Wavell had planned to form an interim government of six congress Hindus (including one untouchable), five Muslim Leaguers, a Sikh, a Parsi and an Indian Christian. Jinnah had already accepted the plan, but Gandhi rejected it. The Muslim League mistrust of Gandhi reached a fever pitch, from then on; The Partition was inevitable. However Nehru informed Wavell that he was prepared to form a government. But soon the more experienced Viceroy Wavell was removed from his lucrative post and called back to Britain; and replaced by the inexperienced Mountbatten, due to some mysterious reason, by the new elected Prime Minister Clement Attlee of Labour Party.

Mountbatten arrived at New Delhi on 22 March 1947 brimming with delight, along with his wife Edwina. According to General Montgomery 'Dickie was delightful person, has a quick and alert brain and has many good ideas. But his knowledge of how to make war is really Nil'. According to Lieutenant Colonel Paul Crook, 'To me Edwina was the famous play girl of the twenties and thirties and some people said, she's only coming out here to pursue an affair'. In the first few days, Edwina sought out and befriended Gandhi's right hand woman, Amrit Kaur who was to become one of her greatest friends and the new government's Minister for Health and the liaison officer between Sikh warriors and Hindu chauvinists. Edwina developed sharp and personal relationship with Congress politicians, especially with Hindu extremist Sardar Patel and more intimately with Jawaharlal

Nehru and his two sisters Nan Pundit and Betty. During the course of their escort from the airport to the Viceroy Palace located in the glorious Mughal Gardens, the Mountbattens noticed the Sikh –hoards showing recklessly provocative behaviour. The Sikhs had arrived in the busy Chandni- Chowk's fashionable Mughal Bazaar, in two lorries and assorted jeeps, and careered about; brandishing swords and shouting Sikh war slogans 'Sarsari Aukar' at the height of their emotions. Jawahar and Edwina became close friends almost immediately on their arrival in Delhi, although they had previously met in Singapore on 18 March 1946 and had some romantic moments over there as well. But now at a first glance, they were genuinely in love. Subsequently Mountbatten had turned into a jelly. Edwina began to find her footing; Dickie rapidly lost his!

'Soon the Mountbattens enthroned themselves in the Viceroy Palace and left for their retreat in Simla to negotiate with different political leaders. Mountbatten used to invite Nehru for tea at the Viceroy's Retreat on his own and over there they would have some secluded and solitude moments. This charming, secluded cottage, hidden among dense forests near the village of Mashobra, was about half an hour's drive from Simla, along precipitous roads. It was set among some the most captivating scenery in the whole of India. Lush green gorges plunged dramatically down thousands of feet to glittering Saphire tributaries of the mighty Sutlej River and colossal mountains rose up thousands of feet behind them. Wild Cacti and delicate orchids sprouted forth from the roots of conifers, families of monkeys swung through the pines and picked keenly at strawberry bushes; above the tree tops, eagles circled.' They spent nights together and sometimes in pairs; and in this soothing and charming environment Nehru and his colleagues had drawn the Partition Plan, under the consent of the Mountbatten, on 17 May 1947, in just three hours.

On 18 May, Mountbatten and his Hindu assistant V.P. Mennon left for London by air for British Government's approval of the ultimate Partition Plan. Churchill saw Mountbatten on 22 May, but his feelings about him were ambivalent. When Mountbatten had returned from India in 1948, he never spoke to him for seven years because of his devious planning about the Independence of India.

'On 30 April 1947, Jinnah made a statement demanding that Pakistan consist of all Muslim –majority provinces; Sindh, the Punjab, the North west frontier province and Baluchistan in the west and Bengal and Assam in the east. It could have included the historically Muslim –majority land of the East, and culturally business centres of Delhi, Lucknow, Aligarh, Agra and Cawnpur. Any partition of Bengal or the Punjab, would result in a truncated or mutilated, moth-eaten Pakistan. Jinnah held the Press Conference in his elegant Delhi's villa. But Bengal and the Punjab; each had large areas of non-Muslim majority population, yet not clear majority at all.' Alex narrated.

After the announcement of the Partition, the well planned massacres and atrocities began in earnest. Alex Tunzelmann continues to describe in her book, 'Indian Summer.' "In Amritsar, on the Indian side of the border, a large group of Muslim women was stripped naked, paraded through the streets, and raped by a Sikh mob. Some Sikhs were able to rescue a few of the women and hide them in the Golden Temple, until the army could arrive. The rest of the women were burnt alive. Murders were running at several hundred a day and a bonfire had been made of Muslim houses. The police either stood by or, in many cases, joined in. One officer joined was confronted with sight of four babies that had been roasted to death over fire."

'The Sikh campaign was being organised with striking efficiency, recruiting and mobilising ex-servicemen and arming them from private stockpiles. Groups of anywhere between 20 and 5,000 men (sometime women and children) would meet in Gurdawaras and organise themselves into Jathas, or fighting mobs, to raze Muslim villages .They were well armed with machine guns, rifles, and shotguns, as well as grenades, spears, axes and kirpans; the ceremonial blade carried by all Sikhs. Usually their Muslim adversaries only had staves. The pattern of attack was well established. When Muslim villagers saw a Jatha coming, they would climb to their roofs and beat gongs to alert neighbouring villages. The Sikh would send in a first wave to shoot them off roofs, a second wave to bob grenades over the walls, and a third wave to cut survivors to pieces with kirpans and spears. A fourth wave of older men would then go in and set light to the village, while outriders would ride around swinging their kirpans to fell any escapees. Mountbatten has been widely held responsible for the scale of the Partition disaster and for failing to deal with it once it started. Sikh Minister of Defence, Baldev Singh, Akali- Dal leaders, Tara Singh and Kartar Singh and Maharaja of Patiala as well as Maharaja of Kashmir, and Home Minister Sardar Patel were fully implicated in the communal violence'.

'There was similar turmoil in the State of Jammu and Kashmir. Kashmir had come into existence as a princely state on 16 March 1846.The British had acquired the territory following the First Sikh War, but East India Company lacked the resources or inclination to administer it. Instead they sold it under the treaty of Amritsar to Gulab Singh, the Raja of Jammu, for 750,000 Rupees. But the Hindu Raja had no guts to rule over the Muslims, so he requested the East India Company to provide him escort of the Company's soldiers; the request was duly granted and Raja steadily brought the area under his control. It is sometimes said that this illogical sale was the root cause of the Kashmir conflict, either because Gulab Singh was a Dogra Hindu and most of the people were Muslims, or because he was, in the words of the Viceroy Hardinge, the greatest rascal in Asia'.

Though around three-quarter Muslim, the population was neither homogenous nor especially orthodox. Budhists formed the majority in the remote Ladakh, perched high among the slopes of Himalayas, while most of the population of the lower lying Jammu was Hindu. It had always been assumed by the British, by the Muslims League, and indeed largely by Congress party apart from Nehru himself, that Kashmir would eventually go to Pakistan. There were only three roads running in and out of Kashmir, two of them went into Pakistan and the third one from the Muslim district of Gurdaspur, which had been unfairly granted to India at time of Independence; this is the same location from where the Mughal- Emperor Akbar the Great had ascended his throne.

'During September and October 1947, the Maharaja's Dogra-led troops carried out a campaign of sustained harassment, arson, physical violence, and genocide, against Muslim Kashmiris in at least two areas- Poonch, right on the border with Pakistan and pockets of southern Jammu. According to some sources, more or less the entire Muslim population of Jammu, amounting to around half a million people, was displaced, with 200,000 of these disappearing completely; having presumably been butchered, or dying from epidemics or exposure; noted Ian Stephens, the Editor of Calcutta Stateman. The Maharaja meant to create a buffer zone of uninhabited land, approximately three miles wide, between Kashmir and Pakistan. Muslims were pushed into Pakistan or killed. Hindus were sent the other way, deeper into Kashmir. C.B. Duke, the British High Commissioner in Lahore, went to assess the situation in the third week of October, 1947. He saw around twenty burnt-out villages along the Chenab River inside the Kashmir border and noted that many of them contained the ashes of mosques. 'It was the Muslims who were suffering', he concluded. The Maharaja had ordered ethnic cleansing under the guise of a defence strategy. India had secretly been providing arms to the Dogra side'.

'Thousands of Muslim refugees from Jammu began to pour into Pakistan's Sialkot district, bringing with them sickening tales of atrocities. In the tribal areas, the Pathans, who had for months been hearing tales of Sikhs and Hindus outrage against their Muslim brothers and sisters in the Punjab, were already gearing up for what they did best; making war. In tribal groups, the warrior swept down from the mountains and massed on the Kashmir border'.

'The tribesmen headed for Srinager, sacking towns and villages on the way. They were held at Baramula by the Maharaja's army on 25 October. The result was a massacre, during which the town was reduced to ashes by Mahsud tribesmen. Maharaja and V.P. Mennon packed up and left for security of Jammu. In Delhi, pressure to send troops grew, led by the hawkish Vallabhbhai Patel and on 27 October, India flew numbers of its Sikh battalions into Srinagar and they quickly secured the Vale of Kashmir'.

'Incensed, Jinnah ordered Pakistan troops in to defend Kashmir against India, but was persuaded to cancel his order when Auchinleck threatened to withdraw all British officers from the Pakistan army. Most of the weapons and stocks owed to Pakistan army were still in India. In Kashmir fighting had spread to Uri at the mouth of the valley and into south-west. On 5 November, 120 trucks mysteriously arrived in the city of Jammu. Local Muslims were rounded up and told that they would be taken to the Pakistan border, then released across it. Five thousand men, women, and children complied and got into the trucks. Instead of driving to the border, the trucks turned the other way, and took the Muslims further into the heart of Jammu. The convoy halted, the guards got out, and then, with machine guns and blasts, massacred their charge. A few hundred escaped by hiding in fields and canals; the rest were killed.'

'Military of the Government of India and the best of the British generals and commanders are, therefore, co-operating to crush a tiny half-organised ill-equipped, general-less force, the people of Kashmir have mustered, it said. Sir Lawrence Graffety-Smith and Duke, as two most senior British diplomats in Pakistan, both warned Mountbatten about involvement in Kashmir. Churchill told Mountbatten categorically that his sending British Soldiers to crush and oppress the Muslims in Kashmir was an act of great betrayal. He described Nehru and Patel as 'enemies of Britain' and accused Mountbatten of fighting against Pakistan.'

According to Nehru's secretary, M.O. Mathai, Nehru said, "After Kashmir, the tribesmen's next objective would be Patiala, then East Punjab; then Delhi itself."

'The U.N. Security Council Resolution on Kashmir, required India to withdraw as well as Pakistan. It was a huge disappointment for Nehru, more so because it had the backing of the British Government; Pakistan was disappointed, too, because under the new resolution, it was required to call off the tribesmen before India withdraw. Jawahar arranged to visit Kashmir in May 1948 to celebrate victory over Pakistan tribesmen'. Alex Tunzelmann added.

On 11 September 1948, Mohammed Ali Jinnah finally succumbed to his illness and died. Two days after his death, India swooped on landlocked Muslim State of Hyderabad. The Nizam appealed to the U.N.O, but they had turned deaf ears. After Jinnah's death relatively inexperienced political leader, Liaqat Ali Khan took over in Pakistan; but he had failed to resolve the Kashmir dispute which was supposed to have been resolved through plebiscite, as had been promised in the U.N.O. resolutions, supported by the U.K and U.S.A.. He too was assassinated on 16 October 1951, by a disgruntled tribesman called Syed Akbar; but before any investigations could have been launched for the cause of assassination, the volatile crowd, tore Akbar, alive into pieces.

As I had observed the outgoing caravans myself at Depalpur (West Punjab) which is some fifteen miles away from the border, the refugees' exodus towards India was completed in one day and in a very orderly manner. All Hindu and Sikhs migrants were escorted by the regular army; I do not know whether they were Indian or Pakistani soldiers, but only thing I can describe is that they were looking a bit darkish. I was only seven years old at that time. However I must thank my eldest brother Yaqoob again who was a teenager himself at that time; an 'O' Level student and captain of the football team of his school, who brought me here from my Grandma's village(East Punjab), only three weeks before. In the refugee caravans I had noticed none of the Akalis (Sikh Militants) mounting on the horses and none of the armed Hindu hoards; I found no one drunk or shouting slogans, but rather I had discovered them as very quiet and drowned in depression.. Our rented house (rent Rs 14 per month) was located just on the edge of the metalled road leading to Indian border. It was a blazing red hot day, the sun glittered and glared just on top of our heads; even the soldiers were sheltering under the shade of the mighty clump of the Bur trees, near the canal bridge-head. The refugees were carrying their household goods, food, clothes and pots on their bull-carts, with children and old people sitting on the top of them. The caravan was lead by two army trucks in the front and an escort of foot soldiers at each furlong or so. The local residents were ordered to lock their doors and stay inside their houses and it was further announced that anybody peeping out of their houses or climbing on their roofs will be shot dead without warning. It was a strict military curfew indeed and we locked ourselves securely in the house. The refugees' faces looked sad and sombre; and trails and seas of human cargo toiled slowly, but surely and steadily. No one was allowed to pause for convenience breaks or stop for a quick chat with their old neighbours or mates. I am certain most of them were still friends and did not hate each other; they were not interested in the glory or power of the four or five of the politicians or high priests; they were happy as they were, just like their forefathers had been and they had no love for the place to where they were drifting. The trail of refugee 'caravans began early in the morning and the exodus had finished by the evening. This is how this should have been on the other side of the border. In hindsight I question myself why those people were uprooted as they had lived there happily for centuries and certainly no one would have welcomed them on the other side. I think there should have been no division of the country or at least on the provincial level. The indigenous people would have lived peacefully together where ever they were. People in power come and go, who would have bothered about them at a later date.

However while the caravans were creeping like ants we peeped through the thin cracks and gaps of our doors and sometimes opened the door a little and had taken the heads out for a quick glimpse. My three elder brothers said good-bye to their school mates and to the neighbours; they also (refugees) waved back. My brothers and some others kept on breaking the curfew and ran out to shake hands with their friends; this happened, even in the presence of the soldiers standing next to them, shouting at them to go in, 'otherwise I will shoot you' warnings' To a kid like me the refugees gave the impression as if they are being herded like cattle or sheep by the shepherds. They were simply forced into this disaster against their will. They appeared like dust particles being lifted by the dust storm in the air or like straws tumbling and tossing in the flash flood, just like spume. My eldest brother got simply carried away and went beyond the boundary of our house; he was hugging his closest friend and wailing consistently. The soldier pushed him back towards our house and my brother returned with tears trickling down his cheeks and he was wiping his eyes with his handkerchief.

That long line of bull-carts and trotters, perhaps few miles long, was not from Depalpur alone, but from the surrounding villages and far distant places as well. On top of that there were some other exit points along the hundreds of miles of the border. It is difficult to say whether they had stopped in a camp on their route, but I am sure they would not have stopped more than one day on either camp-site; and there was no reason for that. It was a mass movement and must have continued just like a dust storm or flash flood, till that died out. However to keep the refugees at one point for months at a stretch was definitely planned to cause maximum misery. For example the distance between Delhi and Lahore is about 280 miles, and with a slow trail of ten miles per day, could have taken average of twenty eight days or four weeks, but my Grandmother took five months to cover a distance of 120 miles, instead of taking 12 days; even if walking. This is really shocking to notice that her journey included buses and trains as well. Why on earth these refugees were kept in the concentration camps for months, rather than hours or maximum few days?; while the top brand enjoyed the cocktail parties, dancing, merry-making, shopping in the Mall of Shimla, Delhi and Bombay. I do not perceive them having the slightest humanity. I wonder what the UNO is waiting for; they must lift the shroud from this dark hole as soon as possible?

Just before a day the caravans had passed, one of the servants of a Hindu rich man was still hiding in his master's lodge in our neighbourhood. He was slaughtered mercilessly by one of the Muslim thugs. He wanted to grab the mare from their big lodge. Certainly he could have taken the mare without killing the poor man. The poor servant was left behind while his master had already fled to India along with his family. The greedy maniac broke the doors and entered the house. He first stabbed the servant to death, this happened in spite of plea for mercy and shouting 'Haul-O-Hoy'(Ram I am dead), he bent on his knees with his hands clasped, but the killer was a cold-blooded. He dragged the wretched man to the canal and came back for the mare. Later someone told him that the victim was still alive and clinging to the embankment. He rushed again to the canal and this time he completely finished him. Everyone in the town was heartbroken and mournful and felt sympathy for the victim. I could see some women going from door to door and describing the tragic incident, most of the residents were in a shock. There was nothing achieved out of that slaughter, as even the mare was taken in custody by the police to give it to the refugees as part of compensation . The poor servant was only obeying the orders of his master, who perhaps promised him that he will be picked up soon under army escort! I did see no more refugee caravans or any more slaughters of innocent refugees in Depalpur. However we did observe some corpses floating in the canal; it could be of the Muslims or Hindus, the simple reason was that the source of the canals or the barrage, built by the British on the gigantic Sutlej River, which was now on the Indian side in the District of Ferozpur (a Muslim majority District) . I did not see anybody checking the rotten corpses, they were quietly and eerily floating with the currents; this was a kind of freedom from the complexities of the life; now they were far away from the deadly beasts.

Soon after the Indian refugees had departed the refugees start pouring in from India to Pakistan, most of them on foot, some on donkeys, some on bull-carts, but many more still beleaguered in India rotting in the concentration camps.. The influential came by army-convoys and buses, trucks and most elite by air. The countless commuting by the trains were intercepted and massacred, but some were lucky to arrive to the safety of their freedom. They also included my own relatives, uncles, cousins and widowed aunts. Some of them had been robbed of their young daughters from the camps and villages. Everyone was in tears and told countless stories of atrocities committed by the cowardly Sikhs and timidly Hindus. They proved themselves as warriors by killing the unarmed; children, pregnant women, sick and the lame. The rape and plunder was widespread. There were series of killing grounds one after the other all across the routes and it continued right up to the last leg of their journey. Those alleged warriors were so excited that they are really free; after being subservient for over twelve hundred years to the Muslims; they could not believe their eyes. One thing puzzles me even today, why the exodus of Indian refugees was finished in one day; while the refugees coming to Pakistan continued for six months. This I can witness and testify it myself. It is one possibility that there were not many Sikhs or Hindus going to India and many more Muslims were forced towards Pakistan, especially Muslim dominated areas of the East Punjab. It was definitely planned on top to cause a greater number of fatalities and so far no one has questioned those culprits or raised any enquiry, although most of them have perished by now Another question pricks my mind perennially why mostly this happened in the East Punjab only; because there are still some odd 150 million Muslims living in other parts of India at the moment!

Some of our closest relatives who arrived in our house in Depalpur, told us that the atrocities were only stopped when the wild tribes-men had arrived in the concentration camps, as well as the Pakistani army, especially the Baluch Regiment.; they started rounding up the hooligans besieging the camps and shot them dead by forcing them to stand in one queue, so that minimum bullets were consumed. My uncle told us that one of the Sikhs was so fat and sturdy that the tribes-men had to use a few bullets to finish him off, one bullet was not sufficient. "There were thick layers of fat and oil and whisky protecting his soul", he quoted with an eerie burst of dark smile on his scarred cheeks.. Those wild tribes-men were so angry that they even started the rampage of the Muslim camps and stripped the men naked to prove that they are circumcised; if they were not; then they would simply dagger them to death. To them anybody could carry the copy of the Quran; because even the others could carry this book to escape execution. These genuine and brave fighters finished off all the rioters and gave these people a bit of taste of atrocities; which they had been unleashing against the beleaguered Muslims for months, weeks, days and nights. Some of those refugees coming to Pakistan narrated that these tribal- fighters were even forcing the Sikhs and Hindus to eat the cooked flesh of their own dead. These are the actual narrations or accounts; which I had heard myself in the first person within minutes of arrival of the refugees (our relatives) in our house and I do not think it was false propaganda or fabrication, as they were also telling similar kind of tales about their own people. It is definitely true that many thousands Muslims were burnt alive, all over India.

Again the questions rise in my head again and again, where was the bulk of the Pakistan Army; they used to be the main body of the British Indian Army. It is because of them that East India Company had defeated the Sikhs in the Punjab in 1849 and later the mutineers in Delhi in 1857. They were the major bravery awards winners in the Great World War One and Two; they fought for the British Empire all over the world including Europe, the Middle East and Africa. Do we call it bravery or treachery! If these people are genuinely warriors, then what was happening for the last twelve hundred years? The biggest question of all, why only Muslim dominant provinces of the Bengal and Assam and the Punjab were partitioned off in the whole of India; and why Kashmir(85% Muslims) and which is contiguous to Pakistan's territory was left in limbo???.

The communal rioting began in the Punjab, soon after the arrival of the new Viceroy of India Lord Mountbatten. His seventeen years old daughter Pamela, who was accompanying him wrote, "We went to see Kahutal near Rawalpindi, one of the typical small towns which have now been completely burned down and destroyed by the Muslims. On 30ᵗʰ of April 1947: we went to visit the refugee camp at Wah (some twenty kilometre from Islamabad), where over eight thousands Sikhs and Hindus have now taken refuge. Our visit provoked mass weeping and wailing; with people kissing Mummy's feet and showing all their scars, or their shaven heads, which of course to a Sikh means the breaking of one of the sacred five K's through the weakness of his spirit (a terrible dishonour for a Sikh). All sides exaggerate, it is almost impossible to judge clearly." She continues, "On Friday 25 July 1947. Jinnah comes to dinner. His attitude to the Sikhs situation was dangerously unsound. My mother was also becoming frustrated by him." She vented her feelings in her diary. "He has already become Meglo-Maniac——so God help Pakistan! The date for transfer of power came around all too quickly, originally it was meant for completion by June 1948, not on the 14/15 August 1947. It is all dramatised and sensational." She added. "In Simla on 1ˢᵗ September 1947; firstly the shocking news of carnage in train taking refugees. The train was stopped and 150 Muslims were killed. Tuesday 2ⁿᵈ September 1947. Last night the old treasurer's son was killed returning from college in Delhi. They were killed in spite of Hindu Chaprassi (attendant) with them. He himself arrived naked, stripped as a suspect Muslim. The situation in Bengal is better although the Punjab is still terrible." On page 171, there is a photograph of those who were killed in New Delhi being loaded in the trucks by the Chumars (untouchables).

She narrated further details, "On Friday 24th October 1947: Bad news from Kashmir as reports say that N.W.F.P tribesmen are marching up Srinagar and on Monday 27th October: Indian troops have been sent to Kashmir to face the invasion of tribesmen. On Saturday 1st November: Daddy has flown to Lahore to discuss Kashmir crisis with Jinnah. On Tuesday 4th November: Kashmir crisis. Baldev's (Indian defence Minister, a Sikh) report from the front to the Defence Committee was not at all good about the situation there. Sunday 9th November: We fly to London for Philip and Lilibet's wedding on the 20th Nov. We had taken with us, a gift for Princess Elizabeth and Philip from Gandhiji, and a piece of white fabric which he had woven especially for them. When the gifts were displayed later; Queen Mary was horrified to discover what she took to be a 'loin cloth'. On Friday 30th January, 1948: Gandhiji has been assassinated. My father went to Birla house. As he got out of the car, someone in the crowd shouted out to him, 'A Muslim did it!' my father had the presence of mind to shout back, 'You fool it was a Hindu!'"

In her book, 'India remembered' Pamela has displayed many pictures of Nehru, especially about his standing on his head, as well as strolling in his tight swimming trunks. There are also many more diary entries about him attending for private lunches, dinners and secret walks in the Mughal Gardens. Pamela also describes about Quaid-i-Azam, "Jinnah was extremely sophisticated and unlike the others Indian leaders, he always dressed in an immaculate English style rather than national dress. He was a Muslim, but only spoke English, which he spoke perfectly, whatever he condescended to speak. He did not fall for my father's charm offensive. My father could talk of nothing else because he could not crack Jinnah and this had never happened to him before. He later admitted that he did't realise how impossible his task was going to be until he met Jinnah." She reiterated.

Stanley Wolpert has narrated in his book, a fellow barrister of Bombay's high court. He says this about it (about Jinnah), "He was a great pleader. He had a sixth sense: he could see around corners. That is where his talents lay... He was a very clear thinker... But he drove his points chosen with exquisite selection-slow delivery, word by word." Another contemporary noted, "When he stood up in court, slowly looking towards the judge; placing his monocle in his eye-with sense of timing, you would expect from an actor he became omnipotent. He cast a spell on the court room... head erect, unruffled by the worst circumstances. He has been our boldest advocate." Jinnah most famous legal apprentice, M.C.Chagla, the first Indian Muslim appointed chief justice of Bombay's high court, reminisced that his leader, "presentation of a case; was nothing less a piece of art."

Wolpert narrates further, "The Mountbattens flew up to Simla for a week's holiday, taking Nehru and his daughter, Indira, as his house guests." Having made a real friendship with the Nehru's during their stay here. "This was the time when final decision was made." He added. However in the hindsight, I personally have a feeling that before Mountbatten departed for India, he already had plan of partition; as well as the boundary line of India. Its blue print was perhaps prepared by Krishna Menon; a humble labour party Hindu councillor in the London Borough; He was also head of India League in the UK and he was Nehru's representative in London. Nehru was so much pleased with his performance that he had already appointed him as the Indian first High Commissioner to the Great Britain. This is far ahead of the independence, while at the same time he had appointed his sister as ambassador to the USA and later to the UNO. India was in his hands already; thanks to the British. According to Pamela, "He (Krishna Mennon) was the first person whom Mountbatten had contacted before going on his new job as Viceroy of India in Simla. There was another incredible and brilliant Mennon(V.P); who was Mountbatten's ADC (attendant/civil servant) who further amended the plan, dictated by Nehru; While Jinnah was completely kept in the dark, as well as Churchill (then opposition leader) was not taken into confidence... Mountbatten personally went to London and got this plan approved. It is exactly the same thing as if a judge in the 'Old Baily' would give authority to one of the contesting parties to write a verdict as they wish; then how the other party will react! Radcliffe (a barrister) arrived in Delhi on the 8th of July but his decision of boundary demarcation was kept secret till after independence. I am certain again that it was lying in his brief case before the time of his arrival in India. These people came to enjoy the glorious free holidays in the glorious last days of the empire of India; free service from thousands of servants and coolies in Simla (next to my grandma's village) and Delhi; and had cocktail parties, a bit of romance, exotic hunting and shopping sprees, sightseeing in the Punjab and Kashmir; while hundreds of other Nawabs and rulers were completely ignored. It makes me wonder; sky was the limit. The Mountbatten family had close relationship with the families of Maharaja of Patiala, Kapurthala and Kashmir and frequently exchanged social visits." Pamela has mentioned such historical and hospitable moments in her book and included a few memorable photographs of such meetings.

In his chronicles the popular Indian writer, Narendra Singh Sarila describes, The Great Game was played under Clement Attlee's 'smoke screens'. Or perhaps this could be due to the deep romance between the Jews and the Brahmins. Coincidently they both proclaim to be the 'elite' and 'chosen' people; as well as perhaps accidently 'money lenders' and 'bankers'. There is one more odd or unique reason; they both have been ruled by the Muslims for over one thousand years; however the rulers were not the Punjabis; but happened to be the Arabs, Turks or mostly Afghans.

In addition to the massacres and carnage of the Muslims in the mainland India, especially in the East Punjab, the so called Maharajah of 'Jammu and Kashmir' state started the slaughter of the Muslims in Kashmir as well. Narendra Sarila accounts, "The massacre was instigated by the Prince Hari Singh (Maharajah of Kashmir)." So on the whole Kashmir situation became even worse. There were the tribesmen from Pakistan; almost reaching Srinager, soon the Indian forces landed in Srinagar to stop the tribesmen; this is in addition to the cruelties of the Dogras (Hindus soldiers from Jammu) and the Sikhs already unleashing on the poor Kashmiris. Quaid-i-Azam (Jinnah), although suffering from terminal cancer, was simply furious; and he ordered General Douglas Gracey, the acting Commander-in-chief of Pakistan Army to deploy two regiments of Pakistan Army on the Kashmir front. However it would appear that he made various excuses; one was that the Supreme commander Field Marshal Auchinleck (both of India & Pakistan) is not available, while on the Indian side their Commander-in-chief General Roy Bucher sent full reinforcement to Kashmir; under the new Governor General of India (Lord Mountbatten). It happened that the supreme commander was O.K over there, rather helped the Indian army with all British Equipment and Army. The Tribesmen kept on pressing towards Srinager and there was lot of panic in the Indian camp. This is quite unequivocal in the diary entries of Pamela, (Lord Mountbatten's younger daughter); who had accompanied her father everywhere in India and kept an immaculate diary for him. The romance was just fading away and smoke screens were just lifting under the storm of the tribe-men. The warriors of India were on the run. There were lot of hurdles put on Pakistan by various means. For example India paid only Rs 200 Crores out of total cash share of 550 Crores; the rest of the funds were just withheld by Nehru & co, this is in spite of pleas from Mahatma Gandhi to release the money. Pakistan had no money left in the exchequer and had to borrow Rs 20 Crores from the Muslim ruler; Niizam of Hyderabad (now part of India), this was on top of the British not co-operating for the deployment of its soldiers; rather quite a few of Pakistan soldiers were still kept overseas; after the end of Great Second World War; That's why Churchill was quite annoyed and protested to the Labour Government for not being fair; And it is perturbing that Pakistani soldiers were not available to escort and safeguard their own refugees. After the independence; Pakistan still had 500 British army officers deployed to help Pakistan at the beginning, along with their equipment. Although they were of great help, but on the whole, perhaps in the hole, there was lot of bias and partial politics on international level, tilting in favour of Nehru.

It is difficult to speculate why Muslims were cornered or sidelined? Why only Muslim majority - Provinces of Punjab and Bengal were divided? It could be because of the strong Brahman's lobby in the Great Britain or USA; or because of bribery or flattery; or perhaps it could be due to cider of the romance. According to the greatest poet of Urdu, called Ghalib, who is still buried in Delhi and was lodging there at the time of Great Mutiny of India, "There is no control on passion and intensity of love; this is such a fire; that one can't ablaze, even if someone yearn to and that one cannot extinguish, even if someone yearn to." For the lust of a few idols, the butchery of hundreds and thousands of the innocent patriotic Muslims should not have been allowed by anyone, it did not matter who, and they should not have been uprooted from their sweet motherland.

I do not hesitate to repeat it again that the British would have never ruled over India without the loyal help of the Muslims of the region, now called Pakistan; and various English scholars and historian have written in great details about their contributions. They gave unconditional sacrifices to achieve the great victory of the Soldiers Sahibs of the East India Company. There is no doubt that the Sikhs were also an important part of these expeditions against the mutineers and they got plenty of rewards just like the Muslims had. In addition the Muslims had fought bravely in the great 'Two World Wars' for the British Empire; this included my own uncles from Shamchorasi and Ahrana (both places now in India), as I have already mentioned. Any visitors or tourists to the Tower of London and National Army Museum in London will never miss the names of such warriors. In his book 'Kashmir Gate', Roger Perkins remembers one such loyal warrior, "4th Bn Duke of Connaught's Tenth Baluch Regiment, one of their men was Sepoy Khudad Khan, a machine- gunner; he fought in the first battle of YPRES, on 31 October 1914. His award of the Victorian Cross was the first ever made to an Indian."

On the Kashmir Front, Narendra has described, "Earlier in September 1947 Gandhiji had approached Mountbatten with the suggestion that Attlee be requested to mediate between India and Pakistan to avert a clash between the two countries, as a result of the conflagration in the Punjab." He added, "After the invasion of Jammu and Kashmir in October 1947, Mountbatten had arranged for Nehru, Sardar Patel (Hindu Home Minister) and Baldeo Singh (Sikh defence Minister) to fly to Lahore in order to meet Jinnah." How they could have faced Jinnah with all those treacheries and atrocities! I hazard to guess! He continues, "The fact remains that the complaint was lodged by Nehru to the UNO on 1st January, 1948 and cease fire was effected on 1st January, 1949 (a year later)." By that time Gandhi was dead and Jinnah was dead; the rest of the politicians in Pakistan were just Nawabs and feudal lords, they were far happy with whatever Quaid-i-Azam had achieved for them; now it was the time for them inclusive of the Pakistan Army to relax and enjoy; the hard work which had been done by the single handed Quaid-i- Azam, who toiled hard day and night for over fifty years. He had achieved this great success without having gone to the British or Indian jail. That was an amazing success as compared to his rival politicians.

Now the fact remains that there are over two million soldiers facing each other, always alert on the border; eye to eye, just like Russian Dolls or paper tigers. About one third of them are Pakistani soldiers. On top of them are the most modern navies and air forces; and atom bombs and missiles. India has over six hundred thousand (600,000) soldiers alone deployed in the tiny now disputed state of Jammu and Kashmir always on high alert; to keep the 15 million Kashmiris under their control; this is one soldier for each 25 persons to manage. What a waste of national funds. However these two armies are very lucky; they hardly fight, but they are there on full alert for the last sixty four years. The full scale war between these two countries was in 1965 which had involved their army, air force and navy; they fought for seventeen days and both of them were half dead and both claimed victory for achieving nothing. To me this is a complete waste of tax-payers money or public funds. These colossal billions and trillions of dollars must be diverted to the welfare of its teeming and soaring; poor indigenous people. The Indian subcontinent used to be called a Golden Sparrow of the globe. The Europeans used to hear the remote tales of its glory, glittering prosperity and had dreamed to reach this fabled and glorious land, at least once in their life time. Unfortunately that glory had happened during the Muslim rule. It is just the opposite now. Delhi was a brand new Muslim town and cradle of civilisation in India. On each independence day, the Indian presidents and prime ministers stand proudly in the balcony of the Muslim Red Fort with their tall hats and long cloaks to share the freedom with their people living far and wide; some living in their palaces, some on the severs and most in the villages and shanty towns.

There are slumps all over the main towns and cities of the subcontinent at the moment. In every village and settlement there are pungent heaps of garbage and the overflowing sludge of choking sewage systems. Tourists to the fabled city of Delhi always stare at the sacred cow feeding on the clump of household rubbish and garbage. The air pollution from the factories and Rikshaws are breath choking in whole of the Indian subcontinent. Teeming millions live and eat on these slumps. The young children are abducted, deformed and forced to beg for rest of their lives. This kind of shambles applies more to Pakistan. There are training schools in India and Pakistan to train young children how to beg; and such schools are shown on the television and broadcast all over the world. How degrading and painful! Some of the young boys are sold to the Arabs for camel racings and young girls are taken as brides. The growth of the population needs to be controlled. The crystal clear waters of the rivers, rising from the Himalayas are constantly being polluted from the toxic fluids from the industries as well as from the sluicing pungent water from the homes. The mighty rivers and canals appear like a network of sewer- drains, it has poisonous effect on the fish and other wild life too. It is from these rivers that the canals take their source, farmers grow their crops, animals drink water and the children swim. These eternal fresh water rivers have now become breeding ground for Malaria, cholera, Hepatitis and dysentery. The situation has become very grim at the moment and I yearn and beg someone from somewhere to come and give the politicians and extremely selfish leaders, more especially in Pakistan, some wisdom about how to live in a hygienic environment and look after their natural resources.

The enmity between India and Pakistan is getting to an alarming stage day by day. Every day the politicians repeat the same rhetorical statements and slogans, which they had spoken 64 years ago, perhaps read out from the same written paper; they cash in the public loyalty and support for their personal power and money. Millions of dollars are earned in commissions for buying military equipment by the generals, ministers and agents alike, it helps them to raise their chests. In addition it helps them to build up their palaces not only in their own countries, but also all over the world, especially in the west..They have developed political dynasties on both sides of the border, which linger on from generation to generation. I'm sure that that they are trying to make the common person stupid for their personal gains. For example, if they have Atom Bombs or Missiles, what good are these products are for the common man. Can they eat electrons or protons; even if they land on the moon; what good it is to the common man; can they escape from the slums or pollution! Even if they have huge armies, will they make them comfortable and prosperous! I have a feeling that the only those countries are beneficiaries, who supply arms to these wretched countries. Arms suppliers make sure that these skirmishes and disputes continue, otherwise how can they earn these easy and eternal handouts. Normally most of the arms are purchased from the loans given by the sellers on an eternal compound interest basis. The Indian subcontinent used to be the 'Golden Sparrow' and most prosperous country of the world, why do they hold begging casket in their hands now a days?

Most of the inhabitants on this gifted planet are not aware that India and Pakistan (amongst the poorest countries in the world) have the highest battle ground on it as well; because of their dispute over Kashmir. The both armies are on high alert in the

Siachin Glacier, its meaning, ' The Red Rose', (average height 20,000 feet) over the 'The roof of the world'. Over here the soldiers are not likely to be killed by the enemy combat, but by the glacier itself; one of the largest in the world, after the Poles; over eighty miles long and twenty miles wide; and four miles up in the sky, with a temperature like the North Pole. The Siachen glacier conflict began on 13 April 1984 with India's successful operation in this highly remote and frozen wasteland of Kashmir. It is estimated that there are over 20.000 combat troops stationed on this particular war front. Since then over three thousand Pakistani's troops have been frozen to death or maimed and many time higher than that number, India's soldiers have perished. As recently as 7 April 2012, an avalanche crushed 139 Pakistan's soldiers to death when it overran one of its base camps located at Gyari sector, at the lower reaches of Siachen. Since the disaster struck, the Pakistani Chief of the Army arrived here by helicopter on the avalanche's site and assured the bereaved families that the soldiers' bodies would be recovered, but after almost eight months digging, only 119 frozen bodies have been retrieved, perhaps rest of the fateful soldiers would remain mummified forever just like the fallen climbers of K2 and Nanga Parbat and scores of other high peaks located over here soaring over 26,000 feet high. The Indian casualties are far higher and more frequent because they occupy the Soltoro Ridge crest which overlooks the main flow of the glacier and also they possess bulk of the main glacier and have high concentration of troops to back up their aggressive posture and naturally cost them many folds. The glacier is deadly treacherous, infested with deep crevasses, frequent avalanches, icy lakes, waterfalls, roaring and foaming torrents, frozen biting-blizzards; and constantly mobile in a steady, but unpredictable manner. I hazard to speculate that the commander who planned this operation must be under the influence of opium or whisky. His intention was to take control of the base camps for K2 (second highest peak in the world and controlled by Pakistan), which are located some hundred miles to the northwest. Now his warriors are frozen as well as that of his enemies and have become snowmen of the Himalayas and are now only waiting to be perished or become defrosted and lose their limbs. The soldiers on both sides live in Igloos and exchange chapattis and sweet dishes with each other on their festival celebration days; their body temperature is maintained by modern devices, imported from abroad. However, the next move for these warriors would be to assemble ladders to pierce through the blue atmospheric wrap and get lost in the black hole; this all at tax-payers' expense for the glory and perks of handful elites.

Indian media and hierarchy hate Pakistan so much that recently they had raised doubts and objections, due to fear of security risk and implication, to the appointment of general Bikram Singh (a Sikh) to the lucrative and sought after top job of 'Chief of staff of Indian army with effect from 31 May 2012'. The reason given was that his younger son is married to a girl who is citizen of Pakistan. The general has been serving the army since 1971, now someone had lodged the petition in the court against his promotion, but petition was dismissed by the court, declaring it farce. The agencies rubbished this and informed the ministry that Singh's daughter–in-law was a 'US' citizen, having an Afghan father and Central Asian mother. It is worth recollecting that those who had ruled over India for countless centuries, were the invaders from Afghanistan and Central Asia, not from Pakistan and what guarantee can be afforded to the credibility of US citizen? The man who had appointed General Singh, the current Prime Minister of India, Manmohan Singh (a Sikh), since 2004 and the most brilliant and highly educated of all Prime Ministers since Independence, was himself born in a small village in Pakistan in 1932 and studied in candle light. He was forced to leave his sweet motherland under the command of foreign masters, at the turbulent age of fifteen and migrated reluctantly to Amritsar, which is only sixteen miles away from Lahore. He still appears sprightly and agile like a teenage boy. Before Manmohan Singh, Air Chief Marshall of Indian Air force, Arjan Singh (a Sikh), who fought full scale seventeen days war against Pakistan in 1965, was himself born in Montgomery, Pakistan in 1919. There is no doubt that Indian and Pakistani military forces are mighty and colossal, but they are non-combatant and stagnant and are in dire need of to be pruned without delay and colossal savings thus incurred, need to be filtered at the ordinary grass root level.

The self-indulgent politicians and army generals fly to 'Siachen Front' by the helicopters and take pictures with the soldiers against the lofty snow peaks to be displayed later as souvenirs in the galleries of their palaces. They must be forced by the international community to leave these wonders of nature alone and definitely they cannot conquer. Where are the environmentalists?; And how much money and lives it costs daily and why? Kashmiris' population is increasing day by day; this is their main job under occupation and darkness. The militants are gaining more grounds and new devices are in practice or being tried. So the Kashmir problem is not going to the 'Doldrums'. It needs to be solved.

These two countries must stop squabbling like school kids; they must learn from their European enlightened partners, like the French, the British, Spanish, Italians and the Germans and even the Russians. They all had disputes and killed millions of each other's; in their home grounds and abroad for centuries and did not gain anything. They have become prosperous by uniting together, by becoming united as one vast country, although main-taining their own national integrity, sovereignty and independ-ence. Indians and Pakistanis are the same people, they have the same culture, they eat the same food, drink the same water, they have the same genes and speak the same language. This is the age of freedom and enlightenment; one has to be tolerant about others beliefs and rituals; and all must live in harmony. Like the enlight-ened Europeans they must have their own football tournaments, their own tennis matches, their own golf tournaments, their rugby matches, their own car races, their own joint festivals and even their own joint security on equal rights basis and following the principles of self-determination and human rights, not might. Prosperity does not come by building huge armies or nuclear arsenal, but by harnessing the explosion of population, helping each individual to stand on their feet and give them fair chance to lead a civilised and dignified life. There will be no harm living on the pattern of European Union; weak and mighty live in peace together and support each other.

I close this chapter with the last paragraph of the account of one of our most senior colleague Margaret in our creative writing class. She reminisces in her memoir 'Recalling the Raj', "The war ended (Second World War), my father was recalled to England. We left for the transit camp in New Delhi. Our servants wept, as we did, and begged us to take them with us. They knew only too well the holocaust to come.

We arrived at Southampton in a crowded troopship. I sampled English education; my father entered the Church of England; my mother mourned for her son. We all wept bitterly at the bloody massacre which followed the Independence of India.

I have never been back and I never will."

Chapter V

Seven/Eleven

After having arrived safely at my parents' house in Depalpur, I found the environment quite different. Their living standard was far higher and more civilised. My father being a senior civil servant was highly respected in the town. This ancient town was quite historical and it could easily be compared with that of more famous cities such as Lahore and Multan, the two paramount cities of whole of the Punjab. It is perched on a vast and a high muddy-mound and encircled by a colossal small- brick wall, provided with lofty thick wood and iron doors in each direction. On top of this there is a deep and wide moat around it, to give further protection against invaders. It appears as if many layers, levels, series of cities and settlements have been buried on top of each other under its current foundations; it is also quite possible that the old series of cities had been destroyed either by the invaders or because of local feuds or by the earthquakes or perhaps by floods. I am a bit puzzled why the British did not excavate this hidden and mystical place, just as they did in Harappa (some fifty miles away), Taxilla and Mohenjudaru, to name only few? However I do not expect anything constructive from Pakistan's government; they never exploit or investigate their ancient heritage; it is just the opposite and perhaps there are too many to dig and explore. Over here I have seen the small bricks walls being demolished and taken by the public to be used in their homes; no state protection is given to these invaluable glorious sites. In the 13th century the Mongols had temporarily occupied this citadel city along with Multan, but were later repulsed by the Muslim rulers of Delhi. Depalpur is located in the heart of the Central Punjab's vast alluvial plains and in the middle of two perennial rivers the Sutlej and the Ravi (miles wide), rising from the Himalayas. I am certain that Depalpur had its glorious past stretching over thousands of years. It could have been the capital of the western side of the Indian subcontinent or one of the regional kingdoms of the Punjab.

My parents dwelled in a spacious rented flat roofed house comprising four bedrooms and affiliated with a good sized square dusty yard; having two trees, one thorny and the other like an umbrella. The water was supplied by a hand pump which was sited under the thorny Kikkar tree. In the house lodged my paternal grandmother, three elder brothers and a sister; as well as my step mother and her young son who was about two years younger than me. In addition there were two servants, one male and a female, a cow and a calf, a goat, two cockerels, over a dozen of hens, a cat and a dog called Jack. I felt rejuvenated here. However at the beginning, I had felt slightly inferior, nervous and neglected, but soon caught up; rather went higher and higher like a bud. Over here also lodged some widows and orphans from immediate relatives and more were added after the carnage of partition. In summer most of the people slept on the flat roof of the house, except my father, his wife and young son, as well as my grandmother; who normally slept in the main yard. As I had already arrived in Depalpur few days before partition, I did not observe any violence or communal upheaval in the town. However I did see some Sikhs wearing Kirpans slung on their shoulders, standing nervously next to their houses, as if waiting for any odd eventuality to happen or waiting anxiously for the mass evacuation, but normally peace and tranquillity prevailed in the town. I did not notice any Hindus having been armed in any way, but they were cleverer than the others, perhaps they had already vacated their houses, especially the most resourceful ones. There is a very popular proverb about the Hindus, although they were a part of our indigenous population, "Mounh Mein Ram Ram, Baghal Mein Chhourie: While in their mouth is Ram, Ram (peace be on you or god bless you), under their armpit is hidden a sword".

My father being a taxman had to visit scores of villages and towns in the subdivision under his control, most of them were far distant and in remote areas.. At that time collection of revenue was normally made in cash. He used to be accompanied by two gunmen or spies, as well as a clerk to keep records for the revenue collected. The catchment area was spread over hundreds of squares of miles of the alluvial plain. Luckily most of the villages were at a walking distance from each other. A large part of the area under his control was situated along the river Sutlej which borders Pakistan and India in that region. This particular tract along the river was full of wild reeds and shrubs which thrived in the marshy flood plain and also infested with crocodiles and wild boars. However there were lots of good quality fish also caught from the river and when my father used to return home, a pack of donkeys loaded with sacks full of fresh fish followed him. However in that wild region gangs of dangerous robbers and criminals also used to take shelter there even in peace time. But at the time of partition the area was involved in far more serious crime like mass murder and organised plunder on both sides of the border.

My father and his team used to stagger to the payees by bus horse-coach on horse-back and perhaps on foot. When my father used to come back, his clothes as well as he himself were full of dust and fully soiled. The first thing he would do after arriving home was to have a quick splash under the water pump and change his clothes. They would continue collection over the long periods; spread over weeks and months. Although there were some government rest houses dotted through the area, normally they stayed with some local big landlord or with the headman of the village, as there were no other facilities available for overnight stay. However soon after the partition he was suspended from duty without pay for few days for refusing to collect revenue from the border areas; as there were still odd killings taking place on either side of the border; especially at night time ambushes took place along the river belt of the border. I speculate that he might have thought that it was too dangerous to travel in that area with cash and also because of health and safety reasons for his staff as well as for himself; and no doubt because it was a completely a turbulent and lawless territory and thus fiercely frightening to him. In hindsight I have a feeling that he was terribly depressed by listening to the continuous harrowing stories of carnage and atrocities not only of his first cousins and nieces, but also of the hundreds and thousands of others whose caravans were passing through Depalpur and amongst them quite a few of them must have had sought his help and guidance. As a result he had become simply physically a broken and mentally shattered person. Just visualise when he heard from the wives and children of his close relatives having been murdered in a most cruel way or their innocent daughters taken away in front of their eyes crying helplessly when being dragged in the fields in the blanket of dark, he must be extremely depressed, while he would try to help and sympathise with them as much as he could. Most of the times I was sitting with him while he was listening to those stories; and later on those painful descriptions had caused my own nightmares which have continued for years. However it was not the fault of his boss to reprimand him, as there was no money left in Pakistan's exchequer. It was still being held by New Delhi to give maximum torture to Pakistan and any odd money scrounged from the taxpayers was just like a goldmine.

While on duty he used to wear either an English safari suit or a native baggy suit; and on his head always used to wear either a hardback broad rimmed bowler hat; usually of khaki, or white, which normally matched the colour of his suites or alternating with a fine white-muslin or a khaki turban with a flare; one side of it rose to the sky like a peacock head and the other side covered his spine. On duty he always held a dark brown baton in his right hand and normally wore sunglasses when trailing. He used to trot on foot to his office which was located about a mile away from our house. He was a perfect noble person and was highly regarded wherever he went. He was extremely honest, generous and a caring person. I recollect one evening, after partition, there were no provisions left in the house to feed the family and the guests; like the flour, pulses, spices or salt. There was nothing available in the shops to buy, but food rations were issued to the refugees.

My brothers had to rush to the nearby village to my aunt, a refugee herself, to get some pulses and flour to eat. He himself was one of the controllers of rationing supplies of food, clothing and accommodation to the refugees. His own supplies had run out because of the constant influx of refugee-relatives to his house. While the refugees at large and our migrant relatives got allotments of their farm lands, houses, businesses; the situation had started becoming normal at a steady pace. However there were still lot of people stuck in the concentration camps in India and one of my uncles was being held in the jail in Ambala. He was a Special Ticket Examiner in the British Indian Railways (a civil servant), but was charged with possessing a spear in his house. His wife and children were fearful for his safety. However he was released from the jail after about six months; he appeared to be skinny and lean, but was thankful to be alive. I heard him saying, "Quite a few Muslim prisoners were killed in the jail by stabbing from the Hindu and Sikh inmates. I was expecting myself to be dead any day; but luck favoured me."

In Depalpur, Lahore or Multan, most of the businesses, farming lands and good quality houses belonged to the Hindus and Sikhs, the majority of Muslims were underdogs, dispossessed or subservient to them; however there were quite a few Muslim feudal lords as well, but they behaved in the same exploiting manner. At that time only a few Muslims were educated or employed in the senior civil service departments or banks. Only few Muslims owned the industries or business corporations. Most of the money was possessed by the Lalas (Brahmans) and they were the most educated people. In the Punjab the bulk of the farming lands were owned by the Sikhs; this had happened since the time of Ranjit Singh, the charismatic Sikh ruler of the Punjab (1799-1839) and they had flourished even more under the British. There were some Muslim landowners as well who owned huge land estates. Once the Hindus and Sikhs left their properties like shops and houses, they were immediately locked up and sealed by the local Muslim league leaders and the Government officials and later allotted to the refugees arriving from India. That allotment depended on the category and value of the assets left behind whether commercial, residential or farming. No one was allowed to loot or plunder or break into the discarded premises. However in one instance, one of the local Muslim chiefs, living next to our house did break into a rich Hindu's house and managed to take out lot of valuable jewellery and other goods. He was immediately arrested by the police and handcuffed in his own house and in front of his family. However he refused to disclose his booty or surrender it to the authorities. He was consequently flogged in his own house, by tying him with his own charpie; and was wailing and shrieking, as well as his family. Soon the people gathered in front of his house and became panicky and nervous at hearing his cries. Soon he came to his senses and revealed the plunder; and thanked his interrogators for releasing him and his family from the pains and suffering of the terrible punishment of interrogation, unleashed on him and his family by the police.

In the post-partition era, there was lot of chaos and confusion in the Pakistan's community; refugees kicked out from the East Punjab especially and other parts of Bharat were most adversely affected. The orphaned children not only had lost their parents, but also their assets were grabbed either by their relatives or friends or they failed to claim their proper assets left behind and nobody helped them either. They were not mature enough to claim the loss of their properties. However there were so many instances where the residents of West Punjab or other parts of Pakistan who were not refugees, but had claimed lot of lost assets left in India by defrauding their claims and as a result became very rich. Thus similarly hundreds of the families who did not claim also became destitute and wretched. However most of the Muslims in other parts of India except Punjab managed to stay in their places and remained Indian citizens; but a part of their families migrated to Pakistan, so they managed to claim the loss of their property after arriving in Pakistan. Therefore their assets in India remained intact with their families as well as they claimed concurrent assets in Pakistan, thus millions of them enjoy double assets on the basis of their divided families. I think they are cleverest of all. Sometimes they get confused whether they are Indian or Pakistani citizens, especially after migration to the UK. Initially the Pakistan government allotted some twenty acres of land to the families whose breadwinners were killed by the Sikhs and Hindus in India at the time partition. This was done on compassionate grounds. Even this compassionate benefit was misused by some fraudulent people. I remember one of my first cousins claiming such benefit by declaring that his wife's husband was killed during the course of communal violence. He himself was a bank official working in the West Punjab. They continued claiming the benefit till some jealous relative or a friend drew to the attention of the relevant authorities. Then he was slightly embarrassed and smiled blushingly. However during the course of the claim some benefit had been reaped, it kept his wife in a pleasant mood. There was more than ample agricultural land that had been discarded behind by the fleeing rich Hindu and Sikh families.

While I was enjoying a comparatively higher living standard and more sophisticated way of life in my parents' home, some more tribulation struck me; this time from mother nature. May be at that moment I was too vulnerable or susceptible to disease or perhaps I was too gaunt or cadaverous. This happened within six months of partition of India. My body became rotten with the epidemic of small-pox. Our house was bustling with the influx of so many people and I was the only one who was picked up by this most cruel disease. Unfortunately it is an infectious and deadly ailment and most of the people flee from it just like a gazelle would do from the pouncing tigress. This is more dangerous than malaria. I was just playing in the dusty yard of our house when I felt sudden itching all over my body and I started scratching. I had a terrible temperature and was almost half unconscious and went straight to bed. Within days small thorny and conical blisters turned into boils full of puss oozing with pungent sticky fluid. The grave thing about this horrid disease is that a greater number of its sufferers either die or get crippled or blinded. However fortunately I did not fall in either of these categories although every bit of my body was pitted with small-pox. Those pungent and oozing boils were inside my eyes as well as outside; inside my nose as well as outside. Every crevasse and hump of my body was covered like the stars in the dark moonless sky. No doctor visited me perhaps it was too late to do anything. I could not open my eyes for at least two weeks and I was completely blind. In our environment and culture they call small-pox as 'phul-Mata' meaning 'Flowery-Mother' as it blazes the whole body with the blisters and boils. Why would they call it as mother, I do not know. In ancient Indian pagan culture everything in nature appears to be either a god or mother.

From among my family, no one came forward to give me any comfort or support. I was segregated in my grandmother's bedroom. My withering body was stuck with the bed-sheets and it was decaying like a corpse. I was relieving myself on the bed as well. And who was my saviour? My sister, who was only ten years old, was my nurse.. She did not worry about getting infected with this fierce disease and luckily she was not. She got full guidance and moral support from my grandmother who herself was very frail and brittle. My sister not only well fed me during the time of this crisis, but also kept me physically cleaned. Her most daunting and dirty task would have been to change my bed-sheets. The bed-sheets had become a part of my body because of the sticky fluids oozing out of my body. She was an amazing self-trained nurse at the age of ten, others were simply too scared to enter my bedroom. She helped me to sail through this perilous tempest safely and yet again I had a lucky escape. Great commendations go to my sister for endowing her invaluable diligence and dedication to me. However I must admit that this unpleasant episode might have happened due to my own fault. This could be due to an incident which happened back in my grandmother's village near Viceroy's summer capital of Simla. A few months before I departed from my grandmother, almost all kids from our village were rounded up for small-pox vaccination. It was done through the public pronouncement. We stood in a long queue along with our guardians and waiting for our turn. There were doctors and nurses in their proper gears.

There appeared to use a kind of sharp round grill to drill in the upper arm at three points and making round scars. I watched many kids in panic and agitated. I was moving forward slowly in the queue while my grandmother caressed me. But I was getting nervous and got startled; then escaped from the queue. My grandmother tried to get hold of me, but I proved myself persistently stubborn and refused to be vaccinated. This blatant blunder proved almost fatal at the end.

After over two weeks of oozing, itching and scratching, I came out of my bed and had a shower under the water-pump. It was bright winter day and I basked in the cool and crispy morning. Our relatives and friends commenced their visit to our house, especially to sympathise with me. The first thing I did was to check my eyesight, which seemed perfect. Although I was not fully recovered yet, there were still some raw sores, but most of the itching and scratching was gone. It took another two weeks to recover fully. At the beginning the decayed skin was being flaked off and replaced by the fresh cells. This is a great wonder of nature which happens automatically and made me nice and bright as normal, apart from leaving some deep scars. My scalp was also being replaced and lot of scales and debris were falling off. Unfortunately there was a great swarm of fleas which were infested in my hair and they were crawling not only in my head, but also in my clothes as well. So I had to help myself by raking my hair with the comb. Any fleas coming to hand, I would put them on my nails and nail them down and squeeze blood out of them with lot of tics. Again this was a unique experience, although it was much more hated and I had uncomfortable feelings, but I never gave up till they were all wiped out.

At that moment my paternal grandma must be in her late seventies or early eighties. She was a unique character. She was of pure white skin, of average height, but strongly built; her eyes brows and plaits were also white like cotton; even her eyes were white like her eye-brows. It would appear that her two eldest sons had died, as well as her husband (my grandfather), at fairly a young age. She suffered a lot of grief as a result of these heartbreaks and I could often hear her wailing while sitting on her own in her room. The silver grey cataract in her eyes did not help either; she could not see, not even her own fingers. She never ventured to walk in the open yard. She just grovelled and cringed along the wall of her bedroom to go to her bathroom. She normally wore a black, white or patterned baggy shalwars and the matching colour muslin loose shirts and wrapped herself in fine muslin, but simple dopatta on her head and chest. She appeared to be very skinny and almost without any fat or muscles. However she was quite tough and very active and often volunteered herself to take rice seeds out from their shells by thumping them with a thick wooden thumper, which is normally quite heavy to lift. I often admire her dialogue which she often used to narrate when she was doing hard physical work, "I do not want the worms in my grave to eat my flesh and fat; I just want to leave with a bare minimum skeleton!" She would say with a laugh, but seriously. She simply hated lazy persons. She also helped us to make 'Swaiyyan' which also require a lot of muscular power to make them from the wheat dough; A kind of shredding of viscous dough through a manual process of wielding a handle of the machine, which needs a great muscular mobility. These ingredients are required to make delicious and exotic sweet- dishes on great festivals like Eid.

Grandma controlled all catering and food raw materials and products herself. At that particular time white sugar, almonds, sultanas, rice were expensive and still are and much sought after by the kids and the servants; she kept them under lock and key; and issued them as and when required, otherwise they would have disappeared in one day. She also guided the ladies in the house how to prepare different exotic sweet dishes and meat products and personally supervised them. She made sure that the quality is maintained and supply of different products was readily available, especially for her grandchildren and her son. Although grandma was blind at that time, but was alert like a snake. She could see if anybody had sneaked into the house and could hear any whispers or perceive any gestures. She was a towering figure and had full command in the house, in-charge of all provisions and ran the house with full discipline. Most of her teeth were gone, but still some left for the sharp bites. When she used to have her meals, she appeared to be fully camouflaged, as if sitting in a tent alone. She would normally sit cross-legged on the charpie; fully covered by her big shawl or a blanket and eat food without having been noticed by anybody. She soaked her chapatti segments into the meat or vegetable curry or in pulse soup or eat rice, as she desired. However all those ingredients were blended in a spacious grey white metallic bowl; almost three times bigger than a normal bowl; so that no liquid is spilled or food falls out. Any bones she would sling to 'Jack' who always crouched next to her ready to pounce at the bones and crunch them with few dribbles and munches; he jumped in the air to keep the birds away with quick few barks and by waggling its tail and ears on full alert.

One day she called me with her usual commanding voice, yelling, "Anwer Khhhaaan". She never called me directly before, so I was taken by surprise and was little bit startled. She was fully aware I was prowling somewhere in the house. At that moment I still possessed the remote village rough manners and interpersonal skills; and was not up to the standard of sophisticated etiquettes of urban life which prevailed in our house.

I instantly responded, "Hoa". My heart fluttered and I rushed towards her from the far side of the yard where I was playing on my own with marbles. I was the youngest in the house, apart from my step brother but most ignored. 'Hoa' was the dialogue between a 'Haa' and a 'Hoo'. She instantly burst into laughter and admonished me," I think, you will be Chaprassi (collie) to your brothers. You must say, 'Haanji (meaning yes grandma)'. She continued bursting into laughter and laughter and laughter; covering her lips with her hand wrapped with her white muslin dopatta; while I stood next to her gazing and blushing like wet cat. I had become flushed and embarrassed, reviewed my manners of speech and its etiquettes; raised a brave shoulder, my cheeks submerged in a cold smile, promised to be civilised in future by nodding 'Haanji and wrenched my hands. It was the first time that someone had told me how to talk to the elders and how to behave with the others.

One day grandma's personal female part-time caretaker named 'Janu' called me 'Annu', a kind of pet name; not rudely but with pleasant gestures and in a friendly tone. She belonged to a farming family lodging in the adjoining small village. She also used to earn extra money by selling some fresh fruit and vegetables to our family which she used to bring from her fields in the village. However I straight away reacted, "Bund Teri Pannu." Which literally means, "I will smack your bum". It had happened next to the grandma in her room. She bursts into laughter again covering her chin as usual with her white muslin dopatta, I think she was doing so to disguise her missing teeth. While the others sitting nearby just gestured and glared in reaction to the rare unusual dialogue from a youngster especially one quiet and shy like me. They were surprised by the speed and how I had reacted; its rhythm and its rhyme. I stood spellbound myself amongst them and my cheeks were glowing in queer gleeful feelings after observing the reaction from the grandma as well as from Janu as she seemed a bit embarrassed by my little rude remark. They were all taken by surprise and could not believe their ears.

Although my parents' home was exhilarating and uplifting for me, there were some different kind of complex sensuous emotions and feelings. I experienced the biased and tendentious behaviour of my father, as well of my step mother. For example my father would only cuddle my younger brother and chatter with him; I was completely ignored. On top of that my mother (step) would give special drinks and food to her son; again I was completely bypassed. She would make arrangements for his tuition and even teach him herself; but again no one paid any attention to me; even in the supply of my clothes and shoes. My other brothers were in their teens and they managed to look after themselves, as well as my elder sister; but I was the odd man out and it hurt me and my nerves! My grandma was not much aware as well because of her frail and fragile structure. Nobody gave me any pocket money to buy some sweets or ice cream or fruit. So I had no one to demand from or to express my feelings; apart from to myself, so I became a self–sympathizer. At that moment, my priority was to have some pocket money; which I started by pick-pocketing my father's vault, there was always plenty of money; I just sneaked in when no one was watching and pinched just a few coins which were far more than my requirements. I did not need any tuition; I taught myself and had become top of the class. Soon my school mates, who used to live next to us started coming to me for free tuition; so it was just the opposite.

On one odd blazing and burning day in June, I left for the bazaar to buy some fizzy cold drink; along with my younger brother. When we were on our way back, near to the rear of home and next to the graveyard; some argument developed between me and my brother. We were both insisting to hold the drink bottle and yearned to grab and possess it. Naturally being the younger and a pet, my brother had the upper hand and took the trophy as he started crying. In the reaction I became boisterous and agitated. Unfortunately, at that moment, I was holding a very tender and green twig of a tree in my hand and lashed him two or three times; it was thin like a thread, but very lethal and made scars on the tender skin. It must have had caused a burning pain and my brother had cried at the pitch of his voice. His shrieks and wails are heard in our house and had startled my father and his wife, who were relaxing in their bedroom. By the time we reached home, in the next two minutes or so, I noticed momentarily that my father was parked doggedly along with his wife in the middle of the yard, while the sun glared overhead like silver disc. He was completely furious and was holding his leather shoe in his right hand. His face was glowing with fury and snarled at me; "why, why, why; you rascal?" I just stood there stunned and dumb; I simply gazed at my father and mother. In fact that was the first time he had addressed to me directly, so it was a unique experience as far I was concerned. On arrival my brother was immediately grabbed and caressed by my mother. "What has happened and why?" She enquired from him by rubbing his scars. "Anwer bashed me with the twig." He replied with his perennial sobs and sheds of tears. Within seconds my sister (two years older than me) camouflage me within her arms and started screaming; my brothers who luckily happened to be there (normally they were out playing with friends), rushed to my rescue as well as my frail grandma was standing next to me in the bright sun. They all begged together to my father for the clemency and forgiveness to me and kept on repeating, "It will never happen again, please forgive him, we will not allow him to be flogged!" Thankfully for me, the united pleas from my grandma, sister and brothers were accepted; my father had eventually cooled down, as well as my mother and younger brother gave a nod to the agreement. I had crossed one more hurdle and had a narrow escape again. However earlier I had some momentous joy out of that crisis as well. While I was holding the fizzy bottle in my hand, I had managed few cool fizzy sips as the lid had already been removed by the shopkeeper and we were trying to seal the bottle by the stiff pressure of our palms on the neck of the bottle. By the time we had reached home, almost one third of the sparkling as well the fizzy drink had already disappeared.

However in the third week of January 1949, my father was lying in state, next to the water hand-pump; located under the thorny Kikkar tree and in the middle of dusty square- yard of our house. He was only forty four years of age; ready to be washed and given the final shower by the local Imam. The perimeter of the pump was cordoned off by four men by spreading four cotton sheets around it; the Imam and his assistant performed the ablution. Then the deceased person body was wrapped with two white cotton sheets and a further black cover was spread over the coffin with some inscriptions from the Quran; but his face was left uncovered for the bereaved persons to pay their last respects. The coffin was laid on a Charpie, surrounded by the mourners paying their condolences to the bereaved and the relatives. There were wails and shrieks by the children and females; the men just shed tears with moans and groans. I cried too so much that no more tears were left in my eyes, my throat became dry and started croaking as if I had been strangled or choked.

Earliest that morning my father had died in the lap of his wife (my step mother) at about three after midnight. Previously for the last few days I had noticed him suffering from a bad cold; or perhaps it might have been pneumonia or flu. In my opinion it was not serious at all and yesterday I observed him having a shower under the hand-pump and having been washed by my mother. He seemed giggling and happy as usual. It is possible that he was overconfident about his good health or perhaps my step mother was a simpleton. They had never visited the doctor or called him; who lodged in his hospital residence only at a walking distance of ten minutes from our house .He normally used his bike to visit his seriously ill patients as he had no car. The doctor's sons were very close friends of my brothers, being class fellows; they played together in the school football team and used to visit each other on almost daily or frequent basis. At that time I used to share the bedroom with my parents, as well as my sister and younger brother. While we were fast asleep, momentously we were startled by the shriek of my mother, "I have been robbed, he's expired. He is no longer in this world. He had only few cool breaths and then became silent. Your father is dead. Oh. I am robbed, I am dead. Oh. I am a widow. He did not say or advise anything, he just raised his hand to me, meaning do not panic and be patient and everything will be alright. Nothing else!" She explained by wailing. The soonest my grandma had heard those wails and had been woken up from her deep sleep and crept into our bedroom to have a chat with him, but was too late even for her, there was no response from her son. Now she had more to moan and groan; more to wail and cry. My brothers rushed to the doctor on foot in the midst of the freezing dark night and he had arrived on his bike within minutes of him having been woken up; he immediately felt the pulse, his heart as well as his eyes but no response and declared my father dead. The doctor who was a friend of my father could not believe that and returned to his lodge with a fierce grief. He was rather shocked and subdued that no one had ever approached him earlier about that ailment or even asked about any medicine. To him it was not a serious disease and only a bit of proper medication and a little care was needed. He was simply stunned and stuttered as he was investigating.

In the Punjab and indeed in whole of India, Charpie is normally used as a bed. It is a network of strings of jute or cane fibres strung together into a wooden frame, supported by four wooden legs. Charpie is kind of a mobile tent or a sleeping bag; it can be easily taken to the top of the flat roof in summer or in the yard; or even the farmers use them in the fields. Also because of lack of space in the houses, some of the men use them in the night to sleep, just outside the house in the street. I myself enjoyed sleeping on the embankment of the canal or in the open fields when I used to visit my aunt or uncle in the village; it fetched lot of cool breeze and fresh air from the canal and the fields. Sleeping in the desert on the charpie, especially in the moonlit night is an amazing experience; full of peace and tranquil. In the scorching and blazing hot summer day, most of the men and males cluster together under the shade of the trees, whether on the embankments or in the fields or a communal areas. Also there are so many sizes and designs of the Charpies; some of them are very colourful and fascinating. Even if the Charpie gets wet because of heavy Monsoon-rains, they can be dried out quickly without any damage to them. In the remote village areas, patients are also carried on the Charpie to the hospitals located far away in the towns or cities. The charpies are carried by four men just like the dolees and so too are the deceased persons being carried to the graveyards for burial.

However the arrangements were made for a truck to transport my father to Montgomery about fifty miles away, the place of my birth; where our grandfather, grandmother and uncles and aunts are buried. This is the real place of our ancestors after leaving East Punjab. After loading the corpse of my father in the truck, whole of family had accompanied him too in the same truck. We stood around in the truck holding the vehicle's frame, while the coffin was lying in the middle. The road was bumpy and humpy; so there were plenty of tumbles and jostles as it was full of potholes and lairs. That caused further pains and jerks, but was not hurting more than the terrible grief and shock, which we already had. However there were no more tears left now to shed. We had suffered so much grief that we had become utterly immune to any further mishaps. The journey had to continue without any U-turn.

After the painful burial we returned home by the night coach. It would appear that we were running short of funds for the bus fares and there appeared so many penniless people travelling in our group. My mother endeavoured to camouflage me under her Burkha, but the bus conductor was vigilant and had demanded for the full fares to be paid or get down! All my three elder brothers were in their teens and sister only eleven. However in the confusion and panic, some of our uncles and aunts scrounged some coins and managed to pay for the fares for all of us and thus had managed to reach home safely. But that was just a prelude for what was about to follow and at that time I was not aware of the complexities of life and especially the lack of help from the uncles and aunts and of course other close relatives.

On the third day after my father's death, a religious gathering was held in our house. All our closest relatives and friends and neighbours attended with great emotion. There was a recitation from the Quran by the congregation and the meeting was wound up by the blessing- prayers from the local Imam; and then the best possible affordable food, fruit and drinks were served as refreshment and thanks giving before the final departure. Just before leaving, an uncle of mine, who was well fed, quite prosperous and plump, gazed at me in compassion and narrated with a smile on his swollen cheeks, "Allah always cares for the orphans, so do not worry, you will be looked after." However he never visited our house again with any support, nor did any soul! He did not live far away from us and quite often used to glimpse me going to school and returning home, as I trailed along a dusty path adjoining to his flour mill.

For the next forty days, on every Thursday, a prayer service was held by the local Imam for the peace and tranquillity of the departed soul. The Imam visited our house for the blessing of the soul, which was believed to have returned to the house on Thursdays from the 'Other World'; and would be pleased if delicious food liked by the deceased person was cooked and verses of the Holy Quran were read on it. In the process the best portion of the food was then given to the Imam for him to take away to his family and the remainder was consumed by the orphans. However that specific period or phase lasted for forty days only and the Imam did not elaborate what was going to happen to the departed soul after that specific mourning period. Even at that moment different kinds of tradition varied from family to family and from venue to venue and from Imam to Imam; perhaps most of the faithful do not practice it nowadays or practice a different version of it.

After the untimely death of my father, our family began to steadily disintegrate. My three elder brothers who had hardly completed their education were struggling to find some sort of jobs to earn money to live and eventually they left the house. My grandma had to endure some more sufferings and hardships. Unfortunately for us, we did not get any pension or help from the government. At that moment there was no money left in the government exchequer, Pakistan being a new born country. My father's dependents got only five thousand Rupees in lieu of his contribution to his GP Fund and that money was subdivided into hundreds. Most of his savings if any and jewellery was collected by the step mother or relatives and soon she started lodging with her father and brothers along with her son. I regret to say that that kind of wretched life was sometimes unwittingly created by the local traditions and culture. Our culture is based on the ancient culture of the pagans of India who had brought those traditions with them from Central Asia. For example the caste system, the superiority of man, no share in property for the females, are to name only few. My mother might have died when I was only two years old, but we did not get any share of her inheritance from her parents; it all went to her brother, which was quite a large acreage of the fertile cultivated land. In addition to that nothing came forward from their house. In other words I was not only deprived of the love of my mother, but also from her wealth as well. As I have highlighted earlier my father was doing such a sought after civil service job, he could have earned extra substantial money, this is considering the corrupt Indian culture, but he was just the opposite. At the time of his death, he did not have his own house or any mentionable savings. He even did not have allotment of a house in lieu of his wonderful ancestors' house (a palace) back in East Punjab, perhaps this could be that he died too prematurely and had no time to reclaim his inherited property at that early stage of Pakistan's creation. On top of that he made another serious blunder; he had got the allotment of his four acres of urban and invaluable land, in the remote rural area. This he did because his sister-in-law and brother-in –law were living there. From that farming land nothing was forthcoming, it was just swallowed up there; thus it was no assistance to us; this invaluable land could have fetched many millions of Rupees in the cities and towns because of ever expanding urban population.

After the fateful death of her son my paternal grandma, although very resilient and tough, became very anguished, depressed and frail. She had not only suffered from the unsuitable loss of her husband and two elder sons; but had lost the last glow of her eyes which had fallen now into oblivion as well. She had no desire to live anymore. She had nothing left now to command or control. She simply gave up like a defeated warrior and wanted to join the company of her loved ones. She departed within a year of the death of my father. I watched her dwindle and fade away like a setting sun from this horizon. Normally she used to relax in her bedroom by squatting on her bed mincing with her prayers beads. She had always loved her solitude and privacy; but on that last critical day she was helplessly lying straight on the bare charpie next to mud wall in the dusty yard. To me she seemed to be relaxing on her Charpie and basking in the crisp December day and warm sunlight. She just lay in a comfortable and relaxed manner; and I, my mother and her daughter-in-law, stood around her Charpie and gazed at her quietly. Momentarily she had asked for some water for her ablution because she wanted to say her prayers at the usual time. That was the time for the Zuhr (Noon prayers). At that time she had no strength left, but she had appeared to be performing the ablution to her arms and hands; while lying straight in the charpie. She would have been in the last half hour of her life and in her subconscious awareness; had performed her prayers. However what follows next is a very upsetting and painful memory for me. My mother, a widow herself, gave a laughing smile and asked her, "Buaji (Auntie), if you recover, would you still admonish or fight with us?" She reacted in an aggressive manner and amazingly in a hard and determined tone. Grandma retaliated with towering a response, "Definitely!". She had steadily raised her hand to her mouth and demonstrated to bite her palm under her teeth (She simply meant that 'I will bite you like this'). An amazing response to a most callous and a heartless question. Within minutes she was fast asleep; there is no unpleasant change or turbulence on her face, indeed it was unbelievable that she had expired. She had been just responding with her usual vigour, personality and domination! However her last desire was to have some water, as her lips were getting dehydrated, but after having few sips, there was no more time left. I still see her departure from us with a great contented face and without fear of anybody.

In summer days we used to break off from school at 1PM and used to leave our satchels at home and then rushed straight to the canal to cool down. The canal was only three minutes away from our home, a magnificent and eternal gift from the British; they had constructed a vast network of canals all over India, especially on Pakistan' s side. The sun used to glitter like a mirror at its zenith and the temperature soared to over 40 centigrade and everything felt like a furnace. The canal used to flow with an open heart through the vast fertile alluvial plains, quenching the thirsty soil around it, including the humans and the creatures alike. A pack of us, eight or nine used to jump together in the canal completely stripped. We used to dive in and out, play hide and seek, in the cool fresh water cruising down from the mighty Himalayas; most of the water was from the melted glaciers, some five miles up in the sky, as well as from the Monsoons. We normally used to swim about ten yards away from the bridge-head, as the water near it was very violent and turbulent. It gushed down the bridge barriers with series of waterfalls thumping with great roars and fury. It created very powerful water spumes, whirl pools, eddies; it swirled round and round, and up and down; and finally was pushed out to the main flow. We used to ride over water buffaloes sheltering in the canal and used to swing to and fro with their tails. We used to make lot of noise, laughs and jokes. We used to splash and splatter water on each other, especially in the eyes with both hands. We used to swim for at least two hours and then come back to do our homework.

We frequently used to notice the fish thrusting against the flow of the current and going upstream, creating a v-shape ripple in the water.. Near the bridge-head, it used to flutter and flap in the air and stroked the wall. In the evenings some people just used to stand over the bridge and catch fish by dangling straw or twig baskets tied to the rope and bending over the bridge. There used to be lot of excitement, applause and roars at the catch; the fish simply slithered in the baskets and in no time it was pulled up. We always looked forward to this fascinating moment and clapped with wild gestures.

While we were swimming as usual one day a very serious and tragic incident happened. A young girl roughly of our age was washing her family clothes by squatting on the brick-platform; only few yards away from the bridge-head. Although she was sitting comfortably on a flat, brick-laid part of the barrier; it was adjoined to the turbulent area. While she chattered with her friend or daydreamed, one of her cotton or silk garments, perhaps a dopatta, shirt or shalwar was just blown away by a gust of the wind and into the troubled waters. The water curled and swirled like a serpent; spitting spume with fury. The water used to hurtle down the bridgehead with a gigantic roar and thunder. She tried to grab it in panic and forgot the danger of the treacherous waterfall. She simply got snatched away by the whirl pools and eddies. She had tried hard to reach the embankment, but in vain; the thrust of the water was too overpowering and rampant with killer waves. She yelled and shouted for help, but was swallowed within a matter of seconds. After some minutes a diver turned up when the alarm was raised and had dragged the floating girl out. The water had tossed and tumbled her just like a straw or perhaps like the way a crocodile strangles and dangles a young fawn. Now she was lying flat on the dusty embankment of the canal; I think she could have been easily saved if proper first aid was given in time. Her stomach was swollen with water and now she looked like a balloon. Her clothes still lay crumpled on the embankment, waiting to be washed; instead her life was washed away.

On one other hot summer day while I was swimming on the same spot, I tried to venture into the turbulent area, but not in the middle; I only dangled my legs in the turbulent water by clinging tightly to the edge of the platform and half submerged in the water. Suddenly the powerful undercurrents hugging against the brick- barrier or platform plucked me away from the edge of the embankment like a hair from the butter and tried to throttle me by dragging me towards the bridgehead; but I toiled very hard and quickly clung back to the embankment. After that I never ventured again and found myself lucky to be alive. To me those feelings were so sensuous and startling as if I had been fighting a dual with a cobra. That was the area where even the grown- ups and mature swimmers had never ventured, apart from the professional divers. I had inadvertently ventured into that death trap just out of thrill or adventure into the unknown. However I am lucky to be alive otherwise I would have been squatting with that young girl washing family clothes.

In the summer there were always lot of school children in the main canal as well as in its sub-canals. A furlong distance upstream from the bridge, there was one bifurcation or offshoot of the main canal. Over that point another barrier had been built and the water level was raised and then was pushed through a narrow channel with great speed and thrust. In that upstream bifurcation we almost daily used to slide through this steep waterfall, it cruised through two narrow and high brick barriers. At the lower end of the fall, the water level was not much deeper and the ferocity of the whirlpools was far less intensive as compared to the main canal bridgehead's falls; so the young swimmers at our age could survive with a bit of skill and courage; it was all enjoyable, it appeared to us as if we were travelling by air, there used to be lot of thrill and excitement.

However the glitter and glare of the summer sun was a great blessing in disguise for the spouses. While the kids were away to the canal, the parents just bolted themselves in their bedrooms; cool their emotions, sweating head to tail. In the joint family system they were normally denuded of their privacy and tranquillity of the night because of joint family sleeping area in the open yard or over the flat roof. The couples rather yearned for the rare chance of having a romantic time

In the Monsoon time I used to observe the farmers bending in the muddy fields clad in their minimum clothes and bare footed; planting rice seedlings by fixing each stem one by one in the soil stooping for hours at a stretch. While toiling hard in the muddy fields, the wretched farmers were vulnerable to the snake' bites as well stings from the thorns. However the panoramic view of the canal, the green swaying fields and the groves laden with fruit had become a comfort of my life and I used to stroll for miles with my friends as well as alone while holding a book in my hand and study, in the mornings and in the evenings. Sometimes I used to sleep on the grass on the embankment or just relaxed under the shade of the trees. In the harvest season I enjoyed picking up cotton wool from the cotton stems in the fields, in dry and crispy winter days, along with other youngsters and females from the village. It was the tradition that only females and kids were employed to do pick the cotton wool from the plants, the reason might be the cheap labour and extra savings for the farmers. It helped me to earn some pocket money to buy some ice cream or sweets during my school breaks. I used to look forward to such a season, which I enjoyed with the village folks. I used to be overjoyed after getting the money which I had earned with my own effort and tucked it safely in my pocket.

In that particular era there were no restrictions imposed on the border crossings between Afghanistan and Pakistan. In winter when the temperature was almost freezing in Afghanistan and Central Asia, caravans of nomads or gypsies used to trail to Pakistan or perhaps to India; men holding spades on their shoulders, with their beautiful and blonde children perched on the mobile cradles and tents, fixed on the humps of their camels; and of course in the pleasant company of their females, their faces camouflaged, in search of fortunes in the fertile plains .Again each winter I always looked forward to such movements of nomad' caravans and fancied their freedom, resilience and dynamic life style. There is no doubt that they are handsome and charming people. I still dream about those caravans and those amazing people, the adventurers, the wayfarers and ever mobile nomads.

In my parent house, we had quite a few hens and I liked to collect their eggs from various locations of the house. I knew exactly when a hen was going to lay an egg. She simply used to get a little agitated or restless and commence croaking and that was at the same tempo at the time of their mating. They always laid eggs in quiet, comfortable and mundane locations. For example they lay eggs on dry fodder's straws or on top of hay or somewhere in the corner of the grain store or in their own enclosures. They never drop or lay eggs in the middle of the yard or the bedroom. Being a large family, we consumed a lot of eggs and of course they were free and exotic. I used to like boiled eggs and potatoes curry, it was quite delicious, certainly my grandma liked it as it was easy for her to chew. On top of that there was a great variety of sweet dishes made from them and they are all well sought after in the house, especially the home made cakes. I used to notice my dad eating two boiled eggs with his afternoon tea on a regular daily basis; this might have clogged up his arteries and resulted in his fatality! One odd day I had collected a peacock egg from the fields and put it with the eggs, underneath the hen, being hatched. I kept a regular vigilance on the hatching and to my surprise the peacock egg did hatch out along with others. I had become excited and had shown it to everyone in the house. I looked after my special innovative prize and cuddled it; and even used to take it in the fields. However after few days, it simply sneaked away in the bush and disappeared from my eyes forever. This was my ignorance that I should not have taken it out in the fields. I was really baffled by the genetics of its nature. I had fancied taming that colourful and fascinating chick, but his built in instinct momentarily startled me, and I had to bear some more pains of separation.

I liked baby animals so much that I used to sleep with the goat kid in my bed, under the same quilt. It made everyone in the house laugh at me. I did so to make them warm in the severe cold winter. Their company in my bed made a very fascinating moment. On top of that being the youngest and least significant in the house, I was also assigned to take the goats to the herd before going to school and bring them back in the evening just before sunset. The shepherd herd was stationed some one mile away in a thorny enclosure in the wild fields. However it did not bother me as I was used to such activities in my maternal grandma's village. Again this is a very happy and pleasant memory for me which will last forever.

After the storm was settled between India and Pakistan, the prisoners were exchanged and most importantly some of the abducted women and girls were repatriated. Most of them were pregnant and even brought some children with Sikhs religious bangles on their wrists. I observed one such victim visiting my sister's house in Lahore, she was expecting her baby anytime, her eyes were down and tears trickled down her cheeks; she was accompanied by her mother and aunt. She had a very soft skin and cheeks like apricots. However she was amongst the luckiest ones.

Most young girls returning could not find their parents perhaps they had been slaughtered during the course of their plight, or drowned in the floods or died of diseases. The majority of those orphans and destitute persons were without guardians or claimants; they were therefore kept in the rehabilitation centres and in further isolation; waiting to be adopted by the prospective well-wishers. According to my friend Gogi who was about sixteen at the time of partition and later became a custom officer in the Pakistan Customs in Lahore,' I had seen so many women and teen age girls terribly distorted and disturbed, some with children, when they arrived by trains, buses and trucks; they could not find their own loved ones and no one else was prepared to take custody of them; even their relatives had deliberately disclaimed them. However some of the rich people had come to the rehabilitation centres to pick up some beautiful girls as their concubines or as spouses to their servants; he was not surprised that some of them would have been taken in the brothels; to be exploited further without paying any compensation. These desolate and destitute victims were treated worse than the animals in Pakistan; perhaps such wretched persons could have been better off on the other side of the border.' Gogi born in Lahore himself was so depressed by those unpleasant behaviours and scenes that he simply resigned and migrated to England. Then he later had become a famous cricket player with Pakistan's team and a successful businessman in England. There were countless stories of widespread abuse of children, girls and widows in the concentration camps, not by the Sikhs or Hindus, but by the inmates themselves; as there was a complete breakdown of law and order or morality or ethics in the camps; and it continued for months.

However in the midst of those tragedies and hostilities, some romantic stories did crop up as well; few of them of epic nature. One of the Sardars (a Sikh) had lost his spouse in such exchange of abductees. Although at the beginning he had snatched the young lass from her parents for abusing, but later he genuinely fell in deep love and he had allowed her to keep in touch with her family. One day he had discovered security men arrived at his door who took away his sweet heart to Pakistan. He could not bear this trauma of segregation from her; therefore he followed her to Pakistan, perhaps on foot and with great perseverance found her residence. He yearned and begged her and her family if they could stay together; even if he had to become a Muslim, but his desire was completely shattered. In a matter of hours, he stood in front of a fast cruising train near Lahore and was wrecked to pieces; He did not want to go back to India; he wanted to die in the sweet land of his beloved; he had become a national hero. His tragic love story was printed on the front pages of all major national newspapers. However no one could broadcast it on the television, as this did not exist. Within months a very successful mega-hit film in the Punjabi was also made about his pure love and the sacrifice he had given. This film was named after him 'Kartar Singh', it had created popular songs and still very popular among the brides and bridegrooms and these are still being played and sung especially by national musical orchestras and musical bands, as well as sung on all weddings in the towns or villages in Pakistan.

In the same period lot of rich Sikhs and Lalas (Brahmans) businessmen and landlords had come back to their houses in the towns and villages abandoned in Pakistan; to dig out their jewellery, gold and valuables. They had come under the pre-arranged escort of local police; one such escort had come to my auntie's house in the village near Depalpur, I think it was a Sikh landlord house. I was there by chance because of school holidays. The police asked us to vacate the room and we were not allowed to look at the strangers. They simply locked the doors of the bedroom and started the dig-out. Within half an hour the job was complete and the floor was restored to its original position. Later my aunt had become very depressed and did not speak for the next few days. More instances like this had happened in Montgomery as well as all over Pakistan. The hidden treasure had to be dug out as soon as possible; as there is an ancient belief in India that after over a hundred years, it comes under the jurisdiction of a serpent or cobra gods. In this situation, these gods simply plump on top of the treasure and would not allow anybody to excavate it; anybody violating would simply be blinded or killed!

However in that hurly-burly my nightmares continued almost on daily basis on every other night. I used to have such scary dreams which used to startle me and make me shudder and shiver. After getting up from my bed I often used to describe them to my grandma, she just used to smile and taught me to read some prayers to make me snug against such nightmares and then surely I used to have a peaceful sleep. For example in such weird and spooky dreams, I experienced myself a few times flying in the air with a colossal speed, while a black snake chased me with the speed of a missile, but in the terrific strife I used to manage to stay just ahead. I would see and hear crowds of people having brawls and squabbles; killing each other with swords, knives, spears and lathis in terrible agitated and charged moods. The worst nightmare was when someone had first cut my right arm with a sword, and later my left arm as well; there were many more and they continued till I become a teenager. Then there were plenty of volatile sentiments to fight against them.

However in spite of such odd unpleasant man-made historical moments and scary nightmares, most of this time was of a growing up age and full of freedom, pleasant moments and thrilling experiences. There were far more happy and romantic moments too. It was the real foundation of learning as a glowing boy at school and knowing the society at large, which developed my body and mind. Going to the circus, observing the lions escorted under leash by men clad in costume, watching the elephants being ridden and trotting just in front of you and the men performing various summersaults jumps and swinging from the roof of the sky high tents and the amusing tricks performed by the giggling mystical clowns were very thrilling and out of this world. Also going to the festivals at some saints' shrines and joining the exhilarated crowds and the singing and the dancing of the enthusiasts; enjoying the sweetmeats and buying colourful toys are some of the delightful moments from that era. The last but not the least, going to the live musical and comedy theatre shows were all delightful and filled with soothing emotions and fascinating youthful memories. Most of those scenes and sights still give pleasant impression of that fresh era of life and seem very fascinating and inspiring. Those happy and carefree moments are still there, nice and young and ever refreshing and soft like the fresh bud of the pomegranate. Those feelings and sensations of the young sprouting crops and fruit blossoms, the colours, fragrance and blossoms of the spring, the pouring Monsoons, swimming and jumping in the swaying canals, playing and hiding in the fields, the aromas and sweet smiles of flowers and their presence always make me happy and soothing. I think that was one of the best times of my life. Now I wish if those happy and fresh moments could return again and I rejuvenate back to be a young boy, but won't!

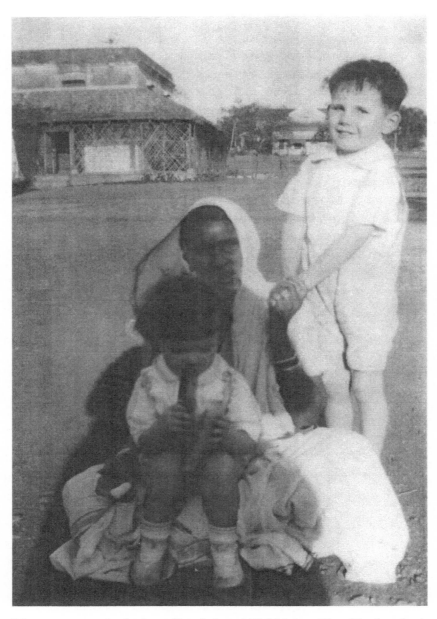

Margaret snugs in the lap of her beloved Nukki Aya. Her elder brother's hands clasped warm-heartedly. She was two when set sail for India. Second World War was three years away.

Mosque in Ahrana {my maternal grandma's village] in East Punjab.
Pictured in January 1978 (31 years after Partition}, at the time of
my visit from Great Britain.

Babu Fazal's residence, who built school adjacent to his house, still
appeared sound in 1978.I stopped for a night in a Sikh noble's house,
who took over the premises. He was tremendously welcoming and
graciously hospitable and did not wish me to depart.

A portion of my ancestral home in Shamchurasi, in shambles in1978, used to be an abode of Hindu Raja in the medieval times and passed on to my grandfather as inheritance. On the right foreground of the picture, the staircase to the palace is crumbling and the forbidden residence occupied by the most wretched people on this earth. It is quite possible that this damage occurred due to volatile communal violence in 1947.

The Great Canal gushing through the heart of Montgomery {A marvellous jewel in the crown}. In the picture Iqbal takes risk for an historic shot.

The neglected and rotting bridgehead in Montgomery.

Scum and slime shines on the crystal clear 'Glacier melted and Monsoon waters'. Industrial waste and municipal sewage outlets are flushed into the canal. In addition toxic industrial waste from India and ashes from cremations are dumped into these waters, as their upper reaches are a part of India's territory. I had instantly turned my face away and shut my eyes at the sight of distressing pollution scarring the great canal.

Milk producers (Gujars) mercilessly violate the embankments at leisure and choke the invaluable lofty trees, planted by the British.

Local Municipal Administration abuses the embankment as dump-yard for household rubble, which metamorphoses soothing hefty trees into skeletons and where wild dogs howl and scrounge.

A modest park along the right bank of mighty canal at Montgomery (Sahiwal), near the bridgehead and railway station.

Central Jail Sahiwal (Montgomery) established in 1873, was not allowed to take picture of main gate due to fear of "Terrorist Attack" (March 2013).

Coal Power Station Montgomery, now derelict, machinery embezzled. Premises occupied at the moment by most unscrupulous administration staff of Electricity Department who causes misery to everyone in Pakistan.

Entrance to Montgomery Railway Station, now terribly decaying and falling apart. Now noisy and unfriendly Rickshaws have taken over the cultured and comfortable horse driven Tongas.

One of the longest platforms, infested with potholes, no trains, no passengers, was once flourishing in business in Montgomery.

Immense orchard of oranges called Mitchell Farms, planted by the British, having its own factory to produce a fine quality of juices, squashes and by-products based at Renala Khurd.

A part of Mitchell's Farms, which are twelve miles long. On the right my nephew Murtaza Sajid; a renowned poet of Sahiwal and on left two farm workers

A view of main rail track from Peshawer to Karachi via Lahore, built by the British 150 years ago; is still single and no single train (baffling!)

A signal tower at Kissan, second station from Renala Khurd, with Karmanwala in the middle. The track is utterly disintegrating and rusting.

A bridgehead on the Great Canal at Renala Khurd, some fifty miles upstream from Montgomery.

A barrier at the back face of the bridge to raise water level for Hydro Electric Project at Renala Khurd.

Hydro Electric Power Project at Renala, inaugurated by Sir Ganga Ram in 1905; bifurcating a flow of main canal into a secondary canal. At the time of my visit in March 2013, only one turbine was operational, out of five or six due to a chronic disease.

A flourishing park segregating the main and bifurcated canals, but the railway station's main ceiling was plumped on its floor, glowing with graffiti of mournful slogans (heart breaking indeed).

A fascinating and foxy fort dominates doggedly in the midst of Cholistan desert in Central Punjab; has survived aggression of invaders as well as sand storms since medieval time.

Traditional way of relaxing and socialising on the outskirt of villages and towns by squatting on a jumbo charpai; playing cards, smoking huqqa (shesha) or having siesta at noon.

The denuded Anarkali Tomb in Lahore. It has been desecrated and stripped of its glory over the last four hundred years, especially during the Sikh rule of Lahore. The right side of it has been squeezed up by government offices and on the left choked by fumes of police fleet.

Great British genius and invention, loved all over the globe for its warm-heartedness and romantic smile. This 1937 model of locomotive has been relaxing for quite a while now, glorifying Lahore Railway Station with its alluring and enchanting image.

The glorious porch and main railway station of Lahore, another superb
and everlasting British Empire's legacy.

One of the grand platforms of Lahore railway station. At the time of
Steam Engine's Empire, these platforms were teeming and overflowing
with commuters, coolies and trains, but now a rare sight.

The classic redbrick building complex of old Punjab University, located at Mall Road, where I was once a student. A cultural and enlightening centre left by the British.

Magnificent and captivating Government College, where most renowned British scholars and professors taught, produced the most patriotic, inspiring and selfless British Indian poet and philosopher, Dr Sir Allama Mohammad Iqbal. He did his PHD in literature from Cambridge and Philosophy from Munich and later glistened in the college.

British Museum in Lahore.

British GPO of Lahore.

British Supreme Court of Justice in Lahore.

Front entrance to the fabulous Gymkhana Complex, opposite to the governor's palaces and next to the biggest zoo in the world, facilitated cocktail parties, ballroom -dances, pubs, all kind of sports, libraries and conference rooms, golf course, walking tracks and horse riding and race course and located on Mall road and heart of Lawrence Gardens.

Just more panoramic view of Gymkhana, now a central library of Lahore.

Flower Show in Lawrence Gardens, March 2013.

Some more colourful and fragrant view of blazing flowers in Lawrence Gardens in the spring of 2013.

Pakistan's soldier thumping and thrusting towards India, a part of daily spectacle when flag is lowered at sunset. This colourful and unique ceremony takes place on both sides of the border simultaneously, amongst the patriotic and emotional uproars and shouts of the spectators from each country.

A barrier on Pakistan's side of border at Wagah check-post. The Indian have the same a few yards away to the east.

Pakistan's Gateway of freedom at Wagah, Lahore.

Mughal "Hall of the Privileged" Shahi Qila, Lahore.

Private and sleeping quarters of the emperor and the empress, called Shesh Mahal {glittering palace} , a main tourist attraction in Shahi Qila, Lahore.

An amazing white marble canopy for cool breeze next to Shesh Mahal, for view of the world at leisure; a Mughal way of flirt and romance. Marble walls jutted with colourful precious stones and inscriptions.

The imposing and superb main gate of Shahi Masjid Lahore.

The fabulous and magical Shalimar Garden of Lahore, which has no parallel in the world.

Coonj-a romantic bird unique to the gifted plains of the Punjab. In the moonlit nights, flocks of them cruise towards the moon for a flying kiss. The lonely Coonj in the picture has been in police custody over 22 years, since has lost her spouse. She stays on guard under eave and does not allow admittance after midnight.

My niece Rabia on her way to the
university.

A family reunion, March 2013.
Sitting L-R: Qamer, Shams, Zia, Imtiaz, Anwer
Standing L-R: Shahnaz, Najma, Afzal, Farkhanda

A tranquil and peaceful moment in cool breeze, on the gregarious yard of the glorious Shahi Masjid Lahore.

Bird's eye view of Islamabad, from the toe of K2. The brand new capital of Pakistan is merely fifty years old, located on the threshold of the "Roof of the World" and having its own dam.

Splendour: World's biggest bouquet made from 3.5 tons of flowers, blossoming outside the main gate of Shahi Qila Lahore, spring festival of 2013.

Arms- wrestling competition in Lahore. Men and women take part equally.

A glimpse of Polo Match raging at Lahore {17 March 2013}.Polo sport originally began in this part of ancient India.

Chapter VI

Hajjo

Only three doors away from my parents' home, there lived a potter with his family. They lodged in a mud and brick house. The house was quite spacious comprising of five large bed rooms, a store, kitchen, a water hand-pump and a gigantic dusty yard split into different terraces. The flat roof was camouflaged by a low brick wall fitted with grilles for the fresh breeze. My friend khushi's house was adjoining to them at the back. He used to peep through the grill of their flat roof wall and had a glimpse of them which was sometimes sensuous and emotive.. On the front were the metalled road and the fields. In the lower terrace of the house were the kiln, potter wheel, bellows and stores of ingredients like clay, colours and moulds. The potter, his wife, two sons, a daughter and a daughter-in –law filled the house to the full. They were a very happy, comfortable and a contented family.

No doubt they were doing a menial job, but were producing skilful, essential and unique products for the community; it did not bother them whether the consumers were very rich or poor, farmers or city dwellers, children or grownups. They produced something for everyone. For example they moulded different models of children toys made of clay like horses, dolls, musical instruments, camels, goats and sheep and many other varieties.. More importantly they produced water containers, chaties, cauldrons, glasses, plates, cups, bowls, spoons, grinding and shredding pots and Haandies (Cooking pots), jars and flower vases.. All these items were diligently created with special skills and ingenuity passed from generation to generation and techniques were updated with the passage of time. They would use different colours, patterns, designs and quality grades for each category of their clients and as demanded from the public. If you think of any household in the Indian subcontinent either in the tiniest settlement or in the largest city, they would need Haandi for cooking dishes and would definitely require water containers for drinking. Haandi is normally used to cook mouth-watering curry or rice, any meat or vegetables dishes and make them most delicious as they are cooked through a slow and steady process; thus retaining the natural flavour and goodness of the ingredients of food. The water container keeps the water cool in the burning hot summers and also maintains its freshness in any season; this is without having to use the fridges which are infrequently available in the rural areas and also in most of the houses in the cities and towns.

The farmer's wife or daughter extracts butter from the yogurt by stirring a wooden disc and the wooden grille fixed to it in a concentric manner to the lower tip of a solid wooden rod which is about 3 inches thickness in diameter and about two feet tall. This 'Buttering and Lassi Device' is called Madhani. There is a special process to how this kind of yogurt is prepared. The milk is boiled in a big clay pot, which of course is moulded by a potter or his wife, on a very low clinker or glow of logs or dried animal dung which has been moulded in the shape of circular fat lumps. This slow process takes nearly whole of the morning and makes a thick curd on the top of the milk full of flavour and delicate taste. In the night time a few spoonful of sour yogurt is blended with the milk and the nicely fermented yogurt is ready by early in the morning. In winter the clay container is wrapped with a thick rag to keep the milk in a reasonable moderate temperature as the temperature outside is sometimes below freezing; in the other months the temperature is just favourable. However I have hardly seen a man or a boy doing this essential and tough duty, not even by mistake. Occasionally I did try to help my aunt or my cousins in the village to do this, but I found this task quite daunting, strenuous and challenging. However the rhythmic alternating arm movements and stirrings in the Chatie with this butter device and the blend of slurps and flaps of churning yogurt thus consequently generated are musical and fascinating; and the neighbours snug in their beds quite a few house away can hear the gurgles which echo like the cooing of a cuckoo. This is the first chore my aunt would do before milking her cattle like cows, buffaloes and goats and after bidding farewell to her husband, who would rise early in the morning far before the dawn and go to his farm for ploughing the fields or feeding his cattle; frequently my aunt would wake him up, but sometimes he would as the need be...while the rest of the family is fast asleep.

This intensely manual stirring wooden device is in turn wrapped with a spiral of rope; the female sits on a low string-stool and pulls the concentric rope manually in a rapid rhythm with alternating hands; in a determined and a constant speed. Both ends of the rope are fixed with the wooden handles or grips. The wooden stirrer is inserted in the Chatie or a big clay container; which is far bigger in girth and circumference as compared to the water container. Chatie is moulded with thicker and stronger layers of clay and far better baked.. The potter moulds it into an open and wide neck and with a bigger circular belly, so that it can take in not only the greater quantity of the yogurt, but it also takes in the stirrer or rotator and the spindle to which it is attached in the front and which normally immerse right in the middle of yogurt to stir and rotate freely. While stirring, churning and rotating; some water is also added to the yogurt and the curd at some intervals. Before the butter is formed, there is lot of spume and foam which forms on the top of now diluted yogurt. Sometimes we used to get a treat from our aunt and she would take out a glassful of this diluted yogurt and this used to be a very delicious and an exotic drink. This exceptional and unique drink is best for the health, quite refreshing and makes you smile. The butter is extracted and separated after an hour or two of arduous spin, grind and twirl of the yogurt. It involves a prolonged strenuous shrugs of the shoulders and constant shakes and sways of the breasts. No doubt the ladies burn lot of calories in this process and harden their muscles. This chore makes them healthy and elegant.

The residue of yogurt left after extraction of butter is in liquid form and is called Lassi. This amazing and blissful by-product is just like cultured milk without fat and can easily be comparable with that of beer in Europe or in the west, but is clear of any whiff or pungent effects and it is full of natural goodness. Its taste is delicious and is an important source of nourishment in whole of India, especially in the Punjab. The potter's family uses the similar manual device for extracting butter and Lassi. They have a cow and a buffalo in their house to provide them dairy products and the supply of these products seems self-sufficient for their consumption.. In my parents' home, Lassi was always in great demand in the long summer red-hot days, especially due to the huge joint family and also due to the addition of some widows and orphans caused by the partition. My father kept on adding bucket-full of water in the Chatie after every few hours when he was at home. The colour of the Lassi kept on changing from pure white to bluish white and at the end to almost darkish blue, plainly speaking at the end of the day it resembled to the tears of the crow! Luckily it maintained its cooling effect and by the evening it was all consumed. I still like its taste and still consume Lassi with the same lust; it keeps me cool even in Great Britain. I remember one of my tutors at Scola, named Margret in the Homeopathy class enlightening us, "More you dilute the vinegar, more powerful and effective it becomes." She emphasised. In my opinion Lassi has the same power and qualities as Homeopathic medicines; they are both based on the natural ingredients. However all my gratitude goes to the potter who moulded the Chatie and which enabled us to make butter and Lassi. Indeed it is a great, useful device for the benefit of masses in the Indian subcontinent, particularly in the burning alluvial plains of Montgomery and Depalpur.

The potter's family used to clad in a variety of dresses, mainly of cotton with deep natural colours. The father himself wore dhotie, shirt, waistcoat, t-shirt and loose muslin turban; his sons just wore dhoti and shirts or t-shirts. The mother normally used to dress in a long baggy skirt, flared frock and dopatta on her chest or head. The daughter and the daughter-in-law just used shalwar, Qamees and dopattas. The whole family looked colourful just like their products. Their youngest son Hanif was of my age and his sister Hajjo about two year older than him. However I cannot remember Hanif or Hajjo going to school; perhaps they were learning the technical family specialised skills from their parents. I used to go to their house to play with my friend and also observe the goods being made. They first used to grind and grate the clay and make dough out of it, then mould on the potter's wheel with constant use of water while the mould was being spun, then dry them in the bright sunshine and later bake them in the kiln or furnace. Once they were baked according to their requirements, the potter and his wife would do colouring or add designs. I used to enjoy the whole process which required lot of patience and perseverance. There used to be co-ordination between all members of the potter's family; although they worked in a flexible way. I frequently used to sneak into their house on the pretext of calling on my friend, but the objective was to have a glimpse of Hajjo and observe her busy at work or at leisure which was fascinating and full of delight as well as captivating. I always yearned to gaze at her walking around, listen to her conversation, observe her pleasant smiles and colourful dresses; and there was a lot to reminisce and enchant. I still feel comfort and peace from those magical moments which keep on spiralling like soft crimson rays of the dawn diffusing through the light and soothing mist of early spring. Those were the best moments of my childhood.

A few days after the mass movement of the Indian refugees' caravans towards the Indian border, which took place during the course of one day only, someone in our neighbourhood, perhaps a tormented refugee arriving from the Indian side might have had a nightmare and shouted wildly, 'Akalie horsemen are on their way to attack Dipalpur.' Hajjo's elder brother Siddique who was busy moulding the clay pots and chatting to his newly wedded wife overheard this. He immediately left his work and rushed out towards the canal with an old rifle grasped in his hand. He must be in his early twenties and had recently got married. The canal bridgehead was one point where the army escorting the Indian refugees had set up their command post under the massive clump of Bur trees. Coincidently I was playing outside Hajjo's house at that moment with my friend Hanif near the edge of the road. The onlookers including myself admired his gallantry when they saw him sprinting on his own towards the ferocious enemy. But luckily it appeared to be a hoax and Siddique returned after half an hour safe and sound. However no alert or alarm was raised by the authorities or any precautionary measures were taken by the police. One single person was running to sustain the deadly aggressors and what chance of success he would have had in case of real scenario! However it would appear that the Akalies (Sikh militants) did have a cluster of villages scattered around Depalpur which were their stronghold a few miles away from Depalpur, but now unfortunately a part of Pakistan. They must have evacuated their villages and joined the refugees' caravans in full security of the armed forces. However it is quite possible that at the time of the hoax those abandoned Akalies were damn busy committing havoc and carnage on their side of the border in Bharat.

The potter, his wife and the eldest son spent days in mixing and moulding clay dough, spinning, sun drying and making the clay toys, pots and water jars. Then they would load their donkeys with their products and sell them in the bazaars and open markets. This is how they earned money for the family. Apparently the quality and durability of their goods was excellent and in great demand. They maintained a good pedigree of donkeys as well for transporting their goods to the market outlets; these resilient beasts of burden are part and parcel of any potter family. Where ever there is a potter, the donkeys would definitely be there. They normally fix a wooden frame, a kind of grating or network of thin wood planks made in a mesh of v-shaped on either side and fitted with a thick wooden joist in the middle. This kind of structure is used for carrying pottery as well bringing the fodder for the animals; but for transporting the clay and other raw material, they normally use thick jute or cotton jumbo sacks. So a healthy fleet of donkeys is an essential part of this cottage industry. They can manage to graze on the rough bush and dry grass in the jungle; so they are easy to maintain and a cheap means of transport. Although the modern day man looks down upon these resilient beasts, once they were a vital means of transport and travelling in the remote and undeveloped areas of the world. However they were also the means of travelling and transport for the prophets, nomads, gypsies and the soldiers in the ancient times. So we are still thankful to these pitiful and hardened beasts for serving the humanity for such a long time and in difficult circumstances, especially over the barren dunes of the deserts and wild bush areas.

However in our eyes Princess Hajjo (potter's only daughter) was the best in the world which the Potter had ever managed to mould, design and produce. Her name was Hajara, but she was so cute and charming that her parents called her Hajjo. The whole family was ecstatic and delighted on their first sight of her. There was a great celebration in the potter's house and since then the house was ever filled with light and it became an enchanting place..She was the heart of the town's enchanted youths, living in the suburb next to the canal and the water wheel-well.. No doubt I was also one amongst the admirers. She was sublime, tall and slim; and of silky brownish white complexion. Her eyes were like that of a fawn and one could easily drown in them. Her face glowing like a new moon and her long black, silky and shiny, plaits dangling at the back slithered like a serpent and curls on her cheeks could easily bite like a cobra. Her teeth glisten like the rays of the dawn, her lips delicate like rose petals and cheeks smiling blossoms. The young and old, boys and girls, men and women were all entangled in her charm; and indeed she was the magnet to the crowd. The flowers and rainbows borrowed the colour of her dresses and whatever she was wearing always become the colour of the moment. The sun borrowed her shine and the flowers begged for her fragrance. The clothes felt comfort on her body. I yearned to be one! Her speech was in a posh dialect and etiquette like a noble person. She would visit our house frequently, sometimes to visit my grandmother like a grown-up person, sometimes meet my sister for a gossip or rope skipping or just a general visit to the family. She prowled like a peacock from her house to our house. A gang of our few friends normally used to play in the front of our houses or indoors; playing marbles, hide and seek or just relax by gossiping. She used to join our company as well and act as an observer; her younger brother normally used to play with us, she might be keeping an eye on him. So this gave us a chance to have a close glimpse of her which I always yearned forward. She stood like a beacon or erected like a lighthouse, we used to forget about our games or gossips and start staring at her and listening to what she was narrating or asking. We were mesmerised, enchanted and become joyful. I used to shudder and smile and looking at my friends' faces, they were in the fantasy world as well. I think she was aware about our reaction and responding in the same manner, but in a subtle way.. Her presence coloured everything that was beautiful in nature. She glowed like the sparkling reddish orange disc of sun sinking down the horizon and cruising helplessly behind the barren edges of sand dunes of the Sahara.

As soon as my father used to see her in our house, he would immediately giggle and ask, "Hello Hajjo. How are you! What are you doing over here? How is your brother, mum and dad? You are looking very pretty." She would simply blush and walk away to meet my sister or grandmother or mother. One day in the crispy winter afternoon, my eldest brother was basking in the bright sun along with his wife, next to the high wall located at the far end of the dusty yard of our house. He had got married only few months ago to a beautiful girl from the clan. I was sitting with them on the same charpie, when Hajjo visited us alone as usual. She was wearing a new orange fine silk dress and looking very beautiful and attractive. My eldest brother and his wife got carried away by her charm and clamour. No doubt I was on the top. She was standing in a stooping posture and camouflaged with a flared dopatta on her chest. My brother appreciated with a smile, "Hajjo your shirt is very beautifully made and stitched by a good tailor and looks very nice, show us your buttons, laces and pleats on the chest and neck. Can you stand straight and remove dopatta, please so that we can see clearly!" She immediately removed her dopatta and stood erected with a smile and ready for the demonstration, just like a model. She was not wearing a bra as per normal. My brother peeped through the transparent fine shirt as well as his wife and they gave smiles to each other. My sister-in-law gave him a dirty look. However I was observing deeply not only Hajjo, but noting their emotions and tempo as well; they were unaware I was intensely focussing on their emotions and hidden lust and indeed I was the epicentre in their triangle. Although my eyes were gazing downwards as was traditionally respectful, I was transfixed from the edges of my eyes, my ears were more attentive; and feeling were biting and boiling, my heart fluttering and mind startling. My emotions were running high and flashing like flash floods and still flashing.

The other day Hajjo was advising us not to run wildly in the fields or push anyone, especially in the dark, while playing hide and seek. She was concerned about the discarded or blind well situated next to the canal and on this side of the embankment (near the houses) . She was asking us, "Have you heard about the buffalo falling in the well last night. The buffalo was stampeding away from the farmer and plunged in the well. There are lot of wild bushes grown around the mouth of the well, so try to avoid hiding there. On top of that there might be snakes sheltering there in the bush as well." She emphasised.

We were fully aware about this incident and the first to reach there. We always played between the canal and the metalled road sprawling in front of our houses. As soon as the buffalo fell, the farmer yelled the distress call for help. He was shrieking and wailing frantically. He was really in panic at losing his valuable beast. It was pitch dark and very quiet, by this time even the birds were sleeping in their nests, the only exception was the occasional splatter and spatter of bats in the starlit sky or squeak of the owls from the lofty trees. Under the blanket of darkness the wolves and foxes howled in the far distant fields and stray dogs barked in the dark streets of the town. Soon the people rushed from all directions and gathered on the site. Sooner the drums were beating and some other spectators started wailing and shrieking as well to draw the maximum attention of the public. The men in the vicinity rushed to the scene and within a matter of minutes there was a huge crowd. Two of the bravest men descended down in the well with the dangling ropes and took two lanterns with them. They tied the puffing and hissing beast with the strong and robust ropes with one end of each rope, while the other ends were held tightly by the men waiting outside on the top mouth of the well. The men inside the well came out and the big pull began. The experts and guides co-ordinated the pull by saying, "Pull the buffalo with maximum force with 'Hayya' (united maximum pull) at one go from all". Unity was the strength and with series of Hayyas the beast was out in good shape, alive and unharmed. Every one clapped and shook hands in excitement congratulating the now relieved farmer as well as the brave men who went down the blind well. That was a thrilling and startling unique historical incident.

The other incident she kept on reminding us about was the vicious and deadly attack of the swarm of honey bees on some ignorant man, which took place last summer; on the edge of the canal and near the orchards. She warned us, "Never try to disturb the bees in their beehives by slinging stones or stirring with the sticks or draw honey without taking the proper precautions and without accompanying an adult and an expert, otherwise you can be dead or seriously stung." She added. "A man tried to extract honey from the beehive without camouflaging himself and without smoking them out. You should extract honey under the cover of the smoke to keep the bees away and make them blind; also cover your arms, face and hands with some cotton sheets." She enlightened us. "This man did not take any precautions and was almost dead. He wailed and wailed, jumped in the canal to avoid the brutal attack from the swarm of furious bees, but he could not escape. Luckily for him a farmer heard his cries for help and rushed with some dried dung and twigs. He immediately lit the fire and smoked them out and saved his life, but anyway children must keep away, never go near them. Most of the

onlookers ran away from the victim in fear of their own safety."
She admonished us. Although, Hajjo was a sprout herself, she
behaved as if she was a guide or a teacher and exhibited far
more maturity than her age. She often used to visit my grandma
and made her smile and delighted her with posh and witty
conversation. She had a special charm and grace in her personality.
To the grandma she was just like a toy and like her granddaughter; she admired her innocent chattering and was enchanted
by her company.

Unfortunately Hajjo was married off at the age of eleven or so
according to her family traditions. We were simply shocked and
stunned. After that we never smiled anymore and our exaltation
was completely swept away. The pleasant environment turned
barren, there was no more fragrance, no more blossoms no
more colours. It was a strange feeling stinging us like the bees. We
could not express our emotions to anyone. We were nothing and
we were simply lucky to have her company; now someone had
snatched her away from us. A bud that was plucked before it
could flower. Princess Hajjo must be unaware about her fate. She
was so naïve, so tender, so innocent. The bridegroom and the
party came on a herd of decorated donkeys like a pack of wolves
howling to swoop on an infant prey. In number so great, like
the swarms of bees, buzzing and humming. To us they all looked
like donkeys, whether they were donkeys or not. As per their
traditions they were beating Dhols(drums), wailing in excitement,
yelling slogans, singing, Bhangra dancing, tinkling and peeling of
bells which were dangling, tied in colourful ribbons, round the
neck of their beast of burden (donkeys). Most of the men, women,
children, boys and girls were clad in colourful dresses; men in
turbans, dhoties, waist coats, women in fine quality of cotton and
silk shalwars, dopattas, skirts, frocks and in brand new shoes.
Additionally the women were decorated with the exotic gold
and silver jewellery. Fists loads of money in the shape of notes and
coins were showered on top of the head of the bridegroom and
packs of children were swooping on the dusty ground to snatch
as much money as possible. Everyone was laughing, smiling and

chattering; there was lot of excitement and the atmosphere was filled with colours and emotions. The guests were welcomed with cuddles, caresses and handshakes. Special drinks and refreshments were being served. Lot of steam and aroma was rising to the sky and filing the atmosphere as the lot of cauldrons were sizzling on the glowing fire of logs where a great variety of mouth-watering and exotic food was being cooked by special chefs.

Inside the house the bride was being decorated with a sumptuous traditional silk bridal red suite and her head was covered with the same matching colour, high quality gold embroidered dopatta, as well as the designer's soft shoes which matched with the tenderness of her delicate feet. She was squatting on a specially decorated high wooden platform covered with thick carpet. The bride was overshadowed by her friends and relatives in their fervour and hustle. First the groom was brought in with his sisters and brothers to be introduced to the bride and her family. Just imagine the excitement of the groom on the first sight, I think he must be wavering and wobbling with emotions. His eyes were stuck on the bride, but the bride was still blushing and her eyes were shut; it was her first glimpse of him and she was reluctant to stare at him, but he could not stop smiling. The bride was decorated with a variety of gold and silver jewellery and looked absolutely stunning and charming. Her face was glowing like new moon. Her body was consoled by the beautiful red rose and fragrant silky dress and her eyes were shrouded under her shadowy lashes. Her face was pale and slim, dry like an egg-shell. When the new couple sat together, it turned into an amazing spectacle. Everyone in the audience felt envious about the luck of the groom and what invaluable prize he was getting.

To introduce the bride to the bridegroom, they performed some unique and interesting rituals. First of all, the bride family wrapped a dopatta round the neck of the groom and had helped the bride to strangle him. The groom consequently promised,' I will earn the living for you and the family and you will enjoy comforts. With this covenant in public, please remove the

strangling or hanging rope from my neck'. In return she showered
smiles to the groom in blushed emotions and relaxed the
stranglehold. Then after that they had sprinkled some coins and
jewellery pieces in a wide and a shallow cauldron filled with water,
blindfolded the groom and the bride and beckoned them to grope
and grab the treasure from the water in the midst of yelling and
cheers. The idea was to find out who was winner and who picked
the most of the valuables. Naturally in the tussle the couple would
touch each other, especially the groom although wet and watery,
but enjoyed the warmth and subtle touch. Then soon after that
another colourful ritual had followed. The girls and young women
had held some empty decorated small water containers under their
armpits and secured against their swinging breasts, made of clay
and moulded by the potter especially for this event and proceeded
to the water wheel-well some two hundred yards away and filled
them with fresh water churning down the well. They prowled
dancing and singing along the edge of the metalled road and in
the midst of the fields crossing the dusty narrow pathway in an
atmosphere full of colours and jubilation and with garlands
dangling round the water containers and under the full view of the
passers-by who were free to stare and enjoy those colourful artists
and shared abundance of their happy feelings. The enchanting
colourful troupe continued the dance at the water-well and also
had been singing songs and dancing all along the dusty route from
the bride's house to the well and back. The whole panoramic view
became aesthetic and filled with joyful moments. They also
continued distributing sweets to the children as well as the toys,
and showered rose petals all along their route.

Even in normal times, the landmark of the water wheel-well used
to be very romantic and some of the town folks used it as a public
bath, indeed I used to be one of them along with my school mates
as well as with my brothers; we had a regular shower with the
fresh water gushing and gurgling down the brick-viaduct. Either
an ox or a pair of them or even a camel, trotted steadily round and
round a central pivotal point blindfolded with pads on their eyes
and drew the water out in tin or clay containers. These beasts

could pull the wheel for hours at a stretch. Again the clay containers were moulded by the potter. The silvery crystal clear water churned and splashed in the wooden or tin trough and then gulped through a narrow wooden or tin channel and then slithered off to the fields. At that time it used to be nice fresh drinking water, cool in summers and warm in winters. The water containers were attached to each other just like prayer beads in a string which were in turn supported by the metallic conveyor grill.. The filled containers emptied themselves in the trough and continued their flow downwards. After refilling the string of containers continued up again from the bottom of the earth and sprinkled water like diamonds. This romantic scene attracted lots of males for bathing and lot of maidens used to come to fill their water- containers (those who did not have water pumps in their homes) or for washing their clothes. As a result they exchanged loads of sentiments, gestures and flirts. While the girls filled their containers with the fresh gushing water, the boys drowned in their eyes or simply yearned to die in dilation. Their eyes sparkled, lips blossomed and sensuous emotions churned.

At Hajjo's wedding, the last but not the least, there was dance and song competition between the groom and the bridal parties. First the boy side danced and followed by the girl side; sometimes solo, sometimes in groups. Each artist or group of artists persevered to marvel on each other. There was lot of exhilaration and jubilation. There were some professional singers too as well as the dancers to amuse the audience. So many enthusiasts also joined in the celebration. These celebrations became further enthralled and captivating with blends of claps, jokes, laughs and some amusing wild story telling. Both groups also tried to make fun of each other by singing and slinging some humorous sarcastic and funny songs against each other. It made everyone in the audience burst into laughter and the atmosphere became hilariously funny and almost everyone had tears in their eyes.

After all those colourful rituals and excitements, now the time had arrived for Hajjo to bid farewell to her beloved parents, brothers and relatives and friends. She was leaving behind her dolls and toys as well as her admiring and loving neighbours. From now onwards her skipping of ropes, playing with the dolls and audience with the youths would become nostalgic and historical moments. Her departure time was very sombre and touching moment. Amidst tears of her parents, family and friends and exaltation of the groom and the alien crowd, she was carried on a Dolee, like a parrot in a cage. She levitated and perched on the shoulders of four men, who carried out their sacred duty like she was a goddess. All colourful donkeys with peeling bells dangling in their necks as well as the riders, trotted briskly on to their destination some ten kilometres away. On their trail they left behind the rising dust on the horizon and a glum atmosphere. A huge reception waited for them on their arrival. The celebrations went on for weeks and months and everyone in her new home was so proud of their new daughter-in-law. Plenty of money was showered over her Dolee at both destinations; at her parents' place as well as at his parents' place.

Alas! within few years of her marriage, she departed from us forever at the time of her child's birth. At her untimely death she was still in middle of her teens and we were utterly shocked and spellbound. I still lived only few doors away from her parent home. To me she had left just few seconds ago. For all of us the world was never the same after that tragic event and I had to endure some more shock waves. Haunted by the fragrance of her memory, I asked why? Perhaps it is the cage of the caste system or the sword of the traditions; echoed the reply. However I can still feel her in the buds of flowers. I can still see her in the smiles of blossoms. I can still smell her in the fragrance of petals.

There are countless instances of child brides in our part of the world and the axe falls only on females, it could be honour killings or slavery. At Hajjo's time a widow was lodging with us and she was not a relative, but one of far distant acquaintances; she must have been abusing the generosity of my parents. She had married her daughter at an even younger age to one of her nephews. He seemed to me a tall, handsome and mature boy. My step mother questioned her about this match and explained to her that her daughter was too young and immature to cope with the pressure of married life. The widow just laughed and commented, "Once the boy meet her and grope about with her, the body will automatically develop to its prime." She further remarked, "The bride is very happy with the groom." She herself had managed to marry with the father of her son-in-law, who was already happily married to some nice woman, now he himself was cruising in two different boats, with one leg in each.

The majority of people in Pakistan still lodge in the rural areas and even those who live in the towns and urban areas are also very sensitive about the love marriages and most of them consider it as taboo and disgraceful. Recently there have been so many cases which have been discussed on the media whereby the young spouses have run away from their homes and had their marriages performed through the courts or some sympathisers. The girls' parents specially and even the boys side consider such cases just like adultery and in majority of cases had killed or slaughtered their daughters on recovery, but normally the boys are just forgiven or slightly admonished. In some instances both boys and girls are massacred wildly. They consider that the consent of the parents is paramount and not the consent of the marrying spouse. It is important to remember that this is not a part of any religion, but clearly a local culture or tradition which is based on ancient pagan convictions. On a daily basis so many males abuse so many females and children right across the board, but hardly any one is caught or punished for their grim crimes and abuses. The majority of the females are still being deprived of their inheritance, education and freedom.

According to the recent reports in the local media, there are thousands of families in the Provinces of Sindh, Baluchistan and some areas of Punjab where the heartless feudal lords first give a tiny amount of loan to the wretched people and when they cannot repay, they enslave not only the headman, but his wife and children as well. Most of the times, these prisoners labour under shackles and therefore live worse than animals for rest of their lives. The Nawabs, Sardars or chiefs and their courtiers not only abuse the slave-women, but also their young sons and daughters; and this abuse continues generation after generation unabated and no institution in the government can question them. The irony is that the ruling elite in Pakistan are the feudal lords or their favourites and they control the law enforcing institutions. The laws are there to protect any member of the public, but these mighty criminals do not obey the laws and have their own private armies who just work as mercenaries at a minimum payment of remuneration and for the glory of their masters. There is one more grim breach of human rights, some of these feudal lords do not marry their daughters to anyone, because they do not want to break their shackles by an estranged son-in-law, but they themselves have more and more wives and concubines on top of slaves. Even after death, they do not share their graves with the rest. They build magnificent shrines on their family tombs and the humble believers come for supplication and prayers and glorify them after their death. That's how the feudal dynasties survive intact generation after generation. However they prefer to educate their sons in the west. When in power, billions of Dollars are robbed from the national treasury and Pakistan requests the more foreign donors for some more. At large in Pakistan, in most cases of adultery and even rape, only females go through the guillotines, but the males are overlooked for the same alleged crime and left uncharged to do some more.

Some of the more desperately impoverished families in Pakistan especially in the Punjab, quite often lease their young sons as old as three or four years to the Arab Sheikhs for running camel races in the Gulf States in return for small salaries. It is quite possible that their parents might have sold them as slaves to their masters and I am certain that there would have been all kind of physical abuses taking place to those innocent kids. These young riders are ideal for camel races for being the lightest jockeys to ride over the racing camels and they normally win the race when they shriek and wail in panic. Some of the young jockeys had been reported killed in those wild races for the excitement of the Sheiks and winning some more money in the gambling. While on a holiday from Great Britain with a touring group to Abu Dhabi I was highly distressed when I observed such races being run in front of us. All these injustices wrench me to the extremes, but the single painful grief concerning Hajjo's departure from this world swallows the lot and hurts for ever.

Chapter VII

The King Cobra

Almost within one year of the death of my father, our family lost coherence and it crumbled. There was no pivotal command or control left then; there was no main breadwinner or guardian on hand to manage day to day maintenance of the denuded family. More than that, in our Indian culture and environment, justice did not prevail. There was no social security system and no pension from my father's civil service department. It was quite possible that at the time of his death at age 44, there was still no money in the Pakistan treasury because perhaps most of its assets and money were still being held by India which Lord Mounbatten should not have allowed it to happen, being first the Viceroy and later the Governor General of India.. It is also possible that the pension laws at that time did not consider the deceased person's family benefits if the employee had happened to die prematurely before the retirement age of sixty. In addition to the above scenario which was beyond our control, there were some inbuilt serious and hidden cultural problems. Any assets due to my mother from her parent's side were automatically taken by my real uncle and it would appear that my own father had let it happen in his life time soon after the partition or perhaps under the ancient pagan laws we were not entitled.

According to the local Muslim inheritance laws two shares of the property go to each male member and one share each goes to the female member of the family; but in reality even now ancient pagan laws of inheritance are applied and normally all assets go to the male member of the family. If any male or female member dies before the death of the parents, even then no property is passed on to the deceased person's family. My maternal grandparents had three off-spring, one male and two females. Hence the total of their assets should have been divided into four shares. Two shares to my uncle and one share each to my mother's family and one to my aunt. In case of my mother, her off spring could have been ignored because she was already dead, but my aunt did not get anything either. So how did my uncle manage to get all the assets of his parents, I do not know. Either he declared himself as the sole surviving descendant of his parents or had taken consent of surrender from his surviving sister. But the crux of the matter is that we were deprived of at least 6 acres of the fertile land and its income. While visiting the village I occasionally used to notice my aunt squabbling with her brother, but I was not aware about the exact cause of the contention. They lodged in the same house, although in their own independent portions. To make the matter worse my father got allotted his own urban inherited land in the rural area next to his brother-in –law and sister-in-law. As a result more valuable urban land was replaced by far cheaper rural land. Even this cheaper land was controlled by my aunt's family and hardly any income was forthcoming. So we were losers all across the board. My uncle and aunt preferred to settle in the village in the West Punjab after migrating from the village in the East Punjab. However no hard cash or crop help was coming towards us living in the town either from my uncle or aunt.

So consequently there was a mass exodus from our house, my grandma died within the year. So did Jack (our dog); he was so upset from her death that I frequently heard him howl and wail every night; so within months of her death, he simply gave up and lain dead. It is quite possible that no one took care of him properly or fed him adequately. In addition to this Janu (grandma's caretaker) was gone, the cow and her calf were gone, the cockerels and hens were gone, the chicks and eggs were gone, the uncles, aunts and cousins were gone, the widows and orphans were gone, the goat and her kid were gone. The Imam and the soul never visited again. My sister was already married at the age of twelve or so. My step mother did not have much interest in us and she starting rolling between our house and her parents' house (few minutes away); so was my sister-in-law, she hibernated between her parents and my eldest brother (her husband) and soon left us to stay with her husband.

Our landlady who used to live in the adjoining house next to us, dropped in at any time for a social chatter; but she never failed to collect her rent and for which she was dot on time. She was gigantic six feet tall; plump and pudgy. She always wore a Burkha and stampeded like an elephant. A few times she had observed me having a shower under the water pump; without shorts or under pants, that could be that I could not afford or perhaps there was no such tradition for the kids but definitely not for a show off. However my attention was drawn to her comment, "It's like a donkey, it is amazing." She gestured and giggled, with her eyes wide open and with her eyebrows raised. Unfortunately our funds had soon dried up; we were unable to pay the rent and therefore were evicted in a cold blooded manner. It would appear that nothing had impressed upon the landlady. The financial restraints smothered and throttled us and we got suffocated in the whirl pool of circumstances; we became destitute and handicapped. Although the rent at this time is only Rs 14 per month, but we simply could not afford that and thus fell into arrears with the rent and became defaulters.

However that forced eviction became a great blessing in disguise. It was just like when an ironsmith strokes a crooked and bent red- hot iron, with a mighty blow of a hammer; and it becomes straight and perfect; or when someone with a bent spine is hit with someone' s leg with a vicious grudge and vengeance, and as a result it loses its deformity and stands straight. It is exactly the same thing which happened to me. It reminds me about the thorny bush, in my maternal- grandmother's village, which had drifted in the dry river bed, firstly by the gust of the wind; and later tossed and tumbled with the flash flood. It never gave up and kept on rolling and trailing, to and fro or up and down; it was still there somewhere when the dust storm was over and the flash-flood had gone.

Eventually we shifted to the Gurdawara which literally means 'The house of the Guru' or the Sikhs Temple. It was only five minutes' walk from our former house and next to the embankment of the canal and adjoining the pedestrian bridge. It was a magnificent building with a vast congregation hall of high ceilings supported with marble pillars. The hall had many fancy wooden doors on all sides and beautiful high quality windows which opened to the canal side at the rear and its gigantic floor was made of black and white marble. In addition it had upstairs galleries, verandas and arches. It had a vast courtyard with the size of the football ground. It was enclosed by a high and a mighty brick wall and fixed with a strong and lofty wooden door; and within the main door itself was fixed a small concentric door for daily use. The main hall was also provided with some side quarters or lodges for the priests or caretakers or admin offices; and those were the side buildings where we got the residence, free of any charges or rents. In reality we were in the possession of whole of the citadel starting from the main lofty door to the main marble hall which became my study and rest room. Immediate to the west side wall of the hall was a high and mighty 'Pepal 'tree which almost overshadowed the roof of the hall as well as the backside yard of the one lodge; it had a massive stem with lofty off shoots of equal girth and height towering to the sky. Within the main yard was another tree and underneath it was water hand-pump. Some lovely lasses from the uptown also used to come to the water pump to fill their clay water containers to quench their thirst; we frequently exchanged smiles and chatters and had light conversation. That property came under Government Jurisdiction and we were allowed in the building on a compassionate ground.

That Gurdawara had its own Persian wheel-well too with attached open bathrooms, situated between the temple and other buildings which housed the dining rooms and restrooms for the pilgrims, which was all part of that extensive religious complex for Sikhs.. In addition on the other side of the well was a Sarai (Inn), a kind of a boarding house for the pilgrims, consisting of about twenty rooms and built on a separate high mound. That was the building where my step mother lodged with her parents and her son. The water from the well was drawn to irrigate the farming land around the temple as well as for washing and bathing. Then every morning we had shower before going to school under the splash and splatter of the water falls shimmering and glistening like a silver fountain; its water was cool in the summer and warm in the winter. The water was brought up in about one hundred tin containers which rotated around the wooden wheel. The wooden lever of the wheel was driven by two blind folded oxen who circum-ambulate round and round for hours and irrigated many acres of farm land, which normally produced vegetables, wheat, corn, rice and sugarcane. The tin containers poured water in the semi-circular wooden trough and the trough was connected to the wooden open viaduct. The area where we used to shower was neatly cemented, spacious and enclosed by high brick and cement walls.

After our move to the temple, the Sikhs from Bharat made a pilgrimage to the temple and they stayed there for few days. We were rather surprised they had returned after all those atrocities only three or four years ago. The whole area, especially the main thoroughfares around the temple were sealed off by the armed police because of what had happened at the time of partition. We were evicted again, along with my step mother, her parents and others. As soon as the convoy of Sikhs had entered the temple, they immediately fetched water from the well and washed the marble floor of the congregation hall as well as cleaned the whole area for their prayers. The singing of the Budgens and songs of prayers continued day and night with a great religious fervour and zeal..I gazed at them along with my school mates perched on top of the edge of the town's mound about a furlong upwards. In hindsight I have a feeling they might have come to excavate their treasures buried somewhere in the temple; as they never came back again. However they left behind plenty of empty bottles and many barrels of brandy and whisky which washed down their souls.

At the event of the Sikhs' pilgrimage we were evicted and shifted to a holy of the holiest places, this time to a Hindu Temple which normally remained completely locked and sealed off at all the times and no one was allowed in the main parapet where the most sacred of the Hindu statues was erected on the first floor. The whole complex of those buildings was constructed of pure dark -red bricks on three stories, with winding narrow stair cases and with dark mysterious rooms; apparently with no open windows or ventilation. We used lanterns to go up and down the narrow dark steep stairways. To me it appeared like a cloister of dark red rooms with ghostly and eerie feelings, perhaps good for meditation and peaceful for the priest to give healings to the faithful in need of blessings, especially to a female. My annual examination was in progress and I realised that I could concentrate better and I came first in the annual results; the whole school clapped when I stood in front of them after the controller of the examination announced my name and I still observe myself over there smiling at the congregation. The top of the main statue contained a casket which dangled the tail (clench of hair) of the head of a god or a guru; the most sacred central point any faithful yearned to see and asked for any wishes to be honoured with an offering of gifts, money and food. However at the time of our stay at the temple, no one tendered any offerings due to the missing believers and the priests.

Opposite to the temple soared a vast and magnificent Sarai (inn) which dominated high and mighty and built on top of the old mound which plumped on the debris of series of the ancient perished settlements of the town. This comprised of over a thousand residential rooms for the pilgrims and the caretakers., 3 stories high and provided with massive gates in each direction from the huge rectangular brick laid - yard in the middle with a cascading wide stairs leading down to the moat. This imposing flight of steps to the Sarai were so wide that even elephants can ascend these scores of cascading wide steps. This is the biggest inn I have ever seen in my life so far. The Sarai is situated within the main strong wall of the citadel town and it is in fact a city within the city. Again this lavish facility for accommodation must be for the pilgrims or the priests or perhaps originally was a barracks for the ancient garrison town; or even a market place for the trading caravans. Historically Depalpur was always a stronghold of all ruling dynasties, especially during Muslim rule. In each era, this town was at the heart of the rulers, invaders and business caravans for whole of India, throughout the history of India. It was also the bread basket of pre partitioned India, especially in the Punjab. After the independence, the refugees from India took over the Inn, as they found it completely vacant on their arrival and hundreds of families could be accommodated.

We returned to the Gurdawara after clearance was given by the authorities and life continued as normal. However within a year, the Hindus had visited their temple too. They performed the pilgrimage just for two days, again escorted by a heavy police guard. However it was not possible for the authorities to dislodge the inmates of the Sarai and put them into concentration camps as before, as it was not so easy to find accommodation for thousands of the refugee families living happily over here. Again just the temple area was sealed off from the common public; I wonder how much treasure was dug out; it must be in tons! Some of the houses left behind by the Hindus in Depalpur were larger than palaces, they were just like giant pyramids with statues of gods protruding and overlooking the houses and protecting them. Some of my refugee -relatives took possession of them and those mighty buildings had to be subdivided amongst them. Most of the shops, properties and businesses in the town belonged to the Hindus; the Muslim came in the lower strata of the society and most of them were squeezed in debt, borrowed from the Lalas (Brahmans) and as a result some of them were living as slaves under their ownership as they could not repay the hefty compound interest on the loans. The Sikh community came in the middle, most of their men worked as soldiers in the British Indian Army; they also possessed huge farming estates since the time of their Sikh leader Maharaja Ranjit Singh; he is considered by the Sikhs as amongst the most intelligent of the rulers of the Punjab and from whose descendants the British took over in the Punjab. The size of the Sarai(Inn) portrays the wealth and prosperity of the Hindus, especially of their business castes of Lalas or Banias, as well as their priestly races.

In the Gurdawara, we lodged in a far more spacious and superior accommodation, so some of my class fellows had shifted their charpies and beddings over there from the centre of the town where they used to live happily with their parents.. Now they were studying in an exclusively quiet and delightful environment and on top that they got free tuition. We used to study not only inside, but also on the canal embankment, as well as in the fields and orchards. In all seasons whether spring, winter, summer or autumn; there was always something different to look forward. There was also freshness and fragrance of varieties of the crops, fruits, flowers and vegetables. The countryside blazed with carpets of purple, orange, yellow, pink, red and pure white flowers and the atmosphere filled with delicate fragrance which kept us fresh and smiling. We trailed the area early in the mornings (before going to school) and late in the afternoons (before sunset). We strolled miles deep in the wilderness, not too close to each other, but some distance apart. However we did a bit of pirating as well, but in a very innocent and subtle way; and we were well fed with fresh fruit and delicious raw vegetables. We also topped the list in every subject in the school and no-one could beat us.

On one fateful pleasant spring evening a farmer who was maintaining surveillance over his orchards, shouted across the fields and had drawn our attention from the far side of the farmhouse in that remote area, "All of you come quickly and have Biryani, it is very delicious." The farmer yelled waving his arm in the air. We were in his orchard picking up some fruit, hidden under the umbrella of fruit laden trees. One or two amongst us who got allured without thinking any consequences soon were made 'Cockerel' and admonished, while the other two or three started sprinting for their safety. 'Cockerel' formation is a kind of physical punishment and very humiliating. The offender is forced to bend on knees, with head down and bottom up; and has to hold each ear with the same side hand by stretching one's arm across the belly. The victim can receive flogging with a baton or slippers or just shudders for few minutes or more. Apparently this is a common practice in schools in India and Pakistan. However we had always used our skills how, when and where to encroach! Anyway the farmers could hardly compete with us in our wild racing. Miles of area came under our domain and we had full freedom to prowl, but not to trample. Together we swam in the canal, caught fish, performed wrestling, played football and Kabaddi. We even used to study Kamasutra sneaked from the bedroom. That was on top of laughing, joking and singing and of course on top of tops of our list was reading the books and studying.

To me the Gurdawara became like the Tower Of London, the canal bridge like Tower Bridge, the embankment of the canal, like Oxford and Cambridge, the fields and orchards like Kew Gardens. All my elder brothers and sister had married in their teens and had their independent family lives. However my middle brother Sarwer, who got a job in the nearby irrigation department, was lodging in the Gurdawara with his wife Mumtaz. She was very brilliant and had looked after the empty house very well and somehow managed to cook fresh meals every day. At that moment the supply of fire logs or wood seemed to be in a short supply and scanty. Sometimes I had collected twigs from the wild bush and trees in the nearby fields, sometimes we managed to buy normal supplies of fire wood from the market, sometimes it came from the farm in the village, which is about two miles away. However infrequently I used to pick up animal dung from the water buffaloes and cows, while they prowled on the embankment returning from their farms and heading to their homes. The farmers used to take them to the farms early in the mornings for grazing all day in the farm lands and bring them back for security reasons and for milking in the mornings and in the evenings. I used to wait and rush with other kids to snatch the dung before it fell on the ground from the large intestine of the beast. I usually used to win the hurdle race and can still feel the warmth and softness of the wet fuel being excreted and used to hold it in tact on my palm before it fell on the soil.

The Gurdawara had a gigantic wooden gate to secure the premises, but we decided to erect a modest brick wall to secure the house, where we lodged. There were plenty of bricks and debris lying in the vast dusty yard next to the western perimeter of the high wall and the lofty trees; they had lain there since the Sikhs had abandoned it. However while clearing the debris and picking up the bricks, the builders noticed the monster. It was a summer morning, the sun was shining as usual like a silver disc,; and the temperature was already rising to 40C.Suddenly the cobra appeared from beneath the debris of the bricks. It started creeping up and curling like a rope with its head in the air. The beast was over nine feet tall with pitch black and grey dabble-back and white chesty front. Its circumference was of over 5 inches radius and body was made of beefy and scaly flesh like a shark; its red tongue with forks flipped and fluttered like a drone. It had shiny, piercing and beady eyes which flashed like lightening. It appeared as if an off spring of a buffalo as its black and white eyes stunned like a bull. It had hidden its venomous fangs and teeth under its shrunken hood. It had been startled by the builders while they were clearing the rubble and picking up the bricks. The beast was relaxing in his lair or hole just like most cold blooded creatures do, but that time someone had disturbed his majesty The King Cobra! He rushed out in great fury and agony, gliding and sliding over the rubble, but was intercepted by the builders. They had tried to kill the monster with their shovels and bricks; but it sneaked and curled back to the furrow and prepared for the counter attack.. The cobra was too fast and shrewd. He rushed back to the hole for protection, sought sanctuary and crammed in the shelter; thus was successful as the builders could not attack him anymore. That retreat could be for tactical reasons, just like an army does on the battle field. I was standing next to the builders gazing, but stayed behind the second line of defence and ready to sprint. The builders persevered to clear the rubble, under red alert, but unable to dislodge The King from its fort. We could easily hear him hissing and observe his glittering eyes. They toiled to shovel him out, but the lair was too narrow and deep; thus risky and scary to go overhead.

While fighting a losing battle one of the builders got a sudden idea how to take him out in the open battle field and that was 'Smoke it out'. Therefore some rags and papers were scrounged and set alight on top of the hide out. Within minutes, the monster shot out like a arrow from his stronghold. It was a crackling dramatic and frightening moment. First it scrambled and clambered on top of the heap of bricks and debris, but found himself besieged and cornered by the humans. Consequently it became desperately furious and ready for a dual. He curled up his tail with great agility and stood erect on his flexible spine; exactly like a wrestler would stand, ready to grab and topple the opponent in the arena. It had appeared like a menacing monster and soared doggedly sweltering and swollen and ready to swoop. The beast stood straight on its folded tail like the thorny, bare and pulpy green-stem of a cactus bush which thrives in the desert. It sprang up like a rocket on ignition, blazing to be fired from the launching pad to the orbit, while a count of ten to one is in process. He was an imposing and utterly uncompromising figure. It fluttered and spluttered its red tongue, twitched and glared its beady and silvery eyes, wriggled and waggled its tail; now his hood was fully dilated and spread just like an umbrella and swollen like a balloon. He was swinging and oscillating his neck sideways and front to back, spitting his venom in extreme vengeance on the Super Monsters (humans) . His eyes were twitching like flashing bulbs and his furious body was soaring and towering. However the builders had kept their nerves, stayed cool and gone on the offensive; before he could pounce upon them. In the skirmish that ensued they did reflect and frisk back without wasting any crucial moment. As I watched the real drama with the beast, my own heart was drumming fast and the soil under my feet was slipping. But I was thrilled to stare at the cobra as well as at the brave builders and waited in the second line of defence in readiness to sprint at any fraction of a second notice, if emergency arose.

The builders had held spades in their hands as well as the bricks. They were taking a great risk and without considering any fatal consequences. The soil continued shuddering under my feet while I shuffled and shivered. The builders were brave enough or perhaps insensitive to the dangers and endeavoured to keep up their nerves and fought back from their defensive positions; but were ready for their flight if necessary. It was a question of 'do or die'. The King Cobra was boisterous and buzzing for the assault. He was not a coward and had put up a brave face in front of the lethal enemy..It had the capability to cruise faster than a racing horse or near to fourteen miles per hour. The flipping red flame of his tongue, the glitter in his eyes and his body slithering movements had created fear in every one's mind. One of the builders was quick enough to land a blow with a brick and the other thumped him with the shovel. In the midst of blows and shrills, the monster was turned into a heap. It fell and curled up, but still slithered and wriggled. Its hood still rose and slump. It finally had shrunk and sunk into the oblivion after some shrivels. Although it lay dead now on the rubble, but its tail continued to wiggle and waggle for few more minutes. "Who can kill this Super Monster?" Whispered the shrewish monster (Cobra) while still sway its tail to the last breath.

News about the death of king-cobra spread like wild fire in the ancient town and spectators rushed for the pilgrimage to the temple. The onlookers were completely stunned and the scene was awe-inspiring; and the humans were still on their guards. It was beyond imagination and rare sight in one's life. Only two nights ago, my class mate Nur and his younger brother Din were startled, descending down the dusty rutted track from their home located in the centre of the old town. They normally used to come after the sunset, after having their dinner. We used to study together under the lantern light by using Kerocene oil. The Gurdawara was located between the Hindu Temple and the canal; and in the middle was the ancient shrine of a Muslim mystic which was situated on the edge of the barren or ghost side of the mound or in a no man's land... The shrine was few hundred years old and appeared to be decaying and crumbling. It was made of small bricks and clump of wild bush and thorny semi desert trees climbed within and around it. It appeared a scary and an eerie place. Only six months ago this shrine was hit by a fierce crackle of lightening and as a consequence some cracks had shown in the dome. However I am not surprised that some serpents and cobras had sheltered there at that time and that might had been one cause of the lightening, especially because the lightening likes the dark colour; this is commonly believed in that part of the world any way. The dusty steep and narrow track ran from the Hindu Temple, sprawled over the mound, down to the moat and the fields, under the trees and then to the Gurdawara. It was near to the shrine that my mate and his brother encountered the frightening and weird noises. They heard a fast moving beast, tumbling and tossing the pebbles; hissing and rustling through the thorny wild bush on the barren edge. They are so startled in the pitch silent dark that they perceived some flares and flashes of some glowing eyes. The ancient mound was shrouded in blanket of darkness and intense stillness had prevailed. Both of them were wailing and shrieking at the wilderness, while fleeing as fast as they could; they had no time to think, just sprint, sprint and sprint down the slope of the steep side of the mound and under the shadowy clumps of trees.

That ghostly incident had happened while I was having a relaxed stroll and chatter in the main yard of the Gurdawara with my school mate Khushi. We got startled on hearing the momentous wails and wild shrieks of our friends somewhere on the edge of the mound which was then covered in utter breathless wintry dark. Normally they used to sing or laugh while trotting down towards us, but that time something strange had happened. That scenario gave us the impression as if someone was strangling them with a great ferocity and they were choking. However that kind of noise I normally used to hear when the police were interrogating the robbers at the nearby investigation branch near to our previous house. While we were wondering about their plight, they soon entered the main mighty door, huffing and puffing; it would appear that they had run just like wild drakes. As soon as they entered the gate, we immediately fired the question, "Why were you crying and howling?" They recounted, "In the cluster of dry and wild bush, there was a peculiar ghostly rustling and hissing sound causing lot of disturbance, the pebbles and debris were tumbling and tossing; it appeared to us as if some giant was slithering and sliding. We could see some lights and flames radiating from the bush. It was an alarming and a scary movement, especially the mix of eerie noises. In the biting dark and sinking quietness, there was no one to help us and we had to make uncontrolled wailing to scare the beasts off or to forget the danger ourselves and run for our life as fast as we could." They responded.

In hindsight, I hazard to guess that they were the King Cobras mating; they do so with great ferocity and zeal, especially under the blanket of darkness and cinder would rise from the burning bush, that's how the primitive cave men would have ignited their fires or their logs.

While startled the Cobras would spray their hidden venom on the victims and make them blind; It can appear to be dead, but not in reality. It has powerful muscles, although the mouth looks small, but flexible muscles make it far bigger. The African python is the biggest of all, it can kill antelope and can swallow it as a whole due to its flexible muscles; everything gets dissolved in the body including horns. This python would not need food for the whole year afterwards.

Cobras can be over 4 meters long, very venomous, pairs fight to catch victims, just like wrestlers. The male cobra can taste the air to find the female snake for mating. They jerk and buck the body at the time of mating; and they remain together for several hours. They take 6-8 weeks to hatch. Cobra can bite while the baby is still in the shell. A tiny drop of poison can kill an animal. Its venom is normally pink. Some snakes give birth to their off-spring like Anaconda the eggs are hatched in the stomach. They are powerful swimmers and can settle in any environment, including the sea. They can absorb oxygen from sea water. They come out every quarter of an hour to have a gulp of air. They are very poisonous and can kill instantly. Because of absence of limbs, they conquer any environment and look very graceful. They eat mice normally.

Personally I have never seen cobras mating, but in my humble observations, the dogs prolong their mating for hours and followed by the donkeys who continue the strokes for countless times and with countless rises and falls, during their mating activity. Thus it appears to me that the cobras top the list!

Just a few months ago one of my nephews called Nazir and who is a farmer described to me another breath-taking, dramatic and overwhelming real time startling story, concerning his personal encounter with a cobra. He was watering his fields in the night time of one odd moist summer day when the dramatic incident happened.. It was deafening dark in the midst of the night and quite hot. What happens is that the farmer has to breach a foot gap in the mud barrier of narrow sub-channel which cruises through the fields and prior to that the water is drawn from the main canal through the distribution viaduct and channels to divert water to his fields and all the farmers have to follow a rota system to irrigate their fields. The time for water usage is dependent on one's cultivated land. The water in the distribution channel becomes less and less as it becomes more and more remote from the main canal. This is the time when serpents and snakes become active and slither out of their lairs; they are desperate to have some fresh air and drink some water as well hunt for fresh meals for stockpiling in their stomach for rest of the year, as they hibernate or sleep for about nine months. After all they are cold blooded, but not in blazing summer of India. Unfortunately the farmers do not wear any hats against the glaring sun or wear any Wellington shoes to protect their legs and feet against muddy waters, thorns and poisonous snakes.

He narrated, "I was dredging alone on the narrow flat pathway built on the barrier of the water channel and far away from the village in the wild countryside. In the night time I try to carry a torch in the middle of the alluvial fields laden with crops, especially at the time of irrigation. I also carry a long stick (Lathi) just in case of an encounter with a robber or any dangerous animals like stray dogs or wolves. The robbers often lie low in the fields and take away the cattle from the barn in the middle of deep dark, just before dawn when the farmers have fast and sweet sleep. While treading I was concentrating on the flow of water from one field to the other and looking forward to a healthy harvest and how much money to earn for the family. Then suddenly something dark stood in front of me and fiercely strangled my legs within a fraction of a second and I was about to tumble on the ground. It seemed to me as if I was fighting a throttling dual with a mighty wrestler who always puffs and hisses. My stick and torch fell on the ground. I was taken aback by an utter surprise ambush of the beast and had to fight a dual. He was just towering in front of me and I was under his shackles. I did not lose nerves. I jostled and shrugged. I moved my legs and feet with great thrift and thrust. We farmers are used to tackling the wild beasts like bulls, buffaloes and cows; even goats, donkeys and horses. But this was unique attack and completely unusual. Others do not strangle you or bite at the same time. It was lucky that I did not notice his red tongue buzzing in the dark. I did not worry about being strangled, but my main concern was being poisoned or bitten and of course having been swallowed alive like a buck; then there was no chance of survival. They normally shelter in the graveyard or relax under the umbrella of thorny bush nearby or hide in some deep holes in the embankments of the canal or viaducts or barriers. It was question of my life and my wife and kids. I did not even know what was happening to me and why?. I simply had no time to think and I fought like a wilder beast and eventually managed to disentangle myself and hopped faster than a baffled ostrich towards the safety of my barn. I slurped and splashed in the irrigated fields like an agitated bull. In the struggle I lost my shoes in the water and did not look back just in case the beast was chasing me. Luckily I was not bitten or poisoned, but that terrible nightmare still overshadows me and I have lost confidence and carry a mate with me for such tasks." He reiterated, "Nearly all the farmers have been bitten by the snakes at least once or twice of their lifetimes while working in the fields especially at the time of irrigation in summer as well as at the harvest time. People have sometimes witnessed them drinking milk from the nipples of buffaloes and cows early in the mornings". He continued with a subdued smile and with twists in his bushy moustaches. I congratulated him for being brave and still living without any snake bites.

But the unique graphic image of King Cobra is always with me since we had the encounter with it in the Gurdawara, I can still gaze at it standing proud and arrogant, fully dilated and dauntlessly erect; swaying and fixed on its tail, fluttering its red tongue like a buzzing blaze rising from the glass furnace; boisterous and brave, raging on the rubble. However I am not sure about its gender; whether it was a male or a female? It is with me all the time whether I am cruising over the Mount Everest, Nanga or K2; whether I stroll over 'The Ice Cap' or have cup of tea over The Iceberg' or sleep in 'The Gher' in the Gobi Desert or climb 'The Pyramids' or trail the foot prints of Moses in the Sinai Desert or hike up 'The Great Wall. It is with me in full grace and glare. It is difficult to say whether it is one of the ancient gods, who sacrifices its life for me and who has been waiting for me for such a long time or it is just an illusion!; but I can state in full confidence and with my hands on my heart that so many calamities fall on me and with such a great intensity and frequency that everything else now seems a 'Peanut'.

It is a common belief in the Indian pagan culture that serpents can transform themselves into the form of the humans, cattle, flowers or birds or to whatever they desire; this is provided they can manage to survive over a hundred years. In our school the story of a weird wood cutter was very popular with all the kids at that time.. It was told about the old and frail woodcutter, who had collected lot of dry wood from the bush and trees, but was unable to carry the huge load to his house which was miles away. It was getting dark and cold. Suddenly he observed a donkey trotting towards him, without any harness. He paused near him and started braying and swaying. The woodcutter had put a rope round his neck and started loading him with all the twigs and logs. The donkey was only too happy to support the old woodcutter and helped him to transport that load to his hut. The wood-cutter was simply overjoyed and had brought some water and fodder for the exhausted donkey, but to his astonishment the donkey had instantly vanished from his view.

In the Indian subcontinent, the deadly bites of cobras, serpents or other snakes are so fearsome that in the pagan culture they revere them as gods. There are numerous ever popular romantic fantasies and thrillers, fables, films, songs and dramas relating to them. The snake worship as gods is an integral part of Hindu belief. The snake charmers and the snake products or medicine flourish in the culture; including the use of their poison in curing impotence and infertility. It is a religious ritual to feed the snakes with milk and meat. They also depict serpents or cobras as protectors of their wealth and their lives against evil and predators.

Most recently a gigantic cobra was trapped by the farmers in the wild bush area of River Chenab. It must be over seventeen feet tall and of colossal weight and girth. It was sighted in the border area of the provinces of Punjab and Kashmir and both provinces claimed its ownership. The professional staff from Lahore Zoo rushed to this arena and eight of its officials held the beast next to their belly- buttons and struggled to clutch it tight with their both arms and posed for the photographs for the media. It was well fed with the wild boar, rabbits, deer, goats or fish. It is alleged that that frequently it siphoned off milk from the buffaloes, cows and even goats. There was lot of excitement and interest shown at the national level. At the end it was decided to set the beast free in the jungle, which was its natural habitation; and it was gravely costly to maintain such a colossal beast in any zoo.

A similar but a romantic story also circulated amongst the teen-age boys and that had further flared up their tense emotions It described a beautiful young lass who was seen sitting alone cross- legged on the embankment of the canal bridge-head. She was described selling beautiful colourful fragrant flowers and exotic tropical juicy fruit. She was dressed in a very fine low neck red silk shirt, green shalwar and a black crinkled dopatta over her head. When someone approached her for some transaction, she instantly splashed in the roaring water and vanished away along with all her goods. At that time I always yearned to have such encounter, but in vain. However my dream was fulfilled while swimming deep in the Mediterranean, just off the coast of Beneden Beech in Spain. Four German girls, fresh buds or recently blossomed, pedal their two boats, cruising smilingly only inches away from me; rippling and uplifting my body and soul. They appeared fully unwrapped and totally exposed to natural forces; swinging and tossing like the cobras or perhaps like the bunch of red and yellow roses. Instead of floating and swimming, I begin sinking and dozing; I am still mesmerising and still dying.

One day when we were washing our clothes and having a shower in the Gurdawara, under the slosh of the well, instantly we observed a stranger entering the bathing area. He gave us the impression as if he was completely dizzy and in agony and could hardly walk as if suffering from a severe fever. He just crouched himself down on the cemented floor and asked us to bring a match box and a sharp knife or a blade. Apparently he had been bitten by the snake near his wrist, while he is cutting the grass or fodder in the adjoining fields or forest. He immediately carved a deep cut at the point of the bite and let it bleed .He had also tied up tightly the upper part of his lower arm (just before the elbow) with a string to slow the flow of the blood going towards the heart; then he had put a lighted match stick on his wound and sizzles the skin We stood gazing at him during all that activity and we are spellbound that he had recovered in matter of minutes and saved his own life. Again what an amazingly cool and bold man! I still remember him squatting on the floor and treating himself in the simplest native way.

While lodging in the previous house, I remember the bravery of my father as well. It was a hot and moist July day, the heavy downpour of Monsoon rain was gusting through the windows of our bedroom in the midst of lightning and thunder storm. My father tried to shut the windows, but could not shut one of them.

Momentarily he noticed a snake trapped between the window door and its ledge and swaying desperately to escape. He immediately came out of the bedroom and signals to me, "Can you run to Hameedan (my real aunt) and ask her to kill the snake. It is there." He pointed. It was just a sheer luck that my aunt was visiting the town to meet some relatives lodging nearby; she herself had lived in the village some two miles away in the countryside. She accompanied me by a brisk and confident trot and with a stick in her hand. She just smiled and laughed at my father's fear. She struck at the snake with a great ease and skill and disentangled it like a piece of rope. "Oh. What a brave lady! I knew she can do it." My father exclaimed with a smile and relief. She also smiled back and enlightened us that such incidents happen almost daily in the village. On another summer day my dad had asked his brother-in-law to kill some other snake which was climbing and creeping up the wall steadily and going towards the top of the flat roof. He must have come out of some crevice or a hole in the brick built wall.

My step auntie Zubaida, who was a resident of the town, was just the opposite of my real aunt Hameedan. She was on a visit to her parents who lodged in the Sarai next to the canal and the Gurdawara. It was Christmas Holidays period and kids were off from school. That time was nearly before dawn and the cool dark night was just fading away steadily with the glimpse of faint daylight and the birds had just started chirping in the trees and the cockerel had just aroused his first croaking and the buds had just started blossoming, when she had noticed the beast under her husband's charpie in the bedroom. She alerted her husband while he was fast asleep and snoring at a high pitch as if cutting a tree with an electric saw. She groped his left shoulder with a slight whisper in his ears, "Can you hear me. Please get up. I think there is a snake!" She startled. He immediately got up and grabbed his lathi (Wooden pole) and asked, "Where. Where. Where is the sssss—snake?' She was terribly embarrassed and smiled with her dopatta covering her chin. "I thought this was a snake". She responded. "You must know that snakes hibernate in winter and have complete rest in the shelters; they only come out in the hot summers for food and drink." He reiterated. "I only kept this lathi just in case if any robber sneaks in the house." He simply mumbled. "However I am upset now because I was having a close encounter with a beautiful woman and you interrupted me, unfortunately she must have gone by now." He giggled. I have a feeling that auntie Zubaida might be having a romantic dream as well, just like her husband. Otherwise how could she had confused the Lathi with the cobra? Even the kids like us were aware that snakes are cold-blooded and they relax for about eight months in their dens and manage to survive without eating and drinking. But these kind of subtle historical and actual amusing moments glow forever and make you smile and they are amusing and full of powerful sensuous memories. I personally like this innocent moment and it inspires me a lot and that's how I recollect auntie Zubaida and it makes me smile in my solitude.

However I do not blame auntie Zubaida for raising the false alarm and for her pre-emptive strike, only few months later a pitch black serpent had really glided through her bathroom's hole, but luckily there was no fatality and it just frisked away when an alarm was raised. The snake must be trying to prey on the well fed mice which normally used to scurry and scuttle in their house. Perhaps the mice themselves were taking shelter in the houses from the cobras and other fearful snakes which often slithered in the fields and were rampant in the wild bush territory. They normally have very sharp ears and disappear very quickly even after a faint whisper. However, recently the residents of the town had become terrified when a young school kid died of a snake bite, while playing hide and seek over and around the mighty Pepil tree in the Gurdawara. This gigantic tree had plenty of holes and burrows and its offshoots were spread in all directions. The poisonous snakes can easily crawl up the furrows or grooves of the stem and make nests over there. The young boy instantly fell to his death while climbing and this had frightened everybody. Normally snakes do not wish to encounter with the humans unless they appear to be threatening. These young boys were not aware about the extreme dangers of the deadly snake bites. When we used to walk on the embankment early in the summer mornings, we often used to observe footprints or signs of snakes' slithers and wriggles on the fine alluvial soil as well as top layer of their discarded dead skins; and they used to be all over the embankment, I think they used to come to the canal for drinking water on daily basis, not in the day time, but in the dark, especially earlier in the mornings just before dawn, when the cool breeze started blowing from the canal to the fields and bushes. Although we had lodged in the wild area infested with serpents and cobras, luckily, we did not suffer any unpleasant incident of snake bites. However when I ponder over those historical moments now, I really get startled with the thought of them and the chill goes down my spine.

I remember quite vividly a man in our neighbourhood who was in his fifties and lodged happily with his family. He used to sell cotton yarn and clothes to the remote villagers. He had fixed some racks on his pedal bicycle and used to load his bicycle with his goods. He would go from village to village and at the end of the day would normally sleep over there; and return home after weeks. In that way he had earned good fortune and had kept his family prosperous. However on one day we got shocked when we saw his dead swollen body. Apparently he had been bitten by a deadly poisonous snake while he was sleeping somewhere in the countryside. But his family were narrating that he was stung by a wasp. His body was completely swollen and appeared like a red brick. In Pakistani or Indian culture the snake bite is considered as a curse from God, the next in line are the bites from mad dogs. When someone is extremely angry or annoyed by someone, then the oppressed person would say, "I hope you are bitten by the snake or by the dog!" So such bites are extreme curses and punishments; although in my opinion this kind of tragedy could happen to anyone, just by sheer luck or coincidence. I can easily quote the terrible massacres at the time of partition just an epic one, although full of madness or cold bloodedness; it does not prove either party as warriors or heroes; in fact just the opposite. While living in the Gurdawara, one day I noticed a long queue of the orphans having been escorted by some men. They came to the Gurdawara for an overnight rest. They slept on the marble floor just like prisoners with bare minimum cotton sheets to sleep on. These were the orphans, a result of the terrible atrocities and slaughters of the refugees; they had lost their parents. Now those poor wretched boys hardly in their teens were being forced to go from town to town for begging and they were being escorted just like war prisoners and marshalled to walk in strict queues. I am certain they would have been sexually abused by their mentors, as well as given the physical and mental torture. They must walk scores of miles daily and their feet must be swollen and full of blisters. This infliction was in addition to the ruthless sufferings due to the tragic loss of their beloved parents. Thus for them pains and sufferings continued to multiply for rest of their lives and who was responsible and who would have been punished?. Those generations were not only physically broken, but more than that their subconscious mind was completely shattered and torn and by who and why? That was simply an act of barbarism.

I might have moaned and groaned so far and might have depressed many sympathizers, but now let us meet a person who had given lot of healing and happiness to all types of sufferers. He was very charismatic and unique and he was a magnificently good looking Pathan and glorified by his bushy and tangled moustaches. His beaming cheeks, shining eyes and glittering teeth made a nice magical triangle. He wore baggy cotton trousers, a long loose shirt and a pair of Peshawari Chapels (open toes leather shoes). He plumped comfortably on a wide cotton spread sheet along with his hidden players. He perched a smart turban over his head, wrapped round a Turkish gold cap; with one end of the turban pierced to the sky and the other end slithered down his shoulders and touched the ground at his back. He used to display some miracle, performing healing medicines, circled round in front of him, along with straw round caskets. He had a cheeky glowing and confident face and enchanted his onlookers by piercing into their eyes with rosy smiles and appeared to be chatting to each one directly in a compassionate manner. He also had his musical instrument called 'Bean' on his side and a long thin rod to point at his medicines. He used to squat crossed -legged on a cotton bed sheet along the pavement and near the edge of the road between our school and the old wall of the ancient town. He was 'Road Side Medicine Seller', who used to manufacture medical products from the snakes, especially from the cobras. He had attracted lot of adult audience and also school kids like us. We enjoyed his way of demonstration, expression and delivery of his dialogues and that was an amazing and a charming gathering and is still unforgettable and still ever glaring. He made everyone in the audience laugh and smile; although the school kids were forbidden to attend his sessions, but we could not help and he was aware that we were breaking the rules and therefore deliberately ignored us; and we had become a vital part of the bewildered audience almost on daily basis. While I recollect that magical gathering and I think from the depth of my mind that he had adored our company and the way we smiled and giggled. His presence as a charismatic person and his delivery of dialogues still amuse me and make me laugh without any restraints while sitting on my own or in a group. Repeating his dialogues in his own accent and gestures are really exhilarating and mesmerising.

He is not only easily compatible with Sir David Attenborough in his scientific narrations about the wild life, but he was also a snake-charmer, client charmer, a salesman as well as the manufacturer of the medicines. He claimed authenticity of his products by fiercely stroking his thighs with his palm and winding his whiskers and I must quote to make everyone laugh and laugh and laugh forever. This is a bit of the healing cream on top of the wounds which I have suffered so far. He asserted to his adult audience that his products could cure impotence, barrenness, revitalise youth, cure blood pressure and keeps one's nerves cool. He used to squat straight on his buttocks and went deep into the emotions and the mind of his audience; and declared, "These products can easily surpass Viagra, and you will feel it as well as she will! After taking these tablets, you will start thrusting and hissing just like a steam engine and people will hear the Ton, Ton,

Ton of the Big Ben. My dear friends the school kids can mistake it as the final chime of the school bell for breaking off their class. The Sunday congregation can misjudge it as the peel of the church bell when the zealot jerks the rope in the tower; or perhaps the faithful can mix it up with the echo of the wakeup call of the muezzin for the morning prayers spiralling from top of the minaret."

He further used to claim by holding his forearm with a tightly clenched fist pointing towards the sky and with his elbow fixed vertically against his thighs,' The tool will become like this, like this...; dilate and sway like a cobra; hiss, sizzle and flutter. The Clinker and cinder will fly everywhere billowing smoke on the horizon!' He declared with his beaming cheeks.

He used to keep different sizes and pedigree of the snakes in the round straw- caskets of various sizes; that was depending upon the size of each snake.. He used to arouse the snakes from their sleep by removing the lid one by one from each casket and by playing the live tunes through his Bean. He played the music in an erratic manner and in a spiral of peculiar rhythms and tunes. He kept on rotating the Bean sometimes close to the beast, sometimes away and kept on doing it till the beast got fully aroused and started hissing and eventually shot out the neck from the casket. Each time each player or participant would dilate, sway, flutter, sizzle, hiss, puff and rise out of the casket. It had a magical, enchanting and captivating impact on the audience, especially on the village folks. That was the time when the congregation would have stopped gazing at the snake charmer and got their eyes fixed on the beasts. That was the most crucial moment when the desperate customers would dig out money from their pockets to buy the amazing snake products. That was the moment when the prospective buyers would have raised their arms in the air with money clutched in their fists. But the medicine seller would beckon them with his long bamboo stick, which he normally continued to use for demonstration of his players and his products, to be patient and wait till the end of whole of the demonstration. For each category he would have given full details of each beast and the medicine he extracted from them; and their healing impact on the patients. The player who was demonstrated at the end was the 'flying snake' and that used to happen after a great suspense and explanation.. "It flies straight on to your forehead and a single bite can kill instantly; it does not allow you to have a second breath if it strikes..." He used to proclaim.

The road side medicine seller was highly an organised person and had planned a successful business enterprise. He used to exhibit and spread his mobile shop on the ground just before our school was about to close for the day, so he could grab a good vibrant crowd, although youngsters were forbidden to attend such gatherings. That was also the moment when the local shop keepers would have achieved their maximum turnovers and also the village farmers were returning home after selling their cash crops like vegetable, fruit and grains. However it is difficult to speculate how he had managed to shift around with his wild creatures and products from place to place; it must be by using a truck or the wagon or perhaps on top of the roof of the bus especially reserved for him... However, at the end of his each unique charismatic and emotive narration, he used to resolutely alert his gathering and emphasized. "Never ever cuddle or love the offspring of a serpent, not even by a mistake; it does not matter how much meat and milk you have fed to them!" He used to warn in absolutely clear and loud words. However that magical Pathan and The King Cobra always glow in my mind just like a brilliantly glaring shooting meteorite or like the brightest evening star and keep me enchanted and enlightened forever.

Chapter VIII

School Match

I was still dwelling in the Gurdawara and hardly eleven years old, when I experienced another and unpredictable twist of life. I remember quite vividly that I was in the fifth year of my school and stood top of my class. My teachers always admired my results and indeed this was well known in the ancient town as it happened year after year.. Our school was located next to the bus station and opposite to the civil hospital and they were both separated by metalled roads. At that time I still had distinct memories of grotesque communal violence at the time of partition, especially the cruel massacre of my uncles and as a result the showers of tears trickling down the cheeks of my cousins and consequently their incessant sighs and screams; as well as the miseries of my aunts. At that time the wounds of the tragic death of my father as well as of my paternal grandmother were still fresh in my mind and were haunting me day and night. I still could not believe that my maternal grandmother had also died even before them in the refugee concentration camps after suffering trauma of more than five months at the hands of secular Hindus and Sikhs; and still I keep on yearning to see her and look forward to cuddle her. At that time I still vividly visualised the overflowing refugee caravans of Hindus and Sikhs crawling like ants on foot and bull carts. While they swarmed towards Bharat they were being fiercely guarded by the army as if they were cattle. At that painful time I was still suffering from the shock of Hajjo having been married at such a tender age. I was still suffering from the hallucinations and nightmares because of those sad events. My nerves were so wrecked that even when any cat or a fox used to chew the food garbage or bones from the tin dustbins of our house in the stillness and quietness of the dark night and made an eerie noise; it made me scared, so much that I used to shiver and shudder like a fish out of water. However it cannot be ruled out that some cobras or serpents were squelching on some scurrying and scuttling rats or hopping rabbits in this wilderness. But somehow I used to get startled and this triggered off shivering automatically; I tried to control my shudders and shakes, but I could not manage. While I am recording my personal emotions and my own experiences and sufferings, my thoughts glide towards the countless Iraqis, Palestinians, Kashmiries and the Afghans and many more people in Africa and Asia at large who have been suffering at the hands of the modern and super powers for decades. These victims come to mind who have been bombarded from the skies, from the sea and from the land not only by the super armies, but also because of their own feuds between different factions committing atrocities on each other for winning power and glory. How much extremely grotesque and pitiable psychological trauma and scars must have been inflicted on these wretched people.

It was just the beginning of the spring -season, the weather was cool and crispy. The dusty school yard was blazing with colourful roses, crocuses and jasmine flowers. The silvery disc of the sun was glaring in the light blue sky overhead. The atmosphere was laden with bright colours of the fresh satsumas, oranges, sugarcanes and a great variety of other exotic fruit and vegetables. The Wooden trolleys, pulled by the donkeys, loaded with different commodities were dotted on both edges of the metalled roads; all along the outskirts of the school and the bus station. There was a great blend of donkey-carts, hand-carts, as well as mobile stalls contiguous to the main shops in the bazaar. The travelling to and from the nearby villages was done mainly through the horse-coaches (tongas), but normally at that time most of the villagers preferred to trot on foot to their destinations as a matter of daily routine. There used to be a great bustle of the shoppers from the surrounding villages as well as from the local residents including males and females. I desperately miss those reminiscing and pleasant crowded moments especially my youth when I used to be carefree. Luckily there were hardly any cars or rickshaws, so the environment was pollution free and without any fumes being emitted from the motor vehicles. Even the buses and trucks were in scanty supply. The environment was simple, clean and friendly. Everyone in the small town knew each other very well and could reach each local destination within short span of time.

At that time Pakistan was less than five years old and there was shortage of public transport, especially buses. We were waiting at the bus station along with other school mates as well as the football team of our school. The match was scheduled to take place in the other town called Okara, located some sixteen miles away from our town. My elder brother Aslam was the captain of our football team. There were quite a few of our school fans who wanted to travel with the team to watch the exciting match, most of them were of higher classes. It would appear that me and my friend Najam, who used to lodge in the great Sarai, had also got carried away and we had decided ourselves to travel to Okara to watch the match and would have returned back home by the same evening. However due to the shortage of buses, the seats for the team were pre booked in advance from the starting station which was about thirteen miles away from us and next to the Indian border. This was done on the payment of extra money to make sure the team members would definitely get in the bus and reach the destination at the scheduled time. As soon as the bus arrived the team got in the bus nice and easy as well as some members of the public and some school spectators too. Some other buses also followed that bus which had carried away our team, but Najam and I could not get in, part of the reason was that the bus conductor was picking up only adult passengers so that he could charge full fares; both of us came under children's half rate fares. There was no queue system, so the most sturdy, tall and strong men from the rural areas just rushed in the buses along with their luggage, perhaps some of them were travelling for the first time in their lives and for them there was excitement and exhilaration to enter the bus. So we had been ignored constantly over and over again and again and had been overrun by more aggressive and powerful commuters. However as a result of that struggle quite a bit of our time had slipped away unnoticed from us, perhaps we were too much involved in the effort to get in the next available bus at least, if not the next and then the next. We never gave up and kept on trying to get in the next coming bus and in each instance we had rushed in the front of the mob, but each time we were unsuccessful. However after about two hours we managed to enter the bus and eventually reached the destination, but it was almost late in the afternoon and it was getting dark already.

After reaching our destination, we had to stagger and sprint to reach the playground where match was taking place. There was one more trap for us we did not know where the match was taking place. We had to ask the public about the venue and there was lot of confusion and conflict in the information provided to us as well as lack of direction from the passers-by; therefore we wasted some more time. Most of the people were not aware or concerned about such a trivial match. By the time the sun was looking orange and had half dipped down the earth's curvature; the redness on the horizon was being overshadowed by sea of greyish darkness. Because of substantial lapse of time the team had already returned after playing the match and we were so disappointed and found ourselves stranded in the dark-ghostly unknown place. We started walking back groping and floundering towards the bus station. By that time it was pitch dark and there were no street lights in the town, but we arrived safely at the bus station.. After reaching there we found the bus station completely deserted, there were no buses arriving or leaving the bus stand and there were only five or six commuters left, one of them was a woman clad in a Burkha. We all waited anxiously for the arrival of the bus, but nothing turned up and with the passage of time the situation was becoming more and more grim and tense. The waiting commuters also kept on slipping away quietly without worrying about our welfare and at the end only two of us were left behind sitting like owls in the dark, but still hoping to see the bus any second, our eyes were staring constantly on the entrance of the parking shed. At that time there was only one bus company running those scanty services; I have a feeling the previous proprietors were either Hindus or Sikhs. The repair workshop-sheds which were located on the outer edge of the dusty parameter of the bus station looked like ghosts. We kept on prowling under the high parking sheds to keep ourselves slightly warm as the temperature was coming down almost to the freezing point now and dark chill had started biting our skins. Normally at this time in our homes, we would be sitting comfy and snug in our quilts and around the cosy heat of glowing hearth of logs-fire. We were gazing at the flickering stars and were yearning for a bus to come and take us to our sweet home. Back in our home, we hardly ventured out in the dark, whether in a winter or a summer. The only exception would have been to see the live circus or theatres for which our whole family would go or at least I would go with my brothers; never alone or with friends only. There was no one from the management staff available at the bus station and not even a caretaker was present to support us. It is also quite possible that the bus driver had driven the bus to his house for overnight parking which would have had saved his travelling time to reach the bus station early in the morning. We completely forgot the match, even forgot about ourselves; we worried about our parents and continuously cursed ourselves for putting our parents in grotesque anxiety and anguish. What would they be thinking about our disappearance because we did not inform anybody about our intention to watch the match in Okara? However we never lost our nerve and kept cool and were hopeful all the time that bus was going to turn up at any moment.

Deep in our mind and in the icy stillness we were asking ourselves, "How will we travel home. Will there be any bus and how quick. Can anybody tell us, give us any clue or help us, tell someone back home". At that moment of the cold dark night all the shops had been shut and every single soul was tucked in their charpies and bedrooms. There was no traffic or any pedestrian moving around, not even a police patrol. While we were sunk in such doom and gloom and stranded like straws in the sea of loneliness, there turned up a man with a blossomed face and with a plume over his head. He was alone and must be in his early twenties, fair skinned like a Kashmiri Brahman and boyish looking. He could have been a businessman or at least a young noble man. He seemed to be a sophisticated and well enlightened. He was wearing western dress, with moustaches and well combed hair. He did not approach us instantly, but he stared at us from a distance and stood still for some minutes and watched us. We had thought that he was waiting for someone, but then slowly he started creeping towards us. We were deadly scared and expected the worse. This was our first experience of meeting a stranger in the dark alien land. It is quite possible that someone had knocked at his door and informed him about us or perhaps he was enjoying a quiet walk after his late dinner. It is also a possibility that initially he might have perceived us as ghosts plumped and crouching in the waiting desks.

As soon as he approached near us, he questioned us politely, "What the hell are you both doing alone so late at the bus stand in the darkness of the icy night? It is so cold. Who are you, how and why? There would be no more buses so late in the night, you can see there is no one here to travel; they will commence about 8 AM again, but there is no guarantee that they would come. At the moment I cannot see any bus parked neither over here, nor in the workshop sheds. How can you sit whole night like this?" He continued. "Come with me, you can stay in our house and leave first thing in the morning, otherwise both of you will freeze to death or perhaps go sick." He escorted us to his house which was located at a distance of about five minutes' walk. We ventured reluctantly for the fear of the unknown. As soon as we entered his house and were settling down in the separate charpies, his mum entered our room and she could not believe her eyes; she was simply stunned and amazed. She stared and stared; interrogated us about our whereabouts and the reason for being stranded. We explained to her in full details and she was very concerned about our health and safety as well as she became anguished about our parents and teachers. She gave us a glass of milk each to drink as this was perhaps too late to cook food. As a matter of compassion and hospitality she did ask if we were hungry, but reluctantly and blushingly, we assured her that we had already eaten and not hungry at all; it was clearly a deliberate lie from us, we did not want to trouble them anymore.

However they provided us with nice quilts and comfy beds; she made sure that both of us were tucked in nicely, but her eyes were showing great concern about the tension back home. She asked us, "Did your parents know that you have come to Okara to watch the football match?" "No, they did not", was the reply. She asked us to secure our bedroom by putting the sling from inside "Just sleep without any fear, I will personally knock at your door and wake you up first thing in the morning, then after breakfast, you can go home, hopefully there will be some buses running." She reassured us before shutting the door and departing along with her son. We got far better accommodation than at our own home and were soon fast asleep, but we were still anguished about our parents and worried about the punishment from the teachers... We were wondering what would happen tomorrow; how our teachers and parents would treat us and how our school mates would react! With these startling and dreadful thoughts, we steadily dozed off.

After a relatively comfortable sleep, we said goodbye and cheerio to our lovely and compassionate hosts with bundle of thanks and got the first available bus and reached our home town about ten in the morning. All classes were in full swing and everyone would have been wondering what might have happened to us and must had been waiting for the news, especially our parents. Both of us went straight to our school, our hearts were beating fast and legs were shaking. We staggered like wet cats. Our class was taking place outside in the dusty yard. The teacher and the students became excited on our first sight as we approached slowly to our class. The students were sitting on the jute rectangular mats as usual alongside of other classes, enjoying the bright sunshine and their lessons. All our class mates and the teacher started staring at us as we approached slowly and there was pin-drop silence. All other teachers and students attention was also momentarily diverted towards us and lessons were interrupted and came to a halt for a fraction of a second. Their faces were inquisitive, but glowing with glee. Our class teacher named Allah Rassie was smiling and felt relieved, we were staring at them and they were also gazing at us in a quiet manner and for a fraction of a second everything looked stationary and awe-inspiring. We pretended as if nothing had happened and took our seats without disturbing the class as normal after saying 'Good morning with our eyes fixed on the ground'. Our teacher beckoned us to come near to him and hold ears (become cockerel).This posture is called cockerel because as a result of it the face and ears become red and glow like a cockerel face. Cockerel punishment is given to most serious offenders in the school. It is quite embarrassing and humiliating means of punishment given in front of whole of the class or school mates. One has to crouch and kneel on the knees, take both arms underneath the belly and hold the ears with the head down and bottom up. It is quite stretching and strenuous; within minutes the legs start shuddering and swaying; the blood circulation is reversed, going from the bottom to the head. Only way to relax is to alternate weight pressure from one leg to the other leg and keep on swaying; but still remain stooped and must not release the ears. If the impact is breached, then flogging and lashes would begin in earnest. Sometimes an extra weight is added on the back of the victim by asking someone to sit on the back or sometimes flogging begins while in cockerel position. In my opinion, this kind of punishment is not justified and must not be practised at least up to the school level.

Allah Rassie literally means' A man who is assigned by the Divine to put the astray person on the right path.' Master (teacher) Allah Rassie was a very unique character. He had a dark brown, grim face with greyish white head, stony neck and was a man without any compassion. Although he used to wear the well pressed traditional baggy shalwar and qamees, but on top always wore English jackets. We had hardly seen him smiling, but he was a man of high calibre and indeed he was a noble person. He was of less than average height and one could only see his teeth when he was grinning or grinding them at the time of lashing with his baton or bashing with his leather shoes. He normally wore a fine pure white but flared muslin turban over his head and walked like a peacock. One end of his turban was rising in the air like a TV tower which was tightly wrapped round a Turkish base hat and the other end sprawled down his back between his shoulders .He lived in the nearby village on a farm a few miles away and travelled via the canal embankment on his well-maintained Raleigh bicycle. A school chaprassi (attendant) used to wait at the main entrance of the school to take his bike for parking while he would walk like a big boss to the class. Everyone stared at him when he used to arrive and our class used to welcome him by standing quietly. At that time his son was a final year medical student at King Edward Medical College Lahore and preparations were in hand to send him to England for further education. His main source of income came from his huge farming acreage, but he was the most disciplined, respected and a dedicated teacher as well.

While both of us were in a cockerel position next to him and the whole of the class was gazing in awe, chill went through my spine for fear of the worst, especially flogging, lashing or slapping. However our conscience was clear and we knew that we were not guilty and it was just an unfortunate mishap. After few minutes of pin drop silence the interrogation began, 'Where did you go without informing your parents and where have you been overnight?.They have been sleepless and panicky; and the police was put on high alert. They had sent errands all over the surrounding villages to ask any school students living there if they had seen you people anywhere. They knocked at each door of the town to find if you might be playing somewhere over there. They searched all over the winding streets in the dark freezing cold beating drums and asking the public if anybody has seen you; even the prayers were broadcast from the minarets. They were in a frenzied hysteria and making everyone aware about their dilemma'. He explained firmly and fairly. My legs were staggering and almost wobbly and I was ready to plump on the ground off balance. My heart started fluttering faster and tears were tipping and dripping quietly on the mat. Luckily our worst fears did not prove to be true. There were no lashes; his baton, shoes or hands were kept away. He was convinced even before our arrival to the class that some kind of misadventure have had taken place. He asked us to stand straight and explain.

We stuttered and stammered, 'We went to the bus-stand with the football team and other boys, but unfortunately could not join them in the bus. We kept on trying to get into the later buses, but the farmers and other adults kept on pushing us back. We did not realise at that moment, how much time span had been elapsed. We embarked the bus after over two hours and expected to return with the team on our way back. By the time we arrived at the destination, we did not know the venue of the match and wasted some more time. By the time we arrived at the venue, the team had already returned and also it was twilight and getting darker. We rushed back to the bus stand and it was quite late and there were not many passengers waiting, eventually they also left the bus stand for some sort of night stay, but unfortunately we were stranded and eventually stayed overnight with some family'. We narrated steadily but assuredly. The misfortune was that we did not inform our parents about our plan, because we had expected return by the evening.

One pleasant spring day, master Allah Rassie failed to arrive in time for his class. All classes had already begun their schedule of lessons, apart from ours. We were waiting and waiting, but still no news about him. The school attendant who used to wait especially for him at the main entrance to welcome him and take his bicycle to the parking bay looked anguished and worried. He had informed the headmaster, who also in turn got perturbed. We in the class were also gazing constantly at the entrance and waiting for him to make his usual glorious entry to the school. He normally used to enter the school not too early and not too late, but dot on time. He was well planned and well organised to manage his time. He used to commute by his Raleigh bicycle via the canal embankment from his village. It would appear that when he was on his way to school, some miscreants waited disguised in the fields and ambushed him somewhere near his village. But he was not a coward and fought like a lion and made them run. However in the skirmish; his hands and face were swollen and bruised. At the end of the fight, he went straight to the police station and reported the violent crime; and from there he arrived at the school. We all sympathised with him about this violence including the teachers and the headmaster and tried to console him. He was aristocratic and arrogant as usual and was determined to take revenge and punish the culprits with an iron hand.

When he arrived at school, he appeared a bit baffled and upset. He was not only the biggest landowner in his village, but he was also the headman, so he was very dominant in the village as well as influential with the hierarchy of the local civil government officials. But some other landowners and residents felt jealousy and antagonism from his status and planned various devices to harm him or take over his position. However it was not easy to overtake the man of his personality and calibre. In the meantime the police arrested his foes and sorted them out by flogging, this is the normal procedure in that culture. However master Allah Rassie soon recovered from this sudden turmoil and commenced teaching as normal without wasting any time. This was really amazing; he was so conscientious that he did not bother about his personal sufferings. He was a wonderful teacher.

However after a year of the 'School Match' episode, my brother Sarwer, with whom now I was lodging in the Gurdawara along with his wife Mumtaz, was transferred to a place called Khudian Khas, some sixty miles away to the north-east from Dipalpur and I had to shift with him over there. Nothing was in my control and I had no harness to control my destiny. After spending a few years over there, we shifted to Montgomery (my place of birth) over a hundred miles away to the west for my further education in the college, then after four years and achieving my graduation, I moved to Lahore for the university education. From there I got a teaching job in the college some two hundred miles away in the west from Lahore. Then after four years teaching I left for the Great Britain and have been living here since. However during this delicate flight of time, although I was visiting my uncle and aunt quite frequently in the village near Depalpur while I was in Pakistan and even after that, but I never visited our honourable teacher Allah Rassie. The simple reason was that he did not lodge in the town of Depalpur, but in the village few miles away. In the subsequent long trail of far distant years, each time I visited Depalpur, I tried to make a pilgrimage to my old teachers who were still living there and derived lot of bliss and delight by paying gratitude to them again and again. Some of the teachers were amazing, they tried to build up our characters and educate us, even out of school hours. One of my teachers even used to teach the whole class during the summer holiday at least for a month out of the three months holidays and did not charge any money.

However after a long lapse of time, perhaps fifty five years or so, I endeavour to visit our teacher Allah Rassie with my school mate Khushi because luckily he was still alive. Although at the time of our visit, he was over one hundred years old and his reflexes were a bit slow, he still appeared to be an imposing and splendid figure. He was sitting in his Charpie like a statue wearing qamees, dhoti, waistcoat and a simple muslin cap over his head, not a flared turban now but just like Mahatama Gandhi would wear in his lifetime. He was enjoying few puffs from his hubly-bubly and continued mincing with his prayers beads. This activity kept him engaged and relaxed in the lone and quiet moments.

Initially he could not recognise me, partly because of the fact that he had not seen me for such a long time and also due to the fact that his memory was steadily declining. I tried to jog his memory by describing about my three elder brothers who were also his students as well as about my father. Momentarily the whole scenario flashed back. He became emotional in nostalgia and he was wiping stream of tears pouring down his cheeks. I was rather baffled to see him shed tears. He was overwhelmed with my visit after such a long time. He was highly thankful to us for paying the visit, especially when he came to know that I had come from London. I asked him whether he remembered about me going to the football match and being missing from my home overnight; and later becoming a cockerel. He simply smiled. There were tears in his eyes again, he kissed my hands and I kissed him. He must have hundreds and thousands of his students spread all over the world, it was not possible for him to remember all of them and all episodes relating to them. Most of his students must have been dead at the time of our last visit to him, but those who were still alive, most of them would be out of touch with him. He was really glad to see us again and was very thrilled. He entertained us with sumptuous tea and biscuits and we spent over an hour with him. On our departure he raised his hands together in supplications and for giving blessings. We bade him farewell for the last time with caresses and kisses. I felt so delighted to meet him after such a long time and grateful to be so lucky to have this unique opportunity for his pilgrimage. However I am still yearning to watch the invisible football match. Just a few months after our visit, he bade farewell to this world. I was depressed to hear the sad news. No one has ever returned after going to that path, but I feel privileged to visit him before he departs us. He left behind a noble record and perfumed memory. I still remember that trauma which was linked to that football match and that has become a unique flash point of my early life. That transient mishap crackles permanently in my mind.

Chapter IX
Dilemma

My teenage years are full of incessant stories and sagas which were loaded with mind bubbling memories and glowing sensuous images. That was the sprouting age, each organ of the body shot and sprang; lot of hidden realities were coming to light and sometimes I used to blush and become embarrassed during discussions with family or friends. That was the age when one felt lusty and lofty; and there were boundless inspirations and vigour. As far as I am concerned that was the threshold of life in every sense. At that time there were no worries or tensions and the sky was the limit. Every moment was the new moment, a fresh moment, an exciting moment, an untold moment and a vast moment. And of course those were the explosive and volcanic moments usually linked to the middle and high school era. When I was living with my middle brother Sarwer and his wife Mumtaz; he was employed by the irrigation department. He was transferred and worked in Khudian Khas, some sixty miles away from Depalpur towards Lahore. In his earliest tempestuous stage, he used to visit his wife every week, then gradually after a fortnight and later after a month or longer. It is quite possible that being a junior officer he might have been paid less and could not afford frequent travelling. Although at that time my step mother was living just opposite to us with her parents and her son: she appeared unconcerned and detached from us. The same was the case with our closest relatives living next door to us. Also my real uncle and aunt lived in the village only two miles away, but they also rarely took any interest in our welfare. Whatever scarce money we used to have, we survived on our own. I used to go shopping for vegetables, meat and other grocery myself, but sometimes we used to run short of money. Thus we had survived on pickle and chutney sometimes.

After a lapse of about two years we migrate again, this time not forcibly. On odd oppressive summer morning, my sister-in-law became exasperated by the situation and made up her mind to say goodbye to Depalpur; for which she would have been planning for sometimes. It was quite possible that she could not live without her husband any longer and must had been missing him desperately. So she packed up her meagre possessions in a tin suite-case and locked up the doors to the house; and off we marched to the bus- stand. I carried the red hot suite-case over my head and trotted like a pony without a saddle or harness; escorted by my sister-in -law camouflaged in a black fashionable silk-Burkha. The bus stand was about a mile away from our house, so we staggered slowly but surely along the dusty pot-holed route on the edge of the ancient small brick city high-wall.. Our relatives saw us walk unsteadily in a subdued state, but no one offered any help. But rather they all stared at us with a kind of funny smiles and gestures on their cheeks and eyes, perhaps wondering how my brother would react to his surprise -visitors; he was a little bit hot tempered and a rigid person. They must also be looking forward to take possession of our house if we do not return to the Gurdawara. In fact that was what had happened later and soon some strange opportunists moved in our house. They did not give any chance to our relatives or even seek any permission from us.

After the adventure of the football match, I was well experienced in travelling on my own by bus and had become quite confident. My voice was already breaking and my body was developing fast with great energy and power. We had never communicated any advance warning to my brother, so he was taken by a great shock to see us standing outside his office and seemed quite agitated. It was really embarrassing for him to see his wife and brother encamped like refugees in front of his office. He got perturbed, panicked and rushed about; and asked us to go back as there was no accommodation available for the family. Perhaps he himself lived in one of the rooms in his office or shared the lodging with his bachelor colleagues.. In the dilemma one of his senior colleagues took us to his house and his wife was also supportive and hospitable to us. It was a sizzling summer day and we had lunch together. In the afternoon they managed to rent a two bedroom house in the middle of the town, in a narrow alleyway and next to the bazaar. I was already missing the Gurdawara which was like a palace, next to the canal and fragrant colourful fields. So I had to endure some more pain. By now I was accustomed to live in the open and wild environment.

In the new town centre the shops were just there and a variety of people lived in a kind of conglomeration, close to each other; some lodging few yards opposite and some with the shared walls on the right and the left. The most annoying thing was the narrow sewage channels which normally overflowed and were full of pungent smell. However there were lots of beautiful girls and women often seen prowling in the narrow streets, peeping through their main entrance doors and sometimes beckoning from top of the stairs. Some of them managed to come out clad in burkha and raised it when passed near me with lot of magnetic blinks and smiles. They had no mixed activity in the locked mysterious society of their houses and tried to enjoy the freedom as innocently as they could. I had intense desires too to see them, but survived on just momentary glimpses. Their unexpected encounter intrigued me. Suddenly I fell in love with them, with their bodies and with their tender and attentive eyes .Their femininity was such as would inevitably touch the heart of a solitary and shy adolescent like myself. 'What was the point of their beauty after all?"Yes, what was the point of their fine breasts, their alluring lips, their magical eyes and their dresses that hugged their bodies so prettily?; disguised under stringent restraints of culture and Hijab. What a fatal blunder is the disappearance of a gorgeous woman, without reflection, without passionate appeal! As I enter my teens; emotions were always running high, in Tsunamis and gushing like flash floods. There were lots of gestures from the other side too, but I was an unfulfilled and neurotic boy and repressed myself to glow like a clinker. This was a different kind of historical moment when I embarked on my middle and high school education. It was an erotic, hypnotic and unconscious moment. At this point blood used to boil and lid was off frequently. However it was the end of the nightmares or frightening dreams and they were replaced by the romantic and ever desired emotional fantasies. I only got rid of them when I was fast asleep or about to.

I remember our opposite neighbour vividly, like the full eclipse of the sun, sitting on his feet fully dilated like a cobra and facing the direction of our house. Errands used to run from the set of the houses next to us, especially from the young daughter of the landlady on our right. He used to wear dhoti and qamees and a muslin cloth wrapped round his head. He had a beard just like a goat, conical and bushy at the chin and becoming thinner as it climbed towards the ears. His eyes were shiny and deep. His untouchable face normally appeared deranged and lost. From his appearance in the street he looked like the simplest and most down to earth man. He had a grocery shop and worked with his old bearded father. His wife was very beautiful and her skin was fine like apricot. He had a few young children and the next one was due any time. We used to gaze at him through the grill of our flat roof just like watching a live x-movie. The other neighbours living opposite did the same and got amused about his stupidity. While sitting in this uncouth and obscene exposed posture, he looked straight on to the horizon as if intoxicated by basking in the sun and hardly moved or blinked his eyes; he seemed completely hooked into the lust or fantasy or perhaps someone in the sky was communicating with him. On the first call of the Muezzin, he would immediately shut his shop and would be the first man to enter the mosque. It is difficult to surmise how he balanced the evil and good faculties with each other. However saying regular prayers was his purely personal matter, but indecent exposure of himself was a public affair. In the circumstances it could have been difficult to punish him in public as I am sure he would have refused to admit it. He planned himself very well, he camouflaged himself from his back which was next to the stairs of his house, as well as he was protected from the other side by the wall of his toilet. If his wife, father or children would have come upstairs, he would have immediately covered himself from the front in a fraction of a second. It became a spectacle as well as a dilemma for the neighbours till someone whispered it to his wife or elderly father. If he was to be punished in public, then it would have been extremely humiliating and degrading for him. They would have pulled his beard, darkened his face and trotted him on a donkey in the bazaars and the streets, midst showers of curses and slinging of shoes on his face and head. However he was very lucky to escape the punishment, but that devious and deranged person still dilates in my highlights of funny and amusing historical moments and still make me smile over his mischievous false pretence.

Sometime later the superintendant of our school hostel was caught up in a dilemma when a young boy complained to him that one of his inmates had sexually abused him last night. The superintendant was highly disgusted and called for the alleged culprit in his office and interrogated him about this gross breach of his conduct and committing very serious offence. He warned him that he would be rusticated, unless he speaks the truth. Most of the students living in the hostel belonged to the surrounding villages, miles away. The declared offender fiercely resisted the allegation against him and proved his innocence and insisted it could have been somebody else; perhaps the victim could not recognise the real culprit in the dark and cold night. Although there was a lot of clamour and hullabaloo amongst the hostel lodgers and the school management, the matter could not be resolved and was nipped in the bud. However a great moral support and special counselling was afforded for the young victim. In the absence of the eye-witness and the proof, the matter remained unresolved.

In the mosque near to our house there was an assistant Imam, who was a genius, but unfortunately was blind. He had memorised the whole of the Quraan by heart, almost one thousand pages of it .His voice was just like a steam engine and very powerful. One could hear the echo of his recitation in the prayers almost half a mile away while rambling on the canal embankment. I do not think he had any regular salary from the management of the mosque, but survived on the support of individual members of the community. He was lodging in a mud enclosure of the mosque. There were no toilet facilities in his accommodation, so he had to go to the nearby fields for a comfort break.. He had to be escorted by a young juvenile who happened to be his student in memorising the Quraan by heart. The young student would hold his walking stick and lead him to his destination. Not only that, he would wash his clothes, make his bed and fill the mosque Hammam for his shower as well. The young student would also cook his meals and sleep in the same room. I recollect that the main Imam did toil hard to get a spouse for him, but in vain. He had no guide dog or any welfare help from the state or the local municipal council. His young student was his guide as well as family. It was catch 22 situation and it is difficult to speculate, how did he manage to sustain himself in simmering of his emotions and lust of life? Unfortunately he had been in a state of pickle and quandary for which I still feel pity.

In our narrow winding street there lived a destitute widow in a tiny house with her lonely daughter. She married her young daughter to a mature person, perhaps in exchange for some remuneration. The groom was like a bull of dark complexion wearing a smartly trimmed dark beard. Soon after his marriage, the man installed his innocent wife into the brothel, located in the nearby ancient town of Qasur some twelve miles away near the Indian border. The wretched mother could not have access to her daughter and had to lodge a law suit in the court for her recovery. She started having fits and getting even more lanky and scraggy. She was highly shocked and hid herself somewhere; she was extremely embarrassed and downgraded. The whole community was stunned and showed verbal sympathy for the unfortunate lady. She had hardly any money to feed herself, how could she pay the lawyer's unending fees. Now she looked to every one for help, but most of the people were spectators and got engaged in discussion about the tragedy and no real help was forthcoming and prayed that God will help the miserable woman. It took almost a year to recover the young girl from the body selling business. However they were never seen again in the public, they simply vanished, nobody knew where! There are countless examples like this in that simple and insensitive society. Most of the indigenous population just mind their own business and there are not many protective laws from the state, which is rather absurd and futile to protest. Even if there are any such laws, no one would obey or practice them, especially the most influential and powerful all across the board.

In the red hot months of May and June, in Pakistan lot of exotic fruit like melons, water melons, plums and mangoes would bloom and blossom the markets with different varieties filled with sumptuous and refreshing juices. Their fresh coloured skins and flavours attract lots of customers in the bazaars and are sold in abundance at affordable prices; so almost all members of the community enjoy them. One day a customer bought some melons and took them home. His mouth was watering by sniffing their flavours and by gazing at the green and blue stripes on the light gold skins of the fruit which appealed to the eyes. There was a play-card declaring in the fruit merchant's shop, 'These melons are very sweet and delicious without any doubt, just enjoy them.' After a few minutes the customer returns with a boiling temper and asked the shopkeeper to refund the money. He yelled at him, "These melons have no taste at all and no sweetness as claimed in your play-card. You are the biggest liar and a professional cheat. Here are your melons. Refund me the money immediately." "But the melons are already cut. I would not be able to sell them. I cannot refund you the money either." The fruit merchant responded. "You sold it to me claiming them as very sweet melons." The customer shouted and slung the melon on the face of the merchant. "I got the same assurance from the wholesale merchant of the main fruit market. I did not go inside the melons to check the authenticity of the product, so it is not my fault. I cannot refund you the money. Just vanish from my eyes immediately otherwise I will slash your belly in a second. Is your brain stuck in your ankles? Do you think that the wholesale merchant will take this fruit back from me and refund the money. You buffoon! You scoundrel! You wretch!" The merchant yelled back. "I think you are an illegitimate child, a bastard and a thug. I would not leave your shop till you refund me the money. You can do whatever you like. Do not threaten me with your knife. I can kill you with my fist." The customer shouted back. The verbal abuses and shouts turned into a physical violence and a terrible brawl. The shopkeeper stabbed the irate customer in his stomach a few times and was knocked bleeding on the narrow alleyway of the bazaar. He was rushed to the local civil hospital, but they were fatal wounds and very deep. The local doctor recommended that the patient be taken immediately to the main hospital in Qasur as it required a major operation. Dreadfully there was no ambulance or taxi available. So the victim's family had to wait for the next arriving bus, but as a result of this crucial lapse of time lot of blood was lost. The man was almost dead when he reached the surgical theatre; all his intestines were dangling out and soon he expired. The shopkeeper was immediately arrested by the police soon after the fight and locked in a cell at the police station next to our school. The melons were worth only few pennies, but the life lost was priceless. The shopkeeper was later imprisoned and his trial for the crime began and he was waiting to be taken to the 'Gallows'.

While wandering in the streets and the bazaars at the weekend, I had witnessed some more interesting episodes full of love and treachery. I noticed some gathering of people and a kind of melee outside a small house in the dusty suburb of the town, situated between the railway station and the lake. The crowd had locked the door of the house from outside by fixing the iron sling in the hook so that the inmates could not escape. It was alleged that a man and woman were besieged inside the house because they were committing adultery in the day time. It is difficult to say who had caught them red handed in that perplexity and quarantine; it might be her husband or some neighbours or perhaps a jealous lover. They were all waiting for the police to arrive and there was pin-drop silence as if they had been sniffed by the serpent. However everyone amongst the besiegers made sure that the lovers could not escape and yearned for them to be stoned to death. I was gazing at the crowd some distance away as a quiet observer, as usual. Soon I noticed two stout and sturdy policemen approaching towards us on foot as if from the horizon and striding forcefully with a blend of smiles as well as grimness on their face. They were dressed in smart uniforms and their moustaches were sprouting across their cheeks like thorny bush and they were wielding batons in their hands. They had been well trained by the British Indian officers to run the Empire in an efficient manner. Everyone stood in awe as they descended. Soon the door was unhooked and the culprits were escorted by them to the nearby police station. The police station was next to our school and was kept in an immaculate condition and appeared like a romantic fort.. The lovers walked subdued and embarrassed under the umbrella of the crowd and the police. They trotted humbly un-handcuffed, one behind the other, with their eyes sunk on to the mother earth and praying for clemency. The woman head was covered with the traditional Dopatta. They looked pale and dejected and worried about the savage pending flogging by the police during the course of interrogation. Statements were taken from the witnesses as well from the suspects. The spouse was locked in separate cells and interrogation continued for days and nights, especially in the dark. There were lots of statements. The woman refused to admit any foul play and rather cursed the wicked witnesses. How these dummies could have witnessed standing outside the perimeter of the house; they were simply dismissed as defaming the lady and her spouse. This incident appeared opposite to the scenario of the young boy living in the hostel which I mentioned earlier. In the absence of actual witness on the scene, no other witnesses were considered reliable in the eyes of the court. So the case was dismissed on poor grounds and naturally the benefit of doubt goes to the defendants. However the police had their days and nights! Nobody amongst the spectators bothered to ask about the outcome of the enquiry and the only beneficiaries were the police in the dungeon.

There is a famous saying in the Punjab and it has the truth in it and I quote, "Jay Kuri Munda Razi, Tay kie Karayga Mullan, Kie Karayga Qazi" Which means, "If the girl and the boy have the sweet will, then what can the Mullah do and what can the Qazi (judge) do!"

After this episode an even more sensuous and more queer, startling and thrilling news was highlighted in bold letters on the front pages of all national newspapers, which said that the daughter of the richest industrialist in Pakistan had run away with their handsome Pathan driver and had married without the consent of her parents and that they were still sheltering somewhere in the country. It is quite possible that the business tycoon was himself enjoying himself with a pretty concubine at that time in some seven star luxury hotel. The newly wedded couple was living in hiding for fear of any fallback from her parents. Initially the business tycoon was in a terrible shock, but later was advised about the complicity of human feelings and emotions. He swallowed all the pride and snobbishness and stooped to the sweet wish of his beloved daughter who simply tumbled herself in the flash flood of her emotions and exhilaration. There were loads of commotions and comments from all corners and walks of the country, but soon died down. The freedom lovers appreciated it as good omen for future generation, but for the traditionalist it sent a shock wave in their spines. Everyone reacted according to their own perception of life and their environment. However the lucky Pathan had already joined equally with the top elite of the country and later he had found himself on the other side of the fence. However afterwards when the dust was settled, he himself was too scared to have a Pathan driver himself for his wife and used to drive the luxury car himself.

Sometime later the students and staff of our reputable national college were stunned by the shocking news that the wife of the vice principal had run away with her chef. They used to lodge in a beautiful bungalow provided by the education authorities and annexed with their own secluded exotic gardens. The learned professor was a man of great dignity and honour. He was highly educated and well respected equally by his colleagues as well as students. He was just like a god-head. However he was keeping very cool and openly discussed the facts of the turmoil like a unique enlightened person. He had nothing to disguise and expressed his feelings quite unemotionally without any false pretence. He narrated,' I had no desire to get married and I explained quite unequivocally to my parents. But some of our acquaintances kept on pestering my parents, sometimes begging to marry their daughter to me. The reason was quite obvious. I was man of fame and part of elite society. I lived in a magnificent official lodge, had gardener, chef and servants to take care of me. She was very contented with her comforts and amenities of life, but I could not physically satisfy her. So she was grossly disgruntled and frustrated most of the time which I could not help; I wish I could, but it was catch 22 situation. Who is so stupid not to enjoy the fantasies, romance and sensuous lust of nature? Obvious result was what you hear now.' He stuttered with regret.

The convention of corporal punishment and 'Cockerel Formation' continued even in the new school. I noticed that regular hard core of students who did not want to study were flogged almost daily, but still would not improve, so it was futile to punish them. The majority of the students were of average ability and they would undulate on a daily basis; and genuinely try to improve with minor smacks on the cheeks or lashes on the hands or pulling of ears. But sometimes when the teacher became frustrated or not in good mood for some reason, perhaps had had a bit of squabble with the wife, then cockerel punishment would come into force. I recollect one day we were attending our 'Drawing' lesson when the teacher became very angry with one of the students because instead of apologising for not doing the home work; the boy tried to make fun of the teacher in front of the class. The teacher became highly charged and asked the student to stand up and bring forward the hand. He started the lashes with great ferocity. The teacher would raise the baton over his head and jump over his feet. We stared in awe. The offender's hands must be sizzling with scars and he kept on rubbing them. Soon the student started Karate on the teacher; hit and punch him ruthlessly. The student belonged to a rich farming community and was a kind of spoilt kid. He was well built and far taller than the teacher whose height was below average. The teacher left the class immediately and reported the most serious incident to the headmaster. Subsequently the father of the student was called in about the serious misconduct of his son and soon he was rusticated from the school.

In our school another painful incident had taken place. We were attending our English lesson when one of the students did not take the teacher seriously and tried to be mischievous. It was a bright sunny day, but cool and crispy. Our class was held in the dusty courtyard of the school to keep us warm because inside the class room it was cold and shivering. His father was also a teacher in our school. Our class mate was a football player as well as a scout. The English teacher was a handsome, well groomed and a smart person; always dressed in western style immaculate suits and used to wear fashionable designers' shoes. He was also a scout master and each year took the scouts to the hill resort of Murree (a hill station just like Shimla, both located in the Punjab and both developed by the British) for training the scouts in the camps during the summer holidays, along with other teams arriving from different parts of the country. The teacher ordered him to make cockerel posture and unleashed his bamboo baton. Our class mate started shrieking and wailing. While in agony, he told the teacher to stop bashing him and raised his arm to stop the baton zooming in his direction. He stumbled from his stooped position and plumped on the ground. While in this skirmish, the teacher kept on showering the lashes unabated as if beating a terrorist and in the process, his elbow was fractured. A fierce crackling noise came along with the deafening shrieks. The whole school rumbled with the echo and the boy's father rushed out to the scene including the headmaster. A fierce argument ensued between the two teachers and the victim was immediately taken to the nearby hospital for the repair of the elbow. There was almost hand to hand fight between his father and the irate teacher. The situation was brought under control through mediation by the other teachers and the headmaster; it stopped the head rolling on the ground. There were lots of apologies from the aggressive teacher and he was really embarrassed in front of the whole school. He also received lot of curses from the boy's mother and other teachers and lot of sympathy for the young boy and his family.

Above of all it was an era of exhilaration, excitement and adventures, but not always free from bitter consequences. Sometimes those could have been the personal emotive factors or from the local interaction of life even across the border from India. It is the Indian factor which I hark back to at this moment, but that time it was uplifting and sensuous for me although it was far more damaging for most people lodging around me. It was month of July and there were heavy Monsoon rains for weeks at a stretch; this was in addition to the excessive heat waves which melted upper layers of the glaciers miles up over the Himalayas. Therefore colossal quantities of the water were flowing in the mighty rivers of the Punjab which were soaring and swirling over the width of miles. It was alleged that so much water had gathered in the Ganda-Singh Barrage on the River Sutluj (part of canal network built by the British), the chances were that that barrage could had been swept away by the great thrust of the river flood. So the Indian Air force was ordered by the government to make a breach on the barrier on the Pakistan side. The simple reason could have been that the lower course of the river meandered through the Pakistan territory, but the barrier could have been breached on the Indian side as well. My ancestors' district of Hoshiarpur was on the higher part of the greater Punjab plains some one hundred miles up in the north east where flash-flood-rivers as well as hundreds of tumbling tributaries were merging into various perennial large rivers at the foot of the Himalayas. It is difficult to speculate whether the Pakistan government was consulted in this matter or any prior agreement was reached. However the emergency was declared by the officials of the irrigation department that the flood waters were on their way to us and every one must shelter on the higher grounds or settlements.

It is quite possible that the Indian side wanted to give another terrible financial blow to Pakistan's economy. This barrage was located on the Indian side of the territory. All this political manoeuvring by India is due to the fact that the Muslim province of the Punjab was partly given to India unfairly. It should have been kept as one province where all indigenous cultures would have flourished in harmony like any other provinces of India and Pakistan., but now there are more everlasting problems, more enmities and squabbles between the two neighbouring countries. To start with it was the area which became the killing grounds for the militant gangs of Hindu and Sikh warriors with the support of their government, where more than one million beleaguered Muslims were butchered in a treacherous way. In addition to those perennial deep scars and disgruntled disputes, now there is continuous political wrangling about the sharing of rivers' waters between India and Pakistan. All these rivers first flow through the upper reaches of Indian Punjab before entering Pakistani Punjab as per gradient of the alluvial plain. Now India is building huge dams on them and in case of war, millions of people in Pakistan could be drowned without exploding an atom bomb if water is gushed out under some mischievous plans; and also Pakistani territory can be turned into a desert if water is completely diverted towards India The part of Indian Punjab is just like a bottle neck and it can be choked against Pakistan at any time.

However on the news that the great Noah's flood was thrusting and roaring towards us, we were so excited that quite a few of our school mates trailed up the upper reaches of great alluvial plain and welcomed the sizzling flood waters few miles up the plain from our small town. We were jumping, yelling and running; and trying to lead the waters. The flood level was building up with great speed and it appeared to slither like a boisterous serpent. The waves began to rise and foam; it started to swallow all the green cropped fields, tumbling the trees and bushes and crumbling the mud houses. It spread across miles in no time. It reminds me the great surge of the flash floods in the Cho in my Grandma's village which eventually used to join the Beas River and Sutluj River; this was the same water which used to gush through my grandma's village. These great perennial rivers are the main rivers where those flash flood Choes(rivers) eventually used to tumble down or empty themselves from the district Hoshiarpur, which is part of India now.

That vast sheet of surging flood ravaged and devastated most of the rural areas which fell in its path. The village folks escorted their families and cattle on war footings; they took shelter on the embankment of the canals which the British had built on a far higher level so that water could reach easily to all the irrigated fields.. The main part of our town was also built on relatively higher ground. Its old buildings appeared as if it was a stronghold of some local feudal war lords. The buildings were structured with small bricks and its streets were narrow, perhaps built like this for security reasons. But the new settlements were developed on the low lying areas, such as the canal colony, school, police station, civil and veterinary hospitals, railway station and private houses. Soon we were besieged by the mighty sway and roar of the vast sway of water. Apart from the centre of the town, most of the buildings in the suburb were lashed with a great ferocity and momentarily submerged in almost six feet depth of water. We witnessed building collapsing and swallowed by the flood. Some of the brave men climbed on top of their flat roofs, but soon they tumbled down and had to struggle to swim to go to the higher grounds for safety. I recollect one person perched on his flat roof far away from us and waving to his son standing next to me who also waved back and shouted, 'The water level is rising, please go to a safer place.' He responded, 'I am far higher up on the strong roof. I am Ok. I worry about you. You look after yourself as well as your mum'. While they were exchanging verbal support and sympathy for each other, the wall of the high roof started crumbling and the man on the roof crashed and splashed. We did not see him again and he just vanished in the middle of the great thrust of twirling and roaring currents of water.

The currents of the flood were so powerful that it was almost impossible to swim. The flood waters were infested with snakes and also carried lot of fish and wild ducks in its waters. There was a colossal loss of valuable properties, crops, railway lines and metalled roads. Hundreds of cattle were swept away and perished along with scores of humans. There was a complete breakdown of communications. Our school and its library were nearly collapsing and all books turned into fodder. Hundreds and thousands of square miles of the fertile plain were in complete a shambles and submerged. The great plain turned into a huge lake and flood waters touched the horizon. Pakistan Air Force was called in to drop supplies of food and blankets. There was chaos and turmoil everywhere. It took months before rail and roads traffic could commence. There was almost little help from the local government or from the UNO indeed. However in this chaos and upheaval, there were some romantic and magical moments as well. Quite a few beautiful women and teenage girls also sheltered in our house. They came from the canal colony and were sophisticated and posh. Before this they did purdah or Hijab from us, now we had a close view of them. Being a red-hot teenager and not outgoing, it was a unique moment for me to exchange smiles and gestures; some of them seemed more keen and alluring to me than I was to them. Even for them this was a unique moment for freedom and coming out of the cage. Their guardians were still on official duty in the canal colony; toiling hard in the strongly built British office buildings to carry out their duties as normal or to deal with any emergency. I still reminisce those everlasting happiest passionate and flushing magical moments in my mind and keep on diving in those icy burning currents and feelings hurt in a savage way.

During the last few months of my school life my brother was transferred again, this time to Qasur, some twelve miles to the north. He shifted over there sooner with his family; naturally I shifted with him too. My final exams were due in less than three months' time and I did not want to shift to the new school. So at the beginning I used to commute to my school by train, but the timings of the train were not much suitable; and also cost money and time. So I requested one of my friends named Gaga if his parents could sustain me for this crucial time of my life. Luckily they agreed and virtually it was almost free. They asked me to contribute just the flour for the chapaties, which I was pleased to do, perhaps they did not want any beggar occupying or sharing the house with their son. Their house was contiguous to one of the main mosques, but none of them hardly attended the mosque for prayers.. They were a kind of secular family and feudal landlords. Gaga's elder sister, mother or grandmother never wore any Hijab, they simply covered their heads with dopattas; used to wear dhoti or shalwar and Qamees as their dress. His father had a grey beard, would normally wear dhoti and qamees; and covered his head with an unflashy muslin turban. He was a permanent member of the jury in the Lahore High Court of Justice; and spent most of his time over there. His grandmother was over six feet tall, sturdy and well built. She used to ride a horse to go to her farms about four miles away without being escorted. She had a pink glowing face and long orangey plaits. He had a beautiful and a charming sister. She had managed a love marriage with the most handsome and one of the richest boys in the town. His elder brother was a kind of a hero and had spent bulk of his life participating in shooting of the films in various film studios of Lahore.

Gaga was a school champion in wrestling, athletics and bodybuilding. He was also a similar champion in the town and well admired by all, especially by the young women. He was quite handsome, pleasant and a likely lad. He spent most his energy in doing press-ups, racing and wrestling. Naturally he paid less attention towards his studies. I have a feeling that Gaga's parents might have had allowed me in their house partly with the consideration that I could be a bit of help in his final exams. His mother did have a quiet whisper with me saying,' Rana you must help Gaga in his studies, he does not concentrate in his books, even though the final exams are just round the corner. Because of you his attitude might change'. The mother gestured. They used to call me Rana as part of tribal traditional name. Living in the vicinity, two more of our class mates named Akbar and Mandu used to join us as well, every night for intensive preparatory studies in our study room. It was winter time, the days were bright, crispy and cool; but in the night time temperature plunged almost below zero. We used to squat on our individual charpies, snug in our soft cotton quilts and around the oil lit- lamp fluttering in the middle which perched on a small wooden table. I did try to help Gaga, but most of the times he looked tired and often dozed off while the book was in his lap. Three of us used to stare at him and smile, but after some struggle he used to tumble in his bed and fall fast asleep like a rabbit. We did try to wake him up, but in vain.

On one dark and freezing night while we were busy studying as usual and Gaga was still awake, someone, outside our study room, momentarily slammed with the iron sling attached to our wooden door and Gaga slipped out quietly. At that time the streets were empty, everyone was huddling in their houses crowding around the fire places which were glowing with the logs of wood. One could only hear the occasional barking and squeaking of the dogs in the dark icy streets and howling of the foxes in the distant fields, mingled with the flickering lights coming from the stars and the new moon shrouded by the floating white clouds. He returned later after over half an hour, looking pale, shaky and nervous.' Ranaji I was trapped. Someone was watching and locked the door from outside'. He stammered with his eyes down and shivering. There was a pin drop silence and we all peeped into his eyes with curiosity.

'What happened?' We enquired with great anxiety.' I went in and when I was returning, I could not get out. Someone was sneaking near the house and locked us in from outside and during the lapse of time quite a few people had gathered out there and waited in suspense.' He described in fright and appeared subdued and baffled.' We were besieged and did not know what to do and what not to do and I was wondering how to escape from this trap.' He gasped. 'I was planning to stand the charpie against the wall and use it as ladder to climb over the wall and jump out. I would have knocked any one down if they had tried to entangle me. It would have been just like playing Kabaddi or pairing in a wrestling.' He remarked with a grim face. 'Some of the spectators in the dark sea outside were peeping through the thin cracks of the door and were whispering amongst themselves.. I was in an extreme confusion and tension. My main worry was if someone had told my parents; then they would have been extremely embarrassed in front of the public and also cross with me. I was not worried about her who had invited me in to start with. While I was wrenching and wrangling in this turmoil and turbulence of emotions and thoughts, someone standing outside opened the door and let me go. They were all scared to touch me and gazed in awe while I quietly trailed back.' He narrated with gloomy smiles on his cheeks.

"But why did you go to her house so late in the night?" We enquired in amazement. "No, I did not. It was her who had slung at our door. She just caressed and carried me away." He smiled. "But why, what was the emergency?" We wondered. "He married her so that she could look after him, cook chapattis for him and look after his house. She has to entertain his parents as well. He is totally impotent and does not quench her emotions. She is terribly frustrated and I am sure her husband is fully aware about this calamity and ignores her secret love affairs." Gaga responded. "This particular incident has taken place because someone else from the neighbourhood or one of the relatives had noticed me going in and got startled. She does not care about them, his family or friends. At the end of the day, it is his fault to marry her without any physical desires and put her in this wretched upheaval." He reiterated in confidence. It was even more amazing that no one had chased him to his room or yelled any abuses. Their heads were in the mud and no one lodged any complaint to Gaga's parents either. The whole episode was buried under the dark blanket of the icy night. If they had reported the matter to the police, they would have welcomed her with the open arms. They would have taken the statement again and again and it would have been swollen at the close of the investigation..

The miserable lady had been imprisoned in her own house without any emotional thrills. She would have definitely yearned for the sturdy and stallion like policemen and would have preferred to stay in the cell of the police station, perhaps she used to dream about going there as soon as possible.

The pitiable woman was stuck in the quagmire. She could not complain to anyone about her trauma that she was not getting anything physical from her husband. One does not normally touch the glass of drink, if there is no urge to drink it! It is a male dominant culture based on the old Indian heathen society and even the lust of intense sensuous emotions belongs to him. By tradition it is a matter of prohibition for the woman to show her sexual hankering or protest about her exploitation by the men. Although it is not a religious taboo but still a deep rooted cultural barrier since the ancient times. Until recently there were reports that women used to commit suicide when their husband had died, but the widower never committed such drastic action. The widowers married more women and enjoy concubines on the top; and had abused and seduced the kids as bonus if ever the opportunity knocked. There are recent reports from the most remote areas of Pakistan that some feudal lords are marrying their daughters with a copy of the Quraan so that their estates remain within their family and does not fragment or disintegrate. There is also rampant, in some tribes and families, honour killing of women in cases of adultery, but not of men; although men and women are equal in Islam and stringent punishment rules must apply equally to the guilty men as well involved in the offence. Again this is not allowed by the religion, but practiced by the most scrupulous and uncivilised landlords and families. It is most detestable and a savage routine which is thriving on the pagan culture of Satti and superiority of men.

However in case of mess relating to Gaga's dilemma and his consequent embarrassment, that woman was gravely depressed who was very hungry, but could not find anything to eat; intensely thirsty, but could not find any drink. She was fully intoxicated, bottle full of wine and ready for a sip by any one and at any time. She lodged just a few doors away from Gaga and developed a friendship with him. I used to observe her coming to Gaga's parents ' home for a social visit to his family wearing a white baggy Burkha, camouflaged from head to tail and tended to stop in front of our room, but I was not aware how much she was involved with him. She used to cook delicious and sumptuous dishes for Gaga and bring them to us; we enjoyed them together, their taste was intensely mouth-watering and we used to lick our fingers. I am sure that his parents were fully aware, but could not help. In that culture most of the boys' parents turn a blind eye towards their son's similar activity, rather feel proud of his manly behaviour. I am certain that the main cause of his weakness in his studies was his involvement with this unfortunate woman. Additionally he was spending too much time in his physical and body building exercises. He was a nice boy of warm and much sought after personality which might had attracted lot of admirers. To his teachers and the school mates, he was a champion and a hero.

Over forty-five years had gone by like a speck of a cloud, since I had left my school and departed from Gaga. Since my retirement from the Royal Mail after over thirty years of a comfortable and prosperous career, I had more time to relax and reflect on the past. It is at this moment that I thought of reunion with old school friends and to visit the old school town. Now I yearned to see Gaga, but wondered whether he might be still there. I was completely out of touch with him for such a long time. When I arrived in the school town along with my other school mate Khushi from Depalpur, we were told that Gaga was luckily still there, although he was retired now. No resident in the area knew me, so I found myself a complete stranger. The town had exploded with population and a lot of expansion had taken place over the span of time. However I went next to the mosque where Gaga used to live with his parents and where once I was a lodger as well. He seemed to have constructed his own house nearby and someone guided me over there.

I was told that he had gone for the afternoon prayers in the mosque and the prayers would be finished in just two minutes, which I could not believe. I waited outside the mosque's main gate along with our guide. I did not enter the mosque and kept on gazing at the gate just in case I miss him coming out and soon he came out with rest of the congregation. Our guide pointed towards him and I recognised him instantly. He had hardly put his shoes on his feet, when I rushed towards him and enquired if he knew about me. Obviously both of us looked like fossils and were stunned to meet again at the same place. He could not believe his eyes. He was fiercely thrilled and exhilarated, just like me. We embraced and caressed each other passionately. His head was covered with simple muslin hat and he appeared like a guru. "I thought you would be in the gym building up your muscles, doing press-ups, perspiring and socialising." I gestured to him smiling and joking. "Gone are the good old days, not much stamina left now." He smiled with his usual brightness in his eyes. "We were told that you had died few years ago, while you were working in the revenue department (in Pakistan)." He quoted from someone with a great thrill and happiness. "No, not in London." I reacted with a teenage laughter. "This is perhaps reincarnation now." He laughed back. "What happened to that woman living in the neighbourhood?" I showered the question impatiently. "She had left him and got married to someone else soon after that incident." He responded with his smiley cheeks. He knew exactly what I meant even after more than forty years.

He wanted to entertain me in his house first, but I was so excited that he took me straight to the bazaars and narrow alleyways, as well as to our school for site seeing and pilgrimage. Nothing could recognise me and I could recognise nothing. No women came camouflaged in the Burkha to have a close encounter with us. The residents of the town at my school time were either dead or migrated to other places. The town was alien to me and I was alien to the town. He took me to the narrow street where I used to live with my brother. It appeared so sad and barren. I did not see any of our acquaintances or hear any familiar voices. I became depressed and disheartened. I have a feeling that subconsciously I must be thinking as if I am still a teenager and the moment has not changed, but the perception in the mind proved me wrong. At that moment it appeared to me as if I had been dead for some centuries and came back to life to visit my school town. The change of population was almost hundred percent and very shocking to me. I did not observe any familiar shopkeepers and indeed any familiar customers. The layout of the shops and their contents had also been changed like ourselves. It was completely a new world order.

The school now had been upgraded to a degree college and one of my class mates had become the Principal of the new college. He was also pleased to meet us. I was also lucky to meet my friend Mandu who had become the main whole sale merchant of fruit and vegetable market. He was sitting on the charpie in the market puffing hubly-bubly and entertained us with fresh fruit and green sumptuous tea. The town had spread up to the canal embankments half a mile away and even beyond. It is a prevalent belief in Pakistan that when a baby is born, "It comes with the food and the fortune in its pocket; these are prearranged even before coming to this world." It is the same canal on whose banks I used to stroll and study; and Gaga used to swim and do press-ups along with us. Gaga served us with nice and cool icy- bottles of coke. Soon it was getting dark and we embarked on a bus going towards Depalpur in midst of cuddles and kisses and hoping to meet again soon. Sadly Gaga and Mandu {my other friend} died one after the other within a few months of my last visit to them. First I was too busy to visit them, but now even if I have the time, still I cannot do so. This is one puzzle and drawback of life and must be swallowed.

Sadly in the 1980s and after over 120 years of its foundations, the name of Montgomery was changed to Sahiwal by some queer politicians or local municipal leaders. It's newly named after some unknown ancient tribe, race or an old settlement which is based on fantasy. However I am in a pickle now as I was born in

Montgomery, I got my graduation in Montgomery, I got married in Montgomery and all my grandparents and parents are buried in Montgomery.

The leaders of Pakistan want to become patriotic on the basis of some fantasy, but not in the real development of the area or welfare of its people. This is clearly a great ingratitude to the person who had endeavoured to develop this barren area and turn it into a most productive land on this planet, especially building up the great canal and the modern settlement of Montgomery, based on the European standards, through which the great canal passes. It was not only Montgomery whose name has been changed, but also the second largest city of the Punjab called Lyallpur and the largest industrial town of Pakistan as well. Lyallpur is now named after another foreigner, King Faisel of Saudi Arabia. It is alleged that King Faisel had given a few million Dollars for the development of this town and in return this new name of the town was dedicated to his name, but I am certain that donation money would have gone in the chests of the corrupt municipal or national leaders. Both of these twin towns on either bank of the River Ravi were originally named after the British Colonial Governors of the Punjab, who laid their foundations and developed these areas; Sir Robert Montgomery and Sir James Lyall. However after leaving my school, there is no doubt that I am completely metamorphosed and would not be able to recognise myself if compared with my school appearance and so would be the admirers.

Chapter X

Chuff-Chuff of the Steam Engine

As a young kid, as a juvenile and as well as a grown up I have a few peculiar and unique emotional and historical memories linked to steam engine journeys. The first historical moment was when my father came to fetch me from my maternal grandmother's village and we travelled together to my father's house about a hundred miles away and I sat in the lap of my grandmother all the way in the train. This was the first and the last time I had travelled with my father in the train. And later my grandmother brought me back to her village after few weeks' holidays. The most historical journey was when my eldest brother came to my grandmother's village and took me to our father's house just a few days before the announcement of partition and this had helped my lucky escape from the grotesque blood baths or having been beleaguered in the refugee camps for months. The main means of travel in the village where I lodged with my grandmother was either walking for short distances or trains for the long distances. However there was infrequent use of Dolees (a kind of doll house carried by four men on their shoulders) for the medium destinations. There were not any metalled roads or buses in its vicinity; even the train station was about ten miles away. Then came the most dilated and evocative encounter with a female passenger at the height and pinnacle of my youth; and last but not the least, but most memorable and enchanting my first wedding night in the most sumptuous and much desired elite coupe of the fastest moving train and one of the longest journeys of my lifetime.

The first railway link was introduced in the British Punjab between Amritsar and Lahore, a journey of some sixteen miles, when Sir john Lawrence, the then Governor of Punjab, opened Lahore railway station on 4 January 1859; eighty years before I was born. And who was pulling the train, it was the celebrated and warm hearted; the steam engine; with clouds of smoke and steam. Initially the bewildered farmers, villagers and town dwellers gazed amazed at the pitch dark 'English Ghost' sizzling, fuming and stroking, gushing and roaring through the dusty alluvial plains, creating whirlpool of dust storms; they thought, 'It's the Englishman smoking the super cigars'. I think they got confused between the bowler hat and the funnel of the steam engine. The indigenous Indian population used to gather around the railway tracks and wait for the train to arrive and have a glimpse of it and the passengers travelling in it. This means of mass transport brought people of the Indian subcontinent closer and it also made it far easier and quicker to transport heavy goods, cattle and armies. In addition it provided new mass employment opportunities, helped the industrial revolution and trade. It also made easier the export of Indian goods to Great Britain and other foreign countries, as well as helping the import of British manufactured goods to India. However at the time of Partition, hundreds and thousands of the fleeing destitute refugees on overflowing trains were also massacred and fluttered in the bloody rivers, canals and roadsides.

The classic, magnificent and glorious railway station of Lahore is no less in grandeur and glory than the everlasting and imposing structures of St Pancras and Victoria Railway Stations in London. The British had built the rail systems in India with exactly the same dedication, standards and ingenuity as they did in Great Britain. Lahore is always said to be the Queen of all cities in India and still is because of an amazing blend of beautiful people, cultures and buildings. This railway station was built four years before the Metropolitan Line; the world's first underground service was opened in London (1863).

My place of birth Montgomery which was a brand new town was crowned as a district headquarters and had been facilitated with a main railway station and located on the main railway line connecting the sea-port of Karachi with Peshawar, which soars over 1200 miles of a straight north to south single railway track, but after the death of my mother when I was only two years old,

I was taken by my maternal grandmother to the remote village at the foothills of the Himalayas near the British Indian summer capital of Shimla (Simla). For travelling from our house to the nearby places or neighbouring villages, she would just pick me up and hold me against her shoulders and breast, gripping and clasping me with her arms, but as 'I grew taller and bigger, she would ask me to walk along with her, which I thoroughly enjoyed and still enjoy, thinking and still reminiscing about those tranquil trails; trotting in the fields, meadows, groves, enjoying the colourful and fragrant fruit trees, crops and wild life, like deer, rabbits, lizards, peacocks and snakes.. However in case of travelling to rather long distant villages, she would travel by a Dolee which I have already described in details earlier and I enjoyed the ride with her and for me it became rather epic journeys while picked up by four men on their shoulders, while we squat comfortably in the nicely decorated and furnished wooden cage. In the village there were no metalled roads, but only dusty tracks and sandy paths with potholes which connected the nearby settlements and villages. The only other means of transport were the oxen-carts or horse rides; but those travels were very bumpy, jerky and full of discomfort, dust; and also primitive and harsh.

Hundreds and thousands of miles of rail tracks were laid by the British, not only in the Punjab, but all over India linking north to south and east to the west and millions of commuters travel daily by trains all over the subcontinent. Being a very vast country it was not possible to connect all towns and settlements by trains, so people desiring a long distance journey have to travel to the railway stations by walking, by tongas (horse driven carts or wagons) or ox-carts or having a ride on beasts like horses, donkeys or camels; and in some cases by Dolees.

In Pakistan there has not been much attention paid to the enhancement or upkeep of the railway networks since partition; it is rather frustrating. The single track laid by the British over 150 years ago still remains the same, although the population has exploded almost six-fold. As I wander around for miles on the embankment of the great canal and gaze at the single rail track, I simply get depressed and feel like wailing as I stand on the edge of the single track which runs parallel to the canal. It is not only still single, but in most dire dilapidation, completely in need of updating and repairs. More than that there are only a few trains which run every few hours, as against Great Britain where trains run every few minutes to any destination. Recently there had been so many instances when the train engine had broken down or its brakes failed while cruising at its normal speed and got stuck in the middle of the countryside or the desert. On other numerous days the destitute commuters are forced to wait desperately, under the open sky for hours enduring the extremities of weather and even have to wait for days to catch the expected train. They have to sleep and squat miserably on the bare floor of the platforms because of lack of contingency plans available to deal with such emergencies. This is clearly due to lack of proper functioning of the governmental institutions and genuineness of the politicians. Due to the lack of law and order, sometime terrorist attacks are instigated on the train by the disgruntled local politicians and even such subversive activities are carried out by foreign agencies to make the country unstable. As a result ordinary innocent people who have nothing to do with power and politics suffer drastically.

It is rather disappointing to observe that some remote areas' tracks and stations have not been maintained and left in shape of disrepair; some have been even discarded and abandoned and rail tracks uprooted and taken to the factories of the corrupt politicians and industrialists to be melted in the forges for the benefit of their lucrative business, perhaps they are waiting for the British to give them a further heavy and fresh hand. How the rulers of the same origin can deprive their own people and prefer to build their own palaces locally and abroad, instead of building and advancing the British built railways and other institutions? However the funds from the national exchequer are diverted to build up the private assets, rather than building up the national infra-structure. The rulers of Pakistan including the bulk of the politicians, generals, feudal lords and industrialists are amongst the richest in the world and have their own private fighting force and have built up their assets not only locally in each popular location, but also in most major and stable economies of the planet. If the plundered wealth is returned to the national exchequer, Pakistan is bound to be one of the richest countries of the world and in gang of the Superpowers. It is a common belief that only 30% of the economy passes through the national exchequer, 70% passes through the black economy like bribery, bureaucratic wrangling and wrongdoings, mafia gangs, smuggling and underhand gratitude payments.

I recollect quite unequivocally when I had the first ride in the steam-train. I must have been about four or five years old. I accompanied my grandmother to meet rest of my family living in West Punjab. The train arrived about midnight at our departing station, we could not see the pitch dark steam-engine as it was moonless night and there were not any lights at the platform. However the dazzling beam of the steam-engine, fixed to its forehead and its sparkling glare appeared like the piercing sharp rays of the rising sun and we had to put our hands on the brows of our eyes to stop squinting our eyes and to have a glimpse of the steam-engine and the wonderful wagons attached to it; but still our eyes shrunk and shrivelled on the first sight and of course these were the subtle feelings of the first night's emotions. This was the first moment I had seen the glint of man- made light. We could easily hear the thrust and hissing of the slowing down steam engine and the clatter of the train in the blanket of dark. It was an amazing sight and full of exhilaration to gaze at the approaching train .There was not much of a rush of passengers at the platform and we easily managed to get into it. I was so excited that I tried to keep my head dangling outside the windows to stare at the landscape, trees, rivers and fields. It was a cold winter night and my grandmother pulled me back cuddling me and soon I fell asleep like a rabbit, snug in her comfortable and warm lap; at least for the night journey wrapped in the blanket. As soon as the first rays of sun flashed, I started peeping out again by dangling my neck. I observed the moving trees and the fields and even thought the train was cruising back towards the station of origin till some different landmarks and physical features proved otherwise. At the end of the journey, my face was fully camouflaged with dust and my clothes needed washing immediately, but I enjoyed every single moment of the ride in the train and this opened my mind and enlightened me as a person to notice so many different places and their features while sitting comfortably in the steam train and seeing such a spectrum of colourful life on our planet. There is a Chinese saying, 'One learns more by travelling a hundred miles as compared to reading a hundred books'.

As a school kid I used to visit my brother at Renala Khurd, a small canal colony settlement, situated upstream along the bank of the mighty canal, some fifty miles away from Montgomery and near to the hydro-electric power house, which the British had very cleverly built by diverting the part of the mighty canal's waters and rejoining it with the main current after a loop of one mile. The great orange groves-Mitchell Farms, almost twelve miles long and provided with four railway stations, soared across the railway track. During those summer holidays it was my compulsive habit to stroll to the railway station daily from the canal colony and wait for the express train to pass and see it roar and gush with a colossal speed and thrust. I was unable to see the passengers sitting in the train, it cruised like a flash with tremendous noise of a tornado, carrying along with it the dust-storm and the atmosphere fully agitated. The smoke and steam rose wildly from the funnel mingled with the shrieks and shrills of its hooter. All the spectators used to stay away on the far sides of the platform. There was one more interesting and a thrilling routine performed by the station master himself. He used to fix a disc, about one foot radius and fixed with a solid leather ball along is circumference and hang it on a special stand. The driver of the train would first throw a similar device manually on the platform which he had picked up from the previous sub railway station and some device attached to the engine would snatch or pluck it, already fixed to the stand, at the colossal speed at this station. Apparently this routine was used to advise the train driver of the steam engine that the single track ahead was clear for the train up to the next station. However the buzz and thud of the steam engine, the rattle and clatter of the train, the hissing and sizzling of the smoke and steam was full of fantasy, thrill and thrust and I thrilled each time I observed the train storming across the small railway station. At a later stage, while travelling myself from Lahore to Montgomery by the fast train, I observed similar crowds waiting to see the express train zoom by them, although the train flashed so fast that I was unable to recognise anyone. On the fast train, one often observed women and children perched on the top of flat roofs of their houses built along the rail track gazing in excitement at how the steam train steamed away on the steel track.

Steam and heat are essential signs of life. As a school kid when I had just learnt few sentences of English and I happened to read through Radio Times magazine my eyes fell on a charming and a smartly dressed radio presenter or announcer; there was no television at that time. I wrote below her picture, 'I like you very much. You are a charming girl. I want to marry you as soon as possible.' I was hardly a teenager then, but the latent heat and steam built in the cells was already there deeply rooted, but sizzling like the Icelandic volcano which fumes desperately underneath the glacier.. Soon one of my brothers picked up the magazine for his perusal and read through my emotions and chuckled at my hissing steam, perhaps he had the same feelings, but I blushed and slipped away quietly fully perturbed. Later on when we were churning through the River Niger in the middle of the Sahara Desert by a speed boat, I noticed the same kind of excitement and uplift of emotions from the indigenous women, children and men when they waved flying kisses and flutters of hands towards us, perched high on the embankment; in excitement and with welcome gestures when we gushed through their mud and bush houses. The emotions were further steamed up and hissed like steam engine with the blow and glow of the stunningly beautiful bare breasts which bit like a pair of agitated cobras. In Lahore which is the second largest city of Pakistan, the airport authority has provided a special viewing gallery at a vintage point on the concourse for the view of the spectators who just flock from far and wide areas of the country, just to enjoy the" take-off and landing of the jumbo aircrafts. Perhaps they cannot afford to fly in the aeroplane or perhaps desire to experience a kind of different uplift in their emotions or admire the wonder of man's creation. They cluster in groups and as individuals to observe and feel the wonder, excitement and magnificence of the big bird, although the spectacle of roars and boom of the supersonic aircraft is far more colossal as compared to the steam engine, but definitely not as romantic, stirring and warm hearted as the good old British steam engine.

As a teenage boy and even after that, I used to yearn, while sitting in the train, for a heavy downpour of monsoons, the wild rumbling and violent dark clouds over the skies, with mighty roar and crackle of thunderstorms; and flash and flares of lightening. This could be because the Punjab is a kind of semi-arid land where rainfall is scanty or perhaps I lived in a country of restraints and restrictions or perhaps I was a person of meagre means and measures. My life was mundane and denuded; and there was not any spur or glow of social or leisure activity; it was rather boring and not much excitement. By travelling in the train, I felt more freedom and refreshed my mind with a great variety of terrain, people and atmosphere. I imagine I was also used to the flash-floods, mountains and wild life while living with my grandmother before the partition. To yearn for the similar environment remains a vital part of my psychology and gives lot of tranquillity, comfort and peace. While travelling in the train, sometimes my wish was fulfilled, there was heavy downpour of rain, the fields and landscape became overflowing with water and turned into pools and ponds. Even if it did not rain, the simple twirl and swirl of the fields and trees going round and round made me equally glad and that also included the fine fresh soil particles falling over my face and clothes, which actually did not bother me. However in the whole of Indian subcontinent, the monsoons are always welcomed with open arms as a blessing from the nature, good for the crops and trees and humans; and indeed a source of life. In the Indian

Subcontinent a great variety of romantic folk and film songs and blockbuster films are based on the monsoons and the train journeys and great many festivities and festivals are arranged during the monsoon showers, this period is definitely connected with the romance and love, especially while travelling in the train. There is a very popular song which says, 'Let us go to a place where there is no man or any of mankind'. Peace, tranquillity and non-interference are the priorities. This can easily be achieved when there is heavy downpour of monsoons, lightning and thunder storms; especially if one is cruising in the train. The first ever romantic film song I recollect listening to from the most popular Indian film before partition, when I was only few years old then, has a lonely lover yearning to her beloved like this '' Thunder rumble of wild clouds flip flap heavy downpour of rain, winds dance, swing and gush, my beloved can you come home sooner, my barren eyes are thirsty for a drop of water, my chest is sizzling, oh you cruel where are you banished, my nerves flash crackle like lightening, yearn you come home before next flash'. The sunken feelings of the lonely dejected lover in the romantic Monsoon clouds and rains, flare and blaze like fumes, glows and hisses of the steam engine.

In Pakistan natural scenery is stunning and bewildering. No other country in the world can match and boast it. It has not only the second highest peak K2, but also next eight or nine highest peaks, apart from one or two, it has series of different deserts, plateaus and mountain ranges spread all over the country as well as vast alluvial plains. So there is a great variety of natural scenes. In addition there are mighty perennial rivers like Indus and its tributaries which hurtle and thrust from the roof of the world. The British tried to build not only the railways, but mighty bridges on the mighty rivers and canals; they also built magnificent tunnels and railway stations over the mountains and remote areas and that includes the much celebrated and world renowned Khyber Pass as well. Although I have not been fortunate or I have not made the effort to travel all over this vast and stunning country, I am highly impressed by the engineering skill and

ingenuity of the British rulers of India, How they made a special
effort to build the magnificent bridges, tunnels and rail tracks
in every corner of the country. While crossing over the rivers
whether in the day or the night time; the mighty soaring rivers,
their vastness and the grandeur of the bridges appear resonant
and sonorous with each other. I remember once crossing the
Chenab River (one of the humble tributary of Indus) during
summer holidays at school during a moonlit night, it was a unique
feeling and experience observing great wonders of nature by
sitting comfortably in the steam engine train. The colossal sheet
of rippling water spread over miles width, glowed submerged in a
mirror of gold, while the moon smiled over the skies, as well
as tossed in the heart of the river. The tranquillity and peace
was only disturbed by the slurp and slap of the waves against the
river banks, which was about to brim its banks because of huge
quantity of water from the melted glaciers and also from the
Monsoon rains. It was an amazing blend of natural goodness and
purity tumbling from the skies; the serene silky gold atmosphere
was only blotted by the lonely night bird called Chikor, a kind of
flamingo, who was buzzing and flapping wildly towards the
moon. However the glow of the full moon and the river and
the lonely flight of the Chikor and the youthful sight from the
windows of the train and the grills of the bridge are still ever
reminiscent, translucent and bite like a serpent. I hypnotised
myself with so many wonders of nature in a single moment, in a
single glance and in a single place sitting snug and safe in the train.

Travelling from Lahore to Islamabad, while circumventing around
the Salt Range (Eighty miles length of solid salt-rock mountain)
one can almost touch the rear coach of the twenty –coach train
while the rear and front steam engines hiss and puff hard to thrust
the piston and the shafts, with lot of chuff-chuff and fumes, as
the train cruises at only a few miles per hour speed because the
contour of the crest of the rock formation is so round and bendy.
And gazing at the pink beauty of the romantic salt range which
teems with wild life and the unique ascent of the train and
admiring the British genius for this spectacular view and unique

experience of a life time. Again travelling by a small gauge train through the wild Pathan territory of the Khyber Pass is another wonderful and unique experience. Again over here the British have done a wonderful job by building forts, tunnels, high bridges on the steep and craggy nude hills and mountains. It is also unique to observe all men slinging the guns from their shoulders as a matter of normal dress, whether at peace or war.

The life at the main railway station is full of hustle and bustle and filled with lot of activities and colours. The first thing is to buy the train tickets and queue up in front of the ticket selling positions, there is a separate queue for the females. Traditionally the Pakistani does not believe in queues even while boarding an aeroplane and will try to push their way up and overtake the waiting passengers. Most of the men use their female accomplices, if any, to buy tickets as there are not many in the female ticket queue; but there is normally one clerk inside the ticket office who issues tickets to both queues. So when one queue is being served, the other queue has to stare on the other queue and pray for their turn. On the men side the uncouth and rough villagers; and even the servants of the influential and bureaucratic people break the queue anyway. Some of them perhaps travelling for the first time fear that the seats will be sold or that they might miss the train; they definitely believe might is right just like the super country does to the rest of the global village. Perhaps sometimes they are on their way to attend a long distant funeral or a wedding party of a close relative or a friend and do not consider the law abiding people who have been waiting patiently for a considerably longer time, even before the window for the ticket sale is open. One gazes in desperation on these trespassers and stone hearted people. In normal circumstances the person waiting sincerely in the front of the queue will be served at the end of the queue. Recently I had been waiting for some time in a queue in front of the window of the ticket office in the glorious Lahore Fort when a Mullah suddenly appeared from nowhere and stood in the front of the queue to get the ticket. There were lot of school kids waiting behind me as well in the same queue and they would have come from far and wide areas of the country to see that wonderful monument. When I and others had asked him to join the queue at the back, he replied, "I am in a hurry because I am getting late for my prayers." I could notice him that he was pretending and his face chuckled due to his blatant excuse. I wondered at that time what kind of lesson school kids were learning from his example as well as the old ones. That simple and insensitive rule of that Mullah prevails all across the board in Pakistan; peoples' rights are not observed.

As soon as one arrives at the main gate for departure or as soon as the train stops and even before the train comes to a complete halt, a swarm of coolies, clad in loose red shirts, baggy trousers and white loose turbans rush to grab the luggage and one has to be quick to draw the attention of the customers. Coolies are unique characters created by the steam- engine train, they are an agile and physically powerful people and can carry lot of heavy items like suite cases, bundles and other heavy items; some carry on their heads, some dangle on the shoulders and some being carried with both arms. They remind me of the tough women in the wild bush areas of Africa, where women trail on foot for long distances in the Sahara desert, carrying at least two heavy loads of grain or water on their heads and an additional load grasped in their hands while also carrying a baby tied at the back. The coolies make the bustling railway station very colourful and help the needy passengers with great perseverance and dedication, although they are not paid adequately enough to have a comfortable living, unless some kind hearted commuter gives them a generous tip. They are expected to be resilient and tough like a donkey and are intensely competitive. They not only climb the steep steps of the overhead British built bridges connecting one platform to the other, they also guide the passengers about the arrival of the trains and to which platform they should go, fully aware of where each particular coach for that particular customer will stop when the train arrives at the station. They will also help the passenger to find the seat while everyone twirls and swirls in the train in their panic. These colourful coolies loiter about desperate to earn fortune for the day, they work very hard to earn very little money to feed their families and this earning is related to their physical ability and there is no security for old age, as they are not officially paid by the railways. There is no welfare state benefit paid to them, which are normally swallowed by the ever more thirsty and hungry, most powerful and selfish rulers, bureaucrats and feudal lords of the country.

There is another colourful character generated by the steam engine, they are the smartly dressed catering men who operate on the fast and long distance express trains. Again they are normally dressed in pure cotton; smart uniforms which consist of nicely pressed white Shalwars (baggy trousers) and long shirts; as well as a crisp smart turban rising like a peacock from their heads. They belong to the catering department of the railways, who cook and supply European, local and Asian food, not only at the main stations, but also in the trains; day and night. The meals like breakfast, lunches and dinners and afternoon teas are supplied under orders to each seat and room location. The money in the train is collected after the meals have been consumed and an invoice and receipts with full details of the menu is provided. Each order of meal, tea or cold drinks or ice cream or fruit is provided in nicely laid trays with a supply of napkins. Each bearer of meals knows exactly how much money to collect and at which station food is to be served and to which cabin or a seat. I think the catering business in the long distance fast trains is vital to the passengers and a successful business on its own. I also hazard to guess that these catering men are descendants of the Chefs and Behras of British Viceroy of India's kitchen and the dining room as far as their appearance, smart uniform and an immaculate service is concerned. There is no difference in the heat and quality of their food and drinks as compared to the meal served on the tables and seats of the actual first class restaurant; but rather this looks more romantic and homely. There seems to be a close co-ordination between the catering restaurant facilitated in the train and the restaurants located all along the railway routes attached to the main stations; if in short supplies of different meals, they can be picked up at the next available restaurant at the next station the train is going to stop. There is one more amazing thing about these legendry catering ghosts, they normally deliver the meals on the trays dangling outside the train while it's speeding up and their smart erected turban still intact. It is really fascinating to observe them entering the car while the straws and dust are already blowing to the sky; they could easily be successfully employed as commandos in the army's elite force or as paratroopers.

There is another unique character born out of the steam engine; that is the train robber. He is terrific, shrewd, mysterious and enigmatic; and on the surface amicable, friendly and helpful. He might appear a simple looking soul having a long beard, sometimes artificial, but not always; and yelping or mincing on prayer beads and is often accompanied by an old, lean and skinny woman or a dying kid. Although they would sit in different segregated compartments for men and women, they would liaise when to plunder and how!; not infrequently men operate on their own, but in a civilised way. First they observe closely where the potential target is and to which compartment they are embarking. They sit next to the target and are most friendly and helpful; however if need be, a minor dose of anaesthesia may be used in a subtle manner, for example some use gas like chloroform or even offer some biscuits or coke mixed with some drugs making the victim unconscious or dizzy. However the police always advise the commuters not to take any drink or food from strange fellow passengers, but while travelling, everybody is not conscious about these culprits or spooky figures and inadvertently can become pitiful victims. However it is a not uncommon practice amongst the travellers to feel relaxed while enjoying the ride, like any other ride, may be in the aeroplane or a tonga, and feeling peaceful easily doze off. So most of the victims fall in this latest category and become victims themselves. The robbers watch their victims having sweet dreams, especially on long journeys and quietly get away with the booty. In these cases the culprits have plenty of time to plunge out from the train. The most popular victims are brides or women with suite cases full of jewellery and money; even businessmen carrying bags of cash for doing business. This kind of plunder takes place soon after the train starts to speed- up from the station or just before arriving at the next station when the train is cruising at the slowest speed and it is easy for the robbers to escape. However before leaving the train, they normally say goodbye to the fellow commuters, saying, 'God bless you, take care; have a safe journey!' They pretend as if they are close relatives or family friends bidding farewell. Now-a- days the mobile-phone system and text messages have made life far easier for the robbers, they can easily communicate with each other on land as well on the train and from compartment to compartment or from seat to the seat. In most of their roguish adventures they collaborate and liaise with the railway police and share the booty with them in return for safe passage.

Life on the average railway station and its platforms is full of hustle and bustle. There is a mixed gathering of people all hoping to travel to their various destinations together in a comfortable and safe manner. Some passengers relax on the benches, some sleep on the floors and some just doze or gossip or loiter about staring at the signals. In the main waiting halls there are newspaper stalls selling all kinds of newspapers and magazines, another stall selling fruit, cakes, tea, and drinks. There are flurries of coolies, travellers, relatives and friends who come to drop or pick up their acquaintances even some sight seers who come for leisure to have a casual look at the crowd and the train, especially the most fascinating steam engine. On the precinct of the station, the taxis, rickshaws, tongas wait for prospective customers. The horses squelch and munch on their fodder and sway their bushy tails to ward off any flies, while the donkey carts are also there. They pick up any heavy goods, the donkeys bray and sway and keep cool; they also grind on their food during their break and flap their ears to escape from the flies. The donkeys are wonderful and resilient beasts; they can survive on a small amount of cheap food and carry burdens in the most difficult terrain. They may not hiss or puff like the horses, but can easily stroke and thrust; and thus are not less than the steam engine in performance and can easily beat off the British. In addition to the main stalls, there are some vendors and hawkers, having their own stalls fixed on pivots and hand carts, laden with oranges, grapes, melons, bananas, peanuts, onion bhaji, chapattis, kebabs, a variety of meat curries, vegetables and fish dishes, with nice mouth-watering aromas. They are dotted at strategic locations across the platforms and are always mobile, depending upon the movement of the train and its stoppage position.

Sometimes the Burkha clad women bring their own stools made of lighter material like canes or bamboo skin and squat casually somewhere away in a remote corner of the station or platform and let their baby suckle at their breasts under camouflage. While the baby is suckling, the woman is also watching the world go by around her from her grill, like an SAS soldier would observe from the observation post. While she sits stationary, her husband will stroll about and feel free to stare at something else. A bride can also be sitting in the similar kind of strategic position laden with the jewellery and money, while submerged in emotions and gazing at the bridegroom. He wears a crispy turban, one end of which rises like K2, piercing the sky and the other end making an erected pigtail covering his spine. There is wild bush around his nose, with his long extending spiky black moustaches bushing out around his pinkish –shiny cheeks and piercing eyes, but drowned in emotions too and looking forward to the sizzling, fluttering and romantic nights.

Burkha clad women are not always as pious and pure as they pretend to be or depict, now a days so many criminal elements camouflage or hide under Burkha, some of them could be men with long beards belonging to a terrorist organisation.. Recently my sister–in-law was scurrying in the fashionable shopping centre in Lahore to buy some flashy and fashionable garments to wear at her nephew's forthcoming wedding in Karachi. She lodges in the USA and had changed a substantial amount of US Dollars into Rupees after her arrival and managed to plump and squeeze them in her designer purse. She accompanied her young daughter Bushra shopping. She is in her late sixties and her daughter in her mid-forties. While searching and haggling from shop to shop, she noticed three women in Burkhas hovering around her and performing the same rituals and rather shared their thoughts and choices. Once she arrived at the decision making stage and got involved in intense haggling with the shopkeeper, one of the women slashed her swollen purse, which was comfortably tucked on her back and slung from her left shoulder, with a sharp razor or knife and the bundles of notes tumbled and thumped on the shop floor with a thud. The rogue women managed to pinch quite a few packs of money and hid them under their Burkha and frisked towards other shops in the basement and abandoned some bundles behind in panic when my niece challenged them. She chased them with great ferocity and managed to catch them and started slapping them and pulled their Burkhas away. In the tussle that ensued, the bundles of Rupees splashed on the floor, which were hidden in their bosoms and armpits. But still they pleaded not guilty and the shopkeeper in whose shop they were sheltering was siding with the criminals and pleaded for their innocence as well. He reiterated that the criminals must be somewhere else and they would not hide over here. Perhaps the shopkeepers collaborated with the criminals and assured them that police would be called in to investigate. My sister-in-law and her daughter departed the scene baffled and thanking their stars for lucky recovery of money. After arriving in the house, she handed her damaged purse to her maid as a souvenir and transferred the bulky Rupee bundles to a new purse.

Momentarily the station attendant bangs the brass disc with the wooden hammer, hung in the wooden gallows erected on the platform. He does so under the command of the station master who gets confirmation about the departure of the train from the previous station, conveyed to him on phone. Then the signalman will proceed to the signal tower which has been built far away along the track on either edge of the platforms. After ascending the high tower, which is just like a control tower, he will pull the relevant liver to diagonally stooping the rectangular signal arm. This is not only the clearance entry granted to the incoming train driver, but good news for the commuters as well; that the train is on its way to the platform and will be approaching in the next a few minutes. While gazing at the signal sign, the jubilant commuters will also try to spot the smoke and fumes of the approaching steam train as well as lots of rising dust having been stormed and stirred along its path. The signalman will also shunt the track on which the train will be entering the station. This is operated manually as devised by British 150 years ago. If the arm of the signal is erected in the horizontal position, it means no train is arriving at the station or if it has arrived outside the station, it cannot enter the station because of some operational and security reason. The rectangular signal metal arm, itself is attached to a lofty and an imposing metal frame which soars next to the tower. As soon as the train arrives near the tower, the signalman also waves a green flag from the air to assure the driver that the train is safe to enter the station.

All passengers and coolies are alerted and take their positions to enter the train. The sight of the train on the horizon is a special moment and thrilling one. The train leaves behind the fields, the countryside, rivers and canals, as well as clouds of dust and agitated air and forests and meadows. Some spectators gather around the railway barriers and gates to have a glimpse of the roaring and soaring train entering the railway station parameter. Some children and women stare and wave from top of the flat roofs of their houses or peeping from behind the pergolas. The hiss and puff of the steam engine, its thrift and thud and slowing down of the pistons and shafts seem all captivating and full of warm emotions. The pitch dark steam engine brings the train and its passengers to a halt with last few sluggish strokes, the pistons and shafts become lifeless. Hissing and sizzling stops with a sigh, ready for the embarking and disembarking. Again there is no discipline or patience among the commuters on the platform; they rush and push without letting the disembarking passengers out first and get stuck in the doors and in the corridors. The exhausted passengers and the coolies wait patiently to come out or go in. This causes chaos not only for the new passengers to find their seats and get settled in the train, but also for the outgoing passengers as well. Why did the British not train them how to queue up and teach etiquette, how to deal with other humans and respect their rights, I do not know!

The train journey in Pakistan reminds me about the Arabian Nights; full of fantasy and magic. The train looks like a picnic area too. The passengers, especially long- distance ones bring with them their food, drinks, blankets, cassette players and even hubly-bubly from which the addicted smokers cannot stay apart. In the night time, some passengers tend to sleep on the floors of the entrance and the corridors; they normally have no seat or sleeper-reservations and cannot afford to stand on their legs dozing whole night,, thus it is impossible to enter the train; police and special train travelling inspectors need to be called in to gain access. Sometimes the wild tribesmen under the influence of snuff, opium or hashish occupy the whole compartment and spread their legs as if the train belongs to them; they apparently pretend as if the whole cabin or compartment has been reserved for them; and normally they are long distance travellers, perhaps travelling for days at a stretch carrying business goods with them. They snug comfortably in their quilts and camouflage in a mysterious way with the lights off. In most of the cases it is possible that they are without tickets or reservations and are not allowing in the genuine passengers who have actually paid the money for the sleepers to have a comfortable night journey; again police and special help is needed from the railway inspectors. They are skilful ticket dodgers, a kind of mafia people and well organised; and having a nomadic life in the train and flourish in business. At the sight of the ticket inspectors, they try to hide in the toilet in a subtle way or pretend to be fast asleep and not to be disturbed. This image of the tribesmen in the train can easily be reflected, taking place right across the board in Pakistan, in the day to day pattern of domestic life and in the official business and dealings in the public services and various national institutions Lots of business routines in

Pakistan are done under hand and through shrouded malpractices, lubricated with courtesy and gratitude to each other.

When everybody is settled the guard waves the green flag to the driver. The engine hisses and sizzles and brakes are released off, again the pistons and shafts thrust and the train clatters slowly and drifts away with a steady acceleration, dust started rising again and the train just disappears in the horizon within a matter of minutes, a miracle performed by the puff-puff and chuff-chuff of the steam engine. There were many atmospheric and euphoric scenes filled with emotions and sentiments which are associated with the steam engine train journeys. There were tears trickling down the cheeks of the departing bride in the train, while the mother had shed tears on the platform and the father wiped his nose and at the same time the bridegroom felt the crispy flag of his turban. There were lots of exchanges of flying cheers, waves and kisses from both sides of the train. In the train there used to be lot of other activities. The regular blind and disabled were already there, holding their fort along with the railway officials on duty. They flitted and flocked in the train with great agility and perseverance from coach to coach, to earn their fortune by begging for themselves as well as for the police and the railway officials who had provided protection to them. They were also allowed to enter the women compartments as they appeared to be harmless and deprived of normal senses. They worked in gangs and mafia groups. I remember once a blind man convincing the travellers and gloating, 'My honourable and lucky brothers and elders, I lost my sight by bad luck and I am unable to earn money for my widowed mother and orphaned brothers and sisters. I assure you, those who fatefully lose their sight, they lose their world and those who lose their teeth, and they lose their taste. So I beg you, my dear friends to donate me generously and take my best wishes and blessings not only in this world, but also life after death where a colossal and unlimited reward will be waiting for you'. He had hardly finished these lampoons of supplications, when a tough and honest travelling ticket inspector entered the coach for normal routine checks on the ticket-dodgers.

This tramp's eyes were tightly shut and the inspector gave him a resounding slap on his face with an angry yell, 'You are a rascal and a rogue; you can see very well, just push off from my sight immediately.' Soon the beggar could see the stars in the dazzling day light and frisked away quietly without any embarrassment, perhaps to the next location. His beard and eyes shook together in front of the bewildered passengers, like the cinders and ashes of the Icelandic Volcano. I wonder why he could not pray for his own prosperity and glory rather than for other fellow commuters in the train!

The medicine vendors also slip into the train to sell their medicine, fully guaranteed, authenticated and government licensed; and fully refundable, if it does not cure. They sell them at sale price and as a limited supply and on a one off basis. They would assure their prospective customers by staring into their eyes and raising the medicines one by one in the air with full confidence and with enchanting smiles on their cheeks like a modern day politician, 'Try it now and see the immediate benefits'. They reassure the customers for better health and ask for their good wishes in return for the cheap treatment provided by a top specialist and a popular medical rep. These medicine vendors carry their products in a rucksack and store them in carefully packed pigeon-holes. The most popular medicine sold in the train is for impotency. He would address and assert to the male audience, "Honourable friends, if you have damaged your organ in your youth by malpractices or abuses, do not worry. I am here to help you. Take me as your Messiah. God willing, it will rectify all weaknesses and you can perform again like a stallion. So please do not despair, and remember it is a sin to despair and try it right from tonight and see the result within two weeks. I can assure you, my honourable dear friends you will thrust and hiss like a steam engine and will InshaAllah (God willing), conquer the fort." The other medicine next in line and in greater demand is concerning decaying teeth and bleeding infectious gums. He would dig out the next patch of medicine and proclaim, "If you have holes in your teeth or your teeth are decaying or your gums are bleeding, use this powder and rub nicely on the gums or fill the holes with this paste, they will become healthy, the teeth will become like a brick and shine like silver, then you can easily peel off the sugarcane and squeeze it within your rock like teeth, there will be no more bleeding and no more smells. Then you can smile and enjoy the taste." The next popular medicine concerns the eyes' ailments. He would dig out some eye drops or ointment in plastic tubes and raise them in the air and proclaim, "These latest inventions based on natural remedies and herbs would improve your eyesight, remove cataracts and cure any infections within days, you will be able to see the stars in the day time and blush like a virgin."

However while returning home from my summer holidays from Lahore to Montgomery, an unusual and one off incident in my life took place in the train. The distance between Montgomery and Lahore is just over one hundred miles and for the fast train at that time was about two and half hours. The train stopped at about four main stations before reaching my town. However because of point failures due to intense heat, two fast trains were badly delayed and even our express train started belatedly. It was near to the happy festivity 'Feast of the sacrifice', which is part of the vital ritual affiliated with the pilgrimage to Mecca, one of the two main Eid festivals of the Muslims. In Pakistan the most popular sacrificial animal is the goat, followed by lamb, sheep, cow and last and not the least camel. However not many people can afford to sacrifice animals because of lack of funds, I think about 60% come into that category; and I am sure I fell in the same group. About 20% sacrifice more than one animal of good pedigree; and 20% use average quality animals. Some believers out of conviction sacrifice the most sought after, beautiful and of extremely rare pedigree and quality animals and pay ten times more for a single beast; they are 'Montgomery Cows and Bulls', the best in the whole of Pakistan. They have special quality of meat and deliver fine and great quantity of milk and have gentle habits and features, people like to cuddle them and feel delighted to have a glimpse of them. However the people who cannot afford sacrifices get their fair share too, because two thirds of the meat is supposed to be distributed to friends, neighbours and the poor. Amongst the most popular beneficiaries are the beggars who appear to be poor and reach each household and beg for their entitlement in person. They work hard and collect meat for the whole year and make different products from the dried meat. The beggars swarm like bees in each locality and sometimes hire youngsters and the unemployed; and they transport their donations on donkey-carts which are provided with the music players. They definitely outdo the persons who actually perform the sacrifice of the animals. It is quite possible that they sell their booty at a sale price to the local butchers ready for selling to the beef-eaters the following morning. All across the board, the Mullahs reassure the believers that the better the pedigree and better the health of the animal, better will be the reward and better will be the peace and tranquillity to the departing soul. However it is difficult to surmise about the fate of 60% of faithful who cannot afford any such sacrifices and what is going to happen to the millions of beggars who buzz and boom at every corner of Pakistan!

As soon as our train arrived at the platform, everyone travelling in that direction rushed to the train to have a seat or at least some space to stand between the seats or stand in the corridors. There were wild and startled crowds on the platform and everyone hustles and jostles each other to embark the train and as a result a great chaos ensued. Normally the women would go to the ladies compartment and the men to the men-side; but in this skirmish and squabble, all gender rules were discarded and fortunately or unfortunately there were some mixed gathering in our men's compartment. I managed to stand in the corridor and a family also rushed and squeezed next to me. I was only twenty years old and red hot in every sense. I was a college student and wore my usual jeans and shirt and in that hot weather and scorching heat I never wore any underwear, even in winter; perhaps I could not afford or I was not much a cultured person. The train was so overcrowded that no one else could manage to come in when the train stopped at the next due main stations, although the people struggled to get in, but in vain; the commuters were even hanging on the doors. Most of the passengers seem to be long distance ones; so for hours and hours there was no change and the squeeze continued unhindered. The young lady squeezed in front of me stood with her cushion like back pressed against me. Luckily it was not a financial squeeze or crunch at that moment, I had none anyway. She must be slightly older than me, but not too old or might be even younger, it is difficult to recollect and it did not worry me the least or even cross my mind. She kept on chattering with one of her male relatives standing opposite to her face and I noticed her gesturing and smiling all the way. She was not wearing any Burkha, but simple cotton Shalwar, Qamees and Dopatta. While the engine chuffed, puffed and huffed, the train rattled and clattered; my emotions were in high tide and brimming the banks and burst like flash floods. The tides rose and fell incessantly and spiralled and dilated like wild bush fire. My heart fluttered and emotions soared and whole body roared in subtle feelings and still do; the soothing cushion like squeeze still evokes my feelings. I arrived in Montgomery, after almost three hours standing in the corridor which went like seconds or a flash. Soon after disembarking at the platform, I cursed myself for the folly of disembarking too soon. I could have easily continued another hundred miles and then made a U-turn, even at the cost of penalty for fare dodging. However I had abandoned the train reluctantly. When I reached home I was drenched and dripping to the ankles, toes and the heels. That unique peaceful and thrilling moment has turned into a glowing moment easily compatible with the bursts, sizzles and fumes of the steam engine.

A few more years elapsed quietly after this incident, till I experience another evocative and graphic historical moment in the steam engine train; this time I was on a far longer journey and far more reaching, exciting and plausible. This is the moment which changed the course of my life. That was the moment which overshadows the rest of my life. I got married on 26 June, 1966, I was only twenty six and had my first wedding night in the train in a special air conditioned coupe, meant only for a couple; the most exclusive and luxurious train journey if one could afford it in the fastest train of the country.. This special and high class accommodation is meant only for the elite and special people and who can be more special than the first wedding night's couple. I travelled with my bride from Karachi to Montgomery a nonstop journey of about seven hundred miles lasting over seventeen hours. The steam engine had to replenish its supply of coal and water at three main junctions. The furnishing and facilities affiliated to this accommodation were immaculate, stunning and amazing. The attendants were there all the times waiting in the corridors or cabins and normally attended to their customers clad in special uniforms and magnificent turbans. Special buttons or bells were fixed inside the coupe to call for the attendants for a glass of cool refreshing water or any other item. Again this unique and one off special night went like a flash and a flare. We had a good supply of juicy mangoes nicely packed in a crate to suck and lot of enchanting moments to recollect. My in-laws very kindly paid for this exclusive romantic trip. My other members of the family travelled separately in economy class. I was completely a virgin and did not know how to grope or fumble about with a woman and was overexcited, but shy. The train departed about 8 PM and we were on our own and settled down quickly and felt rather at home. After few introductory pleasant moments, the bride opened her suitcase to change her posh and hefty bridal dress which was traditional Indian red silk dress embroidered with gold fibres. She was wearing matching dopatta which was heavily laced with silver laces on the edges and some intricate embroidery on rest of it. She also removed her jewellery pieces and carefully secured them in appropriate jewellery boxes. She took her night suite out and unexpectedly handed one for me. Before this moment I never used any night suite; but in the coupe I expected to wear the normal Qamees and Shalwar. I was rather stunned by her gestures and preparation. On the other end no one guided me for anything or any eventuality. From amongst my family no one gave any gift to me or the bride, even I failed to give her any gold ring or wedding night gift as I was not made aware about it or the importance of it; for which I was highly embarrassed and she was upset too.

On top of that I had no money to buy any such sensitive historical gifts, but I had no worries and I am sure she did not care either; at least for the time being.

Then something funny and weird happened, the bride went to the toilet to refresh and also to change herself to her night dress, but for some unknown reasons, she was taking excessive time to come out. I do not know why, perhaps she was missing her parents and crying or perhaps she simply endeavoured to shy away from me or perhaps it might be due to some other reason. It is quite possible that in my mind I was subconsciously exaggerating the time lapse, after all I was waiting and in intense pressure, the wait for a minute could be more than a year. In the bafflement I started knocking on the toilet doors, but still no response, but thankfully she came out eventually and I felt relief. The lights were turned out and we lay snug in the posh velvet sleeper-bed, wrapped comfortably in posh and soft blankets. However due to lack of expertise, confidence and compromise and also being autocratic, initial attempts were aborted. According to the old popular sayings, "Two hands are needed to clap." I was terribly dejected and in the pursuit sucked one or two delicious, juicy fragrant mangoes on my own to refresh myself and turned out the lights again. In such a nervous and tense moment I inadvertently pressed the wrong button as well. To my surprise and more confusion, as well as doom and gloom, the attendant was knocking at our door constantly and asking politely, "Sir, what can I do for you. What is your order, sir?" I opened the door and asked, "What's the matter? We have not demanded anything from you or rang the bell." I responded blushingly and gazing at his solemn face. He said smilingly, "Sir, you did ring the bell..." I replied, "It must be by mishap or unintentional. It just happened in the dark." The attendant chuckled and left with some funny smiles on his cheeks. I was more embarrassed in front of the bride who assured me that I did call for the attendant by pressing the button, fixed next to the seats. She just beckoned towards the button with a whisper. I tittered and chuckled at myself in a tizzy, luckily the lights were off. It was simply lack of handling experience or lack of knowledge, but stuck to my gun and kept cool. However I cursed myself for being ignorant and unacquainted in every sense. This time I felt squeeze and sensation from different angles and perspectives, but not pleasant like the earlier squeeze of the packed crowd in the train, that was different kind of sensation and one off incident. These unique historical moments in the coupe were a blessing in disguise, otherwise they would not flash and crackle so wildly even now after over four decades from the dark and peaceful coupe of the fast thrusting and bursting stem engine train.

At that moment I was working as a lecturer in a government college over two hundred miles away from Montgomery on the banks of icy River Jhelum and the college was about to close in about two weeks' time for almost three months summer holidays . So every one of my colleagues was asking, "Can't you wait another few more days and then there would be almost three months holidays." Some of them were enquiring, "Is this a love marriage that you cannot wait for? Also why are you doing the marriage so far away and in such a scorching hot weather?" In the extreme weather of Pakistan, people normally gets married in the cool and refreshing weather of spring or winter, preferably in November or March when the temperature is mild and flowers blossom everywhere and atmosphere is laden with colours and fragrance. One of my colleagues remarked, "Even if he gets married in December, they would still be inside in June!" They all burst into laughter and made fun of me. It would appear that perhaps they were equally excited too.

Soon after fixing the wedding date, the father of my prospective wife wrote a letter to me in Jhelum, where I was working, and questioned directly, "After the wedding where would the bride would be lodging?" I was rather perplexed about his worries and at that time I was sharing a small house, living in a room with my colleagues. Naturally I would not have kept my wife in that accommodation, but in a separate one whatever I could afford. I think his main concern was whether I would keep her in the joint family home in Montgomery, for which I had no intention, otherwise there was no point in getting married. I replied, "The bride will live in my heart." Later the train journey in a special accommodation was full of colourful emotions and laden with ecstatic romantic reminiscences. However the popular saying goes, 'There are always thorns with the flowers.' There was some snag and enigma attached to it as well, perhaps a dark side As I was a self -made man and still paying back the studentship loans, I could not buy any wedding ring or any jewellery for my wife and as usual no one contributed any help from amongst my closest relatives; and she was rather depressed after listening to the ill remarks of her relatives and friends for not having received the jewellery from the groom-side; and her mother kindly gave her some more to compensate for this discrepancy; but for her it was not the same feelings. So there is one more stigma attached to the Indian social traditions which gives too much importance to the possession of gold and consider these assets as sign of good luck and closest to the goddess of luck. If someone denudes his bride of golden jewellery, it is a bad omen and sign of disaster in future. The liability on the bride family even gets worse. However I was more interested in my bride and getting married without wasting any more time. The opportunity was knocking and I wanted to knock as well; and I did not waste a single moment. To me it was a good omen as I thought she was a good match and I was right because our life has flourished many folds since. Any way I had a glorious start by having seventeen hours of the first night in a superb excluded place; I was a winner all across the way. I had broken the chains and shackles of the local culture and traditions; and I think these unwanted evils and restraints cause more misery and problems at the end. However the majority of parties come under the crunch of loans and people sometimes sell their meagre assets to keep the world happy around them and they themselves with suffering for the rest of their lives. In my case the bride was not worried about this superficial tragedy herself as she was well educated and enlightened, but her relatives and friends kept on nagging her about the bad omen to come. Luckily she is far better off now than her forecasting friends and relatives. Again thanks to the puff-puff and chuff-chuff of the steam engine and the epic wedding night in the train. I perceive human life like a steam engine and the passage of life as a train. The steam engine drags the train on a single track, hissing, sizzling and fuming. It puffs chuffs and strokes while the steam lasts. Life is just like a single track; the moments, the feelings, the joys and sorrows, the rise and fall of eddies and ebbs never return. The last breath and sigh is like the last panting and gasping of the steam engine and the last stroke of its journey. Life cruises on its orbit, but never U-Turns.

Chapter XI

Cascading Flames and Flickers

Spending first few years of my childhood with my maternal grandmother, made me a great admirer of nature and enlightened me as a child. I was hypnotised and enchanted by the sight of the great, soaring dark brown wall of the Himalayas which was not far away from us. Over there as soon as I came out from our house, instantly my eyes would turn in the direction of the mountains and I admired their grandeur each time I stared at them; and indeed we were not far away from Shimla, the then summer capital of British India; although at that time I was not aware of its political significance. In addition I mesmerised myself by staring at the great surge and roars of the flash floods and admired their freedom. At that moment I became aware about the connection of the black clouds and the flash floods. It was enthralling and exciting to stare at the thundering and lightening clouds gushing towards the mountains. As soon as there was a crackle of thunder and a flash of lightening over the mountains, there started the heavy downpour of rain and within half an hour the flash flood swirled towards our village. All those wonderful, captivating and thrilling moments affiliated with the natural phenomena gave me a lot of happiness and hope; and the thoughts of them still arouse my feelings. Even the arrival of dust and sandstorms used to uplift my feelings and I preferred to stroll on my own in the blanket of the storm which enveloped the whole earth and the sky. I do not know why, but it could be the loneliness of a child or the comfort of freedom. However I always yearned for the flash floods, wild clouds and dust storms. As soon as I started walking, I favoured to trot with my grandmother or my uncle, rather than to be picked up. I often strolled on my own in the street of the small village going from my grandmother's house to my aunt's house which was located in the next street at the back of our house.. However, her abode was not far away from us, but in a different street. Luckily the community in that little settlement lived like relatives and close friends, so there was not much danger to the lonely child, but naturally risk was there even from within the close fabric of the relatives, friends, stray dogs or wild animals.

In that tender and sprouting age, I observed the different stages of the crops growth from the seedlings, buds and blossoms to the sprouting, stems and the harvests and enjoyed every single moment. I marvelled at the wonders of nature and was aware how the earth became colourful and full of life with the rotation of the weather. I was bewitched, lured and captivated by the fragrance and colours of the flowering of the mangoes, pomegranate, linseed and wheat. I wondered and admired at the delicate pink and red buds of the pomegranate, how red turns into pinkish white flowers or petals and into a shell of the far bigger golden fruit containing colourful and juicy diamonds inside. I often chose to walk in the green fields of maize to admire the cobs dangling with their dark brown pony tail from the side pockets of their straight stems; I drew pleasure from walking alone in the green fields, orchards and in the dry river bed, as if I was a part of nature and its goodness. I felt more relaxed by wandering in the fields laden with different crops and swaying with fresh breeze swooping down from the soaring heights of the Himalayas; thus most of my spare time was consumed in the fields, orchards or dry river bed rather than squatting in the mundane enclosure of the house. I felt myself more relaxed and comfortable outdoors rather than inside the limited space. While rambling or strolling in the wild environment, I frequently observed leveret hopping around as well as young fawns jumping past me, perhaps they were slightly younger than me, but they gave me an everlasting dream -like partnership, entourage or fellowship. However I was not alone, the precincts of the village teemed with captivating wild life, colourful birds as well as a great variety of flowers. The atmosphere and landscape was filled with a fascinating variety of charming and peaceful fellow creatures. I recollect climbing a low stooping mango tree with my friends and groping into the deep hole carved into its stem; and snatching out some baby parrots, caressing and cuddling and kissing them while they chattered and screeched. It was an amazing experience as a young child to observe the colourful and innocent looking parents of the equally similar fascinating chicks, staying very cool and trying to chatter with us without getting agitated or boisterous. It was a unique privilege to have a chat with these colourful and innocent looking birds without any prior knowledge or guidance. All those delightful and unique historical moments became a part of my happy glittering memory. Those creatures or crops may not be with me now, but they accompany me all the time and subconsciously are a part of my feelings and thoughts. The unique sight of peacocks prowling and blotting the green fields and spreading colourful wings and dancing sprightly in the frenzy and spree of mating, enhanced by their croaking, are few joyful moments to recollect, reminisce and describe. Although the terrible stab and prick of the long thorn piercing the sole of my left foot is fiercely agonising and even now the thought of which makes chills go down my spine, but the moment of respite and pullout by the Imam's beautiful teenage daughter is more gratifying and comfortable and relieves my pain by visualising the snugness and warmth of her lap; the caresses and cuddles of a dream-like maiden. I still feel comfy and cosy clenched next to her heart. To call her fragrant flower would be not fair and would be an insult to her as she deserves far more than that; but her presence gives me lot of peace and comfort. These are all wonders of the grandma's village and add to the great wealth of my childhood experience. I still recollect distinctly staring closely at the seasonal mating of water-buffaloes, cows, mares, goats and bitches in that rural environment and still seem everlasting unique moments. The sight and sound of them have created a colourful zoo in the depth of my mind and they flash forever in the orbit of my vision.

On top of this I was frequently delighted with the melodious songs of the Koel, a kind of black magical bird which perched and fluttered from tree to tree in the midst of the freshness of cool Monsoon breezes slapping down from the mountains, as well as filled with the perfume of the subtle and delicate aroma of the exotic tropical fruit such as mangoes. This is the most romantic moment in the subcontinent when a beloved is dying of in the tempest of volatile emotions and yearns in desperation to meet her lover to quench her thirst, but he seems to be far away in the growling and violent clouds. She becomes so turbulent and distorted that she calls him a cruel person for not quenching her thirst. The echoes of her intensely pulsating and fluttering body resonate with the melodies of the Koel. She feels the crackle, thunder and lightning of the Monsoons and keeps on turning in bed in her wretched agony, disappointment and frustration. Just visualise the close sight of the mighty Himalayas, the colourful wild life as well as the rambling and growling dark monsoon clouds; it creates a magical place and is so captivating and enchanting that one can easily forget the rest of the world. While reminiscing about those nostalgic moments, their peace and tranquillity, I am not surprised that I hardly missed my mother. The sights and scenes in the village endowed motherly comfort and care to me. The other reason for not missing her might be that I had never seen her either in real life or glimpsed her picture; but even if I had seen her, it was not in my memorable age.

After Partition when I was only seven years old, luckily a similar contact with the rural terrain and wild life was maintained, although our new dwelling was nowhere near the Himalayas. We resided just on the edge of the fields, canals as well as the orchards, groves, meadows teeming with a great variety of wild life. But now I began to miss my grandma who had died miserably in the refugees' camps and she had died without having seen me and therefore I yearn more and more to meet her, as I was emotionally attached to her after having spent the last few years with her in the village. At the time of my departure from grandma's village, she was assured by my brother that she would meet me sooner and at that time my feelings were the same to rejoin her at the earliest. However I did not mention about my wretchedness, torture or misery to anyone in my family as I did not expect any sympathy or condolences from anyone, perhaps they might have made fun of me and rather laughed at my gestures. I suppose this is an integral part of that multi-strata primitive culture. However I was not alone who suffered like this so desperately, there must be millions of other people whose relatives or loved ones were slaughtered in the communal atrocities or who had drowned in the great floods in the Punjab or withered away from different ailments' sufferings in the camps during the course of mass migration. And this is the miracle performed by the politicians and the hateful religious leaders who tried to prove that only they are the rightful owners of this wonderful planet and others needed to be wiped out. Luckily they themselves might have been dead by now and I earnestly hope so and those who are still alive, their conscience must be pricking them, provided they have any, before they fade away into the oblivion for good. However after the reunion with my father and the rest of the family, I was soon given the unusual assignment of taking our goats to the pen of a shepherd which lay encamped over a distance of one mile in the remote countryside. The shepherd sheltered his herd of sheep and goats within the lofty enclosure of thorny bush barrier. It was not infrequent for the wolves to ambush the herd and get away with one or two sheep or goats in the stillness of the dark night. My responsibility was to take the goats to the pen, before going to my school first thing early in the morning, after seeing the first rays of the sun and fetch them back just before twilight. Sometimes I accompanied our young servant who was roughly of my age and must have been meagrely paid, as he ran away quite often to his parents' home distant few miles away. Sometimes one of my friends in the neighbourhood gave me a company, but most of the times I was alone and without any fear or hesitation. I had three teenage, real elder brothers in the house, but somehow they had eluded that adventure. However I performed my assignment quite amicably and without any moaning and groaning; rather I felt delight to go through the fields and bushes as I used to do in grandma's village. Later on during the stage of my growing up from childhood to adulthood, my affiliation with the wild bush, fields and orchards continued unabated. I strolled for miles daily at leisure along the canal embankments holding my book in my hand and concentrated better there in my studies; normally I used green fields and greenwood trees as my study room. In the summer time, after school it was our daily routine to swim in the canal with our friends. This was the time when I had encountered the King Cobra and many more snakes, especially on the edge of the canals as well as fields during the scorching summer seasons.

During the course of summer holidays the temperature in the sweltering plains soared to almost fifty Centigrade and everything burned like a furnace and thus became untouchable. While in college I was full of flesh and boiled with blood; a red-hot and an adventurous person. Coincidently those months were also the season of the romantic Monsoons which rushed and gushed from the Indian Ocean, Arabian Sea and Bay of Bengal towards the Himalayas all across the subcontinent, along the great mountains' walls which stretched to 2,500 miles; but their intensity and ferocity became less and less as they proceeded from the east to the west. They came with the roars, lightning and thunder and heavy downpours of rain causing the perennial rivers into high floods in the low lying plains of the Punjab and Sindh. Luckily for me one of my elder brothers named Aslam was working for the Pakistan Air Force at that time and was stationed at a base near Rawalpindi. At that time the twin city of Rawalpindi, now called Islamabad and also the capital of Pakistan, was not in existence. It was just a conglomeration of low lying undulating hills and flash-flood scarred terrain, but in the process of being built. From this base the Himalayas were just ten to twelve miles away; this is almost the same distance which lay from my grandmother's village, which was located over three hundred miles away to the east from Islamabad, now a part of Indian territory. To the north of Islamabad lay the roof of the world where three great mountain ranges of Himalayas, Hindukush and Karakuram meet; where there is K2 over 28,000 feet and more than eight peaks over 26,000 feet, and where circumvents the highest motor way of the world called Karakuram Highway, starting from Islamabad and terminating at the Chinese town of Kashgher; slithering over 700 kilometres. This is the area where also lies the highest battlefield of the world called Siachin Glacier, where the Indian and Pakistani forces exchange chapattis and live in igloos for shelter. This is the area where the most beautiful and disputed valley of Kashmir lies and has brought the people of the subcontinent to their knees and brink of poverty by spending billions of Dollars annually to boost up their forces, but they hardly fight, two million soldiers of joint force stand alert eye to eye. This is the area where the greatest and mightiest Indus River and its main tributary River Jhelum hurtles and plunges from the Himalayas. This is the area where the snow leopard hunts goats and stags and pounces over the craggy slopes of snow-clad mountains.

My brother already had a quiet word with the driver of the truck who was supposed to carry provisions as well as the senior commanding officer of the air force and his pretty wife to the most remote and secluded outpost of Kalabagh (Black Garden) located at a height of some ten thousand feet and about two hours staggering journey from the British built resort of Murree. This road is carved out of very steep slopes of the mountains and its contours loop at acute angles. One feels awe and fright by gazing down at the steep valleys and the piercing vertical sandstone rocky slopes, but luckily the whole panorama of the mountain slopes and the sheer steep walls of the valleys have been heavily forested with lofty and lush green conifer trees and it is difficult even to ramble or hike through them. It is also not easy for the sunlight to pierce through the trees, just like the Amazon jungles, and the terrain looks like black gardens. .This is the area which is famous and popular for the amazing monkeys, tigers, cheetahs, red and black bears and a great variety of stags and deer; as well as long bearded fascinating goats and last but not the least this area is renowned for its mystics and saints. After travelling here you forget rest of the world. This area consists of thickly forested slopes and charming views of wooden spurs, churning crystal clear and cool water falls, as well as natural springs abound on the slopes, splendidly situated at an altitude of 8,400 feet; which overlook the hissing, sizzling and gushing River Jhelum which enters the Pakistan territory in a u-shaped vertical valley after hurtling and cascading from the ever beautiful vale of Kashmir, some eighty miles away. The British Raj summer capital of Simla and Murree are both located in the Punjab, although about 400 miles apart and having the same altitude of about 8,500 feet in the Himalayas. However Murree was the summer capital of the Punjab, the then British governor would shift his offices to here from his capital of Lahore 250 miles away. The governor had a magnificent palace at Murree and still this grand royal lodge is very prominent, dominating and ever popular amongst the rulers of Pakistan. In addition there is an army garrison as well as an air force training school. There are well established convent schools for boys and girls and horse riding training school for the white residents; but now only the rich and elite children come here for the outstanding education and to learn skills for a bright future in pragmatic life.

Historically Murree is significant and a crown in the jewel from the British perspective. Over here James Abbott and Henry Lawrence had set up guerrilla camps when they were fighting the war against the Sikhs, as employees of East India Company. They were using local Muslims 'mercenaries to fight against the Sikhs, the then rulers of the Punjab. According to Abbott, 'The Sikh rulers of Hazara, held unlimited power to plunder, slay or dishonour any Mohammadan. The garrisons of forty castles and towers, scattered over the country, lived chiefly on plunder from the majority Muslim population, which made two third of the exchequer.' The Muslim mercenaries were fighting free for the British to get rid of the their oppressors and after the defeat of the Sikhs became part and parcel of the main force who were fighting against the Muslims and Hindus freedom fighters at the time of the mutiny in 1857; side by side with the Sikh soldiers who later become a part of the fighting force for the British East India Company as well. James Abbott first went to Hazara in December 1846 charged by his senior colleague Henry Lawrence and became the first British Deputy Commissioner to Hazara. The most beautiful resort town in Pakistan, over two hours breathtaking and picturesque journey from Murree, called Abbottabad located at 4,200 feet altitude and is still named after him and is the headquarter of the world famous military training college called Kakul Academy, later established by the British and further upgraded by Pakistan. Over here are also the world famous and classical British built boarding schools, colleges and elite power houses; now this modern town is even proud of its medical colleges and Karakuram High Way which sprawls through it, soaring up to the skies along the banks of the most glorious, fantastic and amazing Indus River. It takes over twenty hours of nonstop driving on the Karakuram Highway to reach the Khunjrab Pass (17,000 feet altitude) from Abbottabad with meal and convenience breaks included; this is almost the same time taken by the express train to reach Lahore from Karachi. It passes along the foot of the most glorious and imposing Rakapushi Peak (26,000 feet) piercing the skies; while relaxing for few minutes for a high cup of tea, one stares and stares towards the top of the peak, but normally one is not lucky to have a glimpse of it as it is mostly shrouded by the high floating white and grey clouds. It is quite easy to fall down on one's back while trying to reach the top from the KKH; the only comfort one can draw from this effort is to gaze at the glaciers thrusting down from the peak, but even they are distant some 9 miles up of steep hiking.

This Pakistan's resort town came to limelight and world's attention, when two American Black –Hawk helicopters set down at the compound, allegedly belonging to Osama Bin Laden, which was located in the backyard of Military Academy, and a team of 25 Seals breaches at least three walls to reach the main building. Helicopter-borne U.S Navy Seals fly from Afghanistan and kill him on May 2, 2011 shortly after 1.00 A.M. The death of Bin Laden gave rise to various conspiracy theories, hoaxes, and rumours. These include the gestures that Bin Laden had been dead for years or is still alive! Doubts about Bin Laden's death were fuelled by the U.S military disposal of his body at sea. Though the Abbottabad raid has been described in great detail by the U.S officials, no physical evidence constituting actual proof of his death has been offered to the public. The building complex itself was utterly obliterated soon after the assault. According to one of its senior citizens, Roshan Abbassi, who is married to the British wife, "Our family has been living in Abbottabad, since the time of James Abbott. Even River Indus opens its breasts over here after thumping and thrusting for hundreds of miles. Everybody knows each other by name in our peaceful and green mountainous town and can identify any strangers at ease. We only came to know about Osama's episode by watching clips on the television. Any boom or zoom of super military hardware or echoes of guns would have easily startled our peaceful town. Plainly speaking we do not believe an iota. The only activity I can recollect is that the security team had erected some barriers around that area at about 16.00 hours on that evening, without giving any explanation. The images shown on the television were, as if highlights from the "Horror movies of the Hollywood." He declared.

A plaque commemorating James Abbotts's poem, about his own founded town, is displayed at Lady Garden Park within the town itself and I quote:

> I remember the day
> When I first came here
> And smelt the sweet Abbottabad air
> The trees and ground covered with snow
> Gave us indeed a brilliant show
> To me the place seemed like a dream
> And far ran a lonesome stream
> The wind hissed as if welcoming us
> The pine swayed creating a lot of fuss
> And the tiny cuckoo sang it away
> A song very melodious and gay
> I adored the place from the first sight
> And was happy that coming here was right
> And eight good years here passed very soon
> And we leave you perhaps on a sunny noon

Mohammed Khan

Oh Abbottabad we are leaving you now
To your natural beauty do I bow
Perhaps your winds sound will never reach my ears
My gift to you is a few sad tears
I bid you farewell with a heavy heart
Never from my mind will your memories thwart

We embarked on our journey to Kalabagh in the burning July afternoon from Chaklala Air Base, located on the outskirts of Rawalpindi and at the edge of the mountains. I was hardly twenty years old and had been dreaming to cool down at ten thousand feet away from the sweltering plains in the romantic monsoons. The handsome and smart commander accompanying us was clad in his official shipshape air-force uniform and an airy hat. His wife, a tall dream-like, elegant and pleasant fair lady was beautifully dressed in equally posh and expensive clothes; I consumed 50% of my leisurely time by quietly staring at her. I think I had already reaped my reward as far as my hidden romance is concerned. They conversed in English in a very subtle and posh tone and occupied the front seats next to the driver. I just squeezed myself in the narrow -spaced seat provided at the back of the pick-up carrier and this suited me by sheer luck. I wore a very fine muslin shirt and a loose cotton local trouser. They carried a good cargo of crates of whisky and brandy as well for the refreshment and indulgence of the elite staff. Now in hindsight, I wonder why the commandant bothered with such a substantial amount of fine alcoholic drinks as they were no match with his charming and intoxicating wife; who slithered and swayed with dangling bouquets of roses! The driver made me squat there before the arrival of the commandant and his wife, as if I was not a stranger. Normally any extra passengers were not allowed because of security reasons. However for me the view from the back was very pleasant for inside as well as for outside and it later proved to be an extraordinarily unusual and dreamlike breathtaking journey, which anyone can ever dream of or encounter in anyone's life time. I think it was roughly four to five hours drive over the steep spurs of the Himalayas, but extremely evoking and stirring. It was a looping journey of about seventy miles with some stops or breaks for refreshment or cooling off the vehicle's engine which normally starts smoking on such steep ascents. On this tortuous route the vehicle chokes, and grunts while staggering up the steep gravity pulling mountainous slopes.

Within half an hour of the zigzagging and twisting ascent, the swashbuckling and dashing scenery began. A combination of forests of green conifer trees, orchards and terraces of cultivated fields, plunging waterfalls, small clusters of houses and villas. As the pick-up truck groaned and grunted upwards, the panoramic view changed dramatically. Near the waterfalls almost all the vehicles stopped to cool down the engines with the icy cold water plunging from the skies while the passengers stroll off on the narrow edge of the road and enjoy the open hearted v-shaped valleys with low flying cumulous dark clouds blotting the green mountains or most probably proceed to the adjacent restaurants perched on the flat slopes to have some sort of refreshment like tea, meals or just fresh exotic fruit or fizzy drinks or juices; at each stop the journey continued after a pause of 15-20 minutes.

We left behind Murree and were driving on the zigzag road making sharp bends at acute angles. The slopes and valleys seemed an ever blissful blend of twirls and swirls of sublime beauty. We were driving now at the top of the steep face of the valleys and just below the top of the forested slopes and the road appeared like a thin hair line. Although, precipitous and abrupt cliffs were terrifying, but the exultant blanket of the lofty green trees balanced against the frightening and startling view of the dark green valley. The panoramic view was awe-inspiring. However, there was no chance of survival if any vehicle plunged down the steep gradient of the slopes. I was unable to view the bottom of valleys and a continuous blanket of dark green conifer trees blotted our view. Our driver, who appeared to be a veteran of the Second World War, was of a stout body with long bushy moustaches and appeared very confident and skilled.

While I was sunk in the peace and tranquillity of the amazing scenery, I noticed and heard; menacing and swerving dark clouds; thundering, growling and flashing over the far distant lush green peaks and valleys miles far below our road and darkening the horizon. In the far distance down there, it appeared as if it was raining heavily and lightning striking at some villages or perhaps at wild animals such as monkeys, lions or cobras. I was enjoying the flares and flashes and growls and explosion of the thunder and lightning; I felt captivated and euphoric by travelling far higher than the boisterous dark clouds and also at the safe height of the mighty mountains. I instantly felt myself as a high and powerful creature.

The sensation of wild turbulent and thundering clouds and the gushing hurricane wind assaulted the whole of the skyline, atmosphere and the terrain on our left. It appeared to be approaching towards us with an incredible sweeping speed and tremendous thrust. It was fiercely sensational, provoking and an extraordinary sight. The dark plumes of clouds had melted and blended into a dark blanket of sea, but enlightened with lot of thundery flashes and flares. It made lot of roars, groans and growls and was sweeping fast towards us. This time it was more than the roars, waves and slurps of the flash floods; or howls, shrieks or gusts of dust storms; or the ferocious dilation and swaying of the King Cobra, rather they all looked like a mole over the Himalayas in front of this hurricane Monsoon clouds. Back in grandma's village, I used to gaze at the staggering clouds floating and rushing towards the Himalayas, but in this case I was above the Monsoon clouds and above the lightning and thunder. However our driver kept on driving with the usual low speed because of the zigzag and the sharp gradient of the ascent of the road. For moments we felt secure and protected by the sheer perpendicular wall of the spur on our right and behind, but soon we were under attack by the first blast and blaze of the sweeping wind and clouds. The driver immediately applied brakes and we were brought to a sudden halt within a fraction of a second; and we shuddered and waited for the storm to clear. It was almost twilight time and the night fell rather quickly. The dark violent and rampaging clouds ran riot and raced about flashing, lightning, thundering, besieging, swelling, growling, blinding, freezing and cruising up the vales and mountains. There was a ferocious and violent skirmish and dual taking place between the clouds and the hurricane. There were waves and waves of the clouds, as well as the upheavals, spins, whirls, twist and twirls. There was a heavy blinding downpour of rain and water was churning and surging from all directions around us. The trees swayed, wrecked and uprooted with the great might of the most violent and turbulent thunder storm. The boulders and rock debris hurtled down the slopes like wild beasts and straws. The brave driver instantly came out of the truck and tried to bolster the wheels with some boulders in order to stop it sliding down the steep slope with the force of the gusts as well as thrust of rushing torrents of water which poured from all directions. The waterfalls and torrential rain churned, squirted and spurted down the slopes; and washed and drenched the rock face as well as the lofty evergreen conifer trees. The driver used great skill to reverse the truck in order to park it on a comparatively safer part of the road. I also voluntarily jumped out of my seat to help him and the commandant did the same. However his wife was still perched in her nest; snug comfortable in her cradle wrapped now in her English soft woollen purple cardigan, as well as the lucky and cuddly Kashmiri shawl. I heard her panting and grumbling to her husband, while wrapping her breasts and shoulders in cold chill, 'Its bloody cold.' He simply muffled the shawl around her back, but those remote feelings in me still hurt and startle me even now. I very rarely heard them speak in Urdu or other native languages, but only in English. It is alleged that there are 142 languages or dialects spoken in Pakistan. While I stayed rooted on the road helping the driver, I could see nothing, not even my own frozen hands. There was dense blanket of clouds which was only revealed by the flash and flits of momentous sparkles in the violent clouds. There were flares, flashes and flickers all around my body which made my eyes squint. There was a queer, unconventional and eerie blend of buzzes, roars and severe crackles of thunder and lightning all over the valleys and mountains; which then appeared completely vanished and I only reflected and hoped that they were still there intact. A colossal celestial battle and real life melodrama raged over the skies and high altitudes resulting in the gigantic crackles, thunders and lightning; only to be cooled down by the heavy downpour of Monsoons. Every pore of my skin seemed to flash, flicker and blend with the zoom and echo of rumbles and growls of the monsoon clouds. At that time I felt as if I was stranded alone somewhere in the midst of the space and deep in the skies. The flutter, sparkle and buzz of the hurricane storm overtook my body and the lightning' crackles and thunders all around me, I stood still drenched and engulfed in the dark clouds which not only had washed me, but also had swamped the whole mountains side. However with hindsight I still keep on speculating why I was not charred by the lightning! While I groped in the dark mist, shivering and shuddering and persevering to find some boulders to block the truck plunging down the road, but at the same time I feared to be imminently smouldered into ashes at any fraction of a second. The boom and zoom of the winds and clouds echoed and re-echoed in all directions and levels and rebounded in the valleys miles below, over laden with the momentous tiny flashes and flickers, turned into a unique celestial drama of melee, confusion and fight between the infinite and supercilious powers of natural elements. This also proved the meanest significance of man on this wonderful, gifted, glorious and colourful planet. However in the midst of flashes, thunder, clouds and rain of tropical Monsoons, I stood lifeless dumb and deaf in the sea of mist. The trees swayed and swung mercilessly and uprooted without any defence and crumbled on the ground. Suddenly there were gushing torrents everywhere, consequently the paths vanished and the boulders hurtled down the slopes and the roads were blocked with occasional landslides. I had a feeling of floating in the space. My heart and soul not part of me. I stood still, frozen at the mercy of nature. Love and romance fled from my body and soul. The agony of the thunder storm and the aggressive swaggering attack of Monsoons continued for few hours and it was almost time for the muezzin to call for the morning prayers. The driver struggled to clear any intermittent landslides' debris or fallen trees and I volunteered again to help clear the road. I was simply soaking wet and completely drenched when we arrived at the remote air force post. The driver and I slept in sleeping bags which were provided by the staff there, under a mighty workshop shed and departed back home soon after the break of the dawn. The temperature was almost freezing, even in summer, at that great height and the burning heat of my heart engine had helped to dry my muslin shirt and the cotton trouser. We left behind the handsome commanding officer and his equally captivating wife stationed at the high post and drove back home on our five hours trail carrying with us the extraordinary and everlasting memory. However the elite couple was oblivious of us then, as they were welcomed over there by the most obedient servants in their most secluded official lodge and would have been tuck in comfortably in their bed at the time of our departure.

Wandering across the desert was even more captivating, peaceful and bewitching. To sleep in the company of sand dunes in the vast open unruffled and untroubled landscape and hugged by the cool fresh breeze which swept and massaged across the pure silvery sands in the summer moonlit nights is an amazing and exceptionally pleasing and sensuous experience, especially sleeping in the charpie under the open sky; to observe the orange and purplish red disc sinking helplessly down the skyline of the peace of desert is one of the most wonderful, enchanting and glorious spectacles one could ever experience on our mother earth. I also took a great delight in performing the pilgrimage to the perennial rivers while they were in high floods in the Monsoon period which gave me lots of excitement, thrills and inspirations; and it also refreshed my memory about the flash floods in grandma's village. However, my inquisitive adventures into the unknown world continued unhindered; this time into the mystical or incorporeal world. After achieving my adolescence I had no more nightmares about the inexcusable atrocities and savage massacres which took place at the time of the partition or independence of India in

1947. However in this instance I had an eerie and a queer dream about a mystic who appeared flying in the air and momentarily landed at a closer distance in front of me, while I was strolling in the wilderness of a meadow. It appeared to me as if he was trying to brisk away from an aroused crowd of people who gave an impression of being desperate to have an audience with him and seek his blessings. I noticed the lower part of his body was shrouded with white cotton wrappings. I also got startled and joined the enthusiastic crowd without any hesitation. While in pursuit of him with the mob, eventually I left behind the whole crowd and approached nearer to that mysterious person who gave me his blessed, thoughtful and reflective smile; the impact of that was such that I felt lot of relief and peace of mind; and all my worries and tensions simply faded away. However that extraordinary unearthly person disappeared in the horizon without having any conversation with me and without any further gestures, perhaps that was the termination of my dream.

However my thirst and quest to find the mystical men continued, as well as my zeal and compassion to travel over the mountains, deserts and wilderness. While studying in the university, I read in the popular national newspaper about a naked mystical man possessing some extraordinary spiritual powers. It was illustrated that he normally squatted on the upper slopes of a beautiful lush green valley about five to six miles lower down the terraces from the British developed mountains' resort of Murree. It was further narrated that a lion reported to him for duty in the night time to give him a ride and he trotted all around the spectacular mountains on the lion's back. Ramblers and pilgrims from all over the country described about some amazing miracles performed by him. Consequently he attracted lot of visitors throughout the year, not only people from local settlements, but also from all across the country as well as Europeans from other parts of the globe. It was further quoted that even the then president and his family had visited there to pay their respects and homage to him on a regular basis and sought his blessings. Therefore I also made some plans to visit him at the earliest opportunity during the course of my holidays and I accompanied my brother Aslam who was a kind of a wayfarer being a member of the armed services. We arrived at Murree by the bus and from the bus stop there was a taxi service available to Baba Lal Shah, the mystic, but most people preferred to track with some keen and devoted young guides who just charged a nominal tip for about two hours hike. However some of the admirers were so much dedicated and devoted that they travelled for days on foot in groups as well as individuals singing mystical songs, having dervish-dances, beating drums and meditating while on their trails; and reached up to their beloved person to seek his attention and prayers. I noticed quite a few of such devotees trailing slowly up the road leading to Murree. There was no doubt that some of them might have been some drug addicts or perverts or criminals as well who preyed on the innocent believers. After many years later, I observed, the far more dedicated Budhists monks, believers and devotees, doing circumambulation, while staggering on foot from their remote settlements to the Dalai- lama's Potala Palace in Lahsa (Tibet); they sometimes continue such strenuous physical rituals for months and years before they arrive to their destination.

However we hired a young guide instead of taking the taxi, it saved us not only some money, but more than that we had a most pleasant hiking trip down the conifer forests and enchanting terraces and waterfalls; while at the same time we reflected and inspired upon the miracles performed by the saint by hearing various stories from the horse's mouth and really it proved ever so fascinating and relaxing in the cool breeze of the mighty Himalayas.. At the base of the slope where the mystic dwelled, there was a cluster of waterfalls splashing and churning crystal clear icy cool water down the hanging valley, from which place most of the pilgrims drank water to quench themselves before hiking up again on the last trail of their pilgrimage and found it very refreshing and soothing. Some of the more enthusiastic visitors even had a quick dip in the freezing pure distilled water. We drank some cool water with the palms of our hands and splattered some on our faces and heads to refresh and revive us.

Then we followed a narrow steep path stooping on our knees and staggering to climb up the difficult rock formation; but luckily this time it was only a twenty minutes steep ascent and I was excited to do some more, although huffing, choking and puffing. As soon as we reached up the face of the middle spur of the open hanging valley, there we found the Baba (old man) sitting on his feet and holding a twig in his hand, just like a magic wand. He had a group of about thirty people, a blend of males and females, encircling in front of him about thirty feet away, constantly gazing at him and waiting anxiously to be called for blessings at his own will or discretion. However it was quite possible that in spite of plumping in front of him for a long time, even for days, they may not be beckoned or called for his one to one attention; and sometimes the devotees had to return without having a close audience with him. However even in that situation it was a matter of great consolation and inspiration for the visitor and a chance of unique tranquil emotions to sit in his audience and share some peaceful moments and to have a close glimpse of him. Although in the bright sunshine, he never wore any clothes, but in the evenings and mornings some caretaker did cover him with a blanket or a woollen hat and it was quite possible that he was taken to his lodge for a limited sleep in the freezing night. But it is unbelievable to observe him sitting on the stones so bare and naked in the almost freezing and extreme day temperature.

At the time of our visit, the old mystic looked like a skeleton and without any fat or muscles and his skin was so dehydrated that it had become a part of the bones. How did he manage to squat on his feet the whole day without eating and drinking, it is difficult to surmise; perhaps only a supernatural human could do like that. To the onlookers he appeared to be made of wood or metal frame with some built in devices to keep him dealing with the pilgrims and attract so many visitors including the foreigners. It was the universal or widespread and popular conviction of most of the visitors that whosoever was called in by him and given the thump of pats or smack, would be a very lucky person and the blessed one. The more the thumps or stroking, the more would have been the benefits. However it was worth emphasizing that he would never be able to bleed or injure any of his apparent targets; but the devotees themselves yearned for rigorous and stern cosh or cudgel to reap maximum results. It was just like a wrestler who fatigued his body robustly to achieve optimum physical endurance and resilience; but in this case hidden subconscious feelings and hallucinations got one lured or seduced. After reaching the enclave, we took our positions like any other visitor and luckily there was no tradition or ritual for exchange of gifts or monetary offerings; so it was all free to join the spectacle and did not involve any money making business. I just perched myself on my feet on the higher saddle of the fold to have a good glimpse of the mystic. Normally he would sit quietly and make some pivotal move around his feet and buttocks. Sometimes he would mumble something to himself and sometimes call some individual or sometimes just gestured to someone by staring and pointing towards an individual. The best thrill which the visitor derived was to be called closer to him and receive a kind of blessings and prayers; in that case he would try to thump the person with a meagre force or bursts with the hollow cane stick; but most of the times he would say prayers by raising his palms towards the sky and mumble few narrations in the favour of the needy person. However in some unusual cases, he would give a nice thrashing on the head, face or the main body, chest and back. It is the latest example that I got entangled with. I endeavoured to hide my face and head and even tried to escape, but the audience behind me bucked me up to stay and take the pounding for maximum reward. But I ducked and dodged to avoid the pounding and later was congratulated by the pilgrims, assuring me that I was amongst the luckiest people who had received that intensity of the blessings and I subsequently retreated backwards on the crest of the fold shaking and trembling, when allowed or pushed back.

I visited this legendary figure on three different occasions and once stayed overnight in the adjacent free gateless shed or make-shift lodge. This time my idea was, if I was lucky, to observe him riding over the lion's back in the middle of the night, but I was so exhausted and tired that once I lay on the reed-mat on the Himalayan glorious height, I slept so deep that I hardly knew what was happening outside in the icy cold dark night; I just woke up after the sun rise. The last time I visited him was when all of my university classmates as well as teachers and ancillary staff stayed in Murree for over two weeks in connection with doing some study projects which were a part of our assessment for the final examination. In that apparently conservative society, our department was the only department in the whole of our university which had more female teachers and students than the males by sheer luck. We arrived in two coach loads along with chefs and attendants to prepare fresh meals for us and to provide ancillary services. We were doing land use surveys, how much land is cultivated and how much under dairy farming and how much under forests and pastures, how do people spend their winters under the constant fall of heavy snow; this is just to give a few examples. It was the month of November and the weather was nice and crisp. At that time we were full of blood, flesh and fires, anyway. More than that, we had a pleasant company and freedom to wander about to survey the most romantic and popular terrain in Pakistan. We trampled up and down the slopes through the valleys and hike across the romantic and magical terraced fields. However during the course of one deep and sweet night sleep, our deputy head of department, Dr Maryam (Mary in English) had a dream asking her why did she fail to pay tributes! Now Maryam who had achieved her PHD from Oxford University and was still a spinster was baffled when she woke up next morning. At the breakfast table she described her kind of weird dream and reiterated solemnly what command she had received and from whom. She enquired from her audience, 'Does anybody know about this person and how do we reach there?' There was no shortage of students, amongst both genders, to give her information about the mystic and accompany her for the pilgrimage. However after reaching her destination the next day, she found the old man utterly naked, perching on a bare rocky ground, but encircled by a very humble and courteous audience. Naturally she was not impressed and felt disgusted and founds his statue like figure as uncouth and uncivilised, especially in the company of her students. Soon she received some verbal abuses from him and consequently she felt quite embarrassed and uncomfortable in front of her students to whom she was just like a goddess. She felt insulted and soon returned to her base with a long subdued face after her an exceptional and unique day's adventure. She trailed in the company of some of the most favourite students and I was not a part of her entourage. However with the lapse of time, I noticed that she became more compassionate and friendly towards me. After having achieved my post-graduation degree, I was the first one who got his job as a lecturer in a government college without any great effort, although I was not amongst the brightest or the most influential of the candidates and it was considered quite a prestigious job at that time. That opportunity occurred due to the fact that the education minister responsible for the appointments happened to be one of my brother's acquaintances. This was not short of a miracle in that part of the world.

My never-ending thirst for ventures into the unknown spiritual and mystical world continued more and more. This time I travelled by the steam engine train some sixteen miles away from Rawalpindi to attend the death anniversary celebrations of the death of a mystic poet of the Punjab. It is difficult to surmise why they were celebrating to his death anniversary, I would have rather preferred to celebrate his birth. His shrine was a few miles away from the local railway station. After disembarking from the train, I joined the others trailing on foot as no other transport was available to our destination. There appeared a heavy trudge of pilgrims trekking in both directions and they raised a lot of dust in the air by walking on the un-metalled road. When I arrived at the shrine with my brother Aslam, I found a great hustle and bustle of admirers and fans of the mystic poet over there. To my utter surprise all the pilgrims joined the big queue to enter the tomb and pay their tributes to the saint. Most of the devotees had dug into their pockets and donated hard cash in appreciation and as a gesture of good will; I noticed that the tributes were being collected by two bearded men wearing smart crisp and erect turbans and clad in luxurious robes and cloaks fully saturated in exotic perfumes. After passing through the door of the tomb, I further observed that some more huge crowds of devotees were also queuing up in front of some other higher and bigger dormitory where the current chief of the descendants of the deceased mystical poet or dervish was squatting and mincing with his prayer- beads, in a magnificent high chair like a throne with more religious hierarchy sheltered behind and around him. This time there was a far bigger queue and to my surprise far more orderly than I had ever seen in Pakistan. I was rather perplexed and baffled to see such a big queue stretched into furlongs and no one pushed or jostled each other. Normally in Pakistan whosoever stands in a queue is always a loser because in that scenario the person's turn will come at the end because the enthusiasts at the back just keep on taking over by overstretching their mighty arms. I also joined the queue without wasting time along with my brother and our turn came after over half an hour of waiting with patience. Now the routine was that at one's turn, the devotee would step forward with a solemn face and stoop in front of the holy man and handshakes with him, with both hands clasped together, concealing offerings in hard cash, between the palms of the hands. After the handshake, the chief custodian of the shrine would raise his hands for prayers and supplications in favour of the devotee, while still having chatter with his courtiers. In view of the high turnover, this routine took only few seconds to satisfy the believer and then the next man would turn up for the same routine. On my turn I pressed forward with a solemn palpitation of my heart and I tried to shake my hands with hollow palms, but the holy man did not raise his hands for the prayers and I was rather shunted off and the next man in line was called up without any remorse. However rather ignorantly and out of conviction, I expected the reverse. Being a penniless student I had yearned in my mind and the depth of my heart for a kind of monetary gift from the holy man endowed to me and a compassionate handshake. I became disgruntled and cursed myself for being ill-fated. The renowned and greatest Urdu and Persian poet Mirza Ghalib had suffered even a greater turmoil and lamented about his misfortune and I must quote a couple of verses from one of his Ghazals (poems): "Ibn e Mariam Hua Kare Koi; Mare Dukh Ki dawa Kare Koi" ("Let there be 'Son of Mary' (a Saviour or a Messiah), but is there anybody, who can cure my suffering!") Mirza ghalib lived in Delhi at the time of Great Mutiny in the Subcontinent in 1857 and was a contemporary poet and a close associate of the beleaguered and frail Mughal Emperor Bahadar Shah Zafar. I returned to the comfort of my beloved steam train, although this time more rejected and dejected and denuded of spiritual healings; but I derived more sensuous bliss by staring at the wonderful landscape, while travelling back by the steam engine train. I always appreciated the usual chuff chuff and puff puff of the train, as well as the fantasy of the ride.

Earlier during the course of my spring holidays and soon after joining the college at Montgomery, I visited my eldest brother called Yaqub (Jacob in English). This is the same person who escorted me to the safety of Pakistan while he was a teenager himself and I was only seven years old. Then he was working in the irrigation department and dwelled with his family in a remote canal colony settlement, while stationed there in the precinct of cluster of small farming villages and next to the banks of the mighty canal. The British built up those canal colonies to provide full lodging facilities for the staff who were employed to maintain not only the canals, but also to oversee the distribution of the water and charge money to the farmers according to their consumption. Parallel to the canal was also the network of main single rail track and disappointingly it is still single; and a metalled road linking Peshawar to Karachi, while that colony was also facilitated with a railway station not far away from it. In the canal colony there was a well maintained canal rest- house where the government high officials came and stayed while on official inspection of the area or on holidays; and there were special caretakers and gardeners employed to maintain the immaculate flower beds, fruit trees, as well as to grow all kind of vegetables; grown free for the consumption of all staff stationed over there. In fact the facilities provided to the staff over there were far superior than provided to the employees of the irrigation department located in the towns. All those canal colonies were dotted all along the main canal as well as along its offshoots which sprawled over hundreds and thousands of miles across the most fertile alluvial plains. That is an everlasting, glorious and glittering legacy left behind by the British to the lazing indigenous population of Pakistan all across the board. That particular canal colony was called Yusufwala, some eight miles away from Montgomery and once I rambled along the enchanting canal embankment on my own, as I had no money to pay for the bus or train fares and reached my destination in about three hours non-stop, while just gazing at the magnificent canal as well as the lofty trees shrouding her view from the onlookers. While I was studying at my primary school, I heard a real story that one person simply disappeared in the canal while trying to snatch a shot down wild duck from the canal. It was speculated that perhaps he was swallowed or succumbed to an odd crocodile, although it was very rare for the beast to have been siphoned off through that canal system from the mighty perennial river.

In the summer of year 2011, more than twenty college students had perished in the canal, when their boat had capsized. They were merely sailing from one embankment to the other and their joyful and exhilarating journey would not have lasted more than fifteen minutes at a slow cruise. On that disastrous sailing trip about thirty students had embarked on the boat, with a view to have a picnic and excursion across the graceful and glorious canal. As soon as the skipper started steering the boat, the young jubilant passengers became excited and overjoyed; and they started singing, dancing and tossed about the deck. As a result the boat lost its buoyancy, tilted and tumbled in the deep water. Few students survived by swimming, but the rest of their pals just perished in a matter of seconds and were swallowed by the deep strong currents. This was a makeshift boat which had been constructed by an amateur or perhaps an adventurous craftsman to make his living. It is difficult to say whether the skipper was trading under licence from the local municipal council or perhaps ventured illegally by bribing the local officials. It was fascinating to see the odd boat in the canal and I had few rides, on and off, myself during the course of previous years and I was thrilled by the return journey across the canal; although I was not sure about the reliability of the boat and had some doubts about its buoyancy. However in case of a wreck, probably I would have managed myself to the safety of the embankment through a frightful swimming and keeping my nerves cool. This boat had no oars and no engine and it was steered manually in a peculiar and queer manner. Two boat men waited one on each side of the embankment and manoeuvred the boat through the system of ''Pulley and rope, while the skippers in the boat held long poles to control the movement and its direction. So it was quite primitive in its mechanisms and was unusual, but thrilling as if walking on a tight rope. However the local divers had failed to locate and retrieve the fateful bodies and a team of army diving squad was called in to recover the corpses. Although an enquiry was launched about this tragic incident, no compensation was paid to the bereaved families and the case was closed under some more bribery. As a protest the bazaars and courts had remained closed for a couple of days in the memory of the unfortunate and enthusiastic drowned youths of the nation.

Only a few years back I had witnessed a pack of army's stallions and mares, which had plunged in the canal and they were hobbling and struggling to come out of the deep water. Luckily they were drifting only near the edge of the canal where the water was not too deep and it came up to their ears and snouts; and they were neighing in frenzy. It was not frequent for the team of horses to trot along the embankment of the canal. Normally they are kept under guard in the stable or the training camp. This time a team of the beasts was being escorted by the soldiers from the stable to the cantonment. Unfortunately the young horses, male and female, got excited, felt the freedom or perhaps got carried away by the flow of the water and galloped in the canal. Their lives were only saved when the army's officers quickly jumped in the canal and escorted them out to the safety of the embankment; I was simply awestruck at the sight of this incident. However it is disturbing to find out that there are no recreational facilities provided for the public like establishment of boating clubs, canal cruises, swimming clubs or canal guided tours. The customers are there, the business is there, but the government institutions are not there and the local council does not provide any recreational facilities for the masses. So there is nothing for the leisure activity or to enjoy the holidays or the national festivities. Instead there are thousands of policemen and soldiers who have been deployed protecting the rulers, bureaucrats and the army commanders and their families. The feudal lords are a worse part of the mafia who have their own private armies, own prisons, slave families and concubines; and plenty of leisure activities and they follow their own rules and traditions. I discovered that the guided or escorted boat or ferry tours along the river Thames or Danube, more enlightening, romantic and relaxing as compared to the bus tours.

During that memorable adventure and valiant visit, I met a unique person called Ghani. He was a kind of wayfarer valet, wandering and vagabond person. He was recommended to my brother by one of our relatives to work as an assistant to care for the cattle like cows and buffaloes, in return for food and free lodging. I hazard to guess whether he got any wages from my brother, apart from some pocket money on demand. He appeared to be in his early thirties and a kind of wrestler with plenty of muscles and physique. He soon became terribly famous in the surrounding villages as he took part in strenuous duals and kabaddi matches and won top prizes in the local sports. Soon I joined him to walk on the embankment of the canal and performed some tough exercises like press-ups and sit-ups and even swimming. He gave me some skilled training how to ride a bicycle and even taught me how to extract honey from the beehives. He simply wrapped his face and hands with white cotton sheet and used smoke as deterrent against the honey bees and extracted honey from the gigantic beehives without any fear. It happened to be the harvest time for the wheat crop and there were huge stock-piles of wheat in many open field- sites, waiting to be transported to the whole sale markets in the towns, which were normally left unattended by the farmers who tended to go home in the villages to spend the night with their families. However Ghani kept a vigilance and surveillance on the possible sites from where to plunder in the stillness of the night. He kept on pinching a modest quantity of wheat from the nearest sites and hoarded them underneath the charpie in his room. However he strictly took me into confidence and whispered to me not to talk about his ill-gotten booty to anyone. He later sold that stock into the nearest village shop and got some handsome money for his personal expenditure. Soon he was given some cash and ordered by my brother to buy some essential grocery and spices for the house from the main shopping bazaars in Montgomery and I accompanied him by hopping on the back seat of the bicycle, which he drove on the embankment of the canal. Soon after arriving at the main bazaars, he turned his bicycle into an adjacent back-side alleyway and disembarked in front of a massive wooden entrance. There an old lady welcomed him with a smile and an open arm. She must have been a kind of caretaker or a cleaner as she later started sweeping the gigantic brick laid yard. As soon as he entered the yard, he enquired from the old lady, "Where is Sharry. Is she in?" The old lady smiled again and responded, "Please hold for a second and have a seat, and I will inform her." Soon a stunningly pretty, tall and young woman, clad in colourful dress came out of her sheltered room and welcomed him with a wide smile on her lips and escorted him into the room and locked the door behind her. He entered the room with a blend of giggles and some familiar light conversation with her and she equally responded in the same familiar manner. Her head was not covered with dopatta, but she wore full makeup. She appeared as if she belonged to some mountainous regions of Pakistan or foreign lands as she was pure white and had an attractive Aryan features. Ghani just sneaked into the room without wasting any moment and without saying a single word to me. He abandoned me in the open yard in the vigilance and company of the old lady. I was utterly stunned as nothing was pre planned or had been discussed beforehand. I kept on standing in the yard not far away from the room he went in till the old lady guided me pointing towards the couple of chairs to sit, relax and wait. After about half an hour later Ghani and the young lady came out of the room and headed towards me chatting. At the end of their session I heard some more quick laughs and dialogues between the couple and splashes of water on the floor. They both headed towards me, dry and dripping, with deranged smiles on their faces, as well as some cool mysterious gestures. As I watched them coming towards me fully simmering and dilated in emotions, the young woman lurked towards me and held my both arms with her both hands and try to pull me towards her and invite me. "Let us go in. Come on. Do not be nervous or shy. Do not be embarrassed!" She smiled and stared amicably. I earlier had blazed and sizzled for over twenty minutes, but now I blushed, hesitated and shied away. I tried to pull away my arms, although I wanted to venture in desperately, but kept cool and took the antidote and had shown antipathy with a dogged face. At that age I was more potent as compared to Ghani, but thankfully I saved myself by poisoning my feelings. Ghani tried to defend me with a laughter by saying, 'He is too young and feels shy at the moment, but he will visit sometimes later!' She laughed back and reluctantly released my hands. In a way it was blessings in disguise as later in the college life I heard quite a few harrowing stories of some boys suffering from venereal diseases and consequently terrible suffering from severe pains and even dying too early for Hepatitis and Aids. It is difficult to speculate about the suffering of the countless inmates attached to this shrouded business and how fast and quick they decay and wither with the continuous wear and tear of their bodies. This was the first and the last time that I ever went into such a shadowy, steamy and misty place, even by mistake. However there is no doubt that millions of women, children and call girls are involved in this mostly illicit, but lucrative trade through the countless mafia gangs, pimps and even at their own discretion to earn their livings; and this hidden business flourishes in each urban and rural area; blending and camouflaged within the indigenous inhabitants . I recollect quite vividly that it was the important tradition to call the singing and dancing women from these premises along with the musicians to add glamour to the celebration at the time of someone's son's wedding, although now a day some more sophisticated and individual professional groups have taken over this profitable money making business, but the ancient traditions still thrive and prevail concurrently. This spectrum of population has produced some legendry and amazing female singers and film artists who turn into the heart beat of most of the population and are ever in great demand, as well as highly paid. Some of these workers do lot of charity work including contributions towards various religious institutions to recompense for their actions.

I remember my first ever visit to Lahore as a school kid like a bright glaring lamp and the guided tour of its historical monuments and cultural centres. I was being escorted by my brother-in-law on foot to see this magical ancient city as well as the queen of pre-partitioned greater India. When we return from the visit to the ever magnificent Badshahi (Royal) Mosque and its adjoining glorious Lahore Fort, we tripped along lightly near to the famous Shahi-Mohalla (Royal pavilion or Watershed Area); one point of three of the inseparable triangular flash points for the Muslim rulers of the subcontinent and their formidable armies which stretched over a period of more than a thousand years; now an important part of the itinerary for international tourists as well as for the natives. However our house was not far away, barely thirty minutes at a relaxed trot from that area and was called Sharanwala gate (Gate of the lions). This was one of the seven gates of ancient Lahore where the Mughals used to keep their lions for hunting. Only few years ago I was rather awe-inspired to observe a stout middle aged - man, clad in the native white silk and cotton Qamees and Shalwar, strolling in the narrow and winding street with two lions under leash and loosely harnessed on either side of him and strolling in the normal hustle and bustle of the highly congested street, It was an amazing sight and he appeared like a godlike figure of Lahore. I was sure that Shahi Mohalla was a relaxing, thrilling and comfortable place not only for the princes, but also for the indigenous soldiers and interested lured residents.

Lahore was situated at a cross road of the Silk Routes' and the foreign invaders, who used to venture over here from faraway places like Central Asia, Afghanistan, China and Iran and even Mongolia. So that was the place where only eagles landed. Naturally they produced an amazing cross-breed of beautiful children and perhaps used to visit them at a later time as their customers. In an extremely popular Urdu edition published in Pakistan titled 'Parliment se Bazar-e-Husn Tak' (From palaces of the Parliament to Bazaar of the Beauties), the learned scholar revealed, through the enlightenment of the overall supreme caretaker of the Shahi Mohalla and quoted, 'Most of the elite in Lahore including feudal lords, businessmen, politicians and men of power must have had left some footprints in this area, in one way or the other. Some of them might have concurrent or parallel families shrouded in mist and dark clouds, some of them even pay heavy prices to the inmates to suppress their names under the blanket to ensure that it was not revealed to the media or to their alleged families..'However a lot had been revealed in the book and since its first publication, it is being printed again and again just like the spicy dribbles and trickles and selling like hot cakes.

The establishment of the ''Shahi-Mohalla cult'' is complex and intricate. It is like a whirling ocean, sometime deep and sometime shallow; sometime volcanic activity takes place, sometime there is a blend of cold and hot currents; infested with menacing sharks and dolphins swaying and prowling around; swallowing countless small fish. The inner hub and hurly-burly of this business is called 'Heera Mandi' (diamond market). Over here exotic and sophisticated dances (mujras) are performed by some of the most beautiful women in the world. These women not only sing and dance and hypnotize with melodious gestures; they also enchant their admirers with the rhythmic movements of their eyes, lips, cheeks as well as captivating sway of their bosoms, buttocks and arms. The selected audience is also aroused and mesmerised by soft and seductive musical tunes played live by the most talented masters in the classical music industry... Over here intimate massage parlours, sexual orgies and alluring musical sessions for the elite are an integral part of it. It is over here that the top elite come and relax and lust. It is over here where the keen men come to play with the live softness of flesh, especially with young women and kids. The men come in these exclusive sessions with fuming and hissing crates of whisky and bushels loaded with Dollars. They shower the packets of notes under the feet and over the head of the dancers, just like straws and leaves; but by the time they are ready to sneak into the intimate dark coop, they are almost irrational and too intoxicated. Perhaps someone else reaps the reward. The hosts wrap up the money and begin the count. It is over here where three W's converge and blend (woman, wine and wealth) and 'Son of Adam' flutters between life and death. It is over here where the rajas, maharajas, conquerors and men of power melted away their bodies like wax; as well as the common men who sizzled and sighed like serpents.

I have a feeling that historically this kind of business had flourished more since the introduction of the Caste System in the Indian Subcontinent. It was encouraged through hereditary exclusion of masses from the self-alleged superior hierarchy. The men and women belonging to the lower grade committed themselves to the sex trade, the women were the main workers; and perhaps more were bewitched by the petty heartless kings, rajas, maharajas, countless feudal lords, nawabs, religious leaders and nobles, by providing them a bare minimum of clothing, food and lodging and naturally they survived as slaves. Shahi Mohalla is well known for its exotic food, footwear and shops for musical instruments. At the moment a fascinating restaurant called Coocoo, overlooking the Shahi Mosque and the Royal Fort, is considered to be the best in whole of Lahore. It has been established in one of the classical and lofty lodges or palaces belonging to an immensely prosperous whore and the demand for its food is such that booking has to be done in advance. Their food is most delicious and any lovers of good quality food dream of dining there at least once in their life time. I think its fame is further enhanced because of its weird and peculiar historical background and the kind of business which had been done through the centuries; so this is a kind of museum for the common public and the customers come here with special emotions.. Although the main business of Heera Mandi is prostitution, under the veil of dances called Mujras, a branch of South Asian sensual dancing. Only one hundred miles away from Montgomery (currently Sahiwal), an ancient walled sacred-city called Multan, boasts of having over five thousands influential families belonging to this lucrative trade. This city has produced an excellent stock of saints, politicians, poets, musicians, theatres, actors, orators and actresses; and dancers of stunning beauty and calibre. In Pakistan sex outside marriage is not allowed and is considered a great sin, but this business is flourishing beyond any imagination. Some main centres might be regulated under licence from the government and pay nominal taxes, but most of them are not controlled. Call girls or boys can work from homes or hotels, but managed by local mafia under police protection through bribery or without it. Pakistan law is greatly influenced by the Penal Code drawn by the British in 1892, which was imposed to control the Raj and this still remains a major element of the current Pakistan Law. The red-light districts and brothels (popularly known as chaklas) remain illegal business and operate as an open secret and offer huge sums in bribe to the law enforcing agencies. However some fanatical communes, in case of adultery, behead their females in the name of honour, but the males get a pat on their shoulders, which is not a part of any law or a religion. Thousands of females face this doom every year and the murderers easily get away. On top of this hundreds of women' faces are burnt and disfigured with the sprinkle of deadly corroding acids through heinous crimes and the culprits are hardly punished for their inhuman actions and they easily get away with it in the name of false honour; again this punishment does not apply to the men. So where are the mullahs and where is the government? What is happening to the 'daughter of Adam'?

The women are sold for a session of minutes, hours, days and nights or for months and perhaps forever. The price, the customer pays, depends upon the nature or term of the contract. The price can vary from two hundred rupees to a two hundred thousand Rupees for the session of night and cost even millions for the long term benefits. The young boys and eunuchs are also a part of the trade. The eunuchs have their own 'Spiritual Lodges' called Khwaja serai. One chief of the household of eunuchs shocked everybody by declaring on the TV, "Most of our patrons are happily married and they come here to enjoy extra sensation with us." They themselves do this business to earn their living and also to have a bit of fun. "We do this because obviously we cannot get married and also no body offers us any job." It was declared solemnly. Now the question arises from where have these large number of workers gathered? Most probably they are born over there and are the offspring of their clients. Certainly the female can plan when to get pregnant and from which pedigree and from whom she can reap maximum benefit later. However there can be some anomalies, sometime the women and boys can be abducted or lured into this network or sometime woman can establish a link to earn her livelihood because of poverty or to escape from her impotent husband. But unfortunately once they enter this cage, it is not easy to escape and can be easily murdered or tortured or imprisoned if they try to dodge. One of the inmates, a young woman in her twenties, described tears trickling from her eyes, "I was happily married and living comfortably with my family. One day a smart and handsome young man approached me and started flirting and brought some gifts for me and took me out for meals. Gradually I started fancying him and then I was lured into the trap. Now even if I have tried to run away, they beat me and make me seduced through drugs and offer me abuse day and night. My body does not belong to me; it belongs to the clients who pay the price. I cannot sleep when I feel so. Sometime a pack of men abuse me day and night, as they pay the pimp. I have tried to run away, but the police beat me badly and once they broke my arm and on top of that they put me in the prison." She sobbed on the TV. The fate of the male children is not much better from the females; they can be physically and sexually abused and may be deformed to join the squads of beggars who swarm begging at every junction of the thoroughfares and public places; some may end up in the orphanage or adopted by the charitable people. However some of the elite amongst the offspring might become lucky and get higher education to become doctors, teachers, artists, singers, dancers or even community leaders or politicians. It is up to the hierarchy to judge the potential of each gender. Some rise to great national fame and become charismatic because of their beauty and personal achievements; some of them become a part of their management and co-ordinator for their workers.

I hark a long way back to when I was a student in my primary school; soon after the independence of India. One of our class fellows, who used to dwell in our neighbourhood and who was the noblest in whole of our primary school; it was alleged that his stunning mother previously had been a harlot. His father, a tall handsome noble man and a feudal lord and leading member of the Muslim League ruling party was entangled in pure and deep romance with that girl at first sight, perhaps the first night and became obsessed with her magnetic charm and procured her in exchange for a handsome amount of hard cash. After meeting her, he could not part with her. It is difficult to surmise whether he met her on her virgin- night celebration or on later excursions or perhaps he might have made her pregnant during the course of flirting and he would have been dead certain about that. He did not want to leave his future offspring, the future member of parliament and future minister in that uncertain society, unlike some others. However in that murky and grey environment, money plays the major role. Most of the girls are well trained and educated to take over any high class society or any glittering power.

According to an ever brilliant writer of the Subcontinent, the Urdu and Persian poet Ghalib, who is buried in a magnificent mausoleum, next to the Red Fort in Dehli, and I quote, "Ishq per zor nahi hei ye wo atish Ghalib, Ke lagai na lage aur bujhai na baney" ("There is no force on love, this is such a fire that it would not ignite even if you wish to blaze, and it would not extinguish even if you wish to blow it out"). However, our class mate was equally handsome, but far richer than us because of a huge land estate of his father which consisted of thousands of acres of the fertile alluvial land as well as plenty of servants to care for the family. Although everyone in the town envied this handsome young boy for his glamour and status, but still at the first sight of him used to remark, "He is son of the whore." However his mother after her marriage lived behind veil (Purdah) like a pious woman of chastity and we as young kids were not allowed to enter their house, apart from the grown up male servants. He had his eldest step mother from his own feudal tribe as well, but unfortunately she bore no off-spring, perhaps his father was not attracted towards her due to an arranged marriage. It was not uncommon for one of his personal servants to come to school with some Qulfi (a kind of curdled ice cream lolly) or some exotic dessert, fully covered in a decorated tray and interrupt his class to feed him in the middle of the lesson. Although the class teacher was resentful for that disruption and we detested it as well in the depth of our hearts, the teacher allowed him out for a few minutes break from class for this refreshment before lunch time. He is still one of my closest friends and still lives as an honourable feudal lord. He himself married thrice, firstly in his own feudal family, but no off spring was born. He married a second time with the daughter of even bigger landlord, but still no children, although she brought in a huge quantity of her assets. He married a third time, this time in the harlot's family and bore some beautiful boys and girls and eventually they will take over the huge fortunes and will be the lawful heirs of the family. However he kept all his wives in a joint family house. He was so spoilt that he had discarded his studies at his young age.

It was a popular tradition and still is a well-known fact to the common man in the street that once the girl is born over in Shahi-Mohalla (red-light area), she is brought up with a greater care and well groomed to a high standard, till she reaches marriageable age. What is the marriageable age in that closely guarded area, it is anybody's speculation, perhaps it depends upon the pedigree of the girl and the charm of her beauty. However the young lass would be well trained in dancing, singing and etiquettes under the supervision of a charismatic female supervisor. Then special arrangements are made under strict rules and scrupulous plans to sell her for the first night's opening celebrations and for the honeymoon. Preference is given to the top bidder; the better the girl, the higher is the bid. If the bidder prefers, he can bid further for getting married on a permanent or temporary basis or to keep her as part of a hidden family or perhaps prolong the honeymoon. Naturally only the rich and influential people dare to venture into this sensuously thrilling and grilling first night; perhaps they already have the prior inside information through the agents or through regular personal contacts. Nothing is publicised or advertised, it is all camouflaged. The main beneficiaries amongst them would be the industrialists, politicians, businessmen, feudal lords and men in power. Though only few of the inmates are lucky to escape the dormant and ironic life, but most of them would be discarded after the short contract and continue to earn in the lucrative business for their iron -shackles bosses, where they would wear, tear and eventually perish at an early age under the influence of drugs and excessive physical abuse.

Recently, a powerful politician in the Punjab who had been the chief minister of the greatest province of Pakistan and is now downgraded to a minister, is going through a most turbulent time of his life. Apparently he had intimate relationship with a breathtaking actress and a dancer belonging to the film industry in Lahore. During the course of this love affair, he produced a girl which exactly resembles him. It would appear that he was keeping this little family in disguise away from his main family, although fully maintained by him, perhaps at the tax payers' expense.. When this new wife or concubine demanded full and equal rights as a family, he was perturbed and promptly banished her, but took away his young daughter from her mother. Obviously he does not want his daughter to grow up in a mysterious way. Now the father of his ex-wife has lodged a lawsuit in the court claiming that he had murdered their daughter and wanted him to be arrested and hanged for the serious crime. He in turn has lodged a counter allegation lawsuit requesting the law enforcing agencies to arrest this man for lodging a false claim against him and trying to defame him as a respectable politician and belonging to a noble family. Now the judges in the court and law enforcing agencies are stuck in the mud or in the quagmire as they themselves are squeezed between two mafias, who are making different statements on daily basis to the media. He is claiming through the television that he was legally married and had divorced her under legal terms and reiterated he knew exactly where she was hiding and soon it would come to light. The media loves it and interrogates the politician showing the clips of his dances with the women and having cuddles and kisses. Being a politician he just chuckled and claimed, "This is part of our culture." Most of the viewers are waiting for the next interview and some more revealing clips and news; while the law enforcing agencies and the court officials stare at each other while waiting for the next move.

I also recall that during the course of one of the sermons being delivered to the congregation at the time of Friday's prayers by the saint like, religious elderly scholar of Sheranwala Gate Mosque called Molana Ahmed Ali and I quote, "The lust and indulgence of Shahi Mohalla is such that even the Pathans from Peshawar come here leaving behind their beautiful and pious women of chastity." Sometime ago a strict Governor of the Punjab, decorated with bush-like moustaches and a crisp erect turban, tried to close this notorious business due to the series of protests and complaints lodged by the mullahs and the local community leaders, in Lahore. He ordered the closure of this lucrative trade straight away and promised to compensate those apparently homeless wretched women so that they could maintain themselves honourably with the alternative government funds, but he failed miserably to provide any significant assistance. Perhaps their income was far higher than his salary. Subsequently there were hoards and swarms of protesters in front of his British built, prestigious and magnificent palace where once the most powerful of British Governors, most popularly known then as 'Laat Sahib', used to lodge. Most of the protesters were irate and wore hijabs to hide their identity, but some of them were not afraid to show their dogged faces and some wore dopattas over their heads, perhaps they were already well known to the regular visitors. Some of those outlawed and banished workers besiege the governor's palace and went on hunger strike in front of the main gate; and even had a pitch battle with the police. The dictatorial governor lamentably withdrew his orders with immediate effect. He had bent in front of the agitators, clasping his heart with his right palm; shut his eyes with wet smiles on his moustaches and cheeks. From there onwards the vice business began to flourish like wild fire. They appeared to be too deeply rooted and they had already countless of their satellites and outposts sprawled in the town. They gradually melted and mingled away in the more fashionable and posh areas of Lahore and not so easy to be singled out or highlighted. They traditionally had perched on the piles and loads of money and could easily thaw the resilience of law enforcing agencies, especially the police. However the governor was so arrogant that later he slapped the face of the principal of a reputable college, as the latter had refused to give an admission to a candidate recommended by the governor; and who did not qualify for the requirements of entrance to the professional college built by the British. Subsequently the governor was removed from his post because of some political wrangles and despatched to his home over the mountains. He was later shot dead by his own son and in his own bedroom of his own feudal strong and secured lodge, which was located in the most fabulous and romantic pink Salt Range on the edge of the ever gifted Indus River. Now he lay dead like a wild beast. I do not know whether it was the curse of the women or the man, but the murderer was never convicted, he was the son-in-law of the president. In the quandary it was difficult to say whether it was a political or a domestic murder.

By the end of my school studies, I was almost seventeen years old and then I felt myself as an independent and more confident person, but I still continued to mature and enlighten myself almost on the daily basis and still do. I commenced making my own decisions about myself, travelled anywhere I liked and moved around in the society in a company of some modest friends. From then onwards I endeavoured to become self-sufficient in funds through tuition fees and interest free loans from the local district council. I was a kind of a bashful and timorous student and did not take much active part in extra curriculum activities such as sports, debates, dramas or students union. However I always looked forward to enjoying those activities and functions as a most devout spectator. This could be due to the fact that I was a lonely person and without any receipt of parental contribution, apart from having some occasional dialogues with my elder brothers, sister and other relatives; who used to be normally busy in the daily chores of their own private life. However I continued to receive free lodging and food with my brothers, from one or the other, while studying in the college at Montgomery. Luckily the situation changed for the better in Lahore when I got admission to the university. I discovered Lahore, like any other citizen of Pakistan, a more romantic, cultured and beautiful city than any other city in the whole of Pakistan. Our university campus, a classical cluster of red brick buildings, was located on the edge of the most spacious and fashionable Mall Road and not far from the Governor's house. It was built by the British in 1882. I started lodging free in the Sheranwala Gate which was just over two miles walk from the university. On my route I used to trot through a series of very popular shopping bazaars, the most notable was the legendry, famous and fashionable bazaar of Anarkali. The Anarkali (delicate blossom of pomegranate) is as famous in whole of Lahore as is the Oxford Street in London, but has a more romantic and relaxed atmosphere. Lahore is the cradle of the most beautiful and graceful people in the world, especially it can boast of its beautiful and equally stunning women. They are so elegant and attractive that one continues to gaze at them till they disappear from the scene or till the arrival of the next better one. Whenever the village folk from the countryside come to Anarkali for shopping, their sensuous feelings bite them like a cobra and they gesture to themselves helplessly, 'Oh Gosh, we have wasted our life playing with the buffaloes back home.'

The girls over here are normally more confident and stroll around in the shopping centres on their own, clad in the most sophisticated and smart native dress of dopatta, qamees and shalwar, but finely stitched, pressed and matched with their ever charming figures. I think Lahore was the first main centre of the subcontinent of India where the formidable armies of the invading alien countries as well as the camel caravans used to have a good rest and blend with the local indigenous populace. It is simply a melting pot of various ethnic races, cultures and colours, as well as the meeting points of the trading caravans and the gypsies. This particular environment had become a tolerant, graceful and a romantic spot; and as a result a place of unique splendid beauty, sophisticated culture and tasteful charm. It is located on the banks of the celebrated perennial River Ravi which hurtles from the melting glaciers of the mightiest Himalayas. On the right bank of River Ravi are the magnificent and glittering tombs of Emperor Jahangir and Empress of India Noor Jahan and on the left is the breathtaking and glorious Mughal Shalimar Gardens; fascinating like Taj Mahal.

The magnificent white marble tomb of Anarkali herself is located not far from the Anarkali Bazaar itself. This tomb was alleged to have been erected in memory of an attractive, delicate and breathtaking mistress who was the centre of romance, and a love triangle between the greatest Mughal Emperor Akbar and his eldest son Jahangir. This monument of love is so peaceful and comfortable that even the eldest son of Ranjit Singh called Kharak Singh, the then charismatic ruler of Sikhs in the Punjab, made it as his palace to live in, and afterwards this was the residence of the most able commander and administrator of the East India Company, Henry Lawrence, at the time of the great Mutiny in India in 1857. He chose this place as his accommodation to give him peace of mind, tranquillity and complete rest during the most turbulent and violent moment that ever happened in the subcontinent. However lately I was one among the others millions of countless fans who derived inspiration, comfort and peace of mind by trotting through Anarkali Bazaar, as many times as possible in life as possible. Many classic films, dramas and songs have been written on both sides of the border, which portray this epic bazaar, as well as its charming and legendry mistress. My feelings still submerge in the delicate, pure and intoxicant petals, buds and blossoms of the ever bustling, swaying and swinging orchard of Anarkali. A famous Punjabi poet named Anwer Masood was so obsessed with the charm and magic of the Anarkali Bazaar that he wrote an evocative and thrilling poem titled, "Toun ki jane polia mujje Anarkali dian shanan" ("Oh you innocent buffalo, what do you know about the splendours of Anarkali?") Over the centuries its fans have come and gone with the uncontrollable passion of life, but the atmospheric, fragrant and delicate Anarkali still blossoms and smiles as usual. The great Muslim Sultan of India, Qutb-ud-din Aybeck, is buried in the armpit of Anarkali; his humble tomb is located only a few yards away in an off side bazaar. Aybeck died in Lahore in 1210 when he fell from his horse while playing polo in a race course. Earlier Aybeck had built the world famous Qutb Minar in Delhi in 1191, with a soaring height of 250 feet (the tallest minaret in the world), made of red and white marble. Its boldly jutting balconies, alternate angular and rounded fluting, and fine Arabic inscriptions set off the natural contrasts. It is so fascinating that any visitor to Delhi whether an emperor, a prince, superman or ordinary tourist cannot leave without visiting it. It is so magical that even one of the disgruntled wives of Sikh Maharaja of Kapurthala had committed suicide by plunging herself down the minaret, to seek attention of the Maharaja.

Supplementary to the classical beauty, culture and glory of ancient Lahore (named after the eldest son of Hindu god Rama), it can also boast of its captivating and alluring modern settlement of Gulberg (flower petal). It has cropped up and flourished entirely since independence; and originally had been an abode of most popular film stars and melody queen Noor Jahan, as well as housing magnificent spacious bungalows and mansions for some of the richest and most influential people in the land. It also contains a modern sports complex for cricket, hockey and other sports. Its broad avenues and boulevards have been provided with wide flower beds in the middle as well on the sides of the roads and roundabouts as well as at junctions. These bloom in amazing captivating colours and fill the air with a blend of sensuously pleasant fragrance. In addition to it beautiful and graceful trees further enhance its charm and tranquillity and blossom their own colourful and fragrant flowers. Every year, on 14th of February, (Valentine day), tons of fragrant and delicately colourful bunches of rose, marigold, crocus, tulip and numerous other flowers, all home grown, are sold by the florists to the lovers who impress the sense of their deep emotions and warm feeling to their loved ones; this is in spite of austerity measures having been applied to the rest of the city. However those who cannot afford, they must have some other means to seduce the person close to someone's heart and even better. After achieving its fame as a posh and peaceful residential area for the rich and cultured people, it has now become a huge maze and hub of commercial plazas, shopping arcades and banks as well as offices for major companies. Scrupulous businessmen and mafia tycoons are acquiring huge residential houses and plots after paying sky high asking prices and developing them into blocks of high rise flats, hotels, restaurants, coffee shops and boutiques. Gulberg has now become world famous and renowned for its score of elaborate restaurants, banquet halls and Chinese food as well as exotic coffee houses. It has become a fashion now to dine out in the evenings in Lahore, especially in Gulberg. Each dining place can cater for hundreds of customers and a great variety of food is cooked on order while waiting under the canopies or dining halls. The food is served by uniformed behras (attendants) wearing erect turbans and crisp pressed uniforms; although most of these places are self-serviced. Normally these dining places are always full and sometime customers have to wait in the queue, but customers are better off if tables are booked in advance, to save any disappointment. Meals can be eaten in any quantity and of any variety at reasonably affordable prices. There are now almost non-existent residential properties on the main thoroughfares and those which survived have become priceless.

Over the flowering decades this area has also become the main market for fashion and designers clothes and dresses, especially for the women, although the men are not far behind. There are hundreds of shops and stalls selling fine varieties of silk and cotton yarn mainly imported from Japan, China, India and Europe. Pakistan's factories now manufacture even better quality of all kinds of fine embossed, embroidered and exotic fabrics and textiles in cotton, silk, and wool. Pakistan is the third largest producer of fine cotton wool in the world and the bulk of its produce is exported all across the planet, along with its manufactured products. However I was rather perplexed that in one of the arcades, the biggest cloth merchant is a Sikh proprietor and the shop is named 'Guru Nanak Cloth House'; named after their alleged founding guru, who was born in Pakistan in Nankana Sahib (named after the guru) and located about forty miles away from Lahore; and was some 543 years ago during the glorious Muslim rule over India. Most of the shop owners and their assistants are normally male, with the exception of few women. They have to be very fit for the 'roll out and roll in' of the countless packs of yarn, which is quite a laborious and demanding job to pull them out from the racks and later stacking them back in the shelves and it often involve climbing and use of a ladder. Unfortunately most of the time, the customers (who are normally females) may not fancy any of the products as the texture or feel of the cloth or colour may not match with the other clothes may not click or blend. With the tradition of fashion and designer dresses and boutiques, tailor-made clothes have become a necessity; and again the best and ideal skilled professional in tailoring craft are the men. They take measurements of the brides and grooms, as well as of the posh and graceful women and men, wrapping their flexible measuring jean-tape; around the breasts and buttocks as well as inside and outside legs, again most of their customers are females. As it happens so frequently, that they (tailors) do so more than once, after the garment appears rather too tight or loose or long or short and it is often happens in case of female customers; perhaps because they are fussy or demand perfection in return for the huge sum of money they are paying to the tailors or perhaps the tailor does it diplomatically or shrewdly for the return visit for a few times. Their popular slogan is just the opposite, 'make and measure'. With these image enhancing devices, come the most expensive and glittering jewellery shops which mould and design heaps of gold and jewels and create exceptional flare in the person, especially for the ladies. Ancillary services like beauty clinics, hairdressers; provision of handbags, shoes and makeup seem even more vital and are part and parcel of Gulberg. Another amazing character doing successful business and essential for the ladies' fashion, are the dyers. They work perched on the pavements and can apply dye of any colour on any cloth or dress as ordered by their customers, within a few hours on demand, and at an economical price. How many dyes they colour daily, only they know; how many customers they satisfy, only they know and how many desires they fulfil, only they know!

The heart of Pakistan is Lahore and the heart of Lahore is Gulberg and the heart of the hearts of Gulberg is the 'Liberty Market'. It is an enchanting and a bewitching shopping mesh of covered cross-narrow lanes, sprawling at different levels; and soaring with colourful shelves, stalls and shops and arcades. They sell fine quality lace, silk, wool and cotton yarn, dresses, bangles and jewellery. The women come here to find the match of their clothes, whether dopatta, qamees or shalwar or laces and they reach here in pairs, in flocks, or alone. It is so peaceful over here that no one bothers anyone else except for the pickpockets. Although I had visited Liberty countless times as if to a shrine, this time my wife had accompanied her cousin Farkhanda, who is an art teacher in Beacons House English School Lahore. My wife and her cousin flitted and fluttered like butterflies, from one shop to the other, like any other woman gone for shopping over there; and after a while they realised that I had shown up slightly lost as I was following them like a dummy and had advised me to relax near one of the corners. They were carrying two bagsful of loose pieces of yarn to match. When they came back after another half an hour, they found me still standing there as if I was waiting for them in anguish. "Paiji athe kitay bai jao, thak jao gae" ("Brother, have a seat somewhere, you will be exhausted"). Farkhanda beckoned to me compassionately on her return, as they had further, time to consume. I smiled and reacted instantly, "Mannu apni koi hosh nai, mein taan bar bar qatal ho rian" ("I have no clue about myself, I am being slaughtered again and again") I shocked her with my gesture of madness; she just laughed it out with a witty wink, yelling, "I know the feeling." But before her retreat I appealed to her, "Please convey the message, on my behalf, to Zia bhai (who was married to her ever beautiful eldest sister Shahnaz; and who was chief of the police department for the whole of the Province of Punjab, a very powerful post indeed) not to probe to prosecute anyone as it is my own sweet wish to perish over here and no one else was to blame". I declared solemnly. She was amused by my rather perturbed and turbulent state of mind and promised to be sympathetic. I had later conveyed the same sentiments myself to Zia bhai (brother Zia) and Shahnaz, as we were lodging with them anyway.

In Liberty I pitched at that lucky corner, dumbfounded and spellbound by the wave after wave of the breathtaking and delightful women and girls; but the pity was that I was gazing at every single of them, but no one had paid any attention to me. The girls in the Liberty were all princesses of Aryans, Persian, Huns, Mongols, Turks, Arab or Afghan as well as of European blood. As I stood fancied in the corner, I could tell by their fine carriage and smouldering looks. I was being tossed about like a straw by the captivating sway of female gales after gales. I do not know from where they were converging, as if from all across the globe. In Liberty, the women flock together like thousands of birds, who would fly to the water hole or sanctuary in the Amazon for their breakfast; at the flash of first ray of the dawn. However those birds do not get alarmed being preyed from the well fed hundreds of crocodiles, who lay camouflaged comfortably in the water and bask in the sun with their tiny shining eyes popping out of water. Over there all creatures; birds, cattle or reptiles have full meals on the same table without any tussle, because of abundance of fresh fish available in the water hole. In Liberty I felt as if I was parked like an ostrich near the edge of the vast meadow while some birds chirp and flutter, perched on his bulky body drum or some peck seeds and worms from the grass nearby. More than that, it had refreshed and aroused my childhood memories, those amazing and enchanting moments in my grandma's village; the melodious, sweet and fragrant songs of Bulbul echoing from the green and sweet mangos' groves, the flash and hop of a fawn in the green sweet corn field, the flutter of leverets in the glitter of sprouting crops and soaring wild bush, soaked in dew drops, the singing and dancing of freshly distilled, crystal clear water torrent; jumping and twisting with the might of Himalayas and thrust of Monsoons, gushing through the heart of the village, the prowling and croaking of peacocks in the pastures, meadows and fields, under the blue sky and rainbows on the horizon. However I was not within myself and I had completely forgotten whether I was standing or flying or even existing. I was not sure whether I was "I am or not I am". I was lost in oblivion and had totally faded away. I recollect the eternal glittering inscription on the walls of Dewan-e-Khas (Royal Audience Hall) in Mughal Red Fort of Delhi, which highlights: "If there is a paradise on this planet, then it is this, it is this, it is this!" That humble Dewan-e-Khas is a museum now for the admiration and inspiration of world tourists, but this place is the paradise of the paradises. One can easily lose sense of existence in these hypnotizing, amazing and magical lanes. I do not grasp how many calories are burnt daily by the shop assistants or their merchants, but what a peaceful place to get burnt. In addition there are lavish stalls of sumptuous and mouth-watering fruit chaat (fruit salad), made of freshly cut and blended fruit segments of apples, banana, oranges, pomegranate grains, guava, grapes, mixed with freshly squeezed juices and a sprinkle of aromatic spices (all grown locally); a bowlful of which can be guzzled through the gullet with ease by any one, as a refreshment or as an appetizer. However Liberty cares for the poor people as well. Some bountiful mortals from charitable organisations come out with delicious food like baryani, korma, nans, fruit and desserts and distribute them in pre-packed lunch boxes; between twelve and one in the afternoons sharp, on Thursdays. The beneficiaries queue up along the outer parameter of the market in an orderly manner and everyone in the queue is served whether beggars, labourers, shoppers or shop assistants, but in Liberty only deserving folks stand there as mark of self-respect; to me everyone over there is well fed and is a symbol of prosperity and peace.

Lahore is a home to many magnificent and eternal British structures and monuments too, built by them during the course of their own golden empire of India; one of the highlights is the Lahore Zoo. It was established in 1872 and is thought to be the fourth oldest in the world and one of the largest, although after the partition it has been poorly managed and has caused death of many invaluable animals like lions, tigers and giraffes; and even snakes. It houses in nearly two thousand different species of birds, mammals as well as trees. Millions of fans visit here annually, natives as well as foreign and mesmerise themselves with the company of fascinating fellow creatures. A great percentage of these species are from Pakistan itself. Amongst many attractions of the splendid zoo, one is amazed at the skill of the parked elephant when he brings forward his trunk towards the spectators and politely plucks the currency notes and passes them on to its caretaker, who stands quietly like a dwarf next to the mighty beast. He especially likes the picture of the British, Her Majesty the Queen, on the Sterling notes, equally popular are the Dollars. He pays individual attention to each of his fans and makes their day with his breathtaking human feat. After bringing his trunk next to the hand of the showering spectator, he softly grabs the money from the outstretched hand of the fan, curls up the tip of his trunk and after reaching his mentor, uncurls it. All fans get their turn in a systematic way and there are glistening sensuous smiles, on the faces of his audience. The elephant and his mentor collect huge sums of money daily and it is alleged these funds are used for the welfare of wild life as well as to help the poorly paid staff of the zoo (I can only hope that this gesture of goodwill is true). Overlooking the zoo, the Governor's house as well as the world famous Gymkhana club, is the imposing sky high Shimla Pahari (Simla Mound) built by the Great British planners, on one edge of the vast Lawrence Gardens; and named after their glorious Indian summer capital of Simla, which was a part of Punjab and located not more than a hundred and fifty miles away from Lahore, not far away from my maternal Grandma's village of Ahrana. Shimla Pahari appears like physical land features called 'North and South Downs' in England. It has narrow steep tracks for pleasant walks, spiralling round and round its contours and its terraces are covered with colourful flower beds and trees; also some stags and deer graze in the adjoining meadow along its face. It has its own supply of water and a team of gardeners keep it blooming throughout the year. In spring time the whole of the alluvial mound blazes with blissful blossoms of colourful flowers and the cool breeze in the air blows with a glitter and blend of bright sunshine and is filled with sweet fragrance. It appears like an evocative dreamland and I yearn to be there all the time during the spring. It is a popular tourist spot not only for the families, courting couples, bachelors, but also for kids. One cannot find a better romantic place on the earth than this. On the base of the mound, there is a 'Tuck Shop' or tea/coffee shop available where one can relax and talk, along with having sips of delicious tea, coffee or fizzy drink or having light refreshments and all served by uniformed behras (young attendants). However due to exploding population in Pakistan (it appears as if meals and mating is the main trait over here) and poor town planning; as well as thousands upon thousands of buzzing and zooming vehicles around it, the peaceful and tranquil Shimla Pahari is being spoilt and polluted by the poisonous emission of lead and fumes, which is choking not only the flora and fauna of the great hillock, but also poisoning the wild life in the zoo as well. Being a prime area in Lahore, multinational companies, are trying to violate this peaceful area and building up jungles of high rise buildings and commercial power houses. In my view this should not be allowed and new areas should be developed. I have given only a tiny glimpse about the spectacles of Lahore and now there is a popular song available about the glories of

Lahore. The track reflects the unique culture of Lahore, describing the life in Lahore, the people, the food and most famous spots in Lahore. It is titled, "Lahore Lahore aye" ("Lahore is Lahore"); sung by Tariq Tafu, a solo singer who is the Tom Jones of Pakistan. He declares in a rhetoric of patriotic song, "Jinnay L'ore naee tak'ya, o' jamm'ya naee" ("one who has not seen Lahore, is not born"). While he performs solo, singing and dancing in a crazy manner; under the fast and rhythmic beat of the live drums and melodious tunes of his guitar, a great enthusiastic and jubilant crowd join him too, wherever he sings. He goes to the actual site about which he is singing and in typical Punjabi style runs and jumps about with one leg and two arms in the air and with swift rhythmic movement of his body. A huge joyous gathering joins him in bazaars of Shahi Mohalla and he draws their attention towards its lavish food restaurants and sweetmeats' stalls, luxurious shoes' shops and melodious lively songs' performances. He then carries on singing and dancing in other flash points of Lahore like the Shahi Qila, Shahi Mosque, Anarkali, Gulberg and almost in every single settlement of old Lahore as well as the River Ravi. This song has become so popular that he had been invited so many times to London to give live performance in Wembley Arena, fully packed with over 30.000 spectators at a glance, including myself with the wife, all singing, jumping and dancing in front of him. He has also performed in the other major cities of Great Britain, Europe and USA. Although his original music video was filmed in Lahore and its popularity had touched the skies in Pakistan and amongst the Pakistanis abroad, but the same song with the same Punjabi lyrics and the same solo singer was filmed, even in the most popular and cultured city of the globe and twin city of Lahore called London. Tafu sings and dances in the heart of London, in Trafalgar Square, Buckingham Palace, Westminster Bridge, Piccadilly; and has been filmed by the local professional movie makers. Again the local spectators and bystanders join him in his magical fast dances and even sing with him in a rapturous manner. He also dances on top of the gigantic statue of lion under the towering Nelson's column, with his rapid and swift rhythmic movements and singing emotionally, patriotic lyrics of "L'ore L'ore aye". This London video has become even more in demand than the original one filmed in Lahore and luckily it is available free on Google on different websites.

While I lodged in Lahore during the course of my studies at the university, the compassionate glittering stars favoured me even more and something unbelievable happened. I got my free dwelling in the prime and central area of ancient Lahore, not far away from the main railway station, with a highly generous and noble family. They allowed me to shelter in a small secluded, but a little darkish and moist room which was located on the lowest floor of their house and was lying about ten feet below the raised level of the main railway maze of tracks which sprawled like fingers above the terraces of the house and which was only separated by narrow alleyway, while they lived on the upper two stories. So the hiss and sizzle of the steam engines and the roars and thunder of them; clap and clatter of the trains, days and nights, used to remind me about the twirls and swirls of my own emotions and upheavals and flutters of my nerves and heart. Again this was another legacy left behind by the ingenious British worth admiring and remembering and a cause of being indebted, as independent Pakistan cannot perform such an adventure which helps its indigenous population, they rather put up a fierce squabble to resist such a feat. However I had paid a nominal or a meagre amount of money to them for my meals only. Their accommodation enclave with a separate entrance was a part of the huge redbrick mansion which was segregated into other dormitories and blocks of multi-story apartments or blocks and a part of it even housed a very popular and modern soap factory of Lahore. They had been provided with their own communal well to draw the water for their consumption. In the middle of the hanging pergolas and wooden balconies and galleries, there was a beautiful spacious garden blooming and blazing with a great variety of colourful and fragrant flowers. At that moment the overall owner of the complex buildings was an old lady, about eighty years old, a kind of Anglo Indian and of pure white skin and with white curly hair. She spoke in broken Urdu and she was the youngest wife of her late aristocratic husband. She was scrupulous in organising her daily chores, always active and alert; and conversed wearing broad smiles on her shining cheeks. She herself was brought into this house from the orphanage at the time of the British Raj. Infrequently I gave her a hand in the spring time to water the plants at no cost. I liked the flowers and fragrance anyway, so I was too pleased to shower the plants and roam about them, sniff and stare at them. I had a feeling that they too smiled back at me and welcomed me with their pleasant smiles and fragrance. I sniffed, gazed and admired them and in return they gave me lot of smiles, consolation, comfort and relaxation.

Even in that isolated and solitary shelter over there, my tuition sessions continued as usual, that time with the teenage daughter of my benefactors, although free of charge as a compliment and in gratitude. She must have been studying in her middle class in the school and must have just entered into the tempestuous, passionate and bumpy teen age. She was the only child of her parents and had been adopted from one of their closest relatives. She was a fine blend of the buds and blossoms, full of charm and delicacy. She's of fine wheat colour silky skin, dark eyes and snake like tress over her face. The clothes she used to wear were of simple cotton or silk with deep natural rainbow colours. Her eyes were intoxicating, cheeks beamed and her lips blazed like petals of crimson desert rose. One could easily observe the water going down her throat and feel through her flesh. To the onlookers she appeared like a fawn. I used to climb upstairs for the tuition as well as for my evening meals. She lodged on the first floor in a spacious room with her parents sharing the same room, although they had more accommodation available on the other floor. That gigantic room had windows attached to it at the level of the railway tracks for the fresh air and there was plenty of sunshine to keep warm and had been furnished with quite a few charpies of high quality and other furniture and piles of suite cases. This was just opposite to my small room which lacked fresh air and the sun, although it was filled with plenty of books, folders and wild emotions. Their kitchen was opposite to their bedroom, although located on the far end of the vast brick laid yard at the rear of the soap factory. However on one evening it was the turn for the English tuition. I crouched on a wooden chair just in front of her and she was doing the same. There was a small wooden table in between us containing books and note books. The gap between us was not untouchable. That day we were grounding on the 'Indirect or reported speech.'

He said to us, 'The gardens in Lahore blaze and sizzle with the colourful flowers and the atmosphere becomes magical and fills with fragrance during the spring.'

He described to us that the gardens in Lahore blazed and sizzled with colourful flowers and the atmosphere became magical and filled with fragrance during the spring.

I say to you, 'You are beautiful and I love you.'

You express to me that I am beautiful and you love me.

The great Persian creative writer and poet called Sheikh Saadi had once quoted about an old man, who had enlightened his son from the insight that there were three symptoms of deep and pure love; "(1) Pale colour, (2) Wet eyes, (3) Cool gasps".

It is difficult to surmise what had happened or what was the cause, perhaps it was the volatile or turbulent age, but I found myself spellbound and hypnotised by the above parts of speech. Instinctively the heart flared up and palpitated endlessly while I stared at her dawn like face, pure and fresh like green lemons, while her glistening and sparkling eyes were fixed at her note book and she blushed like the glint of her mother. Her cheeks glowed like a clinker from a fire and her lips shivered like a deadly bee. Somehow she managed to keep cool and persevered to scribble on her note book. I myself felt like a snow leopard crouched on the bare- stony crag and in a ready posture to pounce on the gazelle hopping on the face of a steep slope. My own eyes drowned, fingers trembled, tongue stammered and stuttered, heart fluttered and body shivered and simmered like the wavering flame of a lamp hung in the pergola during the dust storm. I was submerged and swamped in a terrific surge of intoxicating emotions and my nerves swayed and swirled with flash floods. I burst and erupted with a forceful passion and joy. The turbulent Monsoon clouds crackled and thundered under the violent hurricane storm and I just flashed and flickered. The sensuous feelings had become dilated and unbending in violent roars and whirls of passions, lusts and itches and drowned in more and more spirals and whirls of thirst, yearning and longing. The table floated, swayed, tumbled and tossed like a wild bush in a flash flood and the books shuddered while I oozed and seeped, dribbled and trickled down the ankle, but who would have rung the bell or taken the initiative? I only wavered, hesitated and vacillated. According to the old local tradition, 'if someone proved to be a shy, would bound to be unlucky'. However she stooped to conquer and startled her family. They made a bid, but fell in the doldrums; and the sword of other family's traditions and culture won the day. However I slithered on reluctantly and felt dejected, perhaps she had the same feelings. When I sneaked upstairs for my evening meals as well as for the tuition, she stood rooted next to the entrance to the staircase with an excuse to clean the banisters with the wet rags and mumbled romantic songs in a soft but hurting deeply like a pincer, while her eyes gazed downwards in a soaked, but snaring posture and appeared like a tigress ready to strangle the grazing lamb. I can still hear the chink of her bangles and the echo of her gripping songs and bewitching smiles. Those savage and unfulfilled momentous desires still resonate very vividly like the violent Icelandic Volcano which erupts from time to time; and has been fuming and igniting under miles thickness of ice of the glaciers since the Ice-age. This chill multiplied especially after the midnight sweet sleep and in the intensity of the dark and cold night of a black hole. The time prolongs into infinite, unending and unbending frustrating sentiments.. It becomes uncontrollable and turning sides in the bed does not salvage the ferocity of the yearnings and sentiments.

I stood choked crumbling on my legs, stunned and dumb, in the middle of the stairs and melted away like a candle would do below the root of the flame. I yearned to crunch her like a raw- tender freshly pulled out carrot; or gnaw on the cob of sweet corn or even juice her out like grinding the peeled- stem of the sugarcane. Then I felt my body and nerves shattered, smashed and crushed, but mercilessly suppressed my feelings in integrity and chastity. There was a burning inbuilt temptation to exploit the precious, invaluable and a lucrative bounty. I did not know what to do and what not to do with her. However that crackling and fluttering captivating moment still growls and thunders like the romantic but violent Monsoon cloud. I still yearn to feel and squeeze the pair of lemons, but not to pluck them and their goodness is still there. Those turbulent and erupting days passed by not without flares and fires.

After returning to Montgomery life was not the same, it was rather distasteful and unsettled. The call of the Muezzin from the nearby mosque, the melodious songs and the hustle and bustle of the bazaars did not amuse me anymore. The pleasant daily walk with the friends on the open avenues guarded by the lofty trees, the ripples and flow of the great canal, the hooters of the steam engine and the swarms of the passengers did not draw my attention anymore. I was simply overtaken by the confused thoughts and shrouded in hopeless feelings. In nostalgia those soaked and emotional moments strangled me like serpents. I was unable to sleep and tossed and turned my sides in the bed and gazed at the stars in the blanket of the dark barren-nights. It appeared as if I had been possessed by the supernatural or alien forces and they clenched me with sharp claws under their wings all the time. The great Urdu poet Mirza Ghalib had suffered similar romantic dilations, as a young man and had gone through well-matched emotional turmoil and uproars. He expresses his grief in numerous fascinating and everlasting poems (odes). I have translated some of his couplets from one of them, expressing the same miserable commotion:

Flirtation with the beloved, was not our destiny

If had lasted longer, hold-up would still be continual

We survived on your promise, then my soul, it is false

We would have drooped in jubilation, had this been true

Someone inquest my heart, about your half-bent arrow

This prick would have not sparked off, had it pierced guts across

What friendship is this, that friends have turned advisor

Someone could have been resource, someone could have consoled

How can I explain to whom what it is, night grief is terrible torture

I would not have minded dying, if it was only for once

However that scorching intensity of unfruitful grim-moment glows an eternal flame spluttering in the swaying casket of life. Though there would have been no shortage of admirers for her, I would not have been a part of that gathering. Even if we were to meet again by any chance, still the moment of further separation would hurt with the same intensity and wilderness. In this confusion and restlessness, the chill will keep on multiplying and going down the spine till we meet again and again and again. That memory keeps on spiralling, swelling and dilating, even now swaying like an agitated cobra which spits venom with the wiggle and waggle of its tongue, while rooted straight on its tail like a minaret. In one's life there are thousands of desires and opportunities which someone fulfils in the life time and even yearns to die to achieve that unique objective of lust and wild emotions, but still there are many more which are not quenched. I have a feeling that if I had fulfilled my desires, then perhaps I might have not even remembered them. That particular crackling and steaming historical moment hurts and turns into gloom and melancholia, which is a blessing in disguise and glows like a brilliant lamp and has turbulent impact on the hidden emotions and subconscious thoughts and ever keep on multiplying and will continue till infinity. This is a miracle and the beauty of non-fulfilment of intense desires and keeps on boiling and keeps on lifting and stirring the lid. This is an amazing gift of nature which can only be achieved by going through the sharp guillotine of personal sacrifice and grim restraint, which becomes rather more enjoyable and everlasting. That volatile and violent moment, that chilling sensuous and grilling moment, that fantasy and untouched sensation, that faint fragrance of the young blossom and its enchanting smiles are finely preserved and still billow and surge with the same ferocity and intensity and will forever, and ever and ever.

The last days in the university were also the last days of my full time studies and from that time onwards I was almost twenty four and the soon I embarked on my completely independent, stable and prosperous life. I never looked back; as the time passed by, though I feel that it has now slipped away like a flash of a far distant star or like the shadow of a small speck of cloud floating over the bright sky. It is rather ironical that my life began with the advent of one of the world's major historical events like World War Two, the Partition of the Indian Subcontinent, the mass migrations of its people and also the mass communal killings, rapes and abductions. It is also ironical that I was a part of the forced migration of people and I witnessed the pitiful caravans of refugees and terrible events which subsequently unfolded. I witnessed the killing of my uncles, the abductions of my aunts and cousins in the East Punjab. Those were also the last few gasping moments for the glorious British Empire as a global super power. Since then I have noticed that it is not only the major powers on the globe which control the lives of its people, but also the religious and political hard cores and epicentres based internationally as well as locally, perhaps for their own personal glories and powers, not for the peace of the individual countries or its indigenous people. A similar kind of roll is played by the vehement individuals at the grass root level in the individual families, communities, settlements and the areas, whether they are relatives, religious hierarchy, social or political; naturally there are always some exceptions. However as a result of self-preservation, each pedigree perceives that they are the rightful people and anybody else is wrong. I have gone through the childhood as well as my boyhood like an SAS soldier, although at that time I had thought that life was perfectly normal, so I did not feel upset or left over. However looking back now I feel strong acrimony against the caste system, hatred between different beliefs, the poor rights of the women and treatment of them just like cattle and unnecessary power of the politicians and superpowers, especially in the developing world. Within two years of leaving the university, I paid off all the loans and even managed to get married to a brilliant young maiden and we have kept on flourishing since. Within another two years, I migrated to Great Britain and am still thriving to the top. I think life is full of wonders, although there are some pitfalls, but it is worth enjoying with a bit of perseverance and hard work coupled with a bit of luck.

Bibliography

Allen, Charles. "The Soldier Sahibs"- The men who made North West Frontier

Cunningham J.D. "The History of the Sikhs"

New Horizon. "Mughal India"

Gascoigne, Bamber. "The Great Mughals"

Sarila, Narendra Singh. "The Shadow of the Great Game"-The untold story of India's Partition

Khan, Imran. "Indus Journey"- A personal view of Pakistan

Gibb, H.A.R., "Travels of Ibn Battuta"

Morgan, Sally. "Pakistan"

Mountbatten, Pamela. 'India Remembered'. A personal account of seventeen years old, younger daughter of Lord Mountbatten, who accompanied her father to India during the transfer of power

Lane-Poole, Stanley. 'Mediaeval India, under Mohammadan Rule (AD 712-1764)"

Marozzi, Justin. 'Tamerlane' Sword of Islam, Conqueror of the World"

Wolpert, Stanley. 'Jinnah of Pakistan'

Khan, Sardar Ali Ahmad. "Hidustan se Pakistan/From India to Pakistan': (Urdu Edition).

Khan, Zaheer Ahmad. "Parliament se Bazaar-i-hussan tak/From Parliament to the Beauties's bazaar": (Urdu Edition).

Qanoongo, Kalkaranjan. "Sher Shah Suri aur ous ka Uhad./Sher Shah Suri and his empire"-The ruler of India who had originally built the "Grand Trunk Road" from Dacca to Peshawar: (Urdu Edition)

Tunzelmann, Alex Von. "Indian Summer"- The secret history of the end of an empire

Paxman, Jeremy. "Empire"- What ruling the world did to The British?

Lightning Source UK Ltd.
Milton Keynes UK
UKOW03f0800111014

239924UK00001B/36/P